HISTORICAL DICTIONARIES OF RELIGIONS, PHILOSOPHIES, AND MOVEMENTS
Edited by Jon Woronoff

1. *Buddhism,* by Charles S. Prebish, 1993
2. *Mormonism,* by Davis Bitton, 1994
3. *Ecumenical Christianity,* by Ans Joachim van der Bent, 1994
4. *Terrorism,* by Sean Anderson and Stephen Sloan, 1995
5. *Sikhism,* by W. H. McLeod, 1995
6. *Feminism,* by Janet K. Boles and Diane Long Hoeveler, 1995
7. *Olympic Movement,* by Ian Buchanan and Bill Mallon, 1995
8. *Methodism,* by Charles Yrigoyen Jr. and Susan E. Warrick, 1996
9. *Orthodox Church,* by Michael Prokurat, Alexander Golitzin, and Michael D. Peterson, 1996
10. *Organized Labor,* by James C. Docherty, 1996
11. *Civil Rights Movement,* by Ralph E. Luker, 1997
12. *Catholicism,* by William J. Collinge, 1997
13. *Hinduism,* by Bruce M. Sullivan, 1997
14. *North American Environmentalism,* by Edward R. Wells and Alan M. Schwartz, 1997
15. *Welfare State,* by Bent Greve, 1998
16. *Socialism,* by James C. Docherty, 1997
17. *Bahá'í Faith,* by Hugh C. Adamson and Philip Hainsworth, 1998
18. *Taoism,* by Julian F. Pas in cooperation with Man Kam Leung, 1998
19. *Judaism,* by Norman Solomon, 1998
20. *Green Movement,* by Elim Papadakis, 1998
21. *Nietzscheanism,* by Carol Diethe, 1999
22. *Gay Liberation Movement,* by Ronald J. Hunt, 1999
23. *Islamic Fundamentalist Movements in the Arab World, Iran, and Turkey,* by Ahmad S. Moussalli, 1999
24. *Reformed Churches,* by Robert Benedetto, Darrell L. Guder, and Donald K. McKim, 1999
25. *Baptists,* by William H. Brackney, 1999
26. *Cooperative Movement,* by Jack Shaffer, 1999
27. *Reformation and Counter-Reformation,* by Hans J. Hillerbrand, 1999
28. *Shakers,* by Holley Gene Duffield, 2000
29. *United States Political Parties,* by Harold F. Bass, Jr., 2000
30. *Heidegger's Philosophy,* by Alfred Denker, 2000
31. *Zionism,* by Rafael Medoff and Chaim I. Waxman, 2000
32. *Historical Dictionary of Mormonism,* by Davis Bitton, 2000

Historical Dictionary of Heidegger's Philosophy

Alfred Denker

Historical Dictionaries of Religions, Philosophies, and Movement, No. 30

The Scarecrow Press, Inc.
Lanham, Maryland, and London
2000

SCARECROW PRESS, INC.

Published in the United States of America
by Scarecrow Press, Inc.
4720 Boston Way, Lanham, Maryland 20706
http://www.scarecrowpress.com

4 Pleydell Gardens, Folkestone
Kent CT20 2DN, England

British Library Cataloguing in Publication Information Available

Library of Congress Cataloging-in-Publication Data

Denker, Alfred, 1960–
    Historical dictionary of Heidegger's philosophy / Alfred Denker.
        p. cm. — (Historical dictionaries of religions, philosophies, and
        movements ; no. 30)
    Includes bibliographical references.
    ISBN 0-8108-3737-4 (alk. paper)
    1. Heidegger, Martin, 1889–1976—Dictionaries. I. Title. II. Series.

B3279.H49 D455 2000
193—dc21   99-054067

♾™ The paper used in this publication meets the minimum requirements of
American National Standard for Information Sciences—Permanence of
Paper for Printed Library Materials, ANSI/NISO Z39.48–1992.
Manufactured in the United States of America.

*I dedicate this book to
the memory of Martin Heidegger
(1889-1976)*

CONTENTS

LIST OF ABBREVIATIONS

GA   *Gesamtausgabe* (Collected Edition of Heidegger's works)
ID   *Identität und Differenz*
KNS   Kriegsnotsemester (War Emergency Semester)
MHDR Martin, Bernd (Hrsg.). *Martin Heidegger und das 'Dritte Reich'. Ein Kompendium.* Darmstadt: Wissenschaftliche Buchgesellschaft 1989.
NzH   Schneeberger, Guido (Hrsg.). *Nachlese zu Heidegger.* Bern: Suhr, 1962.
VA   *Vorträge und Aufsätze*
ZS   *Zollikoner Seminare*
ZSD   *Zur Sache des Denkens*

Arendt/Heidegger
Hannah Arendt / Martin Heidegger. *Briefe 1925 bis 1975 und andere Zeugnisse.* Herausgegeben von Ursula Ludz. Frankfurt am Main: Klostermann, 1998.

Biemel & Herrmann 1989
Biemel, Walter, and Herrmann, Friedrich-Wilhelm von (Hrsg.). *Kunst und Technik. Gedächtnisschrift zum 100. Geburtstag von Martin Heidegger.* Frankfurt am Main: Klostermann, 1989

Buchner 1989
Japan und Heidegger. Gedenkschrift der Stadt Meßkirch zum hundersten Geburtstag Martin Heideggers. Im Auftrag der Stadt Meßkirch herausgegeben von Hartmut Buchner. Sigmaringen: Jan Thorbecke Verlag, 1989

Frings 1968
Frings, Manfred S. (ed.). *Heidegger and the Quest for Truth.* Chicago: Quadrangle, 1968.

Jaspert 1996
Jaspert, Bernd (Hrsg.). *Sachgemässe Exegese. Die Protokolle aus Rudolf Bultmanns Neutestamentlichen Seminaren 1921-1951.* Marburg: N.G. Elwert Verlag, 1996.

Löwith 1981
Löwith, Karl. *Sämtliche Schriften.* Band 1: *Mensch und Menschenwelt.*
Beiträge zur Anthropologie. Stuttgart: Metzler, 1981

Ott 1993
Ott, Hugo. *Martin Heidegger: A Political Life.* Translated by A. Blunden. New York: Basic Books, 1993

Neske & Kettering 1990
Neske, Günther and Kettering, Emil (eds.). *Martin Heidegger and National Socialism: Questions and Answers.* Translated by L. Harries. New York: Paragon House, 1990

Papenfuss & Pöggeler 1990
Papenfuss, Dietrich, and Pöggeler, Otto (Hrsg.). *Zur philosophischen Aktualität Heideggers.* Band 2. *Im Gespräch der Zeit.* Frankfurt am Main: Klostermann, 1990

Papenfuss & Pöggeler 1991
Papenfuss, Dietrich, and Pöggeler, Otto (Hrsg.). *Zur philosophischen Aktualität Heideggers.* Band 1. *Philosophie und Politik.* Frankfurt am Main: Klostermann, 1991

Papenfuss & Pöggeler 1992
Papenfuss, Dietrich, and Pöggeler, Otto (Hrsg.). *Zur philosophischen Aktualität Heideggers.* Band 3. *Im Spiegel der Welt: Sprache, Übersetzung, Auseinandersetzung.* Frankfurt am Main: Klostermann, 1992.

Sallis 1970
Sallis, John (ed.). *Heidegger and the Path of Thinking.* Pittsburgh: Duquesne University Press, 1970.

Sheehan 1988
Sheehan, Thomas. Heidegger's *Lehrjahre.* In: *The Collegium Phaenomenologicum: The First Ten Years*, edited by J.C. Sallis, G. Moneta and J. Taminiaux. (Phaenomenologica 105). Dordrecht: Kluwer, 1988.

EDITOR'S FOREWORD

More than just an outstanding philosopher, in many ways Martin Heidegger was also an exceptional philosopher. He was conversant with more strands of philosophy, from the Ancient Greeks to his German contemporaries, than most. He developed his own thinking by adopting what he approved and rejecting what he disapproved, thereby creating a distinctive path. This path never stopped, nor did Heidegger ever feel satisfied, showing as much growth in his later as his earlier periods. Unlike many philosophers, he could also admit he had not always been right and make a turning. Also, unlike most, he put his philosophy into practice and engaged in politics, arguably his worst mistake, yet one that should not deny his many positive contributions.

Alas, even more than many other philosophers, his writings are considered obscure, especially for beginners. This makes the *Historical Dictionary of Heidegger's Philosophy* particularly helpful. First, in the introduction, it traces the evolution of his thought throughout a long and busy career. The chronology again follows this career, highlighting the more important events in his life and times. The dictionary then explains his contributions, with a primary emphasis on key concepts and works, and a secondary one on contemporaries and others who influenced him or were in turn influenced by him. The glossary provides brief translations of essential terms. And the bibliography presents the basic literature, including works by Heidegger, works about Heidegger and his philosophy, and broader ones, which situate both in their context.

This volume was written by Alfred Denker, who studied philosophy at the Universities of Groningen and Amsterdam. Heidegger's philosophy was a specialization, and Denker's dissertation dealt with the development of Heidegger's philosophy until the publication of his main work, *Being and Time*. After teaching courses on Heidegger at the University of Amsterdam, he moved to Pont de Cirou in France, where he established the philosophical center Les Trois Hiboux, which offers seminars and conferences on philosophy, including that of Heidegger. In addition to various articles on Heidegger and German idealism, Dr. Denker has published his own book of philosophy, *Een Filosofie voor Onderweg* (A Philosophy for Your Journey Through Life), and his dissertation *Omdat Filosoferen Leven Is. Een archeologie van Martin Heideggers 'Sein und Zeit'* (While Philosophizing Means to Live. An Archeology of Martin Heidegger's *Being and Time*).

Jon Woronoff
Series Editor

PREFACE

Martin Heidegger is arguably the most influential and important philosopher of the 20th century. His writings have had an immense impact not only in Europe and the English-speaking world, but in Asia as well. His thought has contributed to phenomenology (Maurice Merleau-Ponty, Emmanuel Lévinas), hermeneutics (Hans-Georg Gadamer, Paul Ricoeur), existentialism (José Ortega y Gasset, Karl Jaspers, Jean-Paul Sartre), political theory (Hannah Arendt, Jürgen Habermas, Herbert Marcuse, Michel Foucault), psychoanalysis (Ludwig Binswanger, Medard Boss, Rollo May), post-modernism (François Lyotard, Richard Rorty), literary theory (Jacques Derrida), ecology (Arne Naess, Michael Zimmermann) and theology (Rudolf Bultmann, Paul Tillich). At the same time he is a controversial figure. His involvement with National Socialism has led to an intense and ongoing debate about the relation between philosophy and politics in general, and Heidegger's thought and Nazism in particular.

When I was asked to prepare the *Historical Dictionary of Heidegger's Philosophy* volume for Scarecrow Press, I was honored and eager to begin what I thought to be an interesting and worthwhile project. I have been studying his life and work for over 20 years now and published books and essays on his work. Only when I started working on the dictionary did I become aware of how daunting my task really was. Heidegger is a notoriously difficult philosopher and to some extent even more so in English. Since this is one of the first dictionaries in the series on a person and not a movement, I had to work out my own concept.

A dictionary on a particular philosopher offers its own opportunities and difficulties. It can be more comprehensive than a dictionary on a religious or philosophical movement. I have tried to offer an exhaustive overview of Heidegger's thought and life. The system of internal reference should enable the reader to find his or her own way through Heidegger's often complex lines of thought. This system makes it necessary to use only one translation of German concepts and titles, although different authors and translators often use different translations. As a rule I follow the most widely used translation. The German-English Glossary should enable the reader to find which translations I have used, since many Heidegger translations contain German-English glossaries as well. This dictionary exhibits probably a greater unity than other dictionaries in the series. After all, I am dealing only with Heidegger. There were still some hard choices to be made in determining just precisely what to include. I have included entries on all of Heidegger's writings that have been translated into English and added a few on the most important works that have not yet been translated.

To help the reader I have included a note on how to use the dictionary. In the photo section the reader will find a portrait of Heidegger and some pictures of the most important places of his life. I have also provided a chronology of his life. There are three appendixes: 1. A list of Heidegger's writing, lectures, courses, and seminars in German; 2. A German-English Glossary; and 3. A Greek-English Glossary. I have prepared an extensive bibliography that I have divided into different sections to make it more convenient to use.

The series editor has offered comprehensive guidelines for the dictionary and much help in the preparation of the final manuscript. I am also indebted to some of my friends and colleagues who were willing to read drafts of the manuscript and provide many insightful critical remarks. They prevented me from making unnecessary errors. All remaining mistakes are of course still my own. I owe special thanks to Tom Rockmore, who introduced me to Scarecrow Press and provided much help, and to Theodore Kisiel, who was always willing to share his incredible knowledge of Heidegger with me and read the manuscript carefully and critically. With Marion Heinz I discussed the introduction and my interpretation of Heidegger's life and thought. Hermann Heidegger offered me not only most of the photographs included in this dictionary, but also commented critically upon the manuscript. I thank him and his wife also for their hospitality during my stay in Freiburg. Parvis Emad and Kenneth Maly made the proof pages of the introduction to their translation of Heidegger's *Beiträge zur Philosophie* available to me. This enabled me to enclose their translations of key terms in the dictionary. I am also grateful to Janet Rabinowitch of Indiana University Press who gave permission to do so. Finally, I owe many thanks to my brother Frank, my parents, and Michael Forman for their help and support over the years. Bobby and Igor kept me company when the going not only got tough, but also sometimes lonely. Marjan, this one is for you.

AUTHOR'S NOTE

How to Use the Dictionary

In the introduction to this Heidegger dictionary, I provide an overview of Heidegger's life and thought, which should enable the reader to situate the entries of the dictionary in the context of his path of think-ing.

In the dictionary, the words printed in bold have their own entry in the dictionary. In some cases I have provided "See alsos" at the end of an entry. These refer to other important entries that are not named as such in the text of that particular entry. This is especially important in the entries on philosophers. In the "See alsos" I list the entries on Hei-degger's most important texts in which he discusses his thought. This system of reference should enable the reader who is not familiar with Heidegger's thought to get a clear idea of his thought. Those readers who are well versed in Heidegger do not have to follow all the refer-ences to other entries. At the same time this system makes it possible to read the dictionary as a book on Heidegger. In all the entries, save those on persons and places, I give the German original in brackets after the title of the entry. I have included entries on all of Heidegger's writings that have been translated into English and a few on the most important texts that have not yet been translated.

In the dictionary I distinguish between Heidegger's own conception of Being (uppercase B) and the traditional concept of being (lowercase b). I use a similar solution to distinguish between temporality with a lowercase t (*Zeitlichkeit*) and Temporality with an uppercase T (*Tem-poralität*).

The titles of Heidegger's lecture courses I use in the dictionary are the ones under which they are published in the *Gesamtausgabe* (Col-lected Edition of Heidegger's works). If this title differs from the one under which Heidegger originally announced his course, I also give the original title in Appendix I.

As a rule I use the translations of key terms found in the different translations of Heidegger's works. The one exception to this rule is the recent translation of *Beiträge zur Philosophie*. Since the translators have introduced many new translations of key terms that differ signifi-cantly from those used in the Heidegger literature, I have included them for reference only. They refer the reader to the more usual translation.

I have provided also three appendixes. The first appendix contains a complete list of Heidegger's German writings, lectures, courses, and seminars. Here I give the titles under which Heidegger's courses were originally announced. I also list every publication separately and refer to the volume or journal in which it was published, as well as the volume of the *Gesamtausgabe* in which it is or will be published. The second appendix is a German-English Glossary that should enable those users who read Heidegger in German to find their way in the dictionary. It also enables the English-speaking reader to check what translation I have used in the dictionary. This may be important, since the same German word is often translated in different ways in the translations of Heidegger's works. The third appendix contains a Greek-English Glossary.

I have included an extensive bibliography at the end of the dictionary, organized so as to be instructive and informative. In the bibliography I give a complete list of the 102 volumes of the *Gesamtausgabe* and a list of the books that were published independently by Heidegger and are still in print. Appendix I will enable the reader to find where all of Heidegger's texts were published. For further details on the bibliography I refer to its own introduction.

Martin Heidegger 1889-1976

The Country Path - *Der Feldweg*

The *Hütte* in Todtnauberg

**Albert-Ludwigs-Universität
Freiburg-im-Breisgau**

CHRONOLOGY

1889   Martin Heidegger is born on September 26 as son of Friedrich Heidegger, cooper and sexton in Meßkirch, and Johanna Heidegger-Kempf.

1892   Heidegger's sister Marie is born.

1894   Heidegger's brother Fritz is born.

1903-1906   Heidegger stays at the Konradihaus in Constance to continue his high school education and start preparations for the priesthood.

1906-1909   Heidegger continues his studies at the Gymnasium in Freiburg and stays at the seminary. In September 1907 Conrad Gröber presents him with a copy of Franz Brentano's dissertation, *On the Several Senses of Being in Aristotle*.

1909   On September 30 Heidegger begins his novitiate with the Jesuits in Tisis. Due to health problems he is released on October 13.

1909-1911   Heidegger studies theology and philosophy at the University of Freiburg. He publishes his first articles and reviews and begins to study the writings of Edmund Husserl and Wilhelm Dilthey in 1910.

1911-1913   In the summer of 1911 Heidegger abandons his plans to become a priest and gives up his theology studies. He obtains an endowment to study Catholic philosophy. He also takes courses in natural science, mathematics, and history.

1913   Heidegger obtains the doctorate in philosophy with his inaugural dissertation *The Doctrine of Judgment in Psychologism.*

1915   Heidegger obtains his 'veni legendi' with his qualifying dissertation *Duns Scotus' Theory of Categories and Meaning.*

1915-1916   Heidegger gives his first lecture course on the basic trends of ancient and scholastic philosophy. During this course he meets his later wife, Elfride Petri, who studied political economy.

1915-1918   Heidegger serves in the army at the military Control Board of the Post Office in Freiburg and for the final months of the war as a meteorologist.

1917   Heidegger marries Elfride Petri on March 21 in a Catholic ceremony officiated by his friend Engelbert Krebs and a week later in a Protestant ceremony in the presence of her parents.

1918   Heidegger befriends Elisabeth Blochmann.

1919   In January Heidegger breaks with the system of Catholicism. His first child Jörg is born. Heidegger and Karl Jaspers meet for the first time on Husserl's birthday in Freiburg.

1919-1923   Heidegger teaches as an unsalaried lecturer and acts as Husserl's private assistant.

1920   Son Hermann is born.

1922   Heidegger writes the introduction to his projected book on Aristotle. Paul Natorp is so impressed with this short text that he gets Heidegger appointed to the junior position in philosophy at the University of Marburg in 1923. Elfride offers Heidegger the later famous wood cabin in Todtnauberg as a present.

1923   Heidegger moves to Marburg and befriends Rudolf Bultmann.

1924   Hannah Arendt comes to Marburg to study under Heidegger's supervision. They fall in love and start an extramarital love affair that would last five years. Heidegger's father dies at the age of 73.

1926   Arendt leaves Marburg to continue her studies under the direction of Karl Jaspers.

1927   *Being and Time* is published. Heidegger's mother dies at the age of 69.

1928   Heidegger is appointed as Husserl's successor to the chair of philosophy at the University of Freiburg.

1929   Heidegger delivers his important inaugural lecture, *What Is Metaphysics?*, and publishes his famous book, *Kant and the Problem of Metaphysics*.

1930   Heidegger rejects his nomination to the chair of philosophy at the University of Berlin.

1933   Heidegger is elected rector of the University of Freiburg on April 21. He becomes a member of the Nazi Party on May 3. In the summer he delivers several lectures in support of the National Socialist revolution and issues a number of statements in support of Hitler and his policies. He visits Jaspers for the last time. In October he rejects his second nomination to the chair of philosophy at the University of Berlin and a nomination to the chair of philosophy at the University of Munich. He writes letters of recommendation for some of his Jewish students like Karl Löwith and friends like Elisabeth Blochmann.

1934   Heidegger hands in his resignation as rector on April 23.

1935   Heidegger delivers his famous lecture on the origin of the work of art in Freiburg for the first time.

1936   Heidegger and Jaspers break off their correspondence. In April he travels to Rome where he meets Löwith and delivers his lectures *Hölderlin and the Essence of Poetry* and *Europe and German Philosophy*.

1936-1938   Heidegger writes his second main work, *Contributions to Philosophy*.

1936-1940   Heidegger gives several lecture courses on Nietzsche in which he comments critically upon the National Socialist doctrine of power. The Gestapo observes his courses.

1944   Heidegger is drafted into the *Volkssturm* in November.

1945   In January and February Heidegger is in Meßkirch to order and safeguard his manuscripts. From April until June the philosophical faculty moves to Wildenstein Castle near Beuron. In July Heidegger faces the commission of de-Nazification. Heidegger asks Professor Friedrich Oehlkers, a member of the de-Nazification committee, to inquire about his supposed anti-Semitism by Jaspers. In reply Jaspers writes a negative report that ultimately leads to Heidegger's forced retirement without license to teach.

1946   Jean Beaufret visits Heidegger for the first time. He would become a close friend and worked on Heidegger's behalf in France. Heidegger writes his *Letter on Humanism* in reply to Beaufret's questions and meets also Medard Boss who would later organize the famous seminars in Zollikon near Zurich. The French military government prohibits Heidegger from teaching on December 28.

1949   In July the French military government issues its final statement on Heidegger's Nazism, classifying him as "a fellow traveler without reconciliation". In September the prohibition against his teaching is lifted. In December Heidegger delivers his four famous lectures *(The Thing-Enframing-The Danger-The Turning)* in Bremen under the common title *Insight Into That Which Is*. The correspondence with Jaspers begins again.

1950   Heidegger delivers lectures at different occasions before the *Bavaria Academy of Fine Arts* and at Bühlerhöhe. Arendt visits Heidegger and they resume their friendship. Heidegger is granted his retirement and publishes *Holzwege (Forest Trails)*.

1951-1952 Heidegger begins to teach again at the University of Freiburg and gives his first course under the title *What Is Called Thinking?* In 1951 the Baden government grants Heidegger emeritus status.

1952   Arendt visits Heidegger for the second time.

1953   Heidegger meets and becomes a friend of Erhard Kästner. He delivers his lecture *The Question Concerning Technology* before the Bavaria Academy of Fine Arts. *Introduction to Metaphysics* is published.

1954   Heidegger publishes *Vorträge und Aufsätze (Lectures and Essays)*.

1955   Heidegger delivers his *Memorial Address* for Conradin Kreutzer in Meßkirch and *What Is Philosophy?* in Cérisy-la-Salle in France. He also visits Paris and Georges Braque in Varengeville.

1958   Heidegger delivers his lecture *Hegel and the Greeks* in Aix-en-Provence where he meets René Char and in Heidelberg at the Academy of Sciences. He travels to Vienna and delivers his lecture *Words* on the poetry of George Trakl.

1959   Heidegger is named honorary citizen of Meßkirch on September 27. He is elected member of the Heidelberg Academy of Sciences.

1961   Heidegger publishes his two-volume work *Nietzsche*.

1962	Heidegger travels to Greece for the first time.
1964	Heidegger travels to Greece for the second time and visits Agina.
1966	Heidegger gives his first seminar in Le Thor, France. On September 23 Heidegger gives an interview to *Der Spiegel* which would be published posthumously in 1976. He travels to Greece for the third time and visits Lesbos and also Istanbul in Turkey.
1967	Heidegger travels to Greece for the fourth time in April and delivers his lecture on the origin of art and the determination of thinking at the Academy of Sciences in Athens. In May he makes his fifth and final trip to Greece and visits the islands in the Aegean Sea. Arendt visits Heidegger and will continue to do so each year until her death in 1975. Heidegger's famous collection of essays, *Pathmarks*, is published.
1968	Second seminar in Le Thor.
1969	Third seminar in Le Thor.
1973	Seminar in Zähringen.
1975	The Summer Semester 1927 lecture course *The Basic Problems of Phenomenology* is published by Vittorio Klostermann as the first volume of the collected edition, the *Gesamtausgabe*, of Heidegger's works.
1976	On May 26 Heidegger dies at home in Freiburg and is buried on May 28 at the cemetery of Meßkirch.

INTRODUCTION

Martin Heidegger's Life and Path of Thinking

Martin Heidegger's philosophical career spans nearly 70 years and the collected edition of his works contains over 100 volumes. It seems therefore a daunting task to present a short overview of his life and thought. Fortunately, he has indicated three ways in which we should approach his lifework. The first indication is the motto that he added just before his death to the edition of his collected works, "Ways, not works." This motto not only reveals a certain modesty and the need to relativize his own achievements; it also underlines the very dynamic character of his thinking. The writings that mark his philosophical career offer us no final results. They indicate pathways on which we can follow Heidegger in his thinking. Sometimes these forest paths lead us to a clearing; at other times they disappear without a trace into the thicket, where we can no longer see the wood for the trees.

The second indication is a line from a poem he published in his *The Thinker as Poet*, "To head toward a star - this only." The one star of his path of thinking is the question of being. In 1907 Conrad Gröber presented Heidegger with a copy of Franz Brentano's *On the Several Senses of Being in Aristotle*. On the title page Brentano set down a sentence from Aristotle: "Being becomes manifest in many ways." Concealed in this sentence is the question that determined the way of Heidegger's thought: what is the simple determination of being that permeates all its manifold meanings? He thus came across the question what is being. His whole path of thinking is a sequence of attempts to answer that question, from the fundamental ontology of *Being and Time* to his reflections on appropriation in the 1930s, and the commemoration of the beginning of philosophy and the search for a new beginning of thinking in his later thought. In this introduction we will follow Heidegger on his path of thinking.

We find the third indication in his dialogue on language. Heidegger tells his Japanese interlocutor that he would never have come upon the path of thinking without his theological background. But origin always comes to meet us from the future. Heidegger's philosophy springs from the source of his theological background. If we want to tell the story of his life and thought, we must return to the beginning of his path of thinking.

The early years: As you were you will remain (1889-1919)

Martin Heidegger was born on September 26, 1889, in the south German town Meßkirch. His father was cooper and sexton of Saint Martin's church, where Heidegger served as an altar boy. His mother was born and raised on a farm in nearby Göggingen where Heidegger spent most of his holidays as a boy. His parents were neither poor nor rich. The family home seems to have been a happy place. The fundamental rule of life was to keep within the bounds and limits that were determined by the Roman Catholic Church. Order ruled God's creation and every human being needed to respect that order in the conduct of his life. The ringing of the church bells determined the rhythm of everyday life and reflected the divine order of creation.

When he was 14 years old, Heidegger left Meßkirch to continue his education in Constance. For boys from modest families the financial support of Roman Catholic endowments was necessary to finish their high school education. In return they were expected to study theology and become priests. While visiting the gymnasium Heidegger lived from 1903 until 1906 at the Konradihaus, the seminary where Conrad Gröber was rector. Gröber became not only Heidegger's fatherly friend who gave him a copy of Brentano's dissertation on Aristotle as a birthday present in 1907, but also the Archbishop of Freiburg. From 1906 until 1909 Heidegger lived in Freiburg, where he graduated from high school in the summer of 1909. As expected he began his novitiate with the Jesuits of Tisis in September, but after two weeks he was dismissed for reasons of health. He moved to the seminary in Freiburg and continued his theological studies at the university.

As a student of theology Heidegger published a number of essays and reviews in Roman Catholic journals that reflect the conflict between modernity and traditional Christianity in his life. We find the same tension in the books he read and authors he studied. On the one hand, he was strongly influenced by Aristotle, Scholasticism and his teacher of dogmatics, Carl Braig. He read the very conservative antimodernist journal *Der Akademiker* in which he published most of his earliest writings. On the other hand, he started studying Edmund Husserl's *Logical Investigations* and the writings of Wilhelm Dilthey as early as 1910. He discovered the poetry of Friedrich Hölderlin and

Rainer Marie Rilke, Friedrich Nietzsche's *The Will to Power* and Fyodor Dostoyevski's novels. He was introduced to Sören Kierkegaard and Georg Trakl in Ludwig von Ficker's avant-garde journal *Der Brenner*. He studied the writings of the well-known German modernist Hermann Schell and Maurice Blondel's *L'Action*.

In February 1911 a deteriorating heart condition forced Heidegger to abandon all plans to become a priest. In October 1911 he also took up studies in mathematics, history, and natural science. In philosophy Professor Heinrich Rickert became his most influential teacher. In his seminars Heidegger learned to understand what philosophical problems are and he also acquired insight into the essence of modern logic. At the same time he acquired a correct understanding of modern philosophy from Immanuel Kant on. Rickert introduced Heidegger also to the writings of Emil Lask, his former student who was killed in action during World War I. On July 26, 1913, Heidegger received a doctorate in philosophy with his inaugural dissertation, entitled *The Doctrine of Judgment in Psychologism*.

Heidegger's future looked promising. Philosophy Professor Arthur Schneider and history Professor Heinrich Finke began grooming the promising young scholar for the Freiburg University's chair of Catholic philosophy. A grant from the Catholic Church enabled Heidegger to start working on his qualifying dissertation. On the advice of his mentors Heidegger decided to write on Duns Scotus' doctrine of categories and meaning. At this time, he still thought his lifework would be taken up with a comprehensive presentation of medieval logic and psychology in the light of modern phenomenology. It came therefore as a great shock and bitter disappointment when a year after he had successfully completed his qualifying dissertation, the department of philosophy accorded the chair to Josef Geyser.

The book *Duns Scotus' Doctrine of Categories and Meaning* is a milestone on Heidegger's path of thinking. It marks the transition in his philosophical development from neo-scholasticism and neo-Kantianism, on the one hand, to phenomenology and life philosophy, on the other. In this original work the influence of Lask reaches its peak. Heidegger discusses the doctrine of categories of Duns Scotus in relation to his doctrine of meaning. He uses the modern logic of Husserl and Lask to interpret a scholastic treatise that was, as was later proven, not written by Scotus himself, but by his pupil Thomas of Erfurt. At the same time he uses the medieval doctrine of categories and meaning to criticize contemporary theories. The great advantage of Scotus' doctrine over modern logic is its metaphysical foundation.

The distinctive form of medieval life experience is anchored in the transcendent relationship of the soul to God. As Heidegger writes in the final chapter, which was later added to the commercial edition, in the long run philosophy cannot do without the insights of metaphysics.

As the final requirement to receive his license to teach at the university level Heidegger delivered his test lecture, *The Concept of Time in the Science of History*, on July 27, 1915. In his lecture he distinguishes between the concept of time in the science of nature and in the science of history. This historic concept of time is of great importance for the development of his thought. Heidegger shows that historic epochs are qualitatively incomparable. This implies that the being of entities is experienced in different ways in different epochs. There can be no *one* truth of Being, or as he was to conclude later, Being must have its history. The factual life experience of primal Christianity is different from that of the Greeks and they both differ from the factual life experience of modern times.

As an unsalaried lecturer Heidegger was set to work at the Control Board of the Post Office of Freiburg by the military authorities. This allowed him to teach at the university. He was thus spared the nightmare of the trenches of World War I. He served only for a couple of months in 1918 as a meteorologist behind the lines of fire. His first lecture course in Winter Semester 1915/16 focused on the basic trends of ancient and scholastic philosophy. During this course he met Elfride Petri who studied political economy. They fell in love and got married on March 21, 1917, in a Catholic ceremony officiated by his friend Engelbert Krebs and a week later in a Protestant ceremony in the presence of Elfride's parents. In June Heidegger learned that he would not be nominated to the chair of Catholic philosophy. This disappointment and the fact that his wife was a Protestant would ultimately lead to his break with Catholicism in 1919. A new start was made possible by the arrival of Husserl as successor of Rickert. Husserl had helped Heidegger with the publication of his qualifying dissertation on Duns Scotus in 1916 and by the end of 1917 he looked forward to the occasions of 'symphilosophein' with his most valuable coworker. During the years 1917-1920 Heidegger constantly learned in his close association with Husserl. The results of their collaboration would become evident in Heidegger's first lecture courses after World War I in which he turned away from neo-Kantianism and neo-scholasticism.

The rumor of the hidden king (1919-1923)

When Heidegger started to teach again after the war, he made a fresh start. Since his break with Catholicism, on the one hand, and neo-scholasticism and neo-Kantianism, on the other, he faced two major problems: 1. What can philosophy be after World War I, the bankruptcy of 19th-century culture and philosophy? 2. Is it still possible to be a Christian in the 20th century and what does it mean to be a Christian? Together these questions became the guiding star of Heidegger's path of thinking. It became the fundamental task of his philosophy to teach us what authentic existence is and how we may achieve it. What is the meaning of life or what is the meaning of being?

In his first lecture courses in Freiburg (1919-1923), Heidegger followed the goal of Husserl's famous *Logos* essay to further philosophy as a rigorous science. Here he first identified and named the subject matter of his philosophy, which would assume a series of different names over the years: the primal something, life in and for itself, the historical I, the situation-I, facticity, being-there, Being, appropriation. Philosophy is the science of life in and for itself, or as he would later call it, being-there. Since this is a more primal phenomenon than either nature or spirit, we can approach it neither with the method of natural science nor with that of the humanities. In principle they are both incapable of disclosing life as the phenomenon from which nature and spirit spring. Life in and for itself can only be disclosed in phenomenology. Philosophy is only possible as phenomenology. However, since phenomenology can only be the pre-theoretical science of life, and not of consciousness, Heidegger had to transform the transcendental phenomenology of Husserl into a hermeneutic phenomenology.

Life is in and for itself historical. Historical development can never be given in intuition; it can only be understood. This is the reason why Heidegger would attempt to integrate Husserl's phenomenology as a strict science and Dilthey's life philosophy and doctrine of understanding in his early lecture courses in Freiburg. Phenomenology became the investigation of life in itself. Despite the appearance of a life philosophy, it is the opposite of a worldview. A worldview objectifies and immobilizes life at a certain point in the life of a culture. In contrast, phenomenology is never closed off; it is always under way in its absolute immersion in life as such. This immersion in life in its genuineness is possible only through the genuineness of a personal life. Philosophy is, in other words, an outstanding possibility of human life.

This intertwining of the philosopher's life and his philosophy is also at the origin of his later political involvement.

In his first lecture course after World War I, *The Idea of Philosophy and the Problem of Worldviews*, Heidegger offers his students a destruction of the critical-teleological method of neo-Kantian value-philosophy. In the second phenomenological part he rejects the neo-Kantian starting point of philosophy in the fact of knowledge and replaces it with the primal fact of life and experience. As the original science, philosophy begins with the original leap from the primal something. The only way to get at this original sphere is by pure dedication to the subject matter, that is, the lived experience of life itself. This environmental experience is the condition of possibility of the neo-Kantian experience of pure givenness, which is nonobjective and impersonal. In a discussion of Paul Natorp's objections to phenomenology, Heidegger transforms Husserl's principle of all principles, that is, the primacy of originary giving and so of intuition, into a non-theoretical and hermeneutic principle, that is, the primacy of understanding. This transformation is the hermeneutical breakthrough in phenomenology. The primal something of philosophy is not a fact but the relation as such. It is not an object at all but the intentional moment of out-toward. We can only experience these intentional structures in our factual life experience. Philosophy itself becomes a distinct possibility of life, which uses formal indications to disclose the orienting comportment of life itself. Life is meaningful and expresses itself in and through its self-experience and spontaneous self-understanding.

The importance of philosophy for Heidegger's personal life becomes evident in his religious crisis of 1919 and the most important question of his personal life: how is an authentic Christian life possible in modern times? This question poses three additional questions: 1. What is a Christian life? 2. What is the essence of modernity? 3. Is an authentic Christian life possible in the modern world? To get to the essence of Christian life Heidegger developed a phenomenology of the lifeworld of primitive Christianity in an interpretation of the letters of Saint Paul. The life of a Christian begins with his acceptance of the gospel. We become Christians when we receive God's word in much affliction and with the joy of the Holy Spirit. The how of this receptivity is characterized by a constant being in trepidation. The receptive appropriating of Christian faith leads to needy distress as the very condition of Christian life. A Christian lives his life for and in hopeful anticipation of the 'Parousia', that is, the Second Coming of Christ. This hopeful anticipation is at the same time a steadfast enduring in the face of the

'Parousia'. This enduring is in turn defined by absolute affliction and need, which define every moment in the life of a Christian. Even Paul himself admits twice that he could endure it no longer. Since we are weak, we need the help and grace of the Lord to remain steadfast and opposed to the power of Satan, who tries to tempt us to sin.

There is no certainty in the life of the first Christians, because the 'Parousia' comes as a thief in the night. Nobody knows when the day of the Lord will come and there is nothing anybody can do to bring it closer. The only possible preparation for Judgment Day is to be ready. Paul incites his fellow Christians therefore to remain watchful and sober. Everyone must remain in the situation in which he was called, follow God's commandments and work with his own hands, so that he will not trouble anybody. This kind of life involves a peculiar moment of insight, 'kairos', that comes with the full alertness to our situation. Christian life begins with the kairological decision to accept God's word and live one's life in anticipation of the 'Parousia'. A Christian makes every decision in his life in the light of the 'Parousia'. The uncertain certainty of the 'Parousia' determines the factual life experience of the Christian. How the 'Parousia' stands in my life refers back to the full temporal actualization of my life. Christian religiosity experiences temporality as such. The life of the primitive Christians was enormously difficult, always actualized in need and affliction. The intensification of need and affliction gives the becoming Christian the feeling that it is beyond him to endure this life. Without God's help and grace he is lost. A Christian life is lived before the face of God. A Christian is never ready. Every day he must relive his conversion and endure in his faith. Is this kind of life still possible in the modern world?

What is the essence of modernity? As Heidegger sees it, science and historical consciousness determine modern times. Science expands ever further into other areas of life and culture like politics, art, and religion. In modern times people expect scientific answers even to existential questions. Modern man no longer creates works of art; he develops esthetic theories about art. He is no longer politically active; he leaves politics to paid experts. He no longer dances for God in fear and trembling; he misuses Him as the keystone of his morality. Theoretical consciousness and the subject-object relation determine science. One of the consequences of this objectifying of reality is that we have begun to regard ourselves as objects in the midst of other objects. According to Heidegger, Greek philosophy is the origin of the theoretical and contemplative attitude toward life. For the Greeks, reality was a cosmos. They enjoyed esthetically the magnificent spectacle that took place before their eyes. The ultimate expression of the factual life experience of the Greeks is Platonism and its doctrine of eternal ideas, which we can behold only in pure contemplation. As a consequence, modern factual life experience is at odds with Christian factual life experience, which is dominated by need and affliction. It seems therefore very unlikely that a Christian life is still possible in modern times.

The other main element in modern life experience, historical consciousness, is, on the contrary, of Christian origin. The Greeks knew no history. In an eternal cosmos there can be no creation and no Last Day. The factual life experience of modern times is an inauthentic mixture of Christian and Greek life experience, which contradict each other. This implies that modern man can no longer live his life in an authentic way. In his early lecture courses in Freiburg Heidegger tried to unravel this interlacing in what he called the destruction of Greek and Christian factual life experience. This de(con)struction is not destructive in the ordinary sense, but a careful scraping off of layers that cover up the original life experience. The intertwining of Christian and Greek life experience began with the Church fathers who used Greek philosophy to explain Christian faith and thus corrupted both Greek and Christian factual life experience. In his Summer Semester 1921 course on Augustine and neo-Platonism Heidegger tried to separate the Greek and Christian elements in the saint's factual life experience. In order to be able to distinguish between original Greek and Christian elements, Heidegger had to disclose also the original factual life experience of the Greeks. This element of his destruction would lead to his yearlong study of Aristotle. The source and the focus of Greek life experience was found by Heidegger in Aristotle and not in Plato or Parmenides.

What did Heidegger find in Aristotle? While interpreting Aristotle's writings on practical philosophy and rhetoric, he discovered that affliction and a kairological experience of time do play an important part in Greek life experience after all. He found an original experience of 'kairos' paralleling that of primitive Christianity in Aristotle's account of 'phronèsis' as a way of beholding the true in *Nicomachean Ethics VI*. 'Phronèsis' is the moment of insight that ends the deliberation about what the right action is towards the right person in this situation. Heidegger identified it as conscience already set in motion to make an action transparent. This discovery would ultimately lead to the demise of Christianity in Heidegger's phenomenology of life in and for itself. The two most important elements of Christian life experience were

expressed more clearly in Greek philosophy and the historical consciousness of modern times. The discussion between Aristotle, Paul
and Heidegger became a Greek-German dialogue. In his *Physics IV*
Aristotle developed an explicit theory of time as a series of nows. This
doctrine became the paradigm for all later theories of time. In Winter
Semester 1922/23 Heidegger discovered that 'ousia' for the Greeks
meant constant presence. Heidegger tried to understand being in terms
of time in its fullest and most fulfilled sense. Through Aristotle he
discovered the relationship between Being and time. Aristotle's conception of logic as a productive science of truth, or the unconcealment
of entities in their being, would ultimately lead to the fundamental
ontology of *Being and Time*. In his final course as an unsalaried lecturer, Heidegger developed for the first time a phenomenology of
human being-there as the condition of the possibility of Greek, Christian, and modern factual life experience.

The existential drift of his phenomenology had also brought him and
Karl Jaspers together after their first meeting in 1919. For more than a
decade they would remain close friends. Heidegger visited Jaspers
regularly in Heidelberg to work together in a joint battle community
against university politics and the 'professors' of philosophy. They
shared a love for Kierkegaard, and Heidegger's critical comments on
Jaspers' book *Psychology of Worldviews* were at the heart of their
discussions.

In January 1922 Husserl learned that Natorp would be retiring
shortly, that Nicolai Hartmann would take his place, and that as a result the junior position in philosophy at the University of Marburg
would be vacant. Natorp had been impressed by Heidegger's book on
Duns Scotus. By 1922, Heidegger was renowned in university circles
as an outstanding teacher. In the student body the rumor of the hidden
king became ever louder. The only problem was that he had published
nothing since the Scotus book. For this reason plans were soon initi-
ated for Heidegger to publish a work on Aristotle. After months of
intense labor over the manuscripts of his courses on Aristotle, he pro-
duced the *Introduction* to the projected book in which he founded and
developed the hermeneutic situation in which he would interpret Aristotle's writings. This introduction has since become famous. When
Natorp read his copy in October of 1922, he marveled over finding so
many of his own ideas there on the development of the German spirit,
from Meister Eckhart to Martin Luther and onto Kant and German
idealism. It was therefore not surprising that Natorp used his consider-
able influence to get Heidegger appointed.

The Marburg years: 'Being and Time' (1923-1928)

The years in Marburg were among the most creative of Heidegger's life. Here he conceived *Being and Time*, delivered important lectures, and gave some of his most interesting courses and seminars. For a short period Heidegger enjoyed the company of Natorp, who was one of the main influences on his early life and thought. They were kindred spirits who could keep silent on their many walks through Marburg. Heidegger and Rudolf Bultmann would soon become close friends. They studied Luther together and jointly held seminars in theological exegesis. Bultmann was strongly influenced by the existential analysis of being-there that he used for his demythologizing interpretation of the Bible.

In 1924 Hannah Arendt came to Marburg as an 18-year-old girl to study with Heidegger, the hidden king of German philosophy. They soon fell in love and had an extramarital and passionate love affair for almost five years. Heidegger was twice her age and had two sons. According to Heidegger she was the only person who understood him and his work. In 1926 Arendt took Heidegger's advice and moved to Heidelberg to study with Jaspers.

The coming of Heidegger put his colleague Nicolai Hartmann under great pressure. He finally gave in and moved to Cologne in 1925 to join forces with his friend Max Scheler. The faculty wanted to name Heidegger as successor of Hartmann to the chair of philosophy, but the ministry of education hesitated since he had not published anything in a decade. Under pressure from his peers Heidegger decided to publish his yearlong phenomenological investigations in the form of a book. In March 1926 he retired to Todtnauberg and wrote in four weeks the first 175 pages of *Being and Time*, the work that would be published in Husserl's *Jahrbuch für Philosophie und phänomenologische Forschung* in 1927 and bring him world fame. Heidegger spent the summer of 1926 in Todtnauberg where he continued to work on *Being and Time* and stayed at the Brender-Hof, a farm where he rented a room, while Elfride and the boys stayed in the cabin.

Being and Time is a milestone on Heidegger's path of thinking and one of the most important and influential philosophical works of this century. In a sense it is the answer to Heidegger's existential question of 1919: how can I live as a Christian in the modern world? This vital question is the most concrete and personal question that we can ask ourselves. But - and this is Heidegger's decisive discovery while he was writing *Being and Time* - the most concrete question, who am I?, can be answered only if we know what is means to be. He reformulates the traditional question of being, what is an entity as entity? as the question about the meaning of being. This question is ambiguous for it can mean both what is the sense of being? and what does to be mean to me?

What it means to be is something we can experience only in our own life. In *Being and Time* Heidegger uses being-there as a formal indication of the way of being of humans. It is important to note that the phenomenon of being-there is determined by its intentionality and is therefore essentially being-in-touch-with. This phenomenon shows itself in its being in the complex structure of care. We care for each other and ourselves. We take care of things and people. We care about. Being human is caring, which indicates that we are not disinterested spectators, but active participants in this great enterprise called being. We care about our being and have to take care of our being. In the complex phenomenon of care three ways of being human are interlaced. Being human is: 1. Being-in-(touch-with)-the-world, 2. Being-(in-touch)-with-other-human-beings, and 3. Being-(in-touch)-with-oneself. Being-in originally means being familiar with. Being-in-the-world is not primarily a spatial quality, like the beer is in a glass and the glass is in a pub. We always find ourselves as being-in-a-world with which we are familiar. Being-with is the phenomenon that we are never alone, but always among other human beings. Finally, the phenomenon of being-in-touch-with-oneself shows factual life experience is always mine. This mineness is a formal and not a material concept.

Being can only reveal itself in being-there. The comportment of being-there towards the being of entities is determined by understanding. In everything we do and say, we have an implicit understanding of the sense of being. According to Heidegger, this vague and implicit understanding is an undeniable fact. However, there is no direct answer to the question of being. We can only experience Being in the interlacing of structures that constitute being-there as the unconcealment of Being. Since being-there is determined by mineness, we can only discover in our own existence what Being is. To ask the question of being is an outstanding possibility of our being-there. To philosophize is in this sense an existential exercise and demands the willingness to pay with ourselves. In philosophy we learn to ask questions that we would rather not ask ourselves. Heidegger's invitation to ask the question of being once again enables us to understand *Being and Time* as his *protrepticus*, that is, an invitation to philosophy, or a summons to start thinking out of need, because we want to know who we are. In this thinking out of need we can hear the echo of his earlier critique of the decadent, modern world. We need to recollect ourselves from the pleasures and divertissements of modern life and care about our own being. This mystic element of reflection runs through Heidegger's whole path of thinking like a guiding thread. The greatest need and gravest danger of our time is that we are threatened by nothing. There is no more need for us.

As Heidegger sees it, Being is a phenomenon that only reveals itself in the being-in-touch-with or understanding of being-there. Being-there is the unconcealment of Being and so the clearing in which Being can be experienced. Being is only if and as long as being-there is. The structure of understanding needs to be explicated in order to disclose the sense of being as meaningfulness. This implies that Being can be revealed only from the whole of the existential structure of being-there. This leads to two major problems. First of all, we are ourselves the entities whose way of being is determined as being-there. In an ontic sense nothing is closer to us than being-there, but in an ontological sense nothing is further from us than being-there. We are, after all, always already beyond ourselves in the world and return, as it were, from the world to ourselves. This is also the reason why we understand our own being in terms of the being of nature or natural entities. This explains why the classical definition of human being is rational animal. In order to get a clear view of the structure of being-there we must first scrape away the deposit of this natural point of view. This destruction is the task that Heidegger wanted to undertake in the second part of *Being and Time* that was never published. The second difficulty is that being-there is always under way and never finished. I can never analyze my whole being-there as long as I am still alive and therefore not yet finished. What we can do, however, is disclose the whole structure of the temporality that makes my being-there possible. Heidegger names the structures of being-there existentials in contrast to the categories of traditional ontology.

The sense of being is temporality. The Temporality (*Temporalität*) of Being expresses itself in the temporality (*Zeitlichkeit*) of being-there. The central problematic of all ontology is rooted in the phenomenon of time. Heidegger characterizes being-there as possibility and can-be. Being-there is its possibility. The essence of being-there lies in its existence, that is, its having to be. Existence is the formal indication of the phenomenon that being-there comports itself in one way or another to its own being as its most unique possibility. Being-there is literately its own having to be. As an entity that is determined by the different possibilities of what it can be, being-there has no material qualities, but possibilities it can actualize and give up. Because it is in each instance its possibility, being-there can choose itself.

Being-there's most basic ability to live and cope skillfully with our world, with each other and ourselves, is understanding. Understanding expresses itself in the disclosedness of being-there that in its getting-around entities uncovers the being of entities and brings them thus into unconcealment. We discover the being of entities that are ready-to-hand as equipment, which is suited for certain uses. A hammer is a piece of equipment that lies ready and is suited for hammering. We discover the being of entities that are present-at-hand objectively as a being in itself independent of its relation to our being-there. This distance characterizes objectifying science that describes entities objectively. These descriptions are objectively valid for all subjects. When we do a scientific experiment, the outcome is independent of the subject that performs the experiment.

We discover the being of other people as being-with. I discover my own being-there as the 'for-the-sake-of-which' of my existence. Existential understanding has always the structure of a projection. Being-there has been thrown into possibilities that it really is and projects itself upon possibilities that it could actualize. Being-there is in its essence freedom and possibility. Because being-there has always other possibilities that it is not yet, it is never finished. It always has to be and always has an outstanding debt it still needs to pay. Our existence makes us guilty. This guilt is the source and condition of possibility of the original sin in the biblical sense. The disclosedness that in its projections creates the leeway within which being-there gets a view of its possibilities is illumination. In *Being and Time* Heidegger describes therefore being-there as the clearing, a formal indication that would come to the fore in his later philosophy. The *a priori* conditions of possibility of the clearing, that is, understanding, disclosedness and projections, form the ecstatic unity of temporality which illuminates being-there originally.

Heidegger analyzes in *Being and Time* the sense of being-there in the light of its temporality in order to provide subsequently an ontic foundation for ontology. The sense of being of being-there is either authentic or inauthentic. And so Heidegger is faced with the question whether he should study authentic or inauthentic being-there in order to analyze the sense of being. We should not mistake authenticity and inauthenticity for moral qualifications. They are equivalent existential characters. Inauthentic existence is not less than authentic existence. In order to be able to analyze the sense of being of being-there, we must disclose it as a whole. Being-there exists first and foremost inauthentically. It understands its own being in terms of the world and the 'they'. We project our possibilities in everyday life out of our concern for entities within the world as 'they' do it. Being-there is first and foremost lost in its concern for the world, fallen to the everydayness of the 'they' and not itself. And yet, mineness remains the condition of possibility of the unity of our being-there. This implies that even in being-there's total dissipation in the world and the 'they', the possibility of authentic existence must be preserved. The ultimate and most unique possibility that is and remains real as long as being-there exists, is death.

In its being-towards-death being-there anticipates the possibility of its death as possibility. The possibility of death is the impossibility of all comportment and as such the possible impossibility of existence as such. In the anticipation of its own death being-there understands the impossibility of its own existence as an inevitable possibility. Being-there is possible nonbeing, is not something and therewith a pure can-be that has to be. I can project my own possibilities and can avoid being determined by anything else, be it the world or the 'they'. Since as finite being-there we remain being-in-the-world and being-with, we can never completely actualize this possibility. It is no coincidence that death as the liberation from all external influence is at the same time the end of my existence. In this possibility, to determine ourselves who we want to be, we disclose the factual fallenness into the world and the 'they' of our everyday existence. Death is related to nothing else than our own most can-be, which is individualized through this relation. Death is a possibility that being-there cannot actualize completely, since the actualization of its death implies the end of its existence. In anticipating my death as the most unique possibility of my existence I become conscious of my own unique and once-only existence. Death is always my death of being-there in its individuality. Heidegger does not found the mineness of being-there upon the soul, the *cogito* or the I, but in the structure of being-towards-death. Authentic existence keeps open all possibilities and makes it possible for being-there to exist as a whole.

The being-towards-death of being-there is at the same time its finding itself in anxiety for its own can-be. Anxiety understands the possibility of existence as ultimate possibility. In being-towards-death the possibility of an authentic potentiality for being a whole is disclosed as an ontological possibility. Because being-there is first and foremost lost in its concern for the world and fallen to the idle talk of the 'they', the liberation from inauthenticity demands a turning. The call of conscience calls to being-there and invites it to heed the possibilities of its own unique existence. The call of conscience calls upon us to remember the possible authenticity of our existence and our responsibility for our own being-there. In the call of conscience, being-there calls to itself. It calls being-there forth into the unique situation of its own can-be. There is no general ideal of being-there. I have to be and I can be authentic or inauthentic. My responsibility is grounded in this having to be. My life is my answer to the call of conscience. This answer is an ongoing story. The authenticity of my existence slips away time and again. It is never my possession. I am not the owner of my existence as some kind of inalienable substance. As understanding being-there I have to be in each instance and I must therefore project and interpret my existence every time anew.

This always having to be is the guilt that is given with the fact of our being-there. Being-there has been thrown into existence, not by itself but to itself. This is the primal facticity of being-there: I find myself with others in a world and have to be, whether I like it or not. I have never asked to be born, but now that I have been born, I have to be what I can be. Existence brings with it the obligation of having to be. I am not the cause of my existence; I must become the author of my existence through the appropriation of my own being. With the gift of being-there is given the obligation of having to be. This having to be is the price I pay continuously for my own existence. Because there is no end to my having to be as long as I exist, I can never fully pay the price and therefore I remain indebted to my existence. Existence is both a pure givenness and a given task. I must appropriate my own existence even if I will never be fully in control.

I have to be and so I am faced with the question of who I have to be in each instance. In resoluteness being-there acquires insight into its situation and discovers the possibility of its authenticity. The situation is always a concrete situation of action that is disclosed in a concrete understanding. This concrete understanding is not the representation of a possible situation and a hypothetical musing on what we might do in such a situation; the concrete understanding of a situation is the projection of a resolution. Being-there already acts resolutely. In every situation it projects a certain ontic resolution of authentic existence. In this way being-there comes into the original truth of its existence. Resoluteness is in its most profound sense that which I have to be in the concrete, unique, and once-only situation of *my* existence. Anticipating resoluteness is the authentic existentiell understanding of the outstanding ultimate possibility that is radically my possibility in its individuality and which is certain to come and whose coming yet remains uncertain: my death. My resoluteness brings me into the situation of my existence as a whole. My existence is an ecstatic standing-out as a whole as I live it from inside. Being-there stands out in the openness of Being.

In *Being and Time* Heidegger formulates four theses with regard to temporality: 1. Temporality is constitutive for the structure of being-there's care. 2. Temporality is ecstatic. 3. Temporality actualizes itself in time originally from the future. 4. Primordial time is finite. The structure of care as a whole is being-ahead-of-itself-already-in-a-world as a being-with. Being-there's being-ahead-of-itself is grounded in the future. In its being-already, having been announces itself. Its being-with is actualized as making present. The primordial unity of the structure of care lies in temporality (thesis 1). Temporality is not made up of past, present and future, but actualizes itself in three ecstases (thesis 2). Being-there projects in its authentic understanding temporality. This is possible only if being-there exists in such a way that its most unique possibility can come towards it and it holds out this coming towards it as possibility. Only because it is futural, can being-there be authentically its having been. Future is the primordial phenomenon of temporality (thesis 3).

Primordial time is disclosed in being-there's authentic existentiell understanding. Heidegger introduces the moment as a formal indication of authentic or kairological present. The moment is the moment of resolute insight. The projection of resolution discloses the situation in the moment. Resoluteness projects a temporal leeway or clearing within which we can become what we have to be. Because I disclose my being-there in a moment in the whole of its temporal extensiveness, primordial time is finite (thesis 4). Authentic existence is the understanding of my own finitude, that is, the temporality of my existence.

Temporality always temporalizes possible ways of itself. These temporalizations make possible the manifold modes of being-there's being and especially the basic possibility of authentic and inauthentic existence. The essence of temporality is the temporalizing in the unity and equiprimordiality of the ecstases, which Heidegger names: future, present, and having-been. Being-there actualizes its being in different ways in time. These different ways are grounded in the uniform structure of care. Temporalizing is the interweaving of intentional structures that Heidegger tries to explain as schematizing. Temporality actualizes its different senses through different horizonal schemas. According to Heidegger traditional ontology failed to understand the being of being-there from temporality and thus made it impossible to disclose the sense of being from original time.

In Heidegger's existential analysis in *Being and Time*, we find also some elements that point ahead to his decision to become politically active. Resoluteness frees us for the world-historical aspects of our situation. Death is the highest jurisdiction of our can-be. In our being futural we shatter against death so that we are at once thrown back upon the 'there' of our facticity. We are free for death, free for fate, and free to commit ourselves at the decisive moments in world-history. We can give up any resolution and therewith also our independence. On the one hand, Heidegger is tenacious of the primacy of our can-be. On the other hand, his analysis is so formal and therefore with respect to content so empty, that it makes every ontic decision possible. Heidegger teaches us finally only that we have to be; who we have to be and what we have to be, he leaves to our own imagination and responsibility. Only resoluteness determines the authenticity or inauthenticity of our existence.

What remains underexposed in Heidegger's analysis is the moment of personal responsibility. There are no universal rules and obligations that can tell me what I have to do. In this sense there is for us no place to hide. My life is a book I have to write myself. Since nothing and nobody can tell us what to do, we can only learn from each other what we can do. It is therefore possible to use Heidegger's existential analysis as an ontological foundation for democracy. This possibility is often overlooked in the discussion of his involvement with National Socialism. In this respect we should learn to understand him better than he understood himself.

In *Being and Time* Heidegger shows how individual being-there can free itself from its obsession with the world and its fallenness to the 'they'. However, since being-there is always also a being-with, a real authentic existence implies an authentic being-with. Heidegger has remarkably little to say about authentic being-with. Our being-with must be actualized in each new generation. The unity of a generation lies in the choice of its heroes. The hero incorporates an ideal of authentic existence. Because the hero has to meet no ethical requirements, he can just as well be Albert Schweizer, Martin Luther King, and Mahatma Gandhi, or Adolf Hitler. From 1929 onward Heidegger will attempt to heal not only the broken existence of the individual human being, but also the broken world of modern times.

For a good understanding of Heidegger's later path of thinking it is important to keep in mind certain shortcomings of his analysis in *Being and Time*. It is remarkable that he describes the being of all entities that are not being-there as either readiness-to-hand or presence-at-hand. Being-in-the-world is essentially pragmatic. We encounter even the being-there of others first and foremost in the traces they have left in our environment. The book reminds me of the friend who gave it to me for my birthday. The nightgown on the chair belongs to the woman I made love to last night. Since being-there's being-in-the-world is pragmatic, the being of nature threatens to be reduced to standing-reserve for human purposes. Heidegger will later try to modify his phenomenology of the thing in order to overcome this technological disclosure of entities.

A second important element in *Being and Time* is Heidegger's mostly negative description of being-with. Modern man leads an impersonal life in the anonymity of the 'they'. He conforms himself to the illusions of the day and devours popular culture and entertainment while moving from one craze to another. Pleasure and distraction have become the highest values of this consumption society. Modern individualism has not led to authentic existence, but to a leveling-off and the dictatorship of mediocrity. Social relations disappear and money makes the world go round. Heidegger contrasts this bleak picture with authentic being-with, which is actualized in solicitude. And yet, he has not much to say about solicitude.

Third, authenticity and inauthenticity are not moral categories. Inauthentic existence is no less than authentic existence. As existentials they are purely formal indications. This is also the reason why we can not deduct any concrete determination from resoluteness. Every existentiell choice is possible and defendable as long as we hang on to it resolutely. And yet, no reader of *Being and Time* can escape the impression that only authentic existence is worthy of human being. In this respect Heidegger reveals himself to be another heir of Plato. It is the task of the philosopher to organize society in such a way that all citizens can lead a life worthy of human being. Heidegger's political involvement is also a consequence of his philosophy. When he will attempt to steer the development of the National Socialist revolution in the right direction, he will be faced with a major problem: the purely formal difference between authenticity and inauthenticity. A comparison with Kant's ethics may clarify this problem. Kant's categorical imperative is also a pure formal principle that does not prescribe for us a specific way to the good life. However, because I must be able to think without contradiction of the maxims of my actions as universal law, the categorical imperative enables us to distinguish between moral and immoral actions. Kant's categorical imperative would have prevented him from becoming a supporter of National Socialism. In Heidegger's philosophy, there was nothing that made this choice impossible, although we can read *Being and Time* as an apology for democracy.

Finally, one of the most remarkable things about *Being and Time* is that it was never finished. There are two reasons why it remained a torso:

1. It only makes sense to develop a fundamental ontology if the sense of being is revealed once and for all in being-there. In other words, the sense of being must be expressed in the a priori structure of the existentials that constitute being-there. Because Heidegger emphasizes the factual and historical character of being-there, the a priori structures of being-there are themselves mediated historically and therefore temporary. They develop and change in time. This implies that Being itself can never be revealed fully in being-there. It always has a more, which it has already been or which it must still become. When Heidegger becomes aware of this contradiction in 1929, he comes to the conclusion that Being itself must have a history and he begins to work out his conception of the history of Being.

2. The second reason why *Being and Time* would remain unfinished is that Heidegger still identifies being-there too much with human being. In this respect he remains within the tradition of Cartesian subjectivism. In his later philosophy he discloses being-there not from the being of humans, but from Being itself. Being-there then becomes the clearing in which Being reveals itself as the mirror-play of the fourfold of earth and sky, divinities and mortals. The 'there' is no longer the 'there' of human being, but the 'there' of Being as the clearing or the play of time-space.

The return to Freiburg and the years of crisis (1928-1933)

When Husserl retired in 1928, Heidegger was the logical choice to succeed him as the chair of philosophy at the University of Freiburg. In the summer of 1928 Heidegger returned to Freiburg and presented himself in his Winter Semester 1928/29 lecture course, *Introduction to Philosophy*, as the man who had brought the phenomenological revolution to its conclusion. In this course he rejected Husserl's project of making philosophy into a rigorous science, because philosophy is not a science and this not out of lack but rather out of excess. It springs from the ever superabundant and ebullient appropriation of being-there itself. After some intense discussions with Jaspers in Heidelberg, Heidegger gave up his attempt to finish the second unpublished part of *Being and Time* in 1929 although he would still publish *Kant and the Problem of Metaphysics*. This turning on his path of thinking is a consequence of his philosophical development and a result of the crisis of 1929. We find the first traces of the turning in his inaugural lecture *What Is Metaphysics?*

Heidegger delivered his inaugural lecture on July 24, 1929, in the assembly hall of the University of Freiburg. It was published the same year. In his lecture Heidegger takes up a particular metaphysical question: why are there entities at all and not rather nothing?

In the first part of the lecture Heidegger distinguishes sharply between science and metaphysics. In metaphysics each question is itself always the whole. This implies that the questioner as such is also there within the question and thus placed in question. Metaphysics must be posed as a whole from the essential position of the being-there that questions. Although there are many different fields of inquiry in science, we always approach what is essential in all things. In the pursuit of science human beings irrupt into the whole of entities in such a way that this irruption breaks open and shows what entities are in their being. Science studies entities and nothing else. In science the questioner remains outside his objective field of study and does not question himself. Science wishes to know nothing of the nothing. And yet, when it tries to express its essence, that is, the study of entities and nothing else, it calls upon the nothing for help. In this duplicitous state of affairs a question has already unfolded: how is it with the nothing?

Heidegger elaborates the question of the nothing in the second part of his lecture. The nothing is not an entity, and so we come face-to-face with the problem of how we can encounter the nothing. Heidegger defines the nothing as the complete negation of the totality of entities and can then ask how entities as a whole can be given to us. Being-there finds itself in the midst of entities as a whole. Although we concern ourselves first and foremost in our everydayness with particular entities, entities as a whole may become manifest in certain moods, for example, deep boredom. Heidegger describes how entities conceal from us the nothing the moment we come face-to-face with them as a whole. Is there an attunement in which we may be brought before the nothing itself? Heidegger can now point to anxiety as the mood that makes the nothing manifest.

In the third part Heidegger answers the question of how it is with the nothing. The nothing reveals itself in anxiety but not as an entity. In anxiety, human beings shrink back before the nothing. This wholly repelling gesture toward entities that are slipping away as a whole in anxiety is the essence of the nothing: nihilation. The nothing itself nihilates (*nichtet*). Nihilation manifests entities in their full. In the clear night of the nothing of anxiety the original openness of entities as such arises: that they are entities and not nothing. The encounter between being-there and entities is made possible by the original manifestation of the nothing. Being-there is being held out into the nothing. Only because the nothing is manifest in the ground of being-there can the strangeness of entities overwhelm us and evoke wonder. Only on the ground of wonder does the 'why' loom before us. Only then can we inquire into the ground and question entities. It is only because we can question and ground things that we ourselves are put in question.

Heidegger's inaugural lecture is in many ways a taste of things to come. This new forest trail will ultimately lead to the clearing of another nonmetaphysical kind of thinking and the attempt to overcome metaphysics. In 1930 Heidegger delivered his lecture, *On the Essence of Truth*, on different occasions. This lecture is a further development of the concept of truth in *Being and Time*. Heidegger claims that primordial truth is not the correspondence between the intellect and the matter which is expressed in judgment. According to this traditional doctrine, the proposition that the table is white is true if the table of which being white is asserted is indeed white. Heidegger harks back to the Greek concept of truth, 'alètheia', which he translates as unconcealment. As the term unconcealment indicates, the being of entities is discovered or unconcealed in truth. The truth of entities is wrested from concealment. Unconcealment is the dynamic interplay of revealment and concealment. Truth can therefore never be fully transparent. In the unconcealment of the being of entities, Being as such remains concealed. As Heidegger sees it, truth is the appropriation of the unconcealment of Being in the being of entities, where entities are preserved and Being itself remains concealed and is as such preserved as mystery.

Being-there and entities encounter each other in the openness of unconcealment. In this openness the leeway comes into being that makes the distance between being-there and entities possible. In this open space or clearing human beings can get in touch with entities.

Heidegger understands being-there now as the 'there' of Being, where human beings and entities encounter each other, and not as the being-there or existence of human beings. In the interplay of human beings and entities he discovers a double-sided kind of freedom or letting-be. On the one hand, entities let themselves be in truth or unconcealment. On the other hand, human beings are free to let entities be what they are in truth. The essence of truth is freedom and as such an open relation and interaction between human beings and entities that need to be actualized time and again. We must experience truth and refrain from establishing the truth once and for all. We must in each instance let entities have the possibility to show themselves as they are in truth.

The essence of freedom manifests itself as the letting-be of entities. Within the open lies the space for revealment and concealment, for truth and errancy, and for being present and being absent. Human beings exist within this dynamic structure. This is the 'there' where they are. When human beings shape the 'there' of their being in the form of the self-revealing concealment of Being as such, they create the movement of history. Truth lies in the open leeway between human beings and entities, where the truth of Being is appropriated. The relation between human beings and entities is determined by moods. These moods can be individual or collective. In the mood of anxiety human beings experience Being as the nothing and the possible impossibility of their own existence. The collective mood of deep boredom determines the being-there of modern man. In this fundamental mood we can hear the sound of the finitude of our existence.

Heidegger's conception of truth is a retrieval of the Greek experience of 'alètheia' as the appropriation of truth. Unconcealment is the 'there' of Being where the encounter of human beings and entities happens. Being-there is no longer the being 'there' of human beings; it has become the 'there' of Being as such. Heidegger will later describe the dynamic structure of unconcealment as the mirror-play of the fourfold. The truth of Being is an appropriation that has its own history. Being's appropriation of the being of entities and human beings will become the central topic of Heidegger's thought after the turning.

The year 1929 marks not only a new beginning on Heidegger's path of thinking, but also a decisive break in the history of Germany. Although World War I had ended with Germany's defeat, the humiliating treaty of Versailles, and political chaos, Heidegger saw in it the dawn of a new day. Another page in the book of life would be opened and, as he wrote to Elisabeth Blochmann, "the chance to make a new start made it a pleasure to be alive". Many people thought Judgment Day had come with the communist revolution in Russia. In Germany, the Republic of Weimar, and not the dictatorship of the proletariat, rose from the total chaos of 1919. Germany followed the way of capitalism and parliamentary democracy. The industrial revolution had gained momentum in Germany at the end of the 19th century and its results only became manifest in their full extent after 1919. The social relations of family, church, and village began to lose their unifying power. Small-scale production in agriculture and manufacture could not compete with industrial production and the power of large capital. The population deserted the countryside and moved to the big cities in search of work in factories. The masses of humanity grew ever larger in the slums where an existence worthy of human being was impossible. Nobody made a product; everybody performed his monotonous task as a part of the process of production. The machine determined the tempo of production, not the worker. The difference between the anonymous worker and the machine became ultimately blurred.

The Weimar Republic, which had been under intense pressure from the beginning, collapsed under the stock market crash and the Great Depression that followed. The ever-increasing problems and disasters led to a mood of crisis among the population. It finally became clear that World War I had not really solved any problems despite its horrors. Around this time, the topic of crisis makes its first appearance in Heidegger's lecture courses. The danger of a mood of crisis is that nobody feels the need for deliberation and discussion. We want only that the crisis be dealt with in an energetic fashion. A crisis demands the interference of the man of action and not the critical reflection of philosophy. The man who would answer the call for leadership of the German people had already begun his march in the beer cellars of Munich. Crisis is a word that we should use reluctantly and carefully. All too often the remedy turns out to be worse than the disease.

Heidegger too was sensitive to the mood of crisis in 1929. He searched for a remedy in the hope of finding a solution. In this year-long search he was for a time influenced by the work of Ernst Jünger. This German writer claimed that World War I marked the beginning of a new era that is determined by the will to power. Like Oswald Spengler, whose book *The Decline of the West* was a best-seller, Jünger was a passionate follower of Nietzsche. The will to power expresses itself in the striving for world dominion of capitalism and communism. The struggle for power between both blocs will lead to war again and again. War is no longer the continuation of politics with different means; peace has become an armament race and as such the continuation of war with other means. Jünger calls this continuous state of war the total mobilization that subordinates everything and everybody to the holy cause: the final victory. The total mobilization blurs the differences between the soldier and the worker. The new overman is a fighting machine. In his work Jünger celebrates the manly virtues of the soldier. During World War I he had experienced the massacres of the battlefields with a macabre kind of esthetic pleasure. In an almost mystic experience he understood the violence and horror of the trenches as the ultimate revelation of Being.

Heidegger agreed to a large extent with Jünger's analysis of modern times. However, on two points he disagreed with Jünger. First of all, he could not find any esthetic pleasure in the vision of the future Jünger painted. He was horrified by it. Furthermore, he rejected the metaphysical necessity of the total mobilization. Hölderlin had taught him that in the gravest danger the saving power also grows.

Heidegger saw an important task for the German people. Contrary to the United States and Russia, Germany was not the land of scientists and technicians, but a people of thinkers and poets. The German people needed to do battle against the total mobilization and the will to power. Heidegger rejected not only communism, but also capitalism and its parliamentary democracy. The total mobilization is made possible by technology, which in turn is founded upon the mathematical science of nature. The mechanization of the world picture is a product of modern times and began with the dream of Descartes and his quest for indubitable knowledge. Real can only be that which I know for certain, and only that which I can calculate mathematically can I know for certain. Ergo, everything real must be measurable and thus calculable. Heidegger crossed out all of the attainments of modern times and in this way threw out the baby with the bathwater. He wanted to undo the leveling-off of human being to labor force and of nature to raw material, and replace them with mutual respect for each other's qualities in a corporate society and a careful and cautious use of natural resources.

The German people had to accomplish their task through a retrieval of the authentic existence of the other people of thinkers and poets, the Greeks. The life of the Greeks was rooted in the 'polis'. Likewise, the being-there of the German people needed to grow roots in its homeland. Heidegger's political solution for the crisis of modern times was a provincial national socialism. It was of course the task of the philosopher, and Heidegger in particular, to ensure that the German people would actualize their being-there in an authentic way. Heidegger's involvement with National Socialism is motivated by both political and philosophical deliberations. The untenable situation of the Weimar Republic and the bankruptcy of the old university system in the early 1930s demanded a solution. Like many Germans, Heidegger saw in the rise of National Socialism the unique possibility of a new beginning. His concept of the history of Being enabled him to interpret the National Socialist revolution as a first and necessary step toward the overcoming of technology and nihilism. When he will later reject National Socialism, he will also do so on philosophical and political grounds. In his view, the historical reality of National Socialism is an appearance of the will to power and has nothing in common with the inner truth and greatness of his own brand of national socialism.

Heidegger's philosophy was strongly influenced by his yearlong and passionate exposition of Nietzsche. We can distinguish two periods in Heidegger's interpretation of Nietzsche. In the beginning he is deeply impressed by Nietzsche's philosophy with its analysis of nihilism and doctrine of the overman. The second phase starts in 1936 with his famous lecture courses on Nietzsche. In these courses he coupled the doctrine of the will to power with the doctrine of the eternal recurrence of the same, and he also interpreted the history of the Western world as a process of decay that expressed itself in nihilism.

In the first phase Heidegger developed a doctrine of the work. In *Being and Time* he had interpreted the being of entities as the readiness-to-hand of equipment and the presence-at-hand of objects. He now rejects this interpretation as too technological. If we can discover the being of all entities only as equipment and raw material for further use, reality does indeed become Jünger's gigantic factory. In his search for an alternative interpretation Heidegger will retrieve once again the philosophy of Aristotle. Aristotle had discovered the being of entities as 'energeia', that is, that which is working. An entity is that which works and has its efficacy: the work.

Heidegger distinguishes between three kinds of work: the work of art, the work of thought, and the work of state. As the work of art is the creation of the artist and the work of thought the creation of the philosophers, the work of state is the creation of the great statesman. This conception of 'great' politics is antidemocratic. It will not come as a big surprise that, according to Heidegger, the political being-there of the German people during the Weimar Republic was inauthentic. Since only the individual can actualize authentic existence in his own being-there, only an individual could liberate the German people from the inauthenticity of their existence. In this respect Heidegger shows himself to be a follower of Plato. In the famous allegory of the cave the locals must be liberated by force and forced to face true reality in the world beyond the cave. Likewise, the German people needed to be forced by their political leader to actualize an authentic existence. Heidegger's own task was to disclose in his work of thought the essence of the authentic being-there of the German people. As Georg Friedrich Wilhelm Hegel saw the world-soul in the person of Napoleon Bonaparte passing through the streets of Jena in 1806, Heidegger saw in Hitler the charismatic *Führer* who could turn his work of thought into political reality.

The metaphysical awakening and the self-assertion of the German University (1933-1936)

Heidegger saw in the rise of National Socialism in the early 1930s a sign that the time had come to put his theory of national socialism into practice. He supported the Nazi Party because the National Socialist movement seemed to promise the possibility of an inner recollection and renewal of the German people and a path that would allow it to discover its historical vocation in the Western world. In Heidegger's view, it was the task of the university to contribute to this inner self-collection of the German people. For this reason he saw in the rectorate an opportunity to lead all capable forces back to this necessary process of reflection and renewal. In this manner he hoped also to counter the advance of unsuited persons and the threatening hegemony of the party apparatus and doctrine. On April 21, 1933, the professors of the University of Freiburg elected Heidegger rector almost unanimously, however, with the exception of their Jewish colleagues who were banned from voting. He was nominated as a candidate for the election by the resigning rector, Professor Wilhelm von Möllendorff, whose position as a Social Democrat had become untenable. As a supporter of Hitler Heidegger lent his name and efforts to the National Socialist revolution as rector. He became for a short time an outspoken propagandist for Hitler's policies. During his rectorate the 'cleansing laws' were applied to the Freiburg University student body and thus ended financial support for anyone who fit the description of non-Aryan in Nazi law. The *Führer* principle was established at the university on October 1, 1933, thereby making Heidegger the virtual dictator of the campus. It is therefore remarkable, and an often-overlooked fact, that he appointed only non-party members (including his predecessor von Möllendorff) as deans of the different departments. He tried to reform the university in conformity with his own ideas that were shared to a large extent by Karl Jaspers. When dealing with Heidegger's political involvement we should not forget that nobody knew what horrors were going to occur later. As late as 1936 the whole world would join Hitler in Berlin for the Olympic Games. Like many people Heidegger believed Hitler would later right the wrongs and excesses that are the unfortunate by-product of any true revolution.

On May 27, 1933, on the occasion of the ceremonial transfer of the rector's office, Heidegger delivered his often misunderstood rectoral address. In this lecture he outlined his thoughts on the essence of the German university and its historical mission. His assumption of the rectorate is the commitment to the spiritual leadership of the university. His following of teachers and students can grow strong only in a true and joint rootedness in the essence of the German University. This essence can gain power only when the leaders themselves are led by the spiritual mission that forces the fate of the German people to bear the stamp of their history. The university should aid the German people to fulfill its historical mission, that is, the retrieval of the awakening of Greek philosophy. This beginning still is, it does not lie in the past but stands before the German people. Greek philosophy is the source from which all sciences have sprung.

The National Socialist revolution is the great awakening of the German people. The university teachers must take the lead and advance to the most extreme posts of danger amid the constant uncertainty of the world. The essential will to knowledge requires that the people be subjected to the greatest inner and outer danger in order to enjoy their true spiritual world, that is, the truth of Being. This world is grounded in the forces of soil and blood as the power of the inmost agitation and greatest shattering of its being-there. The German students are on the march. The academic freedom of the old university will be replaced by a new series of obligations: the labor service, the military service, and the service in knowledge. Teachers and students must form a fighting community in service to the people in their state. All capacities of the heart and the body must be unfolded through struggle, intensified in struggle, and preserved as struggle. Heidegger closes his address with the words of Plato: everything great stands in the storm and thus indicates that the project of a renewal of both the university and the being-there of the German people is threatened from all sides. At this time he still believed the National Socialist revolution could lead to a renewal of the being-there of the German people.

The rectorate is at the heart of Heidegger's involvement with National Socialism. On November 3, 1933, he told the assembled students that "the *Führer* himself and he alone *is* the German reality and its law, today and for the future". A week later he took to the radio to urge ratification of Hitler's withdrawal from the League of Nations. In reply to requests by the Baden Ministry of Culture Heidegger wrote negative reports on Professor Hermann Staudinger and Eduard Baumgarten in 1933. He had known Baumgarten, a distant cousin of Max Weber, personally. In 1930 he had appointed his former student Werner Brock as his assistant rather than Baumgarten, because he thought Brock was the more promising and talented of the two. In 1938 he prevented his student Max Müller from getting an academic position by informing the administration of the Freiburg University that he was unfavorably disposed to the Nazi regime. On the other hand, he helped former students and friends like Karl Löwith, Elisabeth Blochmann, Helene Weiss and Werner Brock to settle abroad, and as rector he tried to avoid the forced retirement of his colleagues Eduard Fraenkel and Georg von Hevesy in 1933. Fraenkel was fired, but von Hevesy could stay on.

At the end of February 1934 Heidegger told the Baden minister of culture, Otto Wacker, that he wanted to resign as rector because he did not want to replace von Möllendorff and Erik Wolf as deans. Wacker asked Heidegger to keep his resignation secret until a successor could be found. After two failed attempts, the minister found Professor Eduard Kern willing to take over. While in the meantime Professor Adolf Lampe had been negotiating behind his back with the Ministry of Culture, Heidegger forced the issue and resigned officially as rector on April 23, 1934. He announced the news to the deans of the different departments on the same day. They resigned as well out of solidarity. Heidegger's attempts to reform the university had been frustrated by both the party apparatus and his colleagues.

On Heidegger's path of thinking a second important turning took place in 1934. He now began to turn away from Nazism as the political reality of National Socialism. This about-face is the result of his further Nietzsche studies and of his becoming aware of the criminal character of the Nazi regime. He was deeply shocked by the lawless killings of June 30. He distanced himself from Nazism in 1934 and formulated in his courses a covert critique of the Nazi movement. Although he considered his involvement with National Socialism to be the biggest mistake of his life, he did not feel obliged to publicly confess his guilt after 1945. In my view, there are several reasons why

Heidegger kept almost completely silent about his involvement with National Socialism after 1945. His main writings on this period in his life, the *Spiegel-Interview* and *The Rectorate: Facts and Thoughts*, were, after all, published posthumously.

First of all, in his political philosophy he used the term people as a unitary concept. He explained the authenticity of the being-there of the German people in as individualistic a way as he did the authentic existence of being-there in *Being and Time*. The unity of the German people was rooted in the will of one leader and one party. Since Hitler and the Nazis had actualized an inauthentic form of German being-there, they had misled the German people. Because 'they' had committed the crimes against humanity, none of the Germans was responsible. The German people were as much a victim of Hitler and the ruse of the will to power as the rest of the world. Nazism had nothing to do with the inner truth and the greatness of Heidegger's national socialism. He thus rejected Karl Jaspers' notion of collective guilt. In his view only those who had committed crimes were guilty. He was not a war criminal and had therefore no reason to protest his innocence publicly. He had defended his actions before the de-Nazification committee, the French military government had lifted the prohibition against his teaching in 1949, and in 1951 the Baden government had granted him emeritus status. For Heidegger this episode in his life was over.

The second reason is that Heidegger's concept of the history of Being reduced all political systems to an expression of the will to power. As he saw it, there was no essential difference between Stalinist communism, American liberalism, and Nazism. They all strove for world-dominion and subjected everything to the total mobilization. As he wrote to his former student Herbert Marcuse in 1948, what happened to the Jews under the Nazi regime was no different from what was happening to the East Germans under Russian occupation. His critique of modernity turned a blind eye to political differences.

Third, Heidegger thought language determined the essence of a people. Each people lived in their own language as their house of Being and disclosed Being in their own, historically unique way. Since the essence of language is poetry, the poets found the being of a people. Each people has its own fate which is destined by Being. During his involvement with National Socialism from 1933 until 1934, Heidegger thought the *Führer*, as the political leader of the German people, could decide their fate. Hitler could recollect the German people in the essence of their being-there and the National Socialist revolution could force them to achieve the authenticity of their being-there. In his history of Being, the Greeks were the people of the first beginning of philosophy. The Germans were the people of the other beginning of commemorative thinking. The great poets Homer, Aeschylus, Euripides, and Sophocles founded the essence of the Greek people. According to Heidegger, the German people had never come into their own. Unlike England, France, and the United States, Germany had never been a political unity and had not actualized its essence in this unity. This is the reason why the great poets of the German people, like Hölderlin and Rilke, had not founded the essence of their being-there. They had only foretold the still future possibility of their authentic being-there. From this it followed that the Holocaust had not tainted the future essence of the German people. Even after 1945 they could remain the people of the poets and the thinkers, and the saving power could still only grow in German soil.

The history of Being and the task of thinking (1936-1976)

After the biggest error of his life Heidegger again got on the track of thinking in 1934. He followed the trace of Nietzsche's word: God is dead. This enormous saying, which may exceed the finitude of human being, is not a verdict about the dying of a god. It refers to the slow decline of Greek-Christian norms and values in modern times, that is, the process of nihilism as the inner movement of Western history. The traditional values have become worthless. This moral 'crisis' is a problem we still have to confront today. We have no answer to the question why. Nietzsche's resolution of the problem of nihilism is in theory as simple as it is effective. However, reality is often more unruly than even great philosophers think. If all values have become worthless, then it becomes necessary to revaluate all values. Since all our values are of Platonic origin, and as he saw it, Christianity was Platonism for the common people, Nietzsche wanted to bring about a reversal of Platonism through his revaluation of all values. In a sense, he stood Plato on his head. We should search for values neither in the transcendent reality of the Ideas nor in heaven as the Kingdom of God, but in our natural desires and inclinations. This revaluation should lead to the birth of a new kind of human being: the overman who has the courage to live his life to the full without paying attention to slavish moral rules and obligations. During his study of Nietzsche's writings Heidegger discovered that Nietzsche, precisely because he turned Platonism upside down, remained fully dependent upon the tradition he tried to overcome. His philosophy as a reversal of Platonism remained nihilistic. With this insight Heidegger could take another step. He identified the history of nihilism and the history of metaphysics from Plato until Nietzsche. Hegel's system of absolute idealism was the consummation of Platonism. Metaphysics comes to an end in Nietzsche's reversal of Platonism as its last and ultimate possibility. This end is at the same time the beginning of our being without measure in our relation to nature, God, and ourselves. The scientific quest for truth has become a shameless pursuit of control over and subjection of nature and no longer attempts to do justice to nature. We have abolished the moral world and now know only the law of money and the strong. We have begun to experiment with our own bodies and accept no limit. This experience was at the origin of Heidegger's conception of the history of Being.

The history of metaphysics starts with Plato and ends with the nightmare of Jünger. This implies also a self-criticism of Heidegger. The thought that we could solve the crisis of the modern world by taking decisive action remains an expression of the will to power and only strengthens nihilism. We cannot overcome the will by force of will. This also implies that politics cannot solve the problem of nihilism. Does this mean that all hope is lost? No, because the history of metaphysics is a distinct era which started only with Plato. The being-there of human being that has been actualized in the history of metaphysics is only a possible and not a necessary being-there. It remains tied to a certain area and a certain time. Heidegger is thus faced with two alternatives. In non-European cultures other ways of being-there may have been actualized. This is the reason why Heidegger attempted to start a dialogue with Chinese and Japanese philosophy on his later path of thinking. This undertaking is difficult and wrought with peril. On the one hand, European culture and technology have begun to dominate all other cultures. This is what Heidegger calls the process of Americanization. On the other hand, a dialogue between East and West is only possible by way of translation. Translation transmits that which is other in Far Eastern culture into our own language and thus absorbs it into our own culture. It is very difficult to safeguard the other as other and understand it in its own identity.

The second alternative is the Greek beginning of European being-there. Greek being-there is older than metaphysics. Heidegger therefore tries to discover another possibility than that of metaphysics in the Greek beginning of our being-there. In his retrieval of the original thinking of Anaximander, Parmenides, and Heraclitus he finds traces of a pre-metaphysical kind of thinking and being-there. The origin of

Greek culture is the experience of 'alètheia' as the unconcealment of Being. The origin of philosophy is the discovery that the ground of Being and the being of the ground of all entities are identical. Being must be disclosed from its own ground and guarded in word and thinking in such a way that human beings can save all entities in their essence. The original Greek thinkers understood the unconcealment of Being as 'physis', which names the process of the unconcealment of entities. The original thinking of Being of Anaximander, Heraclitus, and Parmenides, which spoke from the unconcealment of Being and listened to the address of Being, was transformed into metaphysics by Plato and Aristotle. They explicated Being as the beingness of entities. Beingness is the attribute which makes that something is, just as beauty is the attribute which makes that something is beautiful. In the being of entities Being withdraws itself and is therefore forgotten. This forgetfulness of being is the condition of possibility of metaphysics. In metaphysics, truth is no longer understood as unconcealment; it has become correctness, that is, the correspondence between the intellect and its object in judgment. Thinking decides whether an entity is or is not. Metaphysics is onto-theo-logy because it understands the being of entities as beingness and grounds this beingness in the being of a highest entity. In scholastic philosophy beingness is understood as being created and grounded in the being of God as creator of heaven and earth. In modern times beingness has become measurable quantity, which is grounded in the subjectity of the modern subject that reduces everything to standing-reserve for its technological tricks. We make what we can and not what we need. The era of metaphysics lies clenched between two nonmetaphysical eras. The preceding era has left its traces in primordial Greek being-there. The second era still lies in the future and is announced in the poetry of Hölderlin. Metaphysics is not a result of a philosophical failure. It is the fate of European humanity that has been destined by Being itself.

Heidegger's interpretation of 'alètheia' determines his later path of thinking. Unconcealment is the truth of Being as the clearing where human beings and entities can encounter each other. In this clearing Being reveals itself through its withdrawal into the surrounding darkness. In this way it makes room for the being of entities as a whole. The clearing is the place where Being is 'there'. Being-there is no longer the way of being of human beings; it has become the manifestation of Being. Because Being can be there only if it withdraws itself, Being comes to presence in the clearing as the nothing. It is therefore no coincidence that Being was forgotten in the course of the history of metaphysics. For us Being as Being is not there. We can experience Being only as the nothing. The 'there' of Being is the clearing where earth and sky, divinities and mortals gather and in the mirror-play of their gathering actualize their existence. This appropriation of the unconcealment of Being is the original meaning of truth. Truth is the place where Being happens. Heidegger calls the happening of Being appropriation. This is the formal indication of the mystery of Being and the center around which Heidegger's later thinking revolves.

The ground of authentic Greek being-there, which is not so much a merit of the Greeks as a destiny of Being, is the epic poetry of Homer. The voice of poetry bids all that is - world and things, earth and sky, divinities and mortals - to gather into the simplicity (*Einfalt*) of their intimate belonging together. Poetry is thus the 'founding and giving' (*Stiftung*) of the unconcealment of Being and so the origin of the history of a people. The Greek work of thinking was preceded by the work of poetry. In Heidegger's new conception there is no longer an authentic role for politics. This means also that the poets must lay the ground for the post-metaphysical era. As Heidegger sees it, Hölderlin is the poet of the new authentic being-there of the German people. In his poetry Heidegger discovers hints of the authentic German being-there that is still to come. Hölderlin is the messenger of the last God whose coming he foretells. Since we are finite beings, we cannot overcome metaphysics on our own. Only a god can save us from the triumph of technology. The destiny of human beings is the letting-be of entities in unconcealment. This power to let things be is what Heidegger calls acquiescence. This acquiescence is the only authentic attitude of life that is possible in modern times. Acquiescence is essentially an openness to the mystery of Being. As shepherds of Being we must preserve the being of entities.

Heidegger's later philosophy follows two tracks: 1. He elaborates the history of Being and the history of metaphysics as nihilism in great detail. 2. As a possible answer to the crisis of modernity he begins to develop another, nonmetaphysical kind of thinking. This new thinking is a commemoration of the mystery of Being and a letting-be of entities as they are. As such it is an alternative to the calculative thinking of science and technology and a preparation for a new authentic way of being-there.

1. In the history of Being, Heidegger retraces the successive transformations of the relation between human beings and Being. This originally hidden process determines our history. Being emits the truth of Being. With the Greek experience of 'alètheia' as the unconceal-

ment of Being, the era of philosophy begins. The original thinkers, Anaximander, Heraclitus, and Parmenides, named 'alètheia' as the unconcealment of Being but could not think of 'alètheia' as the clearing of Being in its ontological difference from the being of entities. This was not a failure on their part. It was the destiny of Being itself.

The history of metaphysics begins with Plato and Aristotle. 'Alètheia' becomes truth as correctness and Being becomes the beingness of entities, which is grounded in God as the highest entity. Metaphysics has an onto-theo-logical structure and is determined by the forgetfulness of being. The history of metaphysics finds its consummation in the absolute idealism of Hegel and its end in Nietzsche's reversal of Platonism. The end of philosophy is not a mere stopping, but has to be understood as completion. Philosophy is metaphysics and metaphysics is Platonism. Nietzsche achieved the most extreme possibility of philosophy in his reversal of Platonism. The completion of metaphysics is the triumph of the manipulable arrangement of a scientific-technological world and its social order. The present age of nihilism is determined by the will to power and technology. Being emits itself as enframing into the clearing and withdraws itself as such into concealment. Heidegger tries to overcome metaphysics in an attempt to think of the essence of metaphysics and in a reflection on the hidden possibility of the other beginning. He finds traces of this other beginning in early Greek thinking, mythology, and poetry. The other beginning is also announced in the poetry of Hölderlin who named the gods that have fled. It is the task of nonmetaphysical or commemorative thinking to explore this first possibility and so prepare for another beginning of thinking.

In philosophy's beginning, Parmenides speaks about the clearing of Being as such, although it would remain unthought in philosophy. 'Alètheia', unconcealment, was equated with truth as the correspondence of knowledge with beings or truth as the certainty of knowledge. Unconcealment is, however, not the same as truth. We must think of 'alètheia' as the clearing which first grants Being and thinking their presence to and for each other. The task of thinking is the surrender of metaphysics to the determination of the matter of thinking, that is, appropriation.

Heidegger was holding back this important work in a long hesitation. The set of manuscripts written between 1936 and 1938 was finally published posthumously to commemorate the 100th anniversary of his birthday. The title of this unique and complex work is made up of two parts, one presenting the public title, *Contributions to Philosophy*, and the other the appropriate one, *From Enowning*. His *Contributions to Philosophy* consists of a preview, an order of six arrangements or joinings, and a concluding resume of what preceded. Heidegger attempts to think Being in its essential unfolding as appropriation. He describes the experience of thinking as being stretched out between two beginnings and prepares for the transition from the end of the first beginning to a new beginning. The first beginning is the metaphysical thinking of Being as beingness. The new beginning is the thinking of the truth of Being as the clearing of self-concealment.

In the *Preview* Heidegger elucidates the directives that thinking needs to follow in order to experience Being as appropriation. He distinguishes between the guiding question of metaphysics, what is an entity?, and the basic question of incipient thinking about the ground of metaphysics. The attunement of the first beginning is wonder or astonishment, the Greek 'thaumazein'. That of the new beginning is reservedness (*Verhaltenheit*) or the basic mood of being-there's relation to Being, which holds appropriation back and in reserve.

Heidegger describes being-there's relation to Being as the forgetfulness of being. This relation must be thought through and opened up as what has to be thought. At the end of the history of metaphysics thinking experiences the echo of Being as withdrawal and abandonment. He also shows how the guiding question of metaphysics beckons thought to the basic question of the other beginning of thought. We should no longer try to think the unconcealment of Being as the beingness of entities, but think from the truth of Being as appropriation. The other beginning of thinking is only accessible through a leap of thought into the truth of Being itself. The thinker belongs to Being as the appropriation of thought. We must not try to think Being, but let the silence of Being be heard through our thinking.

Through the leap of thought, the being-there of human beings and the expanse, where the truth of Being comes to pass, are grounded. Heidegger calls for the ones to come (*die Zukünftigen*) to prepare for the historical decision of the appropriation of Being and thus make a new beginning possible. In a careful meditation on the beckoning of the last God, Heidegger prepares for the coming of the last God. This last God will make a turning in the appropriation of Being possible and inaugurate a new era in the history of Being. We can experience his nearness in the withdrawal and flight of the gods. The ones to come must prepare for his coming by leaping into being-there, which at the same time is the grounding of the truth of Being

2. In his lecture *The Origin of the Work of Art* Heidegger tried to understand art as an authentic way in which unconcealment happens. Art can teach us how we can discover the being of entities in a different way than in the calculative thinking of technology. In this sense art may open our eyes to a different world. The aim of the lecture is to arrive at the immediate and full reality of the work of art in order to discover the essence of art within it.

In the first part, *Thing and Work*, Heidegger works out the essential difference between a thing and a work of art. What is a thing? The concepts with which philosophy tries to understand things as things derive their meaning from the being of equipment. Equipment resembles the work of art insofar as it is the product of human work. When we compare van Gogh's painting that depicts a pair of shoes with the shoes themselves, their difference becomes clear. Reliability determines the being of the shoes as equipment. The shoes are there when we need them and we can rely on them to perform their function. When we wear our shoes, we understand what they are. Van Gogh's painting reveals the beingness of shoes. It lets us know what shoes in truth are. The work of art opens up the being of entities. This opening-up is the revealment of the truth of Being and happens in the work of art. In the work of art truth sets itself to work. Heidegger thus comes to the next question: what is truth as the setting-itself-to-work?

In the second part, *The Work and the Truth*, Heidegger first discusses the way of being of the work. A work, like a Greek temple, works in the sense that it sets up a world and at the same time sets this world back again on earth, which itself thus emerges as native ground. This setting-up of a world is making space for the worlding of world, that is, the liberation of the open and the establishment of its structure. The work of art lets the earth be an earth and thus makes the dwelling of human beings possible. We can now ask what truth is. Truth is the essence of the true, that is, the unconcealment of entities. Truth happens as the primal conflict between revealing (world) and concealing (earth). Art and truth are joined since beauty is one of the ways in which truth occurs as unconcealment. But how does truth happen in the work of art?

Heidegger tries to answer this question in the third part, *Truth and Art*. The happening of truth is the struggle of the conflict between world and earth. Truth happens only by establishing itself in this struggle and clearing the open. It sets itself into work and establishes itself in the work of art as the struggle of earth and world. All art as the letting-happen of the advent of the truth of what is is, as such, essentially poetry. Poetry is the saying of world and earth, the saying of the arena of their struggle, and thus the place of all nearness and farness of the gods. The essence of poetry is the grounding of truth and may be considered from three points of view as a gift, a founding, and a beginning.

Heidegger's interpretation of the work of art is the first step on the way to an analysis of possible original and authentic being-there. He begins to free himself from metaphysics and to search for another kind of thinking as an alternative to calculative thinking. This other kind of thinking commemorates the being of entities and is a meditative kind of reflection. And yet, as the struggle between earth and world shows, he is still trapped in the dualism of matter and form. Earth is formless matter that needs to be formed by the artist. Art is in nature and must be wrested from it by the artist. In his later essays Heidegger explores the possibility of an authentic and original being-there of human beings as poetic dwelling.

In his lectures *The Thing* and *Building Dwelling Thinking*, Heidegger attempts to reply to the crisis of modern times and the homelessness of modern mankind. He therefore describes an original dwelling and being at home in the world that is rooted in a homeland. People may only dwell if there is a place where they can be at home. Heidegger formally indicates this abode as the fourfold. It is the primal unity of earth and sky, divinities and mortals that is unfolded and folded together time and again. The unity of the four is a mirror-play. The four do not form a static unity. The fourfold is a dynamic structure that is given form continuously. It gathers the unity of the four on the ground of the homeland and is as such a place where humans may dwell. The mortals dwell on the earth under the sky in the oneness of the fourfold. The sky is not only the vaulting path of the sun and the course of the moon; it is also the clemency and inclemency of the weather, the change of the seasons, the light of day and the gloom of night. Earth is the serving bearer that lets things come to presence. The work of art is the contest between the world that it opens and the sheltering of earth from which it rises. The divinities are the messengers of the godhead. Out of its holy sway, the god appears in his presence or withdraws into concealment. In dwelling the mortals wait for intimations of the coming of the divinities. Divinities and mortals, earth and sky are joined together in the oneness of the fourfold. Human beings are the mortals because they can die. Only humans die, and they die continuously, as long as they dwell on earth, under the sky, before the divinities.

The feast of life is celebrated in the fourfold. The unity of the four-fold is the celebration of the appropriation of the truth of Being. Hei-degger's conception of the fourfold is a retrieval of the Greek cosmos in an attempt to heal our broken world. The being-there of human beings in the fourfold is dwelling. Dwelling is a gathering of the four-fold into the unity of the home. It gives us an anchor that safeguards us and lets us abide in the homeland as the place where we can grow roots. Dwelling is in its most profound sense being at home.

Human dwelling comports two dimensions: mortals are in the four-fold inasmuch as they dwell, and in dwelling they take care of and tend the entities that they encounter. The basic character of dwelling is to spare, to preserve. In dwelling, mortals preserve the fourfold in its essential being, that is, its making present. In dwelling mortals take their measure from the way the world fits together and let entities show themselves as they are. Dwelling is building a home in the world.

According to Heidegger, the stem of the German verb '*bauen*' (to build) bears affinity to the form of the verb 'to be' ('*ich bin, du bist*'). Building is the manner in which human beings dwell in the world. Building as dwelling unfolds into the building that cultivates living things and the building that erects constructions. A construction, for instance a bridge, gathers to itself in its own way earth and sky, divini-ties and mortals. The location of a bridge allows the fourfold to enter into a site by arranging it into different spaces, where everything has its place. Genuine buildings give form to the essence of dwelling. Building lets things be as things and preserves Being in things.

As Heidegger shows in his meticulous phenomenological description of a simple thing like a jug, the jug's jug-character consists in the poured gift of the pouring-out. In the drink of this gift, earth and sky dwell. The gift of the pouring-out can be a drink for mortals or a con-secration for the divinities. In the jugness of the jug, mortals and di-vinities dwell. In the gift of the outpouring dwells the simple single-foldness of the fourfold. A thing gathers and unites earth and sky, divinities and mortals. This gathering brings the four into the light of their mutual belonging. Thing means gathering into nearness. Thinging the thing stays the united four, earth and sky, divinities and mortals, in the simple onefold of their self-unified fourfold. The four mirror each other. The appropriating mirror-play of the single onefold of earth and sky, divinities and mortals, is the world. The world comes to presence through its worlding. Since the thing stays the fourfold, it also things the world. Things appear as things out of the ringing of the world's mirror-play. Human beings attend in their dwelling to the world by responding to the address of Being in their thinking.

Dwelling designates the fundamental structure of being-there as it sojourns in nearness to entities. As Hölderlin says in one of his poems, man dwells between heaven and earth. This between is a dimension that admits of measure. Since man dwells in this dimension, it is his task to do the measuring. Only insofar as man measures out his dwelling can he be in accordance with his essence. But how must we understand this measuring process?

The fundamental sense of measure lies in taking a measure. The measure is an appearing of Being itself. In Hölderlin's poetry Being appears in the guise of an unknown god. The mystery of Being is the process of unconcealment. The ontological difference and the ensuing forgetfulness of being together conceal the measure of man's dwelling. Man can only take this measure by letting it come to him in acquiescence. Man measures out the dimension between earth and heaven wherein he dwells. Thinking lets man dwell in nearness to entities. This kind of dwelling is authentic working. Since the taking of the measure of man's dwelling takes place in language as a response to the address of Being, Heidegger calls this measure-taking poetizing.

Language, poetry, and thinking belong together. Language is in its essence the clearing-concealing advent of Being itself and as such the house of Being. In its home, human beings dwell. Human beings must first let themselves be claimed by Being before they speak and take the risk that under this claim they will seldom have much to say. Language speaks originally and human beings speak when they respond to its address. Since the Greeks, language has been represented in terms of speech. Speaking is one kind of human activity. Heidegger abandons this approach because he wants to understand the manner in which language has being. He wants to experience language *as* language. Language first shows itself as our way of speaking. Speaking must have speakers who are present in the way of speaking. They dwell together in speech and speak about that which concerns them. Everything spoken stems from the unspoken. In the nature of language, speech and what is spoken reveal themselves as that by which and within which something is given voice and language, that is, makes an appearance insofar as something is said. Heidegger insists that saying and speaking are not the same. Speaking *qua* saying belongs to the design (*Aufriß*) of the being of language. The essence of language is saying as showing. Every showing by way of language presupposes the prior presence of that which is shown. In this sense speaking is of itself a hearing. Language speaks by saying. Speaking as the hearing of language lets saying be said to it.

Language achieves its completion in poetry. In poetry it invites things to gather to themselves sky and earth, mortals and divinities, and thus let world be. In thinking being-there responds to this appeal by trying to commemorate the unconcealment of Being and respond to the address of Being. Only in thinking can we reflect upon the ontological difference and experience the appropriation of Being.

Since authentic dwelling takes its measure in a concentrated perception, it is a gathered taking-in that remains a listening. Only this measure gauges the very nature of human being. In this measure we rediscover the concept of order that played such a fundamental role in Heidegger's earliest thinking. Only if human beings comply with the measure of reality can they be human in the fullest sense. This measure resides in the letting-be of entities as entities and a meditative recollection of the appropriation of Being. Heidegger teaches us that our dwelling should be a blending into the mirror-play of the fourfold, which gives us our measure. The fourfold is no human product. It is the place where the dwelling of humans is rooted and preserved. Here human beings may dwell on this earth, full of merit and yet poetically.

When Heidegger passed away on May 26, 1976, he had become the most important and controversial philosopher of his time. The publication of the collected edition of his works was under way and his works were translated into many different languages. Many of his former students, like Hannah Arendt, Walter Biemel, Hans-Georg Gadamer, Hans Jonas, Karl Löwith, Herbert Marcuse, and Otto Pöggeler, had become important philosophers and thinkers in their own right. He had inspired countless others, like Jacques Derrida, Michel Foucault, Emmanuel Lévinas, Jean-Paul Sartre, and Richard Rorty. His greatest legacy is perhaps neither his existential analysis of being-there in *Being and Time* nor his *Contributions to Philosophy*. What truly remains is the way. His path of thinking teaches us what is worthy of questioning and to remain with the matter of thinking as such. And as he once said in his lecture *The Question Concerning Technology*: "Questioning is the piety of thinking".

THE DICTIONARY

- A -

ABGROUND (*Abgrund*). *see* ABYSS

ABSENCE (*Abwesenheit*). The absence of **Being** is the condition of possibility of the **presence** of **entities**. **Being-there** is the nothingness or **clearing** in which entities can be present. In the **unconcealment** of entities Being itself remains concealed. In Heidegger's early writings this clearing is opened up by the ecstatic **temporality** of being-there. After the **turning** Heidegger shifts the emphasis from being-there to Being. The clearing no longer belongs to being-there; we now must understand it as the **appropriation** of Being. *See also* Forgetfulness of being.

ABYSS (*Abgrund*). Abyss is the counterpart of **ground**. Since every ground can only be an **entity**, we can only think of **Being** itself as the abyss from which all entities spring into **presence**.

ACCEPTANCE (*Empfängnis*). Acceptance is a key concept in Heidegger's **philosophy** of **art**. The true artist acknowledges the **address of Being** to which he accedes. He accepts this **gift** of Being by manifesting it in the work of art as the coming-to-pass of **truth**.

ACQUIESCENCE (*Gelassenheit*). Heidegger first introduced acquiescence, a term he had come across during his Eckhart studies in 1916, as a key concept of his philosophy in his ***Conversation on a Country Path about Thinking***. It belongs to the **essence** of **thinking** inasmuch as thinking is **being-there**'s acquiescence of the **expanse** and its release into the expanse. As waiting, peace, **way** and **movement**, acquiescence is the right attitude towards the expanse to which being-there belongs and in which it opens itself up to the **open**. The essence of thinking can neither be understood as transcendental-horizonal **representation** nor as **calculative thinking**; it must be understood as **commemorative thinking** and attentive **reflection**. Acquiescence is the waiting for the expanse as the hidden essence of **truth**. In acquiescence being-there achieves **authenticity** as the culmination of thought.

In his **memorial address** at the commemoration of the 175th anniversary of the birthday of the composer Conradin Kreutzer, Heidegger describes acquiescence as the necessary attitude of simultaneous acceptance and rejection of **technology**. In acquiescence we let things be as they are and open ourselves up to the **mystery** of **Being**. This attitude might enable us to escape the danger of homelessness that threatens us in the age of technology and **nihilism**. Acquiescence may enable us to once again grow roots in the **ground** of our home and make the **autochthony** of our **dwelling** possible.

ACTUALIZATION (*Vollzug*). Actualization is a fundamental element in Heidegger's concept of **phenomenology**. It always refers to the way we enact or fulfill **structures** and functions of our **being-there**. *See also* Actualization sense.

ACTUALIZATION SENSE (*Vollzugssinn*). Heidegger distinguished for the first time between the **content sense**, **relational sense** and actualization sense of **situations** in his Winter Semester 1919-20 lecture course on the basic problems of **phenomenology**. These three directions of the life stream circumscribe the self-sufficiency of **life** and allow us access to life in its **origin**. The actualization sense is the most important one, since it springs from the spontaneity of the **self** and determines the way we live our lives. In the 1920s Heidegger broadened the application of these three senses to include the **factual life experience** of **human beings**. In *Being and Time* Heidegger uses these three senses to analyze the **structure** of **being-there**. *See also* Actualization; Temporalizing sense.

ADDRESS OF BEING (*Zuspruch des Seins*). The address of **Being** to **being-there** takes the form of a voiceless appeal that is made manifest through the **attunement** of being-there. **Anxiety** is one of the most important attunements corresponding to Being, because in this **mood** we experience the nonbeing of **entities**. In the disclosure of Being as the **nothing**, the wonder of all wonders, "that entities are," is revealed. Being-there responds to the address of Being by letting itself be as the 'there' of Being. Being itself calls the tune and being-there should listen to its call.

AFFECT (*Affekt*). The **disposedness** of **being-there** makes it possible that being-there can be touched by something that shows itself in an affect. Our affects and feelings reveal how we are disposed in everyday **life**.

AFFECTEDNESS (*Betroffenheit*). Affectedness belongs to the **existential** constitution of **being-there** and has its **understanding**. The prior **disclosedness** of the **world** belongs to **being-in** and makes it possible that we can encounter **entities** in **circumspection**. Being-there can only live in a meaningful **world**, because the entities it encounters can affect it. The affectedness of being-there makes it possible that we care about entities and **human beings**.

AFFLICTION (*Bekümmerung*). My life concerns me. It matters to me what happens to me. Heidegger discovered the importance of affliction for human **life** during his study of **mysticism**. It is central to the development of his concept of **phenomenology**. We cannot disclose the **phenomenon** of affliction theoretically. We can only relive or retrieve the affliction of human **existence** in our own life. In *Being and Time* Heidegger replaces affliction by **anxiety**. **Being-there** is **ontologically** distinguished from all other **entities** by the fact that, in its very **being**, its being is an issue for it. Being-there has a relationship to its own being and goes about its being. This is the **formal indication** of being-there's **understanding of being**.

AGE OF THE WORLD PICTURE (*Die Zeit des Weltbildes*). In this lecture on the grounding of the world picture of modern times through **metaphysics**, delivered in **Freiburg** on June 9, 1938, Heidegger claims that modernity is the age of the **world** as picture and tries to explain how the world became a picture. Every age is grounded through its metaphysics, which determines the **being** of **entities** and the **essence** of **truth**. Every new age starts with a metaphysical revolution. At the beginning of his lecture Heidegger describes five fundamental **phenomena** of modern times: a. modern **science**, b. mechanical **technology**, c. the **essence** of **art** as **lived experience**, d. the realization of **values** in culture, and e. the 'de-godding' (*Entgötterung*), that is, the disappearance of the **gods**. In his lecture Heidegger only discusses modern science and the metaphysical revolution that made it possible.

Modern science is essentially research and as such is dominated by method. It limits itself to specific regions of **reality** that are grounded in characteristic features of reality, for example **movement**, and each are studied with specific methods. Because modern science limits itself to method, it can achieve levels of strictness and exactness that were unthinkable to Greek 'epistèmè' and medieval 'doctrina et scientia'. In his own little corner every researcher follows the method of his science as strictly and exactly as possible. Modern science has been institutionalized and has thus become business. The metaphysical foundation of modern science is the objectivation of entities, which in turn is grounded through method. Modern science no longer concerns itself with the being of entities, but only with objects. How did entities become objects? This transformation is only possible when entities are no longer disclosed in their being, but represented by subjects. An entity is only an entity if a subject perceives it. Truth can then no longer be '**alètheia**', the **unconcealment** of entities in their being; it becomes the certitude of **representations**.

René Descartes was the first philosopher to determine the being of entities as representations and truth as certitude. The scientific revolution of modern times is at the same time a metaphysical change in the essence of being human. **Human beings** became subjects and as subject the foundation of all entities in their being and truth. The world as the **whole** of entities became a representation or picture. Modern times are the age of the world picture.

ALÈTHEIA. '**Alètheia**' is the Greek **word** for **truth**. Heidegger was first struck by the alpha-privative of 'alètheia' as early as 1921. As **unconcealment** it is related to **concealment**, '**lèthè**'. This insight prompted his recognition of the fundamental trait of '**ousia**', the **being** of **entities**, as **presence**. Truth presupposes a **clearing** or opening in which entities can be unconcealed. The unconcealment of entities is at the same time the concealment of **Being** itself. In every truth something remains hidden. **Plato** and **Aristotle** transformed the original Greek **experience** of truth as 'alètheia'. Through the platonic primacy of idea over 'alètheia' truth became correctness of perception and **expression**. As 'alètheia' truth resided in the entity itself; as correctness it became a characteristic of human comportment with entities. Where Plato and Aristotle were still aware of the **ontological** dimension of truth, medieval philosophers reduced truth to correctness. Truth became the correspondence of the mind and the thing. "Veritas est adequatio intellectus et rei." In modern **philosophy** truth lost all relation to Being and entities. Descartes reduced truth to the certitude of knowledge.

ALÈTHEIA [HERACLITUS, FRAGMENT B 16] (*Alètheia [Heraklit, Fragment 16]*). In this essay on Fragment 16 of **Heraclitus** Heidegger discusses the problem of '**alètheia**' as the interplay of revealing and concealing. Heidegger examines this fragment very closely and inter prets it to mean: "From the **clearing** which never disappears into **concealment** because always emerging from it, how could anyone remain concealed?" The clearing is the **open** in which **entities** reveal themselves. The revealing or coming-to-light (*Lichten*) of entities in the clearing is at the same time the concealment of **Being** as such. The source of the **forgetfulness of being** is not the laxity of **being-there**; it is intrinsic to Being itself. The relationship of being-there to the clearing is nothing else than the clearing itself, insofar as it gathers in and retains being-there. The interplay between the clearing, being-there and Being is the **appropriation** that is not only "the wonder of all wonders" meditated in Heidegger's later thought, but also central to the thought of Heraclitus. They both try to think the **mystery** of Being in an attitude of **openness** and free surrender.

As Heraclitus says in Fragment 123, self-revealment, or '**physis**', needs concealment in order to come to presence as revealment. This self-revealing concealment of Being in the clearing is the common denominator of all the essential **words** and names that characterize Heraclitean thought. The movements of self-revealing and self-concealing form one ('hèn') identical process. In this process the light and the dark complement each other and are in harmony ('harmoniè'). Heraclitus describes the harmony of contrarieties also as discord or contention ('polemos') between the positive and the negative. It is a process in which the opposites are meshed into a single **pattern of arrangement**. Fire ('pur') gathers its force together ('logos') into the process of **coming-to-presence** of Being as ornament ('kosmos'). In the clearing of the world Being emits (*schickt*) itself as **destiny** and withdraws itself into concealment. The movement of concealment and revealment is the coming-to-pass of 'alètheia'. Heraclitus thinks in the multiplicity of different names the fullness of what is the same: the **appropriation** of Being.

AMBIGUITY (*Zweideutigkeit*). In its everyday **being-with, being-there** encounters **entities** in the way they are accessible to everyone and about which everyone can say anything. This also means that our everyday **understanding** becomes ambiguous. It is practically impossible to decide when the **being** of entities is disclosed in a genuine way and when it is described in the **idle talk** of the 'they'. Ambiguity holds sway also in the way being-there projects itself and presents itself with its **possibilities**, because these possibilities have been also publicly interpreted. Thus being-there's understanding in the **publicness** of the 'they' constantly goes wrong in its **projections**, as regards the genuine possibilities of being-there. Being-there is always ambiguously there, torn between **authenticity** and **inauthenticity**.

ANAXIMANDER (611-547 BC). Anaximander, **Parmenides** and **Heraclitus** are the original thinkers in Heidegger's **history of Being**. They speak to us from the earliest **beginning** of **philosophy**. This beginning is not only the **origin** of the **forgetfulness of being**, but contains also the **possibility** of another beginning. In his **interpretation** Heidegger tries to understand the pre-metaphysical thought of the early Greek thinkers from a post-metaphysical standpoint. Anaximander has thought the process by which **entities** are **coming to presence** in unconcealment. Every entity leaves concealment to while in **unconcealment** for some time, before it passes away into **concealment**. The process is ruled by 'dikè' which arranges the pattern of entities in their **being**. *See also* Anaximander Fragment, The.

ANAXIMANDER FRAGMENT, THE (*Der Spruch des Anaximanders*). This essay written in 1946 deals with Heidegger's conception of the self-revealing **concealment** of **Being** and its relationship to **being-there** as its shepherd. Heidegger's essay is a dialogue that takes the form of a translation of the oldest saying of **philosophy**: "...according to necessity; for they pay penalty and retribution to each other for their injustice..." **Anaximander** speaks to us from the earliest **beginning** of the **history of Being** as **metaphysics**, which is at the same time the start of the **forgetfulness of being**. Could it be that at the end of philosophy a new beginning is announced in the saying of Anaximander to those who are listening?

Heidegger's dialogue begins with the **interpretation** of the Greek **understanding** of being: 'eon'. 'Eon' is the **word** for that which is present. Every **entity** is, because it has arrived at its **while** in **unconcealment**, 'alètheia'. Entities are only insofar as they are **coming to presence**; they are coming to presence, insofar as they emerge into unconcealment. Entities that are present through unconcealment remain, however, concealed in what they were and shall be. Heidegger can now interpret two words that bear faithful testimony to Anaximander's thought. 'Genesis' is the coming forth and arriving at the unconcealed. 'Phthora' means for that which has thus arrived to leave the unconcealed and pass into concealment. 'Genesis' and 'phthora' are complementary moments of the same dynamic process by which entities come to presence. Every entity leaves concealment to while in unconcealment for a time, before it passes away into concealment.

'Adikia' denotes literally the privation of 'dikè'. Entities proceed out of concealment to reveal themselves in unconcealment before returning to concealment. This intermingling of revealment and concealment is the whiling of entities: a dynamic process of **arrangement**, 'dikè', of entities in their being. 'Adikia' refers to the tendency of entities to disarrangement by refusing to while away. Since this pull towards disarrangement is only a tendency, the **pattern of arrangement** maintains the upper hand. The pattern of arrangement ensures that entities while in compatibility with each other within the **region** of unconcealment. Heidegger can now interpret the second part of Anaximander's **saying**. All beings come to presence insofar as, in compatibility with each other, they overcome the tendency within themselves to deny their passing away, that is, the condition of their coming to presence. Entities can only emerge into unconcealment, if they make place for each other when their time has come to disappear from unconcealment.

According to Heidegger we have in the first three words of the saying, 'kata to chreon', the oldest name by which **thinking** brings the being of entities into presence. He translates 'to chreon' by '*Brauch*', which means use and handling. Anaximander suggested that Being hands out entities in that by which they come to presence. Being gives entities their limits. As a nonentity Being has no limits, it is limitless, 'apeiron'. Anaximander named Being and its relationship to entities, but the **ontological difference** between Being and entities remained forgotten. In the unconcealment of entities Being itself remains concealed and forgotten.

ANTICIPATE (*Vorlaufen*). Heidegger first analyzed the **phenomenon** of **being-there**'s anticipation in his 1924 lecture *The Concept of Time*. Being-there is truly existent and authentically with itself, when it is persistently anticipating to the certain **possibility** of its being gone (*das Vorbei*). In the Summer Semester 1925 course on the **history of the concept of time** it became the anticipation of my own **death**. The **existential analysis** of being-there's **temporality** in *Being and Time* showed that anticipating is the ontological condition of possibility of authentic **understanding**. It opens up the **future** as coming towards being-there. Anticipation as authentic understanding of the future must win itself from the inauthentic future. In inauthentic understanding of the future being-there does not come towards itself in its most unique **can-be**, but awaits it full of **concern**. In anticipating its death being-there understands its most unique and uttermost potentiality-for-being, that is, the possibility of authentic existence. *See also* Authenticity; Conscience; Resoluteness.

ANXIETY (*Angst*). The fundamental **disposedness** of anxiety is an outstanding **disclosedness** of **being-there** in its **being**. That in the face of which being-there has anxiety is not an **entity** within the **world**, but **being-in-the-world** as such. In the disposedness of anxiety being-there finds itself face-to-face with the **nothing** of the possible impossibility of its **existence**, that is, **death**. **Being-towards-death** is essentially anxiety. Anxiety is anxious about being-there's authentic **can-be**. It takes away from being-there the **possibility** of **understanding** itself in terms of the world and the way things have been publicly interpreted. Anxiety throws being-there back upon itself and discloses it as 'solus ipse'. In anxiety being-there finds itself amidst the indefiniteness of the nothing and nowhere and is no longer at home in the world. In being-there anxiety makes manifest its being-towards its most unique can-be. *See also* Conscience; Fear.

APOPHANTIC AS (*apophantisches Als*). The apophantic as determines the intentional **structure** of the '**logos** kata tinos'. Speaking as 'logos kata tinos' is demonstrative letting-be-seen and discloses something as some thing, for example, this is a table. The apophantic as makes **untruth** possible. When we let something be seen as something, we can be mistaken and disclose it as something it is not, for example, this is not a table, but a chair. The 'as' structure of **truth** must be wrested from **concealment** and guarded from loss. In *Being and Time* the apophantic as is the **horizonal schema** of **presence-at-hand** in its three **ecstases** of inauthentic **temporality: past, present** and **future**.

APPEAL (*Anspruch; Anruf*). *see* ADDRESS OF BEING

APPROPRIATING EVENT (*Ereignis*). *see* APPROPRIATION

APPROPRIATION (*Ereignis*). Appropriation is the central **formal indication** of Heidegger's entire path of thinking. It identifies the very source and primal leap (*Ur-sprung*) of the dynamic relationship between **Being** and **being-there**. In the dictionary sense *Ereignis* is the event, the happening or occurrence. Heidegger makes use of the 'own' meaning of '*eigen*' to read the sense of the verb '*ereignen*' as to make one's own, to appropriate. However, **entities** do not appropriate **being** for themselves; Being appropriates entities in their being. The verb '*ereignen*' is derived from the German '*eräugnen*', that means to place before the eyes, to show. Appropriation is also '*Eräugnung*', the placing before the eyes, that is, the **unconcealment** of Being. The appropriation of Being is the **clearing** in which everything becomes visible.

Heidegger introduced appropriation in his 1919 course, *The Idea of Philosophy and the Problem of Worldviews*, as the most intense **lived experience** of the meaning-bestowing **I** in close conjunction with the meaning-bestowing dynamics of the It which worlds. The I is fully there in the "It worlds" of the **primal something** such that I myself properize (*ereigne*) It to myself and It properizes (*ereignet*) itself according to its **essence**. The intimate involvement with the primal "It gives" of Being thus prompts the distinction between events which matter to myself personally and move me by situating me, and processes which pass before me objectively and do not concern me personally. In *Being and Time* appropriation returned to its mundane sense of historical events past and gone. After a decade of dormancy Heidegger returned to its originally intimate sense in 1928.

Appropriation became the central topic of Heidegger's later thought. Here it means a unique process of appropriating (*aneignen*) and assigning (*zueignen*). Being calls for the authenticity of **commemorative thinking**. With his conception of appropriation Heidegger's thought no longer transcends being-there towards Being; he tries to let Being speak out of itself and make being-there heed its **claim**. This **turning** away from being-there to Being implies a change in the essence of **truth**. Heidegger leaves the identity of Being and **thinking** and **fundamental ontology** behind. His thought is now enacted in a **region** appropriation addresses as '**alètheia**', that is, the clearing of self-revealing **concealment** from which the relationship between Being and being-there is thought in a more original way.

Heidegger's second main work, *Contributions to Philosophy*, written between 1936 and 1938, is a careful meditation on Being as appropriation in which he attempts the turning away from metaphysics towards the commemorative thinking of Being. The turning of appropriation is the turning point and appropriation is the ruling middle in which that which is can be itself and thus can return to its property as its proper place. The propriation (*Ereignung*) of appropriation is the assigning (*Zueignung*) of Being to being-there and the surrender (*Übereignung*) of being-there to Being.

Heidegger's new conception of appropriation leads to three fundamental changes in his thought. 1. He determines **language** no longer as apophantic **assertion**, but as the appropriation that brings being-there to its **essence** and makes it the 'there' of Being. Appropriation grants to **mortals** their abode within their essence, so that they may be capable of being those who speak. Language is the **saying** of Being from the **region** of its essence: the dynamic process of self-revealing concealment. Appropriation by way of saying and language thus always speaks according to the **mode** in which appropriation as such reveals itself or withdraws itself into concealment. 2. The temporal determination of appropriation can neither be **ontological** nor **existential**. Appropriation **temporalizes** itself suddenly and unexpectedly. In this respect it is like lightning; we never know when and where it will strike. The **history of Being** is the sequence of such flashes of lightning. Every appropriation is a clearing. 3. Heidegger determines appropriation in its being as the **fourfold** and its **nearness** to **things**. The unity of the fourfold **comes to presence** as the worlding of the **world**, that is, the region and time where **sky** and **earth** and the **divinities** and the mortals meet. Of groundless appropriation holds: It - appropriation - propriates.

APRIORI, THE (*Apriori, das*). The apriori is the third fundamental breakthrough of **Edmund Husserl**'s **phenomenology**. We live in meaningful **structures** from which we experience the **entities** included within them. These structures are made explicit in **categorial intuition**. **Being** articulates itself and so discloses entities in their **being**. The categorial structure of the **disclosedness** of Being is the condition of possibility, or enabling background, of **lived experience**. In this sense **categories** are earlier than any possible **experience**. Heidegger can thus show the link between Being and **time**. Being is earlier than entities. *See also* Intentionality.

ARENDT, HANNAH (1906-1975). In 1924 Arendt came to **Marburg** as an 18-year-old girl to study with Heidegger, the hidden king of German **philosophy**. They soon fell in love and had an extramarital and passionate love affair for almost five years. Heidegger was twice her age and had two sons. According to Heidegger she was the only person who understood him and his work. In 1926 Arendt took Heidegger's advice and moved to Heidelberg to study with **Karl Jaspers**. Arendt's marriage to Günther Stern in 1929 and Heidegger's involvement with **National Socialism** in 1933 led to a long separation that lasted until 1950, when Arendt resumed contact with Heidegger. She helped him to get his work published in the United States and checked the translations for him. Until her death Arendt was both attracted to and revolted by Heidegger's personality. He was, as Jaspers once said, both someone with whom you could be very close and a friend who would betray you when you were not there. Although Arendt's work is in many ways unthinkable without the influence of Heidegger's philosophy, Heidegger never showed any real interest in her work.

ARISTOTLE (384-322 BC). The famous Greek philosopher was probably the greatest influence on Heidegger's early thought. On a summer day in 1907 Heidegger received from his fatherly friend **Conrad Gröber** a copy of **Franz Brentano**'s dissertation on the manifold **senses** of being in Aristotle. Latent in Brentano's quotation from Aristotle on the title page, "an entity becomes manifest in many ways," was the question that determined Heidegger's way of thought: what is the **sense of being**? From 1922 to 1926 Heidegger worked on a book on Aristotle's **philosophy** that he never managed to finish and abandoned after the publication of *Being and Time*.

According to Heidegger Aristotle was not only the first phenomenologist; he was also more advanced in **phenomenology** than **Husserl** and his circle. While studying and teaching Aristotle and Husserl's *Logical Investigations* together, Heidegger discovered that since the time of the Greek philosophers, philosophical knowing has been defined by **intuition**. Heidegger broke with this model for theoretical **truth** and gave primacy to practical and religious truth as it is experienced in factual **life**. Heidegger found an original **experience** of 'kairos' paralleling that of primitive **Christianity** in Aristotle's account of truth in *Nicomachean Ethics VI*. And yet in *Physics IV* Aristotle also understood **time** as a series of **nows**, which became the paradigm for all later theories of time. In 1922/23 Heidegger discovered that '**ousia**' for the Greeks meant constant **presence**. Heidegger tried to understand being in terms of time in its fullest and most fulfilled **sense**. Through Aristotle Heidegger discovered the relationship between **Being** and time. Finally, Aristotle's conception of **logic** as a productive **science** was at the origin of Heidegger's conception of **fundamental ontology**.

After the publication of *Being and Time* Aristotle became less important to Heidegger. In his conception of the **history of Being**, **Greek philosophy** became the beginning of the age of **metaphysics**. As the last of the Greek philosophers Aristotle was the father of metaphysics. Although the conception of Being in pre-Socratic philosophy became the central topic of Heidegger's studies of Greek philosophy, he would return time and again to the thought of Aristotle. *See also* Aristotle's Metaphysics Θ 1-3: On the Essence and Actuality of Force; On the Essence and Concept of Physis. Aristotle, *Physics* B, 1; Phenomenological Interpretations to Aristotle: Introduction to Phenomenological Research; Phenomenological Interpretations with Respect to Aristotle: Indication of the Hermeneutic Situation; Plato: The Sophist.

ARISTOTLE'S METAPHYSICS Θ 1-3: ON THE ESSENCE AND ACTUALITY OF FORCE (*Aristoteles, Metaphysik Θ 1-3. Von Wesen und Wirklichkeit der Kraft*). This Summer Semester 1931 course, originally given under the title *Interpretations from Ancient Philosophy*, is a reinterpretation of Aristotelian **ontology** that was inspired by Heidegger's reading of **Friedrich Nietzsche**'s account of pre-Socratic **philosophy**. From Nietzsche he borrowed the insight into the fundamental difference between pre-Socratic thought and the philosophy of **Plato** and **Aristotle**. This insight led in turn to his conception of the **history of Being**. The course consists of two parts: an introduction and an **interpretation** of Aristotle's *Metaphysics* Θ.

In the introduction Heidegger searches for an encompassing **horizon** from which Aristotle's thought may be explained. He sketches the basic **structure** of Aristotelian ontology and focuses his attention on the conflict between the Oneness of **Being** and the manifold **senses of being**. Aristotle states, on the one hand, that **being** is said in a fourfold way: 1. To be accidental, 2. To be true or false, 3. According to the figures of **categories**, and 4. To be potentially, 'dunamis', or actually, 'energeia'. On the other hand, he is still under the spell of the **saying** of **Parmenides** that Being is One. The four senses of Being, which determine the being of **entities**, cannot be reduced to each other and stand in opposition to the Oneness of Being. Aristotle tries to explain the relationship between Being as One and as manifold by analogy. However, he fails to explain the **essence** of analogy and to show that the relationship between Being One and manifold can be understood as analogy. He also does not explain why Being unfolds itself in a fourfold way. In the **unconcealment** of Being in the fourfold being of entities, Being as the One remains concealed. The **ontological difference** between Being and the being of entities makes **truth**, 'alètheia', possible and is the forgotten ground of Greek thought and the history of philosophy as **metaphysics**.

The main part of the course is a comprehensive interpretation of Aristotle's conception of the essence and actuality of force. Force is the 'archè', that is, the starting point for a transformation or **movement** of an entity into something else. Force shows itself as the toleration of or resistance against transformation. Heidegger distinguishes between an **ontological** and an **ontic** concept of force in Aristotle's philosophy. Ontologically force is the capacity of acting, 'poiein', and undergoing, 'paschein', as one. It is both the starting point of a capacity to transform and a capacity to be transformed. Ontically force is the actualization of an entity as either the starting point of an action upon another entity, or the undergoing of the action of another entity. The opposite of force is incapacity or impotency.

Aristotle understands the actuality of force as a form of having. Having the force or capacity to do something means being able to do something. The Megaric school, on the other hand, holds that the actuality of force is identical to its actualization. According to Heidegger the real issue between Aristotle and the Megaric school remains implicit. This issue is the basic question of philosophy: What is Being? For Aristotle and the Megaric school as for all Greeks, Being means **presence**. Aristotle claims the Megaric concept of presence is too narrow. He denies that actuality, 'energeia', is the only and fundamental way a force is present and real. He distinguishes three ways in which force can be present: 1. A force can be present as capacity, e.g., a shoemaker has the capacity to make shoes. 2. A force can be present as the actualization of a capacity, e.g., the making of shoes. 3. A force can be present in its product, e.g., the shoe as finished product of shoemaking.

In the next step of his argumentation Aristotle shows that **perception**, 'aisthèsis', actualizes itself as the disclosing of entities in their being. The actuality of something present-at-hand is only possible, if the perceptible is not grounded in the actualization of perception. The unasked question of Aristotle's and all later philosophy is how the unconcealment of Being is possible. 'Aisthèsis' is a form of uncovering, 'alètheuein', that is, to take something as true or to take something from **concealment** in perception. Aristotle defines force in its actuality as that for which nothing is unworkable, when it actualizes the capacity that it is said to have. He thus addresses the problem of the essence of an entity in its fullest sense. The essence of an entity is disclosed when the kind of actuality or **existence** that belongs to this essence is disclosed. After Aristotle philosophy fell prey to the **ambiguity** of this question and forgot to ask about the actuality of the essence. This forgetfulness is at the same the condition of **possibility** of the history of philosophy as metaphysics. *See also* Logos; Physis.

ARRANGEMENT (*Fug*). Arrangement is Heidegger's translation of the Greek 'dikè'. It plays a prominent part in his **interpretation** of '**physis**' and '**logos**'. 'Physis' is the coming-to-pass of '**alètheia**', **unconcealment**. In the **clearing** of the self-revealing **concealment** of **Being**, **entities** are gathered together into an ordered collection. This is only possible when this gathering ('**logos**') is at the same time an arranging (*Fügung*) which terminates in an arrangement that is an articulate **whole**.

ART (*Kunst*). Art became a main topic in Heidegger's thought in 1931/32. His meditation on the **essence** of art is neither an esthetics nor a **philosophy** of art. The thinker responds to and tries to recall the **saying** of the poet in the **language** of **thinking**. **Friedrich Hölderlin**'s creative **poetry** became the touchstone of Heidegger's thinking and in their loving struggle his thinking found a new expressiveness. Art is the setting-into-work of **truth**. In this sense all art is poetic and the **appropriation** of truth. Poetry is the saying of the **unconcealment** of **entities** and the illumination of self-concealing **Being**. This light joins its shining to and into the work of art. Beauty is the way in which truth shines as unconcealment. The voice of poetry bids all that is - **world** and **things**, **earth** and **sky**, **divinities** and **mortals** - to gather into the simplicity (*Einfalt*) of their intimate belonging together. Poetry is thus the founding and giving (*Stiftung*) of the unconcealment of Being and so the **origin** of the history of a **people**. *See also* Art and Space; Origin of the Work of Art, The.

ART AND SPACE (*Die Kunst und der Raum*). Heidegger wrote the text of this essay on stone. It is a reflection on the relationship between sculpture and **space**. A statue embodies space, but what does space mean in this context? It cannot be the space of natural **science**. If **art** is the setting-into-work of **truth**, sculpture should disclose space in its true and most unique **essence**. Heidegger tries to find the characteristic features of space by listening to **language**. In the **word** space (*Raum*) we can still hear the echo of making space (*Räumen*), which means clearing. Clearing of wilderness gives the free and **open** where **mortals** can **dwell** and **divinities** can appear. Making space is the release of a place that opens **regions** where it can gather **things** into their belonging together. Are places the result of making space, or does making space receive its essence from the reign of spaces that gather things? Things themselves are places and do not only belong at a certain place. Sculpture can only be the embodying setting-into-work of places, and so the opening up of regions, where **human beings** may **dwell** and the things that matter to them can gather. Sculpture is the embodiment of the **truth of Being** in its work as the founding and giving of places.

ASSERTION (*Aussage*). Assertion and its **structure**, the **apophantic as**, are grounded in **interpretation** and its structure, the hermeneutic as, and furthermore in **understanding**, the **disclosedness of being-there**. According to traditional **logic**, assertion or **judgment** is the place of **truth**. In *Being and Time*, Heidegger shows that the disclosedness of being-there is the condition of **possibility** of the truth of judgment. The Greek '**logos**' is, in its **essence** as **speech**, assertion: a simple announcing of something (*Kundschaft*). This announcement in its widest sense presupposes the openness of the **clearing**. The **unconcealment** of **Being** is the condition of possibility of the revealing of **entities** in their **being** and of the disclosedness of being-there in its being.

AS-STRUCTURE (*als-Struktur*). The as-structure is the **fore-structure** of **assertion**, **understanding** and **interpretation**. It is grounded in the synthetic nature of **entities**. Because every entity is a collection of different qualities, we can disclose it in different ways as something. For example, this entity shows itself as a table, as a table it shows itself as wooden and three feet high. Another entity, for instance a hammer, shows itself as well suited for hammering.

ATTUNEMENT (*Gestimmtheit*). Attunement is the **ontic** counterpart of **disposedness** and is an everyday and familiar **phenomenon**. **Being-there** is always attuned. It is brought before the 'there' of its **being** in **moods** and attunements. They disclose **being-in-the-world** as a **whole** and make it possible for us to direct ourselves towards something. *See also* Acquiescence; Anxiety; Boredom; Fear.

AUGUSTINE AND NEO-PLATONISM (*Augustinus und der Neuplatonismus*). This Summer Semester 1921 course is one of Heidegger's two courses on the **phenomenology** of **religion**. The thought of Augustine is of utmost importance to Heidegger's **destruction** of **factual life experience**. The **facticity** of modernity is determined by the theoretical attitude of Greek **science** and the **affliction** and **concern** over one's own **life** of primitive **Christianity**. In his writings Augustine explained the life experience of primitive Christianity in

terms he derived from neo-Platonic **philosophy**. The Christian dogmatics of the Church Fathers was already underpinned with a Greek
infrastructure.

The main part of the course is a penetrating **interpretation** of the
tenth book of the *Confessions*, that is, the last of the autobiographical
books. Heidegger schematizes factual life as caring. The basic direction of life, rising from **care**, is delight. Caring is tried by the opposing
tendencies of falling into dispersion in the many or the rising towards
an integrated and unified **self**. The unified self seeks the happy life that
is **truth** and truth is **God** himself. **Ontologically** caring is oriented
toward things of use versus things to be enjoyed for their own sake.
The eternal unchangeable things are to be enjoyed, the temporal
changeable things are to be used as a means to that end. We should not
worship God for the sake of money, but spend money for the sake of
God.

Heidegger's interpretation of Augustine's factual life experience
points to the two extant divisions of ***Being and Time***. His discussion of
'timor castus', pure and noble **fear**, and 'timor servilis', servile fear of
punishment, is the forerunner of the **phenomenology** of **anxiety** and
fear. The three temptations reflect the insecurity of human life. Our life
is a trial in which we lose or find ourselves. We should strive to find
our way to God and thus at the same time find ourselves. Augustine's
account is foremost an account of the **actualization** of Christian life
and not so much of its content. We should not delight in the flesh, but
only in the glory of God. The temptation of **curiosity**, the lust of the
eyes, has a roaming quality that serves to make all accessible to it,
without concern for the value and worth of any particular object. In the
absorption of curiosity the self is lived by its **environment**. In the
temptation of worldly ambition the self as such is the end of the delight. This delight is rooted in the genuine concern for my own life and
myself. This tendency can easily degenerate into the love of praise and
being pleased with myself.

Heidegger ends his course with a discussion of the difference between the 'cogito' in Augustine and **René Descartes**. As Augustine
showed, the evidence of the 'cogito' must be founded in factual life. It
cannot be taken out of this context as Descartes did. Our self-certitude
is ultimately possible only by **faith**. "Crede ut intelligas."

AUTHENTICITY (*Eigentlichkeit*).   Authenticity and **inauthenticity**
are two **modes** of **being** which are grounded in the **mineness** of **being-
there**. All **existentials** of being-there are determined by the tension

between authenticity and inauthenticity. Being-there always exists either in one of these **modes** or in the indifference of both. **Anxiety** makes manifest in being-there its **being-out-for** its most unique **can-be**, that is, its **being** free for the **freedom** of choosing itself and taking hold of itself. Anxiety brings being-there face-to-face with the authenticity of its **being** and for this authenticity as a **possibility**, which it always is.

AUTOCHTHONY (*Bodenständigkeit*) Heidegger introduced this term in his Summer Semester 1924 lecture course on **Aristotle**. The conceptuality of a concept is determined by three moments: fundamental **experience**, leading claim and intelligibility. These three moments constitute together the autochthony of the conceptuality. In his Summer Semester 1925 course, *History of the Concept of Time. Prolegomena*, Heidegger uses autochthony as a phenomenological term. The demand of **Husserl**'s maxim "to the matters themselves" means that phenomenological research must provide demonstrations rooted in the autochthony of the **phenomena** and secure this native soil once more. In the early 1930s Heidegger transforms autochthony into a political term. The **being-there** of a **people** should be rooted in its autochthony or its forces of blood and soil. In his later **philosophy** autochthony becomes a key term in his philosophy of **language**. Language as the **house of Being** determines the autochthony of a people.

AWAITING (*gewärtigen*). The **existential analysis** of being-there's **temporality** in *Being and Time* showed that awaiting is inauthentic **understanding** of the **future**. In inauthentic understanding of the future being-there does not come towards itself in its most unique **can-be**, but awaits it full of **concern** as a **present** that is not yet **now**.

AWE (*Scheu*). Awe is the **attunement** of **being-there** in the **presence** of either **Being** as the **Holy** and the Source or the Extraordinary.

- B -

BASIC CONCEPTS (*Grundbegriffe*). In the first part of this Summer Semester 1941 lecture course, Heidegger understands basic concepts as those concepts that ground everything. They invite us to reflect upon the ultimate **ground** of our **being-there**. Ever since the **beginning** of **metaphysics human beings** have in their **essence** been touched by **Being**. Being-there is the **gift** of the **truth of Being** and thus the true abode of human beings. Being is the ground of all **entities**. The grounding of Being is a double movement. Being reveals itself as the **beingness** of entities and at the same time conceals itself as Being. The **concealment** of Being in the revelation of its truth as being-there is the **origin** of both the **forgetfulness of being** in metaphysics and the abandonment of Being in the age of **nihilism**. Metaphysics can only think Being as the beingness of entities and ground Being in a highest entity. To go beyond the onto-theo-logical **structure** of metaphysics we have to undo the forgetfulness of being. This is only possible by coming to experience fully the distress of the abandonment of Being. We have to return to the beginning of **thinking** and try to commemorate the **saying** of Being in early **Greek philosophy**. In a careful meditation of the Periander's saying, "care about entities as a whole" ('metéta to pan'), Heidegger explains the **ontological difference** between Being, on the one hand, and beingness and entities, on the other, as the differentiation that grounds being-there. Logical thought can never reach Being itself, because we cannot grasp Being with concepts. Every concept would reduce Being to an entity. Being can only be understood as the **abyss** from which everything springs.

The second part of the lecture course is an interpretation of the saying of Anaximander that is a different version of his interpretation in the later published article: The **Anaximander Fragment**. *See also* Contributions to Philosophy.

BASIC PROBLEMS OF PHENOMENOLOGY, THE (*Die Grundprobleme der Phänomenologie*). This Summer Semester 1927 lecture course is an elaboration of the unpublished third division of the first part of *Being and Time*: *Time and Being*. The lecture course circles around the question of the **sense of being** and consists of three parts.

In the introduction Heidegger restates his claim that all **ontology** has an **ontic** fundament. He also discusses phenomenological method. It consists of three parts. Phenomenological reduction is the attempt to grasp **entities** in their **being**. The phenomenological construction is the **projection** of given entities with a view to their being and its **structure**. Phenomenological **destruction** is the critical deconstruction of traditional concepts and points of view.

In the historical part of the course Heidegger offers his students a destruction of four fundamental theses concerning being: 1. **Immanuel Kant**'s thesis that being is not a predicate, 2. **Aristotle**'s thesis that to the being of entities belong **essence** and **existence**, 3. The thesis of

René Descartes that being is either an extensive or thinking **substance**, and 4. The logical thesis that the sense of being is the copula.

Heidegger tries to come to an **understanding** of **time** in the systematic part of the course. He shows in a careful interpretation of Aristotle's vulgar concept of time that it presupposes the **temporality** and **existential** structure of **being-there**. In the next step Heidegger develops the existential-horizonal character of existential temporality. This structure is the unity of **awaiting, retaining** and **making present**. Temporality is the condition of **possibility** of the **understanding of being**. Heidegger regards the temporality (*Zeitlichkeit*) of existence as a kind of inner **horizon** whose outer face at once mirrors the **Temporality** (*Temporalität*) of Being. His attempt to work out a convincing theory of horizonal schematizing fails, because he thinks too spatially about time as his new formal indication '**transcendence**' shows. Transcendence means to understand oneself from a **world**. Thus a temporal horizon is derived by trading off the horizon of a world. This lecture course makes clear why he could not finish *Being and Time*.

BASIC QUESTION (*Grundfrage*). Heidegger distinguishes between the **guiding-question** and the basic question of **thinking**. The guiding-question is the central question of **metaphysics**: what is the **being** of **entities**? The basic question asks back to the **ground** of metaphysics: what is **Being**?

BASIC QUESTIONS OF PHILOSOPHY: SELECTED 'PROBLEMS' OF 'LOGIC' (*Grundfragen der Philosophie. Ausgewählte 'Probleme' der 'Logik'*). In this Winter Semester 1937/38 lecture course Heidegger presents publicly parts of the fifth **arrangement** or fugue of his *Contributions to Philosophy* entitled *The Future Ones*. The basic question of this course is: why and how did the original Greek **understanding** of **truth** as 'alètheia', **unconcealment**, become the metaphysical understanding of truth as correctness? **Plato** and **Aristotle** understood truth no longer as unconcealment, but as correspondence between **thinking** and **entities**. 'Alètheia' no longer referred to **Being** itself, but only to the **being** of entities. Unconcealment belongs to the being of entities. Truth became the correctness of the **judgment** in which we say what entities are in their being. However, in the unconcealment of entities, Being itself remains concealed. The history of **metaphysics** from Plato to **Friedrich Nietzsche** is determined by the **guiding question** of **ontology**: what are entities? Because Plato and Aristotle failed to interpret and ground 'alètheia' in its **essence** as the

appropriation of the **truth of Being**, metaphysics became obsessed with entities and forgot to think the truth of Being. The **forgetfulness of being** in metaphysics is at the same time the abandonment of Being, which in turn leads to the distress of modern times. This distress is the dislocation of **being-there**. Our **existence** has become groundless. In the distress of the abandonment of Being we can experience this distress in its essence and think about it. The task of this nonmetaphysical thinking is to reduce the guiding question of metaphysics to the **basic question** of thinking, that is: what is Being? This question is basic, because it asks back to the **ground** of metaphysics. It inquires after the ground of the truth of Being, that is, the unconcealment of entities in their being. In the meditation on the first **beginning** that experienced truth and posited the truth of entities without asking about truth as such, post-metaphysical thinking prepares the other beginning that experiences the truth of Being and asks about the being of truth in order to thereby ground the essence of Being as appropriation. This preparation tries to overcome the forgetfulness of being and **nihilism** by trying to listen to the **address of Being**.

BEGINNING (*Anfang*). According to Heidegger the beginning is not only of essential importance to everything that comes later, but it also always retains something within itself. Every beginning holds a promise and **possibilities** that have not yet been actualized. The beginning plays a key role in Heidegger's **history of Being**. The beginning of **philosophy** in early Greek **thinking** is both the fateful **ground** of the history of **metaphysics** and the possibility of a new beginning. This other beginning will enable us to experience what was forgotten in metaphysics: the **truth of Being**. The first beginning experienced and posited the **truth** of **entities** without asking about truth as such. The other beginning experiences the truth of Being as the **clearing** and explicitly asks about the **being** of truth. The other beginning is only possible as the **appropriation** of Being. We cannot make it happen; it will happen to us. *See also* Contributions to Philosophy; End of Philosophy and the Task of Thinking, The.

BEING (*Sein*). The traditional concept of being understands being as the attribute that all **entities** share insofar as they are and exist. This attribute is **beingness**; i.e., the attribute, which makes that entities are, just as beauty is the attribute, which makes entities beautiful.

BEING (*Sein; Seyn*). As Heidegger loved to say, every philosopher only thinks one fundamental thought. The guiding star of his entire path of thinking is the **question of being**. What is Being? Being is neither an **entity** nor the quality of **beingness**. Being is broader than all entities. It is nearest to **being-there** and yet in its **nearness** furthest removed from it. It can only be understood as the **abyss** from which everything **comes to presence**. The fundamental **structure** of Being is the **between**, that is, the lightning process in which everything is lighted up. Out of the between, the **clearing** comes to presence. The **structure** of the clearing is the **fourfold** as the outcome of the **play of time-space**. Within the clearing the **truth of Being** can be grasped. In the clearing Being lets entities be and reveals itself as beingness. However, insofar as Being lets entities be, it withdraws itself from the clearing. In the truth of Being, Being itself remains concealed. It always holds back other **possibilities** that have not yet been actualized. The **formal indication** of Being is **appropriation**. Being is not static; it is a factual and historical happening. The **history of Being** is the condition of possibility of human history.

BEING (*Seiendes*). *see* ENTITY

BEING AND TIME (*Sein und Zeit*). When *Being and Time* was published in 1927, it created a sensation. This study established Heidegger as an important and original thinker. *Being and Time* is arguably the most important philosophical work of its century. Of the originally projected two parts, each comprising three divisions, only the first two divisions of part I were published by Heidegger.

In his main work Heidegger raises anew the old question of the **sense of being**; that is, the central problem of general **metaphysics** or **ontology**. The goal of his project is to work out a **fundamental ontology**. The originality of his approach is expressed in his attempt to ground ontology in an **ontic** fundament. This fundament is the **being** of an **entity** for which in its being, its own being is an issue for it. Heidegger formally indicates the **beingness** of this entity as **being-there**. In *Being and Time* Heidegger sets himself two tasks: 1. The development of the **existential analysis** of being-there that should lay bare **time** as the **horizon** for an **interpretation** of the sense of being in general (part I), and 2. The **destruction** of the history of ontology (part II).

The starting point of the existential analysis of being-there is the fact that being-there in its being has an **understanding** of the sense of being. The **facticity** of being-there shows itself in the **equiprimor-**

diality of the **existentials** that constitute its ontological **structure**. This also has important consequences for Heidegger's method. Existentials cannot be deduced from one another; they can only be described phenomenologically as they show themselves; that is, in their facticity.

In the first division of part I, *Preparatory Fundamental Analysis of Being-there*, Heidegger describes the basic constitution of being-there as **being-in-the-world**. Since in **phenomenology** we have to go from the light to the dark, we must start by describing being-there in its usual **everydayness**, that is, inauthentic **existence**. Being-there is first and usually not itself, but absorbed by the **world** and the '**they**'.

Being-in-the-world is a uniform **phenomenon** consisting of three elements: 1. The **worldhood** of the world, 2. The who that is in the world, and 3. **Being-in**. The worldhood of the world expresses itself in the pragmatic structures in which our everyday **life** takes place. **Involvement** and **meaningfulness** characterize worldhood. Every entity in the world concerns us and has **meaning**. The who of being-in-the-world is being-there. **Disposedness**, understanding and **discourse** determine being-there. In the fundamental disposedness **anxiety**, being-there understands its essential finitude. Being-there is first and foremost **thrownness** and exists in inauthentic **modes**. Heidegger describes the uniform basic structure of being-there as **care**.

In the second division, *Being-there and **temporality***, Heidegger describes authentic being-there in its being a **whole**. Being-there's most unique **possibility** is disclosed in its **anticipating** its ultimate possibility: **death**. The possibility of authentic existence is also expressed by the **call of conscience**. Being-there remains guilty, because it always has possibilities that still stand out. All possibilities of being-there spring ultimately from death. Being-there discloses its factual possibilities in authentic **resoluteness**.

The original unity of the structure of care lies in temporality. As being-ahead-of-itself being-there is grounded in the **future**; as being-already-in in **having-been**; and finally as being-among (entities) in the **present**. The primary phenomenon of original and authentic temporality is the future. Original time is finite. In the moment of insight of resoluteness being-there is anticipating the possibility of its death and repeating the possibility of its birth. Temporality temporalizes possible ways of itself that enable the manifold modes of being-there's being and especially the basic possibility of authentic and inauthentic existence. The essence of temporality is the temporalizing in the unity and equiprimordiality of the **ecstases**: future, present, and having-been. Being-there actualizes its being in different ways in time. These different ways are grounded in the uniform structure of care. Temporalizing is an interweaving of intentional structures that Heidegger explains as schematizing. Temporality actualizes its different senses through different **horizonal schemas**. Traditional ontology failed to understand the being of being-there from temporality and thus made it impossible to disclose the sense of being from original time.

Heidegger worked out several versions of the third division, *Time and Being*, of part I. Part II existed in the form of lecture notes and works like *Kant and the Problem of Metaphysics*. Yet Heidegger was unable to finish *Being and Time*. This failure ultimately led to the **turning**. Instead of trying to find a way from original time to the sense of being by way of the existential analysis of being-there, Heidegger would now try to understand time from the **history of Being** as the **appropriation** of being-there as the 'there' of being.

BEING-IN (*In-Sein*). Being-in is an **existential** of **being-there**, which has **being-in-the-world** as its essential state. **Disposedness, discovery** and **interpretedness** determine being-in. Heidegger painstakingly tries to eradicate every vestige of spatial containment. 'In' is derived from 'innan' which means to reside. It is the '*in*' of *in*-timate *in*-terest (**care, concern**) *in* the **world**. Being-in is the way in which being-there is intimately involved in habitative **dwelling**.

BEING-IN-THE-WORLD (*In-der-Welt-sein*). As early as 1919 Heidegger underlined that **life** is always life in a **world**. Being-in-the-world became the **formal indication** of **being-there's** being in a world in 1923. Being-there is not first locked up within itself; neither does it have to step outside itself to meet the external world. Being-there as **existence** is always already standing out *in* a world. This **instance** of being-there is disclosed as a world with which we are familiar.

BEING-OUT-FOR (*Sein-Zu, Aussein-auf*). Heidegger introduced the **formal indication** being-out-for in his Winter Semester 1925/26 course on **logic**. **Existence** is itself being-out-for its own **can-be**. This implies existence can never find its end and will remain unfinished. As long as **being-there** is, there is something in it that still stands out. This outstanding possibility is its own **death** as its very end.

BEING-THERE (*Dasein*). In *Being and Time* being-there is the **formal indication** of the **entity** that is ontologically distinguished from all other entities by the fact that in its very **being**, **Being** is an issue for it. Being-there is the **way of being** of **human beings**. It is determined in its **essence** by **existence** and its existential **structure**. From his *Contributions to Philosophy* onward, Heidegger understands being-there as the 'there' of Being. The 'there' or **truth of Being** is the **clearing** as the **appropriation** of the **play of time-space**. Human beings exist in the 'there' of Being. The emphasis shifts from the way of being of human beings toward Being itself.

BEING-TOWARDS-DEATH (*Sein-zum-Tode*).   Being-towards-death is an **existential**, which makes **being-there**'s **being a whole** possible. Like all existentials, being-towards-death has an authentic and an inauthentic **mode**. Inauthentic being-towards-death flees in **fear** from **death** as its most unique **possibility**: the possible impossibility of being there's **existence**. In fear being-there tries to remain indifferent to its uttermost possibility and consider death as something that does not concern it just yet. In authentic being-towards-death, being-there does not evade death as its most unique possibility. It trembles in **anxiety** for the **nothing** of the possible impossibility of its existence. Anxiety throws being-there back upon itself and thus frees it from its absorption by the **world** and the '**they**'. Authentic being-towards-death makes being-there's anticipating **resoluteness** possible and therewith its authentic being a **whole**. Anticipating resoluteness is the **ontic-ontological** prefiguration for tracing out the **structure** of the original **temporality**. *See also* Anticipate.

BEING-WITH (*Mitsein*).   Heidegger introduced this term in 1925 to articulate the initial encounter with the other in his or her having to do with the **world** and his or her functioning in the world along with me, that is, his or her *Mit-dasein* or being-there-with. In *Being and Time* being-with is one of the equiprimordial **existentials** of **being-there**. As **formal indication** it refers to the reciprocity of mutual comporting. Others are always there with me and I am always there with others.

BEINGNESS (*Seiendheit*).   Beingness is the attribute, which makes that **entities** are, just as beauty is the attribute, which makes entities beautiful. *See also* being.

BEON (*Seyn*). *see* BEING

BETWEEN, THE (*das Zwischen*).   The between is the **formal indication** of the most essential **structure** of **Being**. Being reveals itself in the **clearing** as the between that makes every encounter possible. In the lightning process of Being, that is, **appropriation** of the **truth of Being**, everything is lighted up or cleared. The between is the dimension out of which the **play of time-space** can **come to presence**. This dimension makes the encounter of **being-there** and **entities**, of the **mortals** and the **divinities**, and of **earth** and **sky** possible. The between is the 'there' of Being, that is, the grounding process of being-there.

BLOCHMANN, ELISABETH (1892-1972). Blochmann was a close student friend of **Elfride Heidegger-Petri**. Very soon she and Heidegger became close friends as well. Their friendship started in 1918 and lasted until her death in 1972. The correspondence between the two gives many valuable insights into Heidegger's life and work. In the early years of their friendship Heidegger acted like a mentor. He told her what philosophical books to read and encouraged her in her studies. She was a student of people like Georg Simmel, Georg Misch and Hermann Nohl and became a highly regarded pedagogue in her own time. When Blochmann was forced to leave Germany in 1934, Heidegger gave her letters of recommendation and helped her as much as he could. After World War II they resumed their friendship.

BOREDOM (*Langeweile*). In his Winter Semester 1929/30 lecture course *Fundamental Concepts of Metaphysics* boredom replaces **anxiety** as the basic **mood** of **being-there**. Boredom means literally a long **while**. If **time** becomes long for being-there, it tries to drive time and its boring character away. Being-there does not want to have a long time. Boredom means almost the same as homesickness. The basic mood of modern philosophizing is **homesickness** and no longer the astonishment of **Greek philosophy**. In boredom the temporal **horizon** of **presence** becomes so wide that **entities** manifest themselves indifferently. According to Heidegger the very **Being** of German being-there was transformed by deep boredom after World War I. The **affliction** and profound **need** of German being-there would become so great in boredom that it would be able to experience the **moment** of **truth**. This moment would lead to **authenticity** and inaugurate a new era in the **history of Being**. Heidegger saw in the rise of **National Socialism** a historic opportunity to make this fundamental change in German being-there possible.

BOSS, MEDARD (1903-1990). Medard Boss was a Swiss psychiatrist and psychotherapist. His friendship with Heidegger started in 1947 when Heidegger answered his letter full of questions about *Being and Time*. From 1959 until 1969 Boss organized Heidegger's famous seminars in Zollikon. *See also* Zollikon Seminars.

BRAIG, CARL (1853-1923). This Thomistic theologian was one of the major influences on Heidegger's earliest thought. As a schoolboy he came across Braig's book *On Being* in which he found long citations from **Aristotle**, Thomas Aquinas, and Francisco Suárez and the etymology of **ontological** concepts. Braig developed an **ontology**, which Heidegger could assimilate with **Franz Brentano**'s doctrine of **being**. At the University of **Freiburg** Heidegger attended some of Braig's lecture courses in **theology**. Heidegger at first supported his critique of modernity in his *Youthful Theological Writings*. Braig was, however, also a major catalyst for his interest in German idealism and speculative theology.

BRENTANO, FRANZ (1838-1917). Heidegger worked his way again and again, from 1907 on, through the first philosophical work that he studied: Brentano's dissertation *On the Several Senses of Being in Aristotle*. He received this book as a gift from his fatherly friend, **Conrad Gröber**. From Brentano's study Heidegger learned the fourfold determination of **being** in the Aristotelian corpus. Brentano was not only at the origin of Heidegger's study of **Aristotle**; he was also **Edmund Husserl**'s one and only teacher in **philosophy**. In his psychological studies Brentano developed his celebrated doctrine of **intentionality**, which would become of utmost importance to the phenomenological movement.

BUILDING (*bauen*). According to Heidegger the stem of the German verb '*bauen*' bears affinity to the form of the verb 'to be' ('*ich bin, du bist*'). Building is the manner in which **being-there** dwells in the **world**. Building as **dwelling** unfolds into the building that cultivates living things and the building that erects constructions. A construction, for instance a bridge, gathers to itself in its own way **earth** and **sky**, **divinities** and **mortals**. The **location** of a building allows the **fourfold** to enter into a **site** by arranging the site into different **spaces**, where everything has its place. Genuine buildings give form to the **essence** of dwelling. Building lets **things** be as things and preserves **Being** in things. In building its home in the world and letting things shine forth as what they are, being-there responds to the **address of Being**. Being at home is the **moment** of achieved **authenticity** or **autochthony**. *See also* Building Dwelling Thinking.

BUILDING DWELLING THINKING (*Bauen Wohnen Denken*). In this 1951 lecture Heidegger develops the essential continuity of **Being, building, dwelling** and **thinking** and continues his meditation on the **thing**. Dwelling is now the fundamental **ontological structure** of **being-there**. It is the manner in which **mortals** are on the **earth** and under the **sky** and exist before the **divinities**. Dwelling comports two dimensions: mortals are in the **fourfold** inasmuch as they dwell; and in dwelling they take care of and tend the **entities** that they encounter. The basic character of dwelling is to spare, to preserve. In dwelling mortals preserve the fourfold in its essential **being**, its **making present**. In dwelling mortals take their measure from the way the **world** fits together or 'fugues' and lets entities show themselves as they are. Dwelling is building a home in the world. Building is **being-there**'s response to the **claim** of Being inasmuch as being-there reveals entities in their being. In thinking being-there responds to this appeal by trying to commemorate the **unconcealment** of Being and respond to the address of Being. Only in thinking can we meditate upon the **ontological difference** and experience the **appropriation** of Being. *See also* Thing, The; What Is Called Thinking?

BULTMANN, RUDOLF (1884-1976). Heidegger and Bultmann became close friends after Heidegger's appointment as a professor in **Marburg**. They studied the writings of Martin Luther together and jointly held seminars in theological exegesis. Bultmann was strongly influenced by the **existential analysis** of **being-there** that he used for his demythologizing **interpretation** of the Bible. Heidegger's involvement with **National Socialism** led to an estrangement between the two. After World War II they were able to work out their differences and continue their friendship.

- C -

CALCULATIVE THINKING (*rechnendes Denken*). Calculative thinking is the **essence** of modern **science**. Beginning with **René Descartes** the **beingness** of **entities** was reduced to **being** an object for a self-certain subject. The **sense of being** became being represented. As **representations** entities become measurable. Since modern science is only concerned with measurement, it reduces the being of entities to quantity and thus makes their technological control possible. Entities are used up and reduced to a dull and indistinguishable uniformity. In the age of **nihilism** even **human beings** have become nameless faces that only count as numbers. **Being-there** itself has become a means to the quest for power for its own sake: the sheer **will** to will. The task of **reflection**, or the tracing of **sense**, is not to strive for control and power, but to surrender itself to the **address of Being**. The **thinking** of **Being** is at the same time a giving thanks. In this sense modern science does not think. According to Heidegger, science still has to learn how to think. *See also* Science and Reflection.

CALL OF CONSCIENCE (*Gewissensruf*). Because **being-there** exists first and for most in an inauthentic **mode**, the **fallenness** of the inauthentic **self** has to be broken. **Conscience** calls to being-there and thus frees it from being lost in the '**they**' and the **world**. It calls for being-there to obey the demands of its own unique **situation** and to choose its own **projection**. The call of conscience does not present being-there with a universal ideal of **authenticity**. It summons being-there in its **mineness** to its unique **possibilities**. By the call of conscience being-there is called forth into the original **truth** of its individual **existence**.

CAN-BE (*Seinkönnen*). Heidegger first understood **being-there's way of being** as can-be in his 1924 lecture, *The Concept of Time*. Being-there has the original choice to be or not to be its there, its that it is. It is always what it can be and how it is, that is, in the **mode** of **authenticity** or **inauthenticity**, what it can be! Heidegger describes the very **being** of being-there as being-out-toward what it is not, but can be. This **structure** later gives birth to the **formal indication** of **existence**. As existence, being-there is in its **essence** always an on-toward, still under way toward, a can-be, and therefore it is never finished. It is the **possibility** of being free for its most unique can-be, its **death**. Death is the ultimate can-be of being-there. The **call of conscience** provides being-there with the attestation of authentic can-be. The existence of being-there is in each case mine, my own can-be, mine to own up to and make my own. This is what I ought to do. I owe it to myself to own up to my existence. Existence is in its **givenness**, the gift of the having to be, of being-there as a can-be. **Understanding** discloses to being-there the can-be for the sake of which it is.

CARE (*Sorge*). In his Summer Semester 1925 lecture course, *History of the Concept of Time. Prolegomena*, Heidegger replaces **Edmund Husserl**'s concept of **intentionality** with the **formal indication** of care. Care is, in **being-there**'s relation to its **world, concern** and, in its relation to other being-there, **solicitude**. The formal **structure** of care is being-there's being-ahead-of-itself in its always already being involved in something. For being-there its very **being** is an issue, or in other words, being-there's **existence** matters to it and concerns it.

In *Being and Time* care becomes the **ontological** term for the totality of being-there's structural **whole** of relations that consists of **facticity** or **thrownness (past)**, **being-in-the-world** or **fallenness (present)**, and **existence** or **can-be (future)**. **Temporality** is the **ontological sense** of care and its original condition of **possibility**. The basic constitution of care can only be grounded in temporality.

CASSIRER, ERNST (1874-1945). Ernst Cassirer was the last representative of the **Marburg** school of **neo-Kantianism**. He first met Heidegger in 1923 in Hamburg at the occasion of the latter's December 1 lecture at the **Kant** Society and later in Davos at one of the special courses the university organized each year. They worked together in workshops and gave lectures. The highlight of the conference was the famous *Davos Disputation between Ernst Cassirer and Martin Heidegger*. In 1931 Cassirer wrote a review of Heidegger's book, *Kant and the Problem of Metaphysics*, in which he criticized Heidegger for his failure to see the importance of the *Critique of Practical Reason* for Kant's philosophical system. *See also* Cassirer Review, The; On Odebrecht's and Cassirer's Critique of the Kantbook.

CASSIRER REVIEW, THE (*Die Cassirer Rezension*). In his review of the *Philosophy of Symbolic Forms. Vol. 2: Mythical Thinking*, Heidegger welcomed the attempt by **Ernst Cassirer** to give a systematic philosophical **interpretation** of the myth. Heidegger's main point of criticism is Cassirer's failure to answer the questions how myth belongs to **being-there**, on the one hand, and whether or not myth is a fundamental **phenomenon** for the **understanding** of the **sense of being**, on the other.

CATEGORIAL INTUITION (*kategoriale Anschauung*). In his Summer Semester 1925 lecture course, *History of the Concept of Time. Prolegomena*, Heidegger discusses the three fundamental breakthroughs of **Edmund Husserl**'s **phenomenology**: **intentionality**, categorial intuition and the **apriori**. In categorial intuition the meaningful **structures** from which we experience the **entities** included within them are made explicit through the free variation of ideation. Husserl exemplified categorial intuition through sense **perception**. Sense perception is fulfilled in the bodily **presence** of its object. Categorial intuition is fulfilled in the presence of the categorial forms themselves. In sense perception we see for example a white table; in categorial intuition we see that the table *is* white. This 'is' or **being** is never given in sense perception, although it makes our perception of the white table possible. Heidegger rejects Husserl's concept of categorial intuition, because it leads to the objectivization of **lived experience**. In his hermeneutical phenomenology he transforms categorial intuition into interpretative **understanding**. Lived experiences are through and through expressed experiences. They are expressed in a definite understanding we have of them as we simply live in them without regarding them thematically. Interpretative understanding makes explicit these pregiven meaningful structures developed by life **situations** in which the totality of **life** expresses itself.

CATEGORY (*Kategorie*). The **sense of being** expresses itself in the categorial **structure** of 'logos' that determines both the **being** of **entities** and our **thinking**. We live in a meaningful or categorically structured **world**, and are therefore able to make sense of it. In *Being and Time* Heidegger differentiates carefully between categories and **existentials**. Categories are only valid for entities that are not **being-there** (**nature**, **equipment**, **things**, objects) and should not be used to understand being-there or the sense of being in general. The structure of being-there is not determined by categories, but by existentials.

CHRISTIANITY (*Christentum*). It is not surprising that Christianity is an important factor in the development of Heidegger's thought. He came from a Roman Catholic background and was destined to become a priest. Both Christianity and modernity determined the **facticity** of his **existence**. From 1909 to 1911 he studied **theology** at the University of **Freiburg**. Because of health problems he abandoned his plans for the priesthood and became a philosopher. As a student he was strongly influenced by both scholasticism and **phenomenology**. He used the modern **logic** of **Edmund Husserl** and neo-Kantianism (**Heinrich Rickert**, **Emil Lask**) to interpret scholastic treatises and show their value for modern **philosophy**. The highlight of this approach is his book *Duns Scotus' Doctrine of Categories and Meaning*.

At first Heidegger was a staunch defender of the eternal **truth** of the Catholic **faith**. Although he criticized modernity for its superficiality and lack of **transcendence**, he still strove to remedy the ills of modern society by making the truth of Catholicism available to his fellowmen.

After his marriage to Elfride Petri Heidegger broke with the system of Catholicism in 1919. In his early lecture courses in Freiburg Heidegger developed a phenomenology of religious **experience** in which he highlighted the **affliction** of primal Christianity and contrasted it with the theoretical spectator attitude of modern times. The true insights in the **facticity** of human **life** in primal Christianity were overshadowed by the theological **interpretation** that derived its concepts from **Greek philosophy**. The fundamental difference between the two **factual life experiences** was blurred. To get to the root of primal Christianity Heidegger worked out a **destruction** of Christian factual life experience.

The main result of the destruction of Christianity was the insight that the moment of affliction and the **experience** of **time** as 'kairos' were also expressed in the writings of **Aristotle** on practical philosophy. This led to a change in Heidegger's interpretation of history. The facticity of modern life was no longer the falsification of the factual life experience of primal Christianity by Greek philosophy, but the original factual life experience of the Greeks was falsified by its Christian interpretation. Heidegger later moved away from Christianity. In his 1927 lecture, *Phenomenology and Theology*, Heidegger's final word about Christianity is that it belongs to theology, that is, the archenemy of philosophy. *See also* History of Being.

CIRCUMSPECTION (*Umsicht*). Heidegger's first description of the **environment** is based on looking around rather than getting around. Circumspection is first so named in 1922 in contrast to inspection (*hinsehen*). In *Being and Time* dealings with **equipment** subordinate themselves to the manifold assignments of the **in-order-to**. The sight with which they thus accommodate themselves is circumspection.

CLAIM (*Anspruch*). In **language, human beings** can hear the claim of **Being**. This claim claims that human beings belong to Being. In our **thinking** we can respond to the claim of Being.

CLEARING (*Lichtung*). Under the influence of the **tradition** of 'lumen naturale' Heidegger introduced this central term of his later thought in *Being and Time* to name the **disclosedness** of **being-in**.

According to this tradition the **human being** is lighted within itself and has been cleared. The light that makes being-there open and bright for itself is **care**. Only by this clearedness is any illuminating, awareness, or having of something possible. Heidegger identifies the lighted clearing of **being-there** with the unity of ecstatic **temporality**. Being-there is the temporal clearing of the **sense of being**.

In the 1930s Heidegger rethinks the clearing within the framework of his theory of **truth**. He now interprets '**alètheia**' as clearing, that is, the lightning process in which everything is lighted up. The clearing as the 'there' of being-there is the **unconcealment** of **Being**. Being reveals itself in the clearing as the **beingness** of **entities** and conceals itself as Being. The lightning process of the clearing makes the **history of Being** possible and explains the **forgetfulness of being** in **metaphysics**. The **structure** of the clearing is the **fourfold** as the outcome of the **play of time-space**.

The clearing also plays an important part in Heidegger's theory of **art**. Art is the setting into work of truth, which is only possible when there is a clearing within the **whole** of entities. This clearing as the **nothing** encloses all entities and enables the work of art to let entities shine forth in their simple and essential **being**. In this way the work of art illuminates self-concealing Being.

COMING TO PRESENCE (*wesen*). Heidegger uses *wesen* as a verb, although it is seldom used as such in modern German. *Wesen*, **essence**, as a noun is derived from this verb. Essence does not mean 'quidditas' originally, but rather enduring as **present**. The essence of an **entity** does not simply mean what something is, but also means the way in which something pursues its course, the way in which it remains through **time** as what it is. *Wesen* is the same as *währen*, that is, to last or endure.

COMMEMORATIVE THINKING (*Andenken*). Since the history of **philosophy** has ended in the reign of **technology** and the frenzy of **calculative thinking**, Heidegger opposes commemorative thinking to calculation and **representation** as another kind of nonmetaphysical **thinking**. It does not try to determine and dominate **entities**, but attempts to let them be what they are. In commemorative thinking we open ourselves to the **mystery** of **Being**. It is essentially **reflection** or deliberation of **sense**. As recollection, commemorative thinking does not think the **history of Being** as something of the past; it tries to respond to the **destiny** of the **truth of Being**. Commemorative thinking commemorates the **possibility** of another **beginning** in the history of Being. **Acquiescence** holds sway in the **essence** of commemorative thinking. It is the task of the **shepherd of Being** to commemorate the **appropriation** of Being.

CONCEAL (*verbergen*). *see* CONCEALMENT

CONCEALMENT (*Verborgenheit*). Heidegger interprets the Greek concept of **truth**, 'alètheia', as **unconcealment**. Truth must be wrested from concealment. There are three forms of concealment: 1. Truth brings **entities** forth from their original concealment as the not yet discovered and discloses them in their **being**, 2. The **discovery** of entities may be forgotten and relapse into concealment, and 3. Because truth discloses entities in their being, it may also go astray and conceal rather than reveal entities in their being. The danger of **errancy** always lurks just around the corner of truth. In the unconcealment of entities **Being** reveals itself as **beingness** and at the same time holds itself back in concealment as Being. The **truth of Being** is the **appropriation** of its self-revealing concealing and its self-concealing revealing.

CONCEPT OF TIME, THE (*Der Begriff der Zeit*). Heidegger presented this public address on July 25, 1924, to the **Marburg** Theologians Society. It contains the core **structure** of *Being and Time*. The central topic of the lecture is the question what is **time**? Heidegger analyzes first the everyday concept of time. Time is related to **movement**. **Aristotle** and Albert Einstein agree that time exists only because of the events that happen within it. In natural **science**, time is measured by a **now** that is so much later than an earlier now and so much earlier than a later now. Yet, as Augustine has shown, we can measure time only through our **disposedness**. Time is closely related to the **being-there** of **human beings**.

The **way of being** of being-there is determined by its **particular whileness**. The **life** of a human being is a succession of the particular **whiles** of its **situation** and is extended between its birth and **death**. Being-there is primarily a **being** possible or **can-be**. Death is the undetermined certainty of being-there's most unique **possibility** of being at an end. When being-there **anticipates** the certain possibility of its being gone, it is authentically with itself and truly existent. It thus becomes visible in its unique here-and-now and the once-and-for-all of its unique **fate** in the possibility of its one-and-only goneness. Being-there is its **present** in **everydayness**, its **future** in anticipation and its

past in **historicality**. Being-there is time and therefore the most proper determination of time is that time is temporal. Heidegger rephrases the opening question of his lecture, what is time?, as who is time? Are we ourselves time or am I my time? If I were my time, being-there would become a question for itself. With this statement Heidegger ends his lecture on the threshold of *Being and Time*.

CONCERN (*besorgen*).   Concern is the actualization of **care** as a possible way of **being-in-the-world**. **Being-there** concerns itself with activities which it performs and **things** which it produces. As the relation between being-there and the things it encounters within the **world**, concern is characterized by **circumspection**. *See also* Equipment.

CONSCIENCE (*Gewissen*).   In *Being and Time* conscience makes it possible for **being-there** to free itself from its **fallenness** to the **world** and the 'they'. Conscience calls for being-there to obey the demands of its own unique **situation** and to choose its own **projection**. The **call of conscience** does not present being-there with a universal ideal of **authenticity**. It summons being-there in its **mineness** to its unique **possibilities**. By the call of conscience being-there is called forth into the original **truth** of its individual **existence**. *See also* Guilt; Resoluteness.

CONSTANCE (*Konstanz*).   Constance is the town on the Lake of Constance where Heidegger began his preparation for the Roman Catholic priesthood in October 1903. He entered the equivalent of the freshman year of high school at the Heinrich Suso Gymnasium. At the same time he took up residence in the Konradihaus, the archdiocesan high school seminary that had been named after the city's patron saint. Heidegger's fatherly friend, **Conrad Gröber**, was the rector of the Konradihaus. Heidegger would live in Constance for the next three years while pursuing the first half of his secondary education.

CONTENT SENSE (*Gehaltssinn*).   Heidegger first showed in his Winter Semester 1919-20 course on the basic problems of **phenomenology** that factual **life** has motives and tendencies. Every tendency has a certain content. This content is a **lifeworld** that itself becomes a motive for the **self**. The content sense refers to this motive and shows what it is. *See also* Actualization sense; Relational sense; Temporalizing sense.

CONTRIBUTIONS TO PHILOSOPHY. FROM ENOWNING (*Beiträge zur Philosophie. Vom Ereignis*). Heidegger was holding back and sheltering his second main work in long hesitation. The set of manuscripts written between 1936 and 1938 was finally published posthumously to commemorate the 100th anniversary of his birthday. The title of this unique and complex work is made up of two parts, one presenting the public title, *Contributions to Philosophy*, and the other the appropriate one, *From Enowning*. Heidegger's contributions to **philosophy** consist of a preview, an order of six **arrangements** or joinings, and a concluding resume of what preceded. Heidegger attempts to think **Being** in its essential unfolding as **appropriation**. He describes the **experience** of **thinking** as being stretched out between two **beginnings** and prepares for the transition from the end of the first beginning to a new beginning. The first beginning is the metaphysical thinking of Being as **beingness**. The new beginning is the thinking of the **truth of Being** as the **clearing** of self-**concealment**.

In the *Preview* (*Vorblick*) Heidegger elucidates the directives that thinking needs to follow in order to experience Being as appropriation. He distinguishes between the **guiding question** of **metaphysics**, what is an **entity**?, and the **basic question** of incipient thinking about the **ground** of metaphysics. The **attunement** of the first beginning is wonder or astonishment, the Greek 'thaumazein', that of the new beginning, is reserve or reservedness (*Verhaltenheit*), the basic **mood** of **being-there**'s relation to Being, which holds appropriation back and in reserve.

In the first arrangement or fugue, *Echo* (*Der Anklang*), Heidegger describes **being-there**'s relation to Being as the **forgetfulness of being**. This relation must be thought through and opened up as what has to be thought. At the end of the history of metaphysics thinking experiences the echo of Being as withdrawal and abandonment.

In the second arrangement, *Playing-Forth* (*Das Zuspiel*), Heidegger shows how the guiding question of metaphysics beckons thought to the basic question of the other beginning of thought. We should no longer try to think the **unconcealment** of Being as the beingness of entities, but think from the truth of Being as appropriation.

As Heidegger shows in the third arrangement, *Leap* (*Der Sprung*), the other beginning of thinking is only accessible through a leap of thought into the truth of Being itself. The thinker belongs to Being as the appropriation of thought. We must not try to think Being, but let the **silence** of Being be heard through our thinking.

The fourth arrangement, *Grounding* (*Die Gründung*), describes how through the leap of thought, the being-there of **human beings** and the **expanse**, where the truth of Being comes to pass, are grounded.

In the fifth arrangement, *The Ones to Come* (*Die Zukünftigen*), Heidegger calls for the ones to come to prepare for the historical decision of the appropriation of Being and thus make a new beginning possible.

The sixth arrangement, *The Last God* (*Der letzte Gott*), is a meditation on the beckoning of the last **God**. We can experience his **nearness** in the withdrawal and flight of the **gods**. The future ones must prepare for his coming by leaping into being-there, which simultaneously is the grounding of the truth of Being.

The last part of the *Contributions to Philosophy*, *Be-ing* (*Seyn*), amounts to a final conclusion and culmination of the entire work and the **movement** of thinking accomplished through it.

CONVERSATION ON A COUNTRY PATH ABOUT THINKING (*Zur Erörterung der Gelassenheit. Aus einem Feldweggespräch über das Denken*). In this essay Heidegger introduces the **expanse** as a **formal indication** of **Being**. The expanse is the open domain wherein **entities** may while. In this conversation Heidegger describes the **essence** of thought as the **thinking** of Being as expanse. **Being-there** belongs to the expanse and the expanse would not be what it is without being-there. Being appropriates itself as expanse, which at the same time is the expanding of the 'there' of being-there. The expanding process is both the release (*Gelassenheit*) of being-there into the expanse and being-there's **acquiescence** (*Gelassenheit*) of Being.

Thought as the thinking of Being can have Being as its **origin** and its term. Thinking with Being as its origin is the basic **structure** of being-there's **openness** to the **open** and its expansion to the expanse. Heidegger describes thinking with Being as its term as waiting. Waiting is grounded in the fact that being-there appertains to that for which it waits. The thinker must assume the attitude of being attentive to Being and let Being **come to presence** as expanse. In waiting we must leave that for which we wait to open, because waiting lets the open be. Waiting is both the liberation from representational-horizonal thinking and a release into the open. This liberating movement of thinking requires a touch of willing that disappears in being-there's release into the expanse and is completely extinguished in acquiescence. In acquiescence being-there achieves **authenticity** as the culmination of thought. The **essence** of authentic thinking is **resoluteness** of the **being** of **truth** in its essence. Only when the thinker perseveres in his resoluteness may he be said to repose in himself as what he is. This state of repose is **instance.**

CRITICAL COMMENTS ON KARL JASPERS' 'PSYCHOLOGY OF WORLDVIEWS' (*Anmerkungen zu Karl Jaspers 'Psychologie der Weltanschauungen'*). Heidegger's essay was meant to be a review of **Karl Jaspers'** famous book *Psychology of Worldviews* for publication in the *Göttingsche Gelehrte Anzeigen.* It was first published in 1972, but in June 1919 Heidegger distributed a typescript of it to Jaspers, **Edmund Husserl** and **Heinrich Rickert.** The review is a critique, which tries to bring into sharper focus and contour the true tendency and basic motives of Jaspers' problematic and its method. There is at once a positive and a negative edge to the critique, since it is a destructively self-renewing **appropriation.** In the course of the review Heidegger will time and again amplify and supplement his radical method of critique with other aspects of phenomenological method. The review is thus both a treatise on phenomenological methodology and a critique of Jaspers' book. Jaspers tried to answer the basic question of psychology, what the **human being** is, by way of a psychology of **worldviews**, which seeks to describe the limits of the soul and thus provide a clear and comprehensive **horizon** for the psychic. Jaspers tries to illuminate the **phenomenon** of **existence** in and through **limit situations.** He seeks to understand what ultimate positions the soul can assume in limit situations and what forces move it to do so.

Heidegger's critique of Jaspers centers on two points. Jaspers introduces the term existence as a Kantian idea, that is, something that counts as the **whole**, or existence. He then traces it back to its sources in **Sören Kierkegaard** and **Friedrich Nietzsche** for whom existence refers to the **life** of the present individuality. According to Heidegger Jaspers fails to get at the problem of existence, because he uncritically borrows his concepts from the philosophical **tradition.** He is unaware of the historical **situation** of his **interpretation.** The second point of critique is his method and his lack of concern over this issue. Jaspers assumes he can describe existence objectively by just looking at it. He contemplatively holds the whole of life in its unity and harmony, untroubled by any self-worldly **concern.** Heidegger denies existence can be approached in this basically aesthetic **experience,** since existence is not an object but a particular **way of being**, a certain **sense** of the 'is', which 'is' essentially the sense of 'I am'. I am in having myself. According to Heidegger the truly actualized **ground** of **factual life experience** is that my life concerns me radically and purely. The 'I am' can only be experienced in its full actuality and **facticity**. This having myself assumes different senses in different regards, so that this manifold of sense must be made comprehensible in specifically historical contexts. Only in the infinite process of a radical questioning, which holds itself in the question, can the phenomenon of existence be approached. The genuine insights via limit situations into the genuine problem of existence that Jaspers has to offer in his book are thus obscured by his lack of methodological concern. *See also* Phenomenology.

CURIOSITY (*Neugier*). Curiosity is the tendency of **being-there** towards seeing which belongs to its **everydayness**. In curiosity being-there does not try to see in order to understand, but just for the sake of seeing itself. Curiosity leaps from novelty to novelty and does not tarry alongside the **entities** it encounters. Because curiosity does not tarry, it is always concerned with the constant **possibility** of distraction. When being-there is curious, it never dwells anywhere and is delivered over to **idle talk**.

- D -

DASEIN. *see* BEING-THERE

DAVOS DISPUTATION BETWEEN ERNST CASSIRER AND MARTIN HEIDEGGER (*Davoser Disputation zwischen Ernst Cassirer und Martin Heidegger*). This disputation occurred in connection with Heidegger's and **Ernst Cassirer**'s lectures on **Immanuel Kant** at the second Davos Hochschule. The discussion centers on the **interpretation** of Kant. They both agree that the productive power of the imagination is of great importance to Kant and that it is necessary to raise the central question of **metaphysics** anew: what is **being**? Cassirer shows that the finitude of **human beings** becomes **transcendent** in Kant's ethical writings; Heidegger, on the other hand, raises the problem of whether the inner **structure** of **being-there** is finite or infinite.

DEALINGS (*Umgang*). *see* GETTING AROUND

DEATH (*Tod*). The origin of Heidegger's **understanding** of death is **Karl Jaspers**' description of death as a **limit situation** in his *Psychology of Worldviews*. From 1919 on, and especially in *Being and Time*,

Heidegger described death as the ultimate and most unique **possibility** that is and remains real as long as **being-there** exists. In its **being-towards-death**, being-there **anticipates** the possibility of its death as possibility. The possibility of death is the impossibility of all comportment and as such the possible impossibility of **existence** as such. In the anticipation of its own death being-there understands the impossibility of its own existence as an inevitable possibility. Being-there is possible nonbeing, is not something, and therewith a pure **can-be** that has to be. I can project my own possibilities and can avoid being determined by anything else, be it the **world** or the **'they'**. Since as finite being-there we remain **being-in-the-world** and **being-with**, we can never completely actualize this possibility. It is no coincidence that death, as the liberation from all external influence, is at the same time the end of my existence. In this possibility, to determine ourselves who we want to be, we disclose the factual **fallenness** into the world and the 'they' of our everyday existence.

Death is related to nothing else than our most unique can-be that through this relation is individualized. In anticipating my death as the most unique possibility of my existence I become conscious of my own unique and one-off existence. Death is always my death of being-there in its individuality. Heidegger does not found the **mineness** of being-there upon the soul, the *cogito* or the **I**, but in the **structure** of being-towards-death. Authentic existence keeps open all possibilities and makes it possible for being-there to exist as a **whole**.

In *Being and Time*, death is the highest jurisdiction of our can-be. In our being futural we shatter against death so that we are at once thrown back upon the 'there' of our **facticity**. We are free for death, free for **fate**, and free to commit ourselves at the decisive moments in world history.

After the **turning** and his break with **National Socialism**, Heidegger grounds the finitude of being-there no longer in its being-towards-death, but in its mortality. In the **fourfold** the **mortals** and the **gods** are united. Human beings are now called the mortals, because they can die. Only humans die, and they die continuously, as long as they dwell on **earth**, under the **sky**, before the **divinities**.

DEBT (*Schuld*). *see* GUILT

DESCARTES, RENÉ (1596-1650). The father of modern **philosophy** is a pivotal figure in Heidegger's **history** of philosophy. He grounded the **being** of **entities** in the self-certain subject and determined **truth** as certitude. Every entity is either an object or that which objectifies. Heidegger designates this subject reference of all being **subjectity**. Its three most important consequences are: 1. The **world** becomes a picture, 2. Philosophy becomes anthropology, and 3. **Value** becomes the goal of all intercourse between **being-there** and entities. *See also* Age of the World Picture; Basic Problems of Phenomenology, The; European Nihilism; Introduction to Phenomenological Research; What Is Metaphysics?

DESTINY (*Geschick*). After the **turning**, the **forgetfulness of being** in **metaphysics** is no longer the work of **being-there**; it can only be understood as the destiny of **Being** itself. Being-there could only understand the **sense of being** as **beingness**, because Being revealed itself as the **being** of **entities**. The **overcoming** of metaphysics cannot be achieved by being-there itself; it is only possible as the **appropriation** of a new **beginning** by Being.

DESTRUCTION (*Destruktion*). Destruction is an important element of Heidegger's phenomenological method and makes its first appearance as phenomenological critique in Winter Semester 1919/20. Its goal is to loosen up the hardened **tradition** and to dissolve the **concealment** which tradition has brought about. Destruction aims its criticism at the **present** and its failure to go back to the **origins** of our **interpretation** of **being-there**. Destruction is the **retrieval** of the original **facticity** that was expressed in philosophical concepts. In the course of history the original **meaning** of these concepts as **expressions** of **experience** is covered up, distorted and ultimately lost. After the **turning**, Heidegger no longer considers this concealment and distortion to be the failure of being-there, but as destined by **Being** itself.

DIALOGUE ON LANGUAGE, A (*Aus einem Gespräch von der Sprache*). In this dialogue between a Japanese professor (Tomio Tezuka) and an inquirer (Heidegger) the **possibilities** and dangers of a dialogue between Japanese and German culture are discussed. The great danger of this dialogue is that the relation between the two cultures can only be discussed in either of the two **languages**. Since the Japanese and the Germans speak different languages, they live in two different **houses of Being**. In their search for the **essence** of language Heidegger and his Japanese guest come to the conclusion that the essence of language can only be disclosed in a dialogue that speaks from and out of language, instead of about it. Only in a dialogue that wants to **keep silent** can language reveal itself in its essence as **saying**. Heidegger determines saying in two different ways, as what is said in it and what is to be said. Language as saying hints at **Being** and reveals in its beckoning the **unconcealment** of the **twofold**.

DIFFERENCE (*Differenz*). *see* ONTOLOGICAL DIFFERENCE

DILTHEY, WILHELM (1833-1911). As early as 1910 Heidegger studied the works of Dilthey and continued to do so until the publication of ***Being and Time***. Dilthey had a profound influence on Heidegger's thinking. From Dilthey he learned that **life** has always already expressed itself in forms and **structures** that it can understand. Life is always **lived experience**. Heidegger used Dilthey's concept of **hermeneutics** to turn **Edmund Husserl**'s transcendental conception of **phenomenology** into a hermeneutic phenomenology. He transformed Husserl's three early breakthroughs, **intentionality, categorial intuition** and **apriori**, into **care**, interpretative **understanding** and **time**. He also took over from Dilthey the emphasis on the **historicality** of the **being** of humans and later transformed the historicality of **human being** into the **temporality** of **being-there**. *See also* Life philosophy.

DISCLOSEDNESS (*Erschlossenheit*). Disclosedness is the **ontological** term for **being-there**'s being lighted and cleared within itself. Being-there is in its 'there' disclosedness and not locked within itself. Being-there is a **structure** and it has no inside. In its very **being** it stands open. This fundamental **openness** of its **instance** makes it possible for being-there to encounter anything at all.

DISCOURSE (*Rede*). Discourse is the **existential-ontological** foundation of **language**. It determines equiprimordially the two ways in which **being-there** is its 'there': **disposedness** and **understanding**. **Hearing** is constitutive for discourse, of which **keeping silent** is an essential **possibility**.

DISCOVERY (*Entdecktheit*). The discovery of **entities** within the **world**, which are present-at-hand or ready-to-hand, is grounded in **being-there**'s **disclosedness** of the world. Being-there can only discover entities, because it is familiar with the **meaningfulness** of the world. *See also* Presence-at-hand; Readiness-to-hand.

DISPOSEDNESS (*Befindlichkeit*). Disposedness is the ontological term for **being-there**'s being attuned, its **mood** or **attunement**. It is a fundamental **existential** of being-there. Disposedness discloses being-there in its **thrownness** and proximally and generally in the manner of an evasive turning away. It is an '**existential**' mode of the equiprimordial **disclosedness** of **world, being-with** and **existence**. Being-there's **openness** to the world is constituted existentially by its disposedness. It is the way in which being-there is its there. **Anxiety** is a fundamental and authentic disposedness of being-there.

DISTRESS (*Not*). *see* NEED

DIVINITIES, THE (*die Göttlichen*). The divinities are the messengers of the godhead. Out of its holy sway, the **god** appears in his **presence** or withdraws into **concealment**. In **dwelling**, the **mortals** await the intimations of the coming of the divinities. Divinities and mortals, **earth** and **sky**, are joined together in the oneness of the **fourfold**.

DUNS SCOTUS' DOCTRINE OF CATEGORIES AND MEANING (*Die Kategorien- und Bedeutungslehre des Duns Scotus*). Heidegger wrote his qualifying dissertation on Duns Scotus in 1915. In this original work he discusses the doctrine of **categories** of Duns Scotus in relation to his doctrine of **meaning**. Heidegger uses the modern **logic** of **Edmund Husserl** and **Emil Lask** to interpret a scholastic treatise that was, as was later proven, not written by Scotus himself, but his pupil Thomas of Erfurt. At the same time he uses the medieval doctrine of categories and meaning to criticize contemporary theories. The great advantage of Scotus' doctrine over modern logic is its metaphysical foundation. As Heidegger writes in the final chapter, which is a later addendum to the published edition of 1916, "in the long run **philosophy** cannot do without its optics **metaphysics**". Heidegger's original approach to philosophy and its **history** brought him to the attention of **Paul Natorp**, who in 1923 would play a pivotal role in Heidegger's appointment as a professor at the University of **Marburg**.

DWELLING (*wohnen*). After the **turning**, Heidegger describes the **being-in-the-world** of **being-there** as dwelling in the **fourfold**. In dwelling, being-there builds its home in the **world**. Dwelling is the manner in which **mortals** are on the **earth** and under the **sky**. Dwelling comports two dimensions: mortals are in the **fourfold** inasmuch as they dwell; and in dwelling they take care of and tend the **entities** that they encounter. The basic character of dwelling is to spare, to preserve. In dwelling mortals preserve the fourfold in its essential **being**, its making present, and take their measure from the way the world fits together and let entities show themselves as they are. Saving the earth, receiving the sky, awaiting the **divinities**, and initiating mortals are all the **appropriation** of dwelling. Men dwells poetically. *See also* Building Dwelling Thinking; Poetically Man Dwells.

- E -

EARTH (*Erde*). **Human beings** dwell as **mortals** on the **earth**. Earth constitutes with **sky**, and mortals and **divinities** the simple oneness of the **fourfold**. Earth is the serving bearer that lets things **come to presence**. The work of art is the contest between the **world** that it opens and the sheltering of earth from which it rises.

ECSTASIS (*Ekstase*). In *Being and Time* the ecstases of **temporality** are the **phenomena** of **futurity**, **having been**, and **present**. Temporality temporalizes itself equiprimordially in the unity of the ecstases. Within this **equiprimordiality** the **modes** of temporalizing are different, because temporalizing can determine itself out of the different ecstases. Temporality, as the original out-of-itself in its towards, back to, and among, opens the ecstatic **expanse** that defines the **ontological structure** of **existence**. To every ecstasis belongs a whither to which we are carried away. This whither is the **horizonal schema**. The authentic mode of having been is **retrieval**, of the present the **moment**, and of futurity **anticipation**. The inauthentic mode of having been is **forgottenness**, of the present to **making present**, and of futurity **awaiting**.

EGO, THE. *see* I, THE

END OF PHILOSOPHY AND THE TASK OF THINKING, THE (*Das Ende der Philosophie und die Aufgabe des Denkens*). In this 1964 lecture Heidegger tries to answer two questions: 1. What does it mean that **philosophy** has entered its final stage in our time? and 2. What task is reserved for **thinking** at the end of philosophy?

The end of philosophy is not a mere stopping, but has to be understood as completion. Philosophy is **metaphysics** and metaphysics is **Platonism**. **Friedrich Nietzsche** achieved the most extreme **possibility** of philosophy in his reversal of Platonism. The completion of metaphysics is the triumph of the manipulable arrangement of a scientific-technological **world** and its social order.

The end of philosophy is the complete actualization of the metaphysical possibility of thinking. In the Greek **beginning** of thinking, however, a first nonmetaphysical possibility of thinking remained concealed. It is the task of nonmetaphysical or **commemorative thinking** to explore this first possibility and so prepare for another beginning of thinking.

In philosophy's beginning **Parmenides** speaks about the **clearing** of **Being** as such, although it would remain unthought in philosophy. '**Alètheia**', **unconcealment**, was equated with **truth** as the correspondence of knowledge with **entities** or truth as the certainty of knowledge. Unconcealment is, however, not the same as truth. We must think 'alètheia' as the clearing which first grants Being and thinking their **presence** to and for each other. The task of thinking is the surrender of metaphysics to the determination of the matter of thinking, that is, **appropriation**.

ENFRAMING (*Gestell*). The dominion of enframing is the **essence** of modern **technology** as the end of **metaphysics**. It is the ordering of every **entity** as **standing-reserve**. As standing-reserve every entity is controlled and stands ready for use. Even the **being** of **being-there** is reduced to standing-reserve and therefore needs to be put to good use. Enframing is the **mode** of **Being**'s revealing itself, in which it reveals itself by withdrawing. The **truth of Being** in the age of **nihilism** is the **forgetfulness of being**. Enframing reveals itself most clearly in the **will to power**. Because enframing is a **destiny** of Being, being-there cannot escape from it. All that remains for us to do is to prepare in **acquiescence** for the coming of the last **God**.

ENOWNING (*Ereignis*). see APPROPRIATION

ENTITY (*Seiendes*). Entity is the **ontological** term for every actual being. Everything is an entity.

ENVIRONMENT (*Umwelt*). In his 1919 lecture course, *The Idea of Philosophy and the Problem of Worldviews*, Heidegger describes the environmental **experience** of a chair in a meaningful context that gives us a **world**, or as Heidegger likes to say, it worlds (*es weltet*). We encounter every **entity** in our environment in a referential context as meaningful. In Winter Semester 1919/20 he juxtaposes the environment or world-around to the **with-world** and the **self-world**.

EQUIPMENT (*Zeug*). Heidegger describes the **entities** that **being-there** encounters in **concern** as equipment. Equipment is essentially something **in-order-to**. A knife is something in order to carve. To the **being** of equipment always belongs a totality of equipment, that is, its **involvement**, in which it can be what it is. This totality is constituted by various ways of the in-order-to like serviceability and usability. The **way of being** of equipment is **readiness-to-hand**.

EQUIPRIMORDIAL (*gleichursprünglich*). The **existentials** that constitute the **existence** of **being-there** are equiprimordial and cannot be deduced one from the other. They are all given at the same time with the existence of being-there and can only be interpreted together and through each other.

ERRANCY (*Irre*). In his lecture ***On the Essence of Truth*** Heidegger describes errancy as the essential nonessence to the primordial **essence** of **truth**. It is the condition of **possibility** of error. Truth is in its essence a process of **discovery** and **concealment**. The **forgetfulness of being** is not the fault of **being-there**, but is due to errancy. Because **Being** discloses itself as the **beingness** of **entities**, Being itself remains concealed. In this way being-there is being led astray by errancy. Errancy itself as leading astray can be experienced by being-there. This experience makes it possible for being-there to resist errancy. In **acquiescence** we can experience the **mystery** of Being: **appropriation**.

ESSENCE (*Wesen*). Essence is the quality whereby an **entity** is what it is. In scholastic **ontology** the essence of an entity is its nature or what it is, independent of its **existence** or that it is. In ***Being and Time*** Heidegger overthrows traditional ontology when he says that the essence of **being-there** lies in its existence. In his later work Heidegger puts emphasis on the verbal sense of essence as **coming to presence**. It is not a quality but an activity, a primal act, and a **way of being**.

ETERNAL RECURRENCE OF THE SAME, THE (*Die ewige Wiederkehr des Gleichen*). In the first section of this Summer Semester 1937 lecture course that was published in *Nietzsche I*, Heidegger sketches the four divisions he intends his course to have. The first is a preliminary presentation of the doctrine of the recurrence of the same in terms of its genesis, configuration, and domain. In the second division the **essence** of a metaphysical position is defined and such positions in prior **metaphysics** are discussed. The third division is an **interpretation** of **Friedrich Nietzsche**'s metaphysics of the **will** as the last possible one. In the fourth division the end of **philosophy** and the new **beginning** of **commemorative thinking** are discussed. As is often the case with Heidegger, only the first division receives full treatment. The conclusion of the course is a brief sally into the second division.

Heidegger interprets the doctrine of the eternal recurrence as the fundamental thought of Nietzsche's philosophy. Nietzsche stands in fundamental opposition to **Platonism** and **Christianity**. Nietzsche communicated the thought of the eternal recurrence reluctantly, because it is the hardest of all thoughts to bear. It is important to note the fundamental shift in Heidegger's interpretation. In his preceding lecture course, *The Will to Power as Art*, he understood the will to power as the **being** of **entities** and the eternal recurrence as the temporal **sense of being**. In this course he interprets the being of an entity in its essence as will to power and in its **existence** as eternal recurrence.

Heidegger's interpretation centers on the death of **God** and the humanization of the being of entities. Humanity, and not God, is the center of the eternal return of the becoming **world**. What returns eternally is neither God nor the Platonic idea but the will to power as constant **presence**.

The **guiding question** of philosophy, 'What is being?', is answered in metaphysics without developing it as the **basic question**: 'What makes the **unconcealment** of **Being** possible?' The question 'What is being?' is always answered by naming an entity as the **ground** of the **beingness** of entities. Nietzsche's philosophy is the last **possibility** of metaphysics, because he answers the guiding question by interlocking the answers of **Parmenides** and **Heraclitus** in his doctrine of the eternal recurrence and the will to power. He insists that Being is and becomes. In this sense his philosophy is inverted Platonism and the grandest and most profound gathering of all essential fundamental positions of philosophy.

ETERNAL RECURRENCE OF THE SAME AND THE WILL TO POWER, THE (*Die ewige Wiederkehr des Gleichen und die Wille zur Macht*). Heidegger projected this lecture to serve as a conclusion to his three lecture courses on **Friedrich Nietzsche**: *The Will to Power as Art*; *The Eternal Recurrence of the Same*; and *The Will to Power as Knowledge*. It consists of an introduction and six sections. Heidegger's overriding claim is that Nietzsche's **philosophy** is the consummation of **metaphysics**. The **guiding question** of metaphysics, 'What is **being?**', is answered by determining being as the permanence of the **presence** of **entities**. The doctrines of the **will to power** and the eternal recurrence converge in Nietzsche's philosophy as the final metaphysical position.

In the age of **nihilism**, **Being** refuses to reveal itself as itself and abandons **being-there**. The being of entities is reduced to manipulability and disposability. The meaninglessness of Being expresses itself in the measurelessness of self-overpowering power. And yet we can experience the withdrawal of Being. In the **clearing** Being reveals itself as self-**concealment**. This self-concealing revealing of Being is both dubious and worthy of question. When we accept guardianship over the clearing and refrain from the **will** to dominion, a new and other **beginning** in the **history of Being** becomes possible.

EUROPEAN NIHILISM (*Der europäische Nihilismus*). In this 1940 lecture course, published in *Nietzsche II*, Heidegger confronts **Friedrich Nietzsche**'s **interpretation** of **nihilism**. This course unfolds in three stages. Heidegger first offers an account of nihilism, the **will to power**, and valuation in Nietzsche's thought. Nietzsche understands nihilism as the collapse of all valuation. The revaluation of **values** must revert to the **eternal recurrence of the same**, because the will to power is essentially enhancement. Only the overman (*Übermensch*) is able to affirm the eternal recurrence. Nietzsche tries to overcome nihilism by the will to power's revaluation of all values. His **philosophy** is a **metaphysics** of the will to power. He answers the **guiding question** of metaphysics, 'What is **being?**', by grounding the being of **entities** in the will to power.

In the middle section Heidegger explains the convergence of the will to power and valuative thought. Value **thinking** is the **essence** and fulfillment of the metaphysics of **subjectivity**. Nietzsche's humanization of metaphysics and morals is the consummation of the tradition from Protagoras to **René Descartes**. For Descartes the **human being** is the '*subjectum*' as the **ground** of the **representation** of entities in terms of **truth** as certitude. This quest for certitude is determined by the goal of unconditional dominion over the earth. Nietzsche's metaphysics of the will to power is dependent on Descartes' fundamental metaphysical position. The being of entities remains for Nietzsche representedness. Modern **value-philosophy** conceals the collapse of the **essence** of **Being** and truth.

The third section postulates the end of metaphysics and calls for an inquiry into the **history of Being**. The forgotten condition of the **possibility** of the unfolding of nihilism as the history of Being is the **ontological difference**. The differentiation of Being and entities is the **experience** of Being as the **nothing** and abundance. In the age of nihilism we must try to experience history as the release of Being into machination. This release is the **destiny** of Being. Through the **experience** of the destiny of Being as **appropriation** a new **beginning** of thinking may become possible.

EVERYDAYNESS (*Alltäglichkeit*). Everydayness is the undifferentiated **mode** in which **being-there** first and foremost exists. Heidegger calls this undifferentiated character of being-there averageness (*Durchschnittlichkeit*). *See also* They, the.

EXISTENCE (*Existenz*). In scholastic **ontology** existence is the quality whereby an **entity** is. Heidegger gives existence a new meaning in his *Critical Comments on Karl Jaspers' 'Psychology of Worldviews'*. He suggests that existence can be regarded as the **formal indication** of the **sense of being** of the 'I am'. In his 1923 lecture course, *Ontology: The Hermeneutics of Facticity*, existence is the formal indication of **being-there**'s most unique **possibility**. After assuming a universalized sense of possibility in his Winter Semester 1925/26 course *Logic: The Question of Truth*, existence becomes the formal indication of the **way of being** of **being-there** as *existence*. Being-there stands out in its **being**, its **instance**, and has outstanding possibilities. It understands itself in terms of its existence: the possibility to be itself or not itself.

EXISTENTIAL (*Existenzial*). Heidegger introduced the term existential in *Being and Time* to distinguish between the existentials as the **formal indications** of the ontological characters of **being-there**, which are determined by its **existence**, and **categories** as the concepts that refer to the ontological characters of **entities** other than being-there. *See also* Fundamental ontology; Ontology.

EXISTENTIAL (*existenzial*). In *Being and Time* existential refers to the ontological categorizing of the **existentials** to distinguish them from the **ontic** and **existentiell** level of individual **life**.

EXISTENTIAL ANALYSIS (*existenziale Analytik*). **Being-there** is ontically distinguished from all other **entities** by the fact that in its being it has an **understanding of being**. In his introduction to *Being and Time* Heidegger defines the **way of being** of being-there as **existence**. As existence being-there has the **possibility** to be itself or not itself. The existential analysis is the taking apart of the '**ontological**' **structures** that constitute being-there. Heidegger calls the context of such structures **existentiality**. The existential analysis is a **phenomenology** of the fundamental ways of being, or existentials, of being-there. Because being-there's understanding of being is the condition of possibility of all **ontologies**, the existential analysis is **fundamental ontology**. In the existential analysis **time** is explicated as the **horizon** for an **interpretation** of the **sense of being** in terms of the **temporality** of being-there that understands being. The existential analysis is the first requirement of the **question of being**.

EXISTENTIALISM (*Existentialismus*). Although Heidegger developed in *Being and Time* a **fundamental ontology** by way of an **existential analysis** of **being-there**, his **philosophy** was misinterpreted for many decades as a philosophy of **existence**. Through this fruitful misunderstanding he became one of the founding fathers of existentialism. *Being and Time* is a work on **ontology** and not on human existence or anthropology.

The origin of existentialism is **Friedrich Wilhelm Joseph Schelling**'s distinction between a negative philosophy in which the necessary **categories** of the **essence** of reason are systematically developed, and a positive philosophy, in which the existence of **freedom** in a **world** determined by those categories, is explained. **Sören Kierkegaard**, who attended Schelling's lectures in Berlin in the early 1840s, would later use the distinction between essence and existence, or necessity and freedom, to overcome **Georg Wilhelm Friedrich Hegel**'s system. As Kierkegaard saw it, the relation between **God** and man determined human existence. In the 1920s Kierkegaard became the philosopher in vogue in German **theology** and philosophy. Since both **Karl Jaspers** and Heidegger were strongly influenced by the Danish writer and had made existence a central concept of their philosophy, the existentialist misunderstanding was born. It remains remarkable that Heidegger strenuously avoided the existentialist vocabulary in his early lecture courses and only started to use it while he was writing *Being and Time*.

One of Heidegger's oldest students, **Karl Löwith**, was the first to misinterpret his philosophy as a form of existentialist philosophy. We find the same misunderstanding in **Rudolf Bultmann**'s theological reading of Heidegger's *Being and Time*. In his famous essay *Existentialism is a Humanism*, **Jean-Paul Sartre** claimed wrongly that he and Heidegger belonged to the atheistic wing of existentialism.

EXISTENTIALITY (*Existenzialität*). Existentiality is the context of the **structures** that constitute **existence**.

EXISTENTIELL (*existenziell*). In *Being and Time* existentiell refers to the **ontic** side of **being-there**. The question of **existence** can only be straightened out through existing itself. The **understanding** of one self, which always leads along this way, is called existentiell. *See also* Existential.

EXPANSE (*Gegnet*). Expanse is another **word** for the **truth of Being**. It is that domain which in gathering **entities** together opens itself up in such a way as to establish and maintain the **open**. In the open, every entity can emerge and repose within itself as what it is. **Being** appropriates itself as expanse, which simultaneously is the expanding of the 'there' of **being-there**. The **acquiescence** of being-there is also its release into the expanse where it has to wait and attend to the **mystery** of Being. *See also* Conversation on a Country Path about Thinking.

EXPATRIATION (*Unheimlichkeit*). *see* WEIRDNESS

EXPERIENCE (*Erfahrung*). **Life** is essentially experience. It expresses itself in and lives out of meaningful **structures** that it can **understand**. **Phenomenology** as an understanding **science** (*verstehende Wissenschaft*) can lay bare these structures in a **retrieval** of the original experience. See also Factual life experience; Lived experience.

EXPLANATION (*Erklärung*). In his early lecture courses in **Freiburg** Heidegger often uses **Wilhelm Dilthey**'s influential distinction between the explanatory and the understanding **sciences**. Natural sciences are theoretical and explain events by universal laws of **nature**. The humanities, on the other hand, try to **understand** human **life** in its individual manifestations like the work of art and historical persons and events. Life in its **facticity**, or as Heidegger would later call it, **being-there**, cannot be explained, but only understood. *See also* Lived experience.

EXPRESSION (*Ausdruck*). **Life** is **lived experience** and expresses itself in meaningful **structures**. These expressions can only be understood in hermeneutic **phenomenology** by vital participation in the distress of the **self**. By going back again and again to the original **experience** phenomenology can **understand** these expressions without objectifying them. This constant striving for **retrieval** constitutes the strictness of phenomenology as a **science**.

- F -

FACT (*Faktum*). **Being-there**'s vague and average **understanding** of **Being** is a fact. With the term fact Heidegger indicates that being-there is a last and undeniable **givenness**. It can only be understood through itself. Whenever being-there is, it is as a fact and the factuality of such a fact is being-there's **facticity**.

FACTICITY (*Faktizität*). Facticity is the **formal indication** of **being-there** that is already charged with its hermeneutic **expression** in **structures** that we can **understand**. Facticity is understanding as the matter itself of **phenomenology**. We can understand everything in **life** except the fact that life itself is understandable.

FACTUAL LIFE EXPERIENCE (*faktische Lebenserfahrung*). Factual life experience is Heidegger's **formal indication** of the matter of hermeneutic **phenomenology**. It will later be replaced by **facticity** and in *Being and Time* by **being-there**. **Life** gives itself as **experience**. As **lived experience** life always expresses itself in **structures** it can **understand**. Life experience is factual, because it is the first and last **givenness** that can neither be denied nor explained.

FAITH (*Glaube*). In his famous 1927 lecture, *Phenomenology and Theology*, Heidegger distinguishes **theology** as the positive **science** of faith from **philosophy** as the science of **Being** itself. The 'positum' of theology is the factual **mode** of existing of a believing Christian, whose **existence** is determined by the cross. Faith expresses itself in the rebirth. Only in faith can we experience what it means to be a Christian. Because faith posits the existence of **God** as the **ground** of **being**, faith is the **existentiell** enemy of philosophy. Philosophy has to disclose the **sense of being** and can therefore not be guided by faith. *See also* Christianity.

FALLENNESS (*Verfallenheit*). Fallenness is an '**existential**' **mode** of **being-in-the-world**. In its **everydayness**, **being-there** does not exist in an authentic mode as itself, but in fallenness to the **world** and the '**they**'. As not **being** itself, being-there is absorbed by the world in its **concern** and **understands** itself in terms of the world as a natural **entity**. In its fallenness to the world, being-there is simultaneously absorbed by **curiosity** and the **idle talk** of the 'they'. Being-there in its **facticity** has the tendency to fall from **authenticity**. This falling has itself an existential **possibility** in a mode of its temporalizing.

FARNESS (*Ferne*). The correlation between farness and **nearness** allows Heidegger a wordplay of which he never tires in his later work. For **being-there**, **Being** is far, simply because it is not an **entity** and can never be conceptualized by being-there. Being conceals itself behind the entities, which it gives **presence** in the **clearing**. Being is near, because it is that by which entities that are near are. In this respect Being is the **origin** of all nearness and is thus nearer to being-there than any entity could ever be.

FATE (*Schicksal*). Fate is **being-there**'s authentic **historicality**. Its being free for **death** gives being-there its ultimate goal and throws it back into its finitude. Once being-there has grasped the finitude of its **existence**, it is brought into the simplicity of its fate. In authentic **resoluteness** being-there hands itself down to itself, free for death, in a **possibility** which it has inherited and yet has chosen, that is, its fate.

FEAR (*Furcht*). Fear is an inauthentic **disposedness** of **being-there** that is made possible by **anxiety**. Heidegger considers fear from three points of view: 1. That in the face of which we fear is the threatening. The threatening is always a specific **entity** within the **world**. As fearsome it draws close, but also carries with it the **possibility** that it may pass us by. 2. Fear is the **mood** in which we let something matter to us as fearsome. 3. What the fear is about is the entity that is afraid, i.e., being-there. Fear discloses being-there as endangered and abandoned to itself.

FOR-THE-SAKE-OF-WHICH, THE (*das Worumwillen*). The for-the-sake-of-which pertains to the **being** of **being-there**, for which in its being, that very being is the for-the-sake-of-which of its **existence**. The instrumental series of the '**in-order-to**' and '**for-which**' all find their termination in the 'for-the-sake-of-which' as the end of the environing **world**.

FOR-WHICH, THE (*das Wofür, das Wozu*). The for-which of usability of **equipment** is disclosed in **being-there**'s **circumspection**. That for-which a hammer is usable is hammering and not writing.

FORE-CONCEPTION (*Vorgriff*). The everyday **interpretation** of **circumspection** is grounded in fore-conception, **foresight** and **fore-having**. Fore-conception is something we have grasped in advance and with which we try to conceptualize that which we have in fore-having and foresight.

FORE-HAVING (*Vorhabe*). Everyday circumspective **interpretation** is grounded in **fore-conception**, fore-having and **foresight**. The fore-having is something we have in advance and which fixes that with regard to which what is understood, is to be interpreted.

FORESIGHT (*Vorsicht*). Everyday circumspective **interpretation** is grounded in **fore-conception**, **fore-having** and foresight. Foresight is something we see in advance and takes the first cut out of what has been taken in our fore-having and does so with a view to a definite way in which this can be interpreted.

FORERUNNING (*Vorlaufen*). *see* ANTICIPATE

FOREST TRAILS (*Holzwege*). Forest trails are the paths tracked through the forest that do not lead us to a **clearing**, but lose themselves among the trees for which we can no longer see the woods. They are dead ends. The forest trails belong to Heidegger's path of **thinking**. *Forest Trails* is also the title of one of his collections of essays.

FORGETFULNESS OF BEING (*Seinsvergessenheit*). The history of **metaphysics** is determined by the forgetfulness of being. While **Being** revealed itself in **unconcealment** as the **beingness** of **entities**, **meta-physics** forgot the **ontological difference**. Being became equated with the **presence**, permanence, and usability of entities. Because Being concealed itself, **philosophy** is not to be blamed for its forgetfulness of being, which must be understood as the **destiny** of Being. In the course of the history of philosophy the forgetfulness of being is enhanced. The end of this process is modern **technology**. The abandonment of

Being is the greatest danger. Yet the **experience** of this danger makes the **turning** of the forgetfulness of being to **appropriation** as the **clearing** of Being possible.

FORGOTTENNESS (*Vergessenheit*). In *Being and Time* forgottenness is the inauthentic way of **having been**. It is related to that thrown **being** which is one's own. In forgottenness **being-there** forgets its most unique thrown **can-be** and projects itself inauthentically towards **possibilities** that are drawn from the being of other **entities**. Only on the basis of forgottenness can anything be remembered by our concerned **making present** of entities. *See also* Forgetfulness of being.

FORMAL INDICATION (*formale Anzeige*). Formal indication is an essential part of Heidegger's phenomenological method. It is conducive to the direction of the **understanding** of **phenomenology**. It points the way and guides the deliberation. It makes it possible for us to view a **phenomenon**, but as *formal* indication it has nothing to say content-wise. Formal indication leads us to the matters themselves and guards us against assuming that the **relational sense** between the phenomena and us is theoretical. It makes it possible for us to be drawn into the **situation** out of which we can learn how a phenomenon must be approached.

Formal indication indicates the full immediacy of the individual human **situation** expressed in the indexical particularities I, here, and now and captured in the singular **experience** of **being-there**. By way of the **intentionality** of being-there it indicates the formal **structure** of **relations** that already traverse this immediacy: with others, amidst **entities** and so forth. Formal indication seeks to formalize the immediacy of **time** as the underlying background of intentionality in its full structural dynamics and thus catch it in the act of its individualizing contextualizing.

FORTUNE (*Schicksal*). *see* FATE

FOUNDING (*Begründung*). In his essay *On the Essence of Ground*, Heidegger describes founding as one of the three elements in the process of grounding. This process enables **being-there** to encounter **entities** by making them manifest in and as themselves.

FOUR SEMINARS (*Vier Seminare*). Of the four seminars, the first three (1966, 1968, 1969) took place in Le Thor, where Heidegger also visited his friend René Char, and the last (1973) in Zähringen. In the first seminar Heidegger discusses the poem of **Parmenides** and the fragments of **Heraclitus**. This seminar is to a large extent a finger-exercise for the Winter Semester 1966/67 seminar on Heraclitus which Heidegger conducted with Eugen Fink.

The second seminar is an **interpretation** of **Georg Wilhelm Friedrich Hegel**'s **philosophy** based on his famous early essay on the difference between the systems of Johann Gottlieb Fichte and **Friedrich Wilhelm Joseph Schelling**. This interpretation is a stepping-stone to an explication of the **essence** of philosophy and **metaphysics** and the danger of **ontological difference**. When we see this difference in the light of metaphysics, we tend to represent **Being** as an **entity**.

The third seminar circles around the difference between the Greek and the modern **experience** of the **being** of entities. The starting point is **Immanuel Kant**'s essay on the only possible fundament for a demonstration of the **existence** of **God**. Heidegger sums up also his entire path of **thinking** and searches for ways to overcome the **enframing**.

The seminar in Zähringen is a return to the *Logical Investigations* of **Edmund Husserl**. Heidegger explains how he overcame Husserl's dependence on consciousness. He also develops his concept of **phenomenology** as the making manifest of the invisible. The only question of Heidegger's path of thinking is the question of the **sense of being**: What is Being? *See also* Heraclitus Seminar.

FOURFOLD, THE (*das Geviert*). In Heidegger's later **philosophy**, **being-in-the-world** as the fundamental **ontological structure** of **Being-there** is replaced by the fourfold. The fourfold is the primal oneness of **earth** and **sky**, **divinities** and **mortals**. It is the **appropriation** of the **truth of Being** and so the **clearing** in which **things** can be. *See also* Building Dwelling Thinking; Origin of the Work of Art, The; Thing, The.

FREEDOM (*Freiheit*). Freedom is a central topic of Heidegger's path of thinking. In ***Being and Time*** Heidegger discloses **being-there** as the **possibility** of its being free for its most unique possibilities. The **way of being** of being-there is **can-be**. Being-there has constantly to actualize its possibilities. The essential freedom of being-there expresses itself most clearly in its capacity to give up its actualized possibilities and make a new start. Being-there can be itself in an impassioned freedom towards death, that is, a freedom which has been released from the illusions of the '**they**', and which is factual, certain of itself, and anxious.

In his 1930 essay *On the Essence of Truth*, Heidegger's concept of freedom begins to shift. In *Being and Time* freedom is being-there's most unique possibility to be itself or not itself. In the 1930 essay Heidegger can identify freedom and **truth**, because every **entity** has to be liberated from **concealment** and the resulting **unconcealment** (*alètheia*) is truth. Primarily true and therefore free is being-there. Freedom is the **openness** of being-there toward the **open** and that which is open. To render entities free is to let them be manifest as what they are. Freedom is the letting-be of entities. The condition of possibility of being-there's freedom is the fact that being-there is ecstatic. It lets itself in on the open and its openness where it can let entities be. The open is the **clearing** and thus the **truth of Being**. In the shift from the actualization of possibilities (activity) to the letting-be of entities (passivity), the **movement** of the **turning** in Heidegger's thought announces itself. After the turning, **Being** itself, and no longer being-there, is free in the most original sense, since Being lets being-there be free to heed or refuse its **claim**. The freedom of being-there reposes in the freedom of Being and is no longer something merely human.

FREIBURG-IM-BREISGAU. This city in Baden-Württemberg is the economic and cultural center of the Black Forest, where Heidegger lived most of his life. From 1906 to 1909 he was a pupil at the Berthold-Gymnasium and from 1909 to 1913 a student at the Albert-Ludwigs-University. On July 27, 1915, the university granted Heidegger the license to teach in philosophy. After World War I Heidegger became **Edmund Husserl**'s assistant. After his years in Marburg from 1923 to 1928, Heidegger returned to Freiburg as successor to Husserl's chair and remained there until his death in 1976.

FROM THE LAST MARBURG LECTURE COURSE (*Aus der letzten Marburger Vorlesung*). This essay first published in 1964 is an excerpt from Heidegger's Summer Semester 1928 lecture course *The Metaphysical Foundations of Logic*. In this text Heidegger summarizes his attempt to disclose the guiding thread on the basis of which **Gottfried Wilhelm Leibniz** determines the **being** of **entities**.

FUNDAMENTAL CONCEPTS OF METAPHYSICS: WORLD, FINITUDE, SOLITUDE. THE (*Die Grundbegriffe der Metaphysik. Welt - Endlichkeit - Einsamkeit*). In this Winter Semester 1929/30 lecture course Heidegger determines the **essence** of **philosophy** as **metaphysics**. Metaphysics is not an overstepping of the sensible **world** to another and higher world; it is a revolution in our everyday **thinking** and questioning. In metaphysics our own **being-there** should become a question for us, and in this sense metaphysics is a fundamental occurrence in our lives. Heidegger addresses the question concerning world, finitude, and individualization (*Vereinzelung*).

In the first part Heidegger shows how philosophy springs from a fundamental **mood**. The fundamental mood of his time is deep **boredom**, which expresses itself in the attempt to control and satisfy all **needs**. This defense against need makes it impossible for us to experience our need as a **whole**. As being-there we no longer experience our **being** as the task of having-to-be. The **mystery** of being-there, which gives being-there its greatness, remains hidden. Heidegger tries to evoke the mood of deep boredom in his students. After an extensive analysis of boredom, Heidegger addresses in the second part the fundamental question of metaphysics concerning world, finitude and individualization. As usual Heidegger will not have enough time to address all three questions. He only discusses the question of the world.

What is world? Heidegger distinguishes between the stone that has no world and is worldless, the animal that is poor in world, and being-there that shapes and constitutes world. He formally indicates world as the manifestation (*Offenbarkeit*) of **entities** as such as a whole and analyzes its structural constitution. In the exposition of the essence of **life** Heidegger shows how the manifestness of entities as such is the 'there' of the **openness** of the world. The manifestness of entities as such and the openness of the world are intertwined. Only because being-there exists in the midst of entities can it get close to the essence of life. In our nearness to life, the **phenomenon** of **nature** shows itself.

Heidegger shows next how being-there and nature belong together. The **nearness** of being-there and nature manifests itself in the intertwining of **thrownness** and **projection**. Nature can only be disclosed in the **clearing** of an **understanding** of world. In understanding, the openness of the world is opened up. The phenomenon of world is formally indicated in the fundamental character of the manifestness of entities as such and as a whole. The openness of world happens to entities; it concerns entities as such and as a whole. As a structural moment of manifestness the 'as' refers to the **structure** of the '**logos**'. This explains why metaphysics took the 'logos' as its starting point. In a **destruction** of **logic** Heidegger takes a **step back** into the **ground** of the structure of the 'logos' as **assertion**. This original dimension is the triple structure of the shaping of world as the fundamental appropriating event in being-there. This triple structure is as the holding sway of world at the same time the being of entities as a whole and as such the letting hold sway of being-there's projection of world.

FUNDAMENTAL ONTOLOGY (*Fundamentalontologie*).   For the early Heidegger, **philosophy** is **phenomenology** as the pretheoretical original **science** of original **experience**. This science tries to explicate the **primal something** out of which any **entity** is how it is. Phenomenology is therefore fundamental ontology from which regional ontologies receive their **ground** and **meaning**.

In *Being and Time* Heidegger relates fundamental ontology to an **existential analysis** of **being-there** as end to means. Its aim is to elaborate the question of the **sense of being** from the **understanding of being** that being-there itself is. In his existential analysis Heidegger shows that the being of being-there is **temporality** and that its understanding of being is made possible by the **Temporality** of **Being** itself.

The existential analysis is at the same time a **destruction** of the history of **ontology**, because being-there has always explicated its being through **categories** derived from the natural **world** in which it lives. The categories of traditional ontology are unsuited to lay bare the **structure** of being-there. Fundamental ontology thus becomes the analysis of Temporality and reflects the **ontological difference** between entities and Being itself. Since all ontologies spring from fundamental ontology, which is ontically founded in being-there, fundamental ontology must be supplemented with regional ontologies, or as Heidegger called it in 1928, a **metontology**.

Metontology is a metaphysical ontology of entities as a **whole** and consists of categories and **existentials**. Fundamental ontology, the destruction of the history of ontology, and the metontology constitute the full concept of metaphysics. In 1929 Heidegger abandons the project of fundamental ontology and tries to overcome metaphysics in a **step back** out of its onto-theo-logical structure.

FUTURE (*Zukunft*).   Future is the primary **phenomenon** of original and authentic **temporality**. It is the coming towards itself of **being-there** in its most unique **can-be**.

FUTURITY (*Zukünftigkeit*).   In *Being and Time* futurity is one of the three **ecstases** of **temporality**. The authentic **mode** of futurity is to **anticipate** and its inauthentic mode is to **await**. The unique **possibility** of the futurity of **being-there** is its **death** as the possibility of the impossibility of its **existence**. When being-there anticipates its death, it brings its most unique **can-be** before itself in **resoluteness**. The **horizonal schema** of futurity in which **being-there** comes to itself out of the **future** is the 'for-the-sake-of-which'.

- G -

GADAMER, HANS-GEORG (1900-). In 1922 **Paul Natorp** showed Gadamer his copy of Heidegger's *Phenomenological Interpretations with Respect to Aristotle: Indication of the Hermeneutic Situation*. Gadamer was very impressed by Heidegger's work and decided to move to **Freiburg** to study with him in 1923. Gadamer moved back to **Marburg** with Heidegger and became one of his most important students. He was deeply influenced by Heidegger's hermeneutical turn and his controversial reading of **Greek philosophy**. Gadamer and Heidegger became lifelong friends. After World War II Gadamer played an important part in Heidegger's rehabilitation.

GENERATION (*Generation*). Since **being-there** is always **being-with**, it belongs to a generation. Being-there's fateful **destiny** in and with its generation goes to make up the full authentic coming to pass (*Geschehen*) of being-there. The central event for Heidegger's generation was World War I and the ensuing chaotic times of the Weimar Republic.

GESTELL. *see* ENFRAMING

GETTING AROUND (*Umgang*). In *Being and Time* getting around is the **formal indication** of the different ways in which **being-there** gets around in the **world**. These dealings, interactions, and occupations are disclosed in **circumspection**. Heidegger first thematized the **structure** of getting around in Winter Semester 1921/22.

GIFT (*Schenkung*). In the work of art **truth** sets itself to work. This coming to stand of an **entity** in the light of its **being** is only possible through the emergence of **Being** itself, which bestows itself in pure bounty as gift. The **truth of Being** is a gift of Being and as such is given to **being-there**, which is at the same time given over to its **existence**. The metaphor of gift is also important in Heidegger's analysis of the **fourfold** and the **thing**. The gift of things is the **coming to presence** of the mirror-play of the four.

GIVENNESS (*Gegebenheit*). Givenness is an important moment in Heidegger's conception of **phenomenology** as the **science** of things as they show themselves. It reveals the **thing** itself as it is given in original **experience**. The **phenomenon** is never given as an irrational remainder, which can never be grasped. As immediately given it is determined by its givenness, or the way in which it shows itself. This givenness is a **structure** that can be analyzed and laid bare. For this reason phenomenology only describes its phenomena and does not construct them. Givenness is the condition of **possibility** of any given phenomenon. **Being-there** is given as **existence**. Its givenness is at once an unfinished task. The gift of existence is the having to be of a **can-be**.

GOD (*Gott*). The God of Heidegger's youth is the personal God of Christian revelation. Heidegger became a student of **theology** with the clear intention of becoming a Roman-Catholic priest. He defended the eternal **truth** of the church against the dangers of modernism. For reasons of health Heidegger ended his theology study. He became a scholastic phenomenologist. His marriage to Elfride Petri and the ensuing religious crisis led to his break with the system of Catholicism in 1919. As a 'free Christian' and personal assistant to **Edmund Husserl** he worked on a **phenomenology** of **religion** as a **destruction** of Christian **lived experience**. The religious **experience** was the paradigm of lived experience and thus essential to phenomenology itself.

In *Being and Time* God disappears into the background of Heidegger's thought, from which He would seldom emerge. Out of **awe** Heidegger prefers **keeping silent** about God in the domain of **thinking**. **Philosophy** is unable to disclose the godliness of the living God. The onto-theo-logical **structure** of **metaphysics** reduces God to an **ontological** principle. Heidegger interprets **Friedrich Nietzsche**'s diagnosis of the death of God as the end of the god of metaphysics. He tries to leave room for God within the **truth of Being**. In silence, **reflection** may be nearer to the living God than any metaphysical discussion of God's nature could ever be. The **holy** is the **openness** where **being-there** may encounter God or the **gods**. Heidegger's thought is so attractive to theologians precisely because he limits himself to a description of the **possibility** of the encounter with God. The coming of a last God, which Heidegger announces in his *Contributions to Philosophy*, is the beginning of a new era that can only begin with the mythology of the poets. The task of the thinker is to preserve being-there's **openness** for the coming of the last God. *See also* Christianity.

GODS (*Götter*). The gods make many appearances in Heidegger's writings and lectures on **Friedrich Nietzsche** and **Friedrich Hölderlin** in the 1930s. They are the Greek gods who have fled before the coming of Christ, but who may return. In his later work Heidegger replaces the gods with the **divinities** of the **fourfold**.

GRACE (*Huld*). The **address of Being** takes the form of a voiceless appeal that is disclosed through **being-there's attunement**. In the attunement of **awe, Being** reveals itself as grace. Only when Being is present for being-there as grace is it possible for **human beings** to **dwell** on **earth**. Grace is the **gift** of Being's **presence** in the **fourfold**.

GREEK PHILOSOPHY (*Griechische Philosophie*). With some exaggeration we could say that Heidegger's *Gesamtausgabe* is a series of notes in the margin of Greek **philosophy**. **Franz Brentano**'s dissertation, *On the Several Senses of Being in Aristotle*, kindled his interest in philosophy in 1907. Latent in Brentano's quotation from **Aristotle** on the title page, "an **entity** becomes manifest in many ways," was the question that would determine Heidegger's path of thinking: what is the **sense of being**? We can distinguish three periods in his confrontation with Greek philosophy.

From 1922 until the publication of *Being and Time* Heidegger worked on a book on Aristotle's philosophy that he never managed to finish. According to Heidegger, Aristotle was not only the first phenomenologist; he was also more advanced in **phenomenology** than **Edmund Husserl** and his circle. While studying and teaching Aristotle and Husserl's *Logical Investigations* together, Heidegger discovered that since the Greeks, philosophical knowing has been defined by **intuition**. Heidegger broke with this model for theoretical **truth** and gave primacy to practical and religious truth as it is experienced in factual **life**. Heidegger found an original **experience** of 'kairos' paralleling that of primitive **Christianity** in Aristotle's account of truth in *Nicomachean Ethics VI*. And yet in *Physics IV* Aristotle also understood **time** as a series of **nows**, which became the paradigm for all later theories of time. In 1922/23 Heidegger discovered that 'ousia' for the Greeks meant constant **presence**. Heidegger tried to understand being in terms of time in its fullest and most fulfilled sense. Through Aristotle he discovered the relationship between **Being** and time. Finally, Aristotle's conception of **logic** as a productive **science** was at the origin of Heidegger's conception of **fundamental ontology.**

After the publication of *Being and Time* Aristotle became less important to Heidegger. In his conception of the **history of Being**, Greek philosophy became the **beginning** of the age of **metaphysics.** As the last of the Greek philosophers Aristotle was the father of metaphysics. Although his attention would later turn first to **Plato** and then to pre-Socratic philosophy, he would return time and again to the thought of Aristotle.

Heidegger's reading of **Friedrich Nietzsche**'s diagnosis of the **nihilism** of Western culture and his interpretation of **Platonism** sparked his interest in Plato in the early 1930s. Plato was the pivotal figure who transformed the early Greek **thinking** of Being into metaphysics. He conceived being no longer as '**physis**' but as idea, '**eidos**', that is, the form in which entities show themselves. His new **understanding of being** led also to a transformation in the process of '**alètheia**'. The early Greek thinkers understood 'alètheia' as the **unconcealment** of Being. Plato transformed 'alètheia' into truth, that is, the correctness of the correspondence between idea and entity. For Plato philosophy was no longer a **saying** of Being; it had become the determination of the **beingness** of entities as idea and the **founding** of the **being** of entities in the idea of the good as highest entity.

After the turning, Heidegger began to develop his conception of the history of Being, which in turn led to his decade-long interpretation of pre-Socratic philosophy. **Heraclitus**, **Anaximander** and **Parmenides** are the original thinkers in the history of Being. They speak to us from the earliest beginning of philosophy. This beginning is not only the **origin** of the **forgetfulness of being**, but contains also the **possibility** of another beginning. In his interpretation Heidegger tries to understand the pre-metaphysical thought of the early Greek thinkers from a post-metaphysical standpoint.

Anaximander has thought the process by which entities are **coming to presence** in unconcealment. Every entity leaves concealment to while in unconcealment for some time, before it passes away into **concealment**. The process is ruled by '**dikè**' which arranges the pattern of entities in their being.

Heraclitus disclosed the being of entities as '**physis**', self-revealment that needs concealment in order to come to presence as **revealment**. The movement of concealment and revealment forms one identical process. In the **clearing** of the '**logos**', Being emits itself as **destiny** and withdraws itself into concealment. Heraclitus is the thinker who has named the **appropriation** of Being.

The saying of Parmenides that Being and apprehending are the same has become the **fate** of Western philosophy. Parmenides has named 'alètheia' as the unconcealment of Being. In the revealment of the being of entities, Being as such withdraws itself into concealment. In the poem of Parmenides the being of entities is disclosed as constant presence.

GRÖBER, CONRAD (1872-1948). Conrad Gröber was the rector of the Konradihaus in **Constance**, where Heidegger stayed as a pupil from 1903 to 1906. He became Heidegger's spiritual mentor and a fatherly friend. In 1907 he gave him a copy of **Franz Brentano**'s dissertation on **Aristotle**. Gröber later became archbishop of **Freiburg**. His friendship with Heidegger received a severe blow in 1919, when Heidegger turned his back on the system of Catholicism. In the de-Nazification trials after the war, a besieged Heidegger turned to his old friend for help. He intervened on Heidegger's behalf and wrote several letters to the French military authorities. Despite his efforts Heidegger would not be reinstated as a professor at the university until 1950.

GROUND (*Grund*). In *Being and Time* **temporality** is the ground of **care**. Heidegger first discusses the problem of the ground in depth in his famous essay *On the Essence of Ground*. Here he tries to gain access to the **sense of being** through a meditation on the sense of ground. The ground belongs to the realm of **transcendence** as fundamental **structure** of being-there. The **origin** of the ground is **freedom**, because freedom is freedom to lay the ground or found. This **founding** is orchestrated in terms of **projection** of **world**, taking possession, and **ontological** founding of **entities**. Freedom is the triplex strewing of ground, whose ultimate **meaning** is **time**. Freedom is finally understood as the **abyss** of being-there.

After the **turning**, Heidegger distinguishes between the **guiding question** and the **basic question** of **philosophy**. The former is concerned with the **beingness** of entities; the latter asks about **Being** in respect to its ground. The ground of Being is **truth** as **unconcealment**.

In his 1955/56 lecture course *The Principle of Reason* Heidegger is concerned with the **question of being**. He discusses the principle of reason, i.e., nothing is without reason or a sufficient ground, as **Gottfried Wilhelm Leibniz** first formulated it. He shows that Leibniz's formulation of this principle was a response to the **address of**

Being and thus the result of the history of **metaphysics**. The **history of Being** mirrors itself in the history of the principle of reason.

GUIDING QUESTION (*Leitfrage*). In the 1930s Heidegger begins to distinguish between the guiding question and the **basic question** of **thinking**. The guiding question is the central question of **metaphysics**: what is the **being** of **entities**? The basic question asks back to the **ground** of metaphysics: what is **Being**?

GUILT (*Schuld*). The **call of conscience** imposes on **being-there** in its **everydayness** the demand to live up to its **authenticity** and wholeness. In this call being-there is told about its own guilt, which is not specific and determinate, but general and unconditional. The mere **existence** of being-there makes it guilty, because it is not itself the **ground** of its own **being**. Being-there never has power over its most unique being from the ground up. This inability belongs to being-there's **thrownness**, which is shot through with **nullity**. In **anxiety** this nullity by which being-there is determined in its ground is unveiled as thrownness into **death**. This thrownness is a source of guilt for being-there insofar as it fails to respond to the task of achieving authenticity by shaping its existence within a thrownness it can never master and control.

- H -

HANDINESS (*Zuhandenheit*). *see* READINESS-TO-HAND

HAVING BEEN (*Gewesenheit*). In ***Being and Time*** having been is one of the three **ecstases** of original **temporality**. The authentic coming-towards-itself of anticipatory **resoluteness** is at the same time a coming back to one's most unique **self**, which has been thrown into its individualization. In this **retrieval** or authentic way of having been, **being-there** brings its **thrownness** before itself. Having been makes it possible for being-there to take over resolutely that **entity** which it already is. We should not confuse having been with the **past**, because as long as being-there exists, it is never past, but it always is as already having been in the sense of 'I am as having been'. The inauthentic way of having been is **forgottenness**. Being-there can forget itself in its most unique thrown **can-be**.

HEARING (*hören*). Hearing is an '**existential**' **possibility** of **speech** itself. It is constitutive for **discourse**. Hearing is **being-there**'s existential way of being open as **being-with** for others. It constitutes the authentic way in which being-there is open for its most unique **can-be**. Being-there can only hear because it understands. **Understanding** is the **ground** of **language**. Being-there is in its **being** understanding.

HEGEL, GEORG WILHELM FRIEDRICH (1770-1831). In his history of **metaphysics** Heidegger considers the **philosophy** of Hegel to be the completion of **Platonism**. After Hegel only **Friedrich Nietzsche**'s reversal of Platonism remained as an authentic **possibility** of philosophy. Because Hegel is a pivotal figure in the history of metaphysics, Heidegger interprets his writings time and again. Despite his importance for Heidegger, Hegel had very little influence on the development of his thought. For Heidegger, Hegel was both the villain and the hero of the history of philosophy. *See also* Hegel and the Greeks; Hegel's Concept of Experience; Hegel's Phenomenology of Spirit; Onto-theo-logical Constitution of Metaphysics, The.

HEGEL AND THE GREEKS (*Hegel und die Griechen*). Heidegger gave this lecture on July 26, 1958, at the Heidelberg Academy of Sciences. The title names the whole of the history of **philosophy** from its Greek **beginning** to its Hegelian culmination. Heidegger's lecture is a meditation on the end of philosophy and the matter of **thinking**.

    Georg Wilhelm Friedrich Hegel gave the first philosophical **interpretation** of the whole history of philosophy. According to Hegel the history of philosophy is the necessary progress of **spirit** towards **truth** as absolute knowing, in which the beginning is as important as the culmination. The three dialectical steps of this process determine also the history of philosophy. The first step, or thesis, is the immediate and undetermined consciousness of **objectivity**, which abstracts from the object's relation to the subject. The unfolding of this beginning of philosophy is the history of **Greek philosophy**. The next step, or antithesis, is the reflection on the relation between subject and object in which we become conscious of the fact that the object is a **representation** of the subject. The unfolding of this new beginning is the history of modern philosophy from **René Descartes** to Johann Gottlieb Fichte. The third step, or synthesis, is the becoming conscious of the fact that the mediation of objectivity through the reflection of the subject is itself the inner movement of spirit. This movement determines the method of philosophy. Hegel's philosophy is the synthesis of modern subjective philosophy of reflection (*Reflexionsphilosophie*) and the objective **ontology** of Greek philosophy.

Heidegger discusses next Hegel's interpretation of the four ground **words** of Greek philosophy: 1. 'hèn' or the one of **Parmenides**; 2. '**logos**' or reason of **Heraclitus**; 3. 'idéa' or concept of **Plato**; and 4. 'energeia' or actuality of **Aristotle**. Because Greek philosophy is not grounded in **subjectivity**, it represents philosophy at the level of the 'not yet'. The goal of philosophy is truth, that is, the absolute self-certainty of spirit as the knowing subject. In Greek philosophy, spirit does not know itself as subject. The Greek concept of truth, '**alètheia**', cannot therefore determine truth as certainty. Heidegger shows that 'alètheia' as **revealment** does not have its place in the absolute subject; revealment is the place where a representing subject can be. According to Heidegger **metaphysics** begins with the thinking of **Being** as **presence**, '**ousia**'. The holding sway of 'alètheia' is the condition of **possibility** of presence. 'Alètheia' is earlier than philosophy and is as such the 'not yet' of that which has not yet been thought and remains to be thought as the matter of thinking. *See also* End of Philosophy and the Task of Thinking, The.

HEGEL'S CONCEPT OF EXPERIENCE (*Hegels Begriff der Erfahrung*). This 1950 essay is based on Heidegger's Winter Semester 1942/43 seminar on **Georg Wilhelm Friedrich Hegel** and **Aristotle**. It is both a detailed **interpretation** of the introduction to Hegel's *Phenomenology of Spirit* and a critique of Hegel's **philosophy**.

The starting point of Heidegger's interpretation is **René Descartes'** discovery of **subjectivity** and its absolute self-certainty. If Descartes sighted new land, Hegel takes full possession of it. He elevates philosophy to the level of absolute knowing. Absolute knowing is released from its dependence on objects. This process consists of three steps: 1. Absolvence, that is, the tendency of knowing to release itself from dependence on objects; 2. Absolving, that is, the striving to make this release complete; and 3. Absolution, that is, the actual **freedom** from objects which is achieved in the process of knowing. Knowing is presentation as a form of **presence** or the self-consciousness of the knowing subject. Self-consciousness constitutes as self-manifestation the **being** of the subject, which Heidegger defines as **subjectity**.

The heart of Heidegger's interpretation is his analysis of Hegel's concept of **experience**. The process of absolvence, which constitutes absolute knowing as self-consciousness, is governed by three principles: 1. Consciousness is for itself its own concept. 2. Consciousness supplies of itself its own norm. 3. Consciousness examines itself. Experience is the process by which absolute consciousness comes to presence as itself. Consciousness or **thinking** determines the being of **entities**.

In his implicit critique Heidegger shows the limits of Hegel's philosophy. Because Hegel expands the absolute certainty of consciousness into **Being** itself, the subjectity of modern philosophy culminates in his absolute idealism. Hegel could not disclose **truth**, 'alètheia', as the process by which entities emerge into **unconcealment**. In the history of philosophy the **truth of Being** has remained unthought.

HEGEL'S PHENOMENOLOGY OF SPIRIT (*Hegels Phänomenologie des Geistes*). This 1930/31 lecture course is Heidegger's most comprehensive **interpretation** of **Georg Wilhelm Friedrich Hegel**. Hegel came to be of particular interest to Heidegger in the late twenties, when he replaced the **formal indication** of **being-there, existence**, with **transcendence**. Transcendence is for Hegel the crossing of finitude and infinity and the dialectical liberation of absolute knowing from its dependence on the **objectivity** of entities. Heidegger understands transcendence as the transcending of **entities** by finite being-there. These two conceptions of transcendence form an antithesis.

Heidegger's course is a running commentary on sections B, *Consciousness*, and C, *Self-consciousness* of Hegel's *Phenomenology of Spirit*. His **understanding** of the **essence** of **philosophy** as onto-(ego)-theo-logy is the starting point of his interpretation of Hegel's thought. Philosophy understands **Being** from '**logos**'. The 'logos' is grounded in **God** as the highest entity. In modern philosophy since **René Descartes**, 'logos' is understood as knowing, which is grounded in the self-certainty of the ego or subject.

Heidegger sees in the *Phenomenology* an attempt to overcome and further develop **Immanuel Kant**'s revolutionary philosophy of reflection (*Reflexionsphilosophie*). The central part of the *Phenomenology* is therefore the chapter on *Force and the Understanding: Appearance and the Supersensible World*, in which Hegel discusses the limits of Kant's philosophical position and lays the foundation for the absolute position of his own idealism. This chapter is the transition of the finitude of consciousness to the infinity of the **spirit**. Heidegger pays close attention to Hegel's attempt to not disclose self-consciousness from knowing, but to disclose it in its **sense of being**.

In his discussion of the chapter on self-consciousness, Heidegger focuses his attention not on the objectivity of the object, but on the standing of the **self**, the standing on itself of **being** itself. This standing on itself of self-consciousness is the **reality** of spirit. At the end of the course Heidegger interprets the *Phenomenology* as the **fundamental ontology** of absolute **ontology**. The **question of being** is understood from the 'logos', which is disclosed as 'idein' or representative **thinking**. Philosophy is in essence idealism.

HEIDEGGER, FRIEDRICH (1851-1924). Heidegger's father was sexton of Saint Martin's church in **Meßkirch** and a cooper. Like his wife he was a devout Roman Catholic. He worked hard to provide for his family and to make the family home a happy place. He was introverted and strict. Like his son he knew how to keep silent for days.

HEIDEGGER, FRITZ (1894-1980). Heidegger's brother was a real character with a great sense of humor. He worked his whole life at the local bank of **Meßkirch**. Although he and his brother were in many ways exact opposites, they were very close. He was very popular with all of Heidegger's visitors in Meßkirch. Because he stuttered when he became serious, he pronounced *Dasein* always as *da-da-sein*. He followed his brother's philosophical career with great interest and pride. He not only typed out most of Heidegger's manuscripts and lecture courses; he also understood his brother's work better than most professional philosophers did. His whole life Heidegger would remain grateful to "his only brother".

HEIDEGGER, HERMANN (1920-). Heidegger's sons fought at the Western and Eastern Fronts during World War II. After the end of the war they spent several years in prisoner-of-war camps in the former Soviet Union. Hermann obtained a doctorate in history and was an elementary teacher for three years. Thereafter he became again a professional officer in the German army. Heidegger appointed him executor of his literary estate. Hermann attended several of his father's courses, seminars, and lectures and was closely involved in the working out of the conception of the *Gesamtausgabe*. Since his father's death in 1976 he has been the staunchest defender of his father and his philosophical legacy.

HEIDEGGER, JÖRG (1919-). After serving in the army during World War II and spending several years in a Soviet prisoner-of-war camp, Heidegger's oldest son became a university-trained engineer and then a teacher in the practical arts. Being of a more practical nature, he was much less interested in his father's work than his younger brother Hermann. Heidegger often mailed photographic cards to his friends that were made by Jörg.

HEIDEGGER, MARIE (1892-1956). She was Heidegger's only sister. Her husband was a chimneysweeper. There is very little known about Marie. In most writings on Heidegger's life she is not mentioned at all.

HEIDEGGER-KEMPF, JOHANNA (1858-1927). Heidegger's mother was born and raised on a farm in Göggingen, where Heidegger as a boy would spend most of his holidays in the company of his nephew Gustav Kempf. She was a good-humored woman and proud of her farmer's background. As **Fritz Heidegger** remembered later, she used to say that life was so pleasantly organized that there was always something to look forward to. Heidegger was his mother's darling and often spoiled. She was a strong supporter of his decision to strive for the priesthood. His decision to abandon his study of **theology** and his later break with Roman Catholicism came as a great shock and bitter disappointment to her. When Heidegger became a professor, she seems to have accepted her son's existential decisions. Heidegger presented his mother with a copy of *Being and Time* on her deathbed. As he wrote to **Karl Jaspers**, it was almost an apology.

HEIDEGGER-PETRI, ELFRIDE (1893-1992). Elfride Petri was the daughter of a Saxon officer. She met Heidegger in the fall of 1915 at the University of **Freiburg** where she studied political economy. They were married on March 21, 1917, in a Catholic ceremony and a week later in a Protestant ceremony in the presence of her parents. She belonged to the Protestant church and did not convert to Roman Catholicism. Although she is often depicted as the evil genius of Heidegger's life, she supported him through thick and thin. They lived through the financial difficulties of their early marriage, the tensions caused by Heidegger's love affair with **Hannah Arendt**, and the troubles of the Nazi period and the de-Nazification process after World War II. It is a fitting tribute that Heidegger dedicated the collected edition of his works to his wife.

HERACLITUS (611-547 BC). Heraclitus, **Anaximander** and **Parmenides** are the original thinkers in Heidegger's **history of Being**. They speak to us from the earliest **beginning** of **philosophy**. This beginning is not only the **origin** of the **forgetfulness of being**, but also contains the **possibility** of another beginning. In his **interpretation** Heidegger tries to understand the pre-metaphysical thought of the early Greek thinkers from a post-metaphysical standpoint. Heraclitus disclosed the **being** of **entities** as '**physis**', self-**revealment** that needs **concealment** in order to **come to presence** as revealment. The **movements** of concealment and revealment form one identical process. In the **clearing** of the '**logos**' Being emits itself as **destiny** and withdraws itself into concealment. Heraclitus is the thinker who named the **appropriation** of Being. *See also* Alètheia (Heraclitus, Fragment B 16); Heraclitus Seminar; Logos (Heraclitus, Fragment B 50).

HERACLITUS SEMINAR (*Heraklit Seminar*).   This Winter Semester 1966/67 seminar is Heidegger's last teaching engagement at the University of **Freiburg**. Eugen Fink, **Edmund Husserl**'s last assistant, conducted the seminar. Heidegger commented on Fink's **interpretation**. This seminar offers a wonderful impression of Heidegger's teaching skills. The main thrust of his interventions is the ongoing attempt to understand **Heraclitus** as a pre-metaphysical thinker. This attempt is grounded in our post-metaphysical **hermeneutic situation**. The interpretation of Heraclitus should thus at the same time be an **understanding** of our **being-there**.

HERMENEUTIC CIRCLE (*hermeneutischer Zirkel*).   In *Being and Time* Heidegger discusses the problem of the hermeneutic circle. In order to work out the **question of being** adequately, he must make the **ontological structure** of **being-there** transparent. Heidegger must first define an **entity** in its **being** before he can disclose the **sense of being**. The circularity of this undertaking belongs to the **essence** of **hermeneutics** and is a positive **possibility** of knowledge. Only through an implicit **understanding of being** can we come to an explicit **interpretation** of the sense of being. Every new interpretation leads to a new **understanding**, which in turn makes possible a new interpretation and so on.

HERMENEUTIC SITUATION (*hermeneutische Situation*).   The hermeneutic situation determines the **situation** of our **understanding**. Every **interpretation** is made possible by the **structure** of our **fore-having**, **foresight** and **fore-conception** of the **phenomenon**, which determines the **possibility** of our understanding. This situation can be seized originally or simply assumed and provides us with the way in which past **being-there** is to be apprehended in advance, the regard in which being-there thus apprehended is to be interrogated, and the conceptuality which stands ready for this appropriative understanding. The original seizure of our hermeneutic situation is at the same time a **destruction** of the **tradition** in which we stand and a critique of our time. *See also* Hermeneutics.

HERMENEUTICS (*Hermeneutik*). As a student Heidegger carefully studied the hermeneutics of **Wilhelm Dilthey** and Friedrich Schleiermacher. In his lecture courses in the 1920s he incorporated their teachings in his conception of hermeneutic **phenomenology**. He enlarged the scope of **hermeneutics** and made it fundamental for his phenomenological method. He no longer opposed the scientific methods of **understanding** and **explanation**, but made understanding an **existential** of **being-there** itself. Being-there is **disclosedness**. **Disposedness**, projective understanding, and **discourse** determine this fundamental **openness** of being-there. Being-there has always already understood the **world** into which it is thrown through the **projections** of its **possibilities**. These projections are interpreted in discourse. Interpretation makes the projections of being-there explicit. *See also* Hermeneutic circle.

HERO (*Held*). In ***Being and Time*** Heidegger claims that every **generation** chooses its heroes. The hero is someone who embodies a way of **existence**. Because the hero's **projection** of **being-there** is determining for a generation's conception of existence, the hero gives each generation its distinctive unity. The existence of a hero can be either authentic or inauthentic. Heidegger makes no ethical demands upon the hero.

HISTORICALITY (*Geschichtlichkeit*). Heidegger follows **Wilhelm Dilthey** in making historicality central to his hermeneutic **phenomenology** of **facticity** and later **being-there**. The immanent historicality of our **existence** is the **experience** of **factual life experience** that spontaneously gives us an **understanding** of our **being**. Being-there is **disclosedness**. With the **possibility** of **death** our understanding of the history that we are assumes a future term. Historicality receives its fundamental sense from more comprehensive, kairological **temporality** singling out the historical individual and its **generation**. **Anticipating** one's death is at once anticipating one's **fate** and the fate of one's generation. The **having been** that still is comes to meet us from the **future** in an anticipating **retrieval** of **possibilities** transmitted from an owned heritage. Retrieval is the authentic understanding of our historicality that delivers us over to the unique and decisive **moment** of our **existence**. Retrieval makes possible both the **destruction** of our **tradition** and an understanding of our **hermeneutic situation**.

HISTORICISM (*Historismus*). Historicism is a **worldview** that was strongly opposed by **Edmund Husserl**. It considers all knowledge, culture and **values** to be historical products and as such relative to a particular **time** and place. Historicism denies that there are universal values and truths. Husserl's phenomenological method was also an attempt to overcome historicism and naturalism through a return to the matters themselves. Because **phenomenology** describes only what shows up as it presents itself in our **experience**, its findings are apodictic and universally valid. As a student Heidegger made use of phenomenology to criticize historicism. Although he would later transform Husserl's phenomenology into a hermeneutic phenomenology and emphasize the significance of finitude, worldliness, and **historicality** for our **hermeneutic situation**, his concept of **time** and conception of the **history of Being** kept him from adhering to historicism.

HISTORIOLOGY (*Historie*). Heidegger introduces the concept of historiology in its distinction from **historicality** in his unpublished review of the correspondence between **Wilhelm Dilthey** and Graf York von Wartenburg in 1924. Because **being-there** is determined by its historicality, it has the specific **possibility** to explicitly **uncover** the **past** for its **present**, that is, to study the past in order to gain information and write interesting books about it.

HISTORY OF BEING (*Seinsgeschichte*). Heidegger worked out his conception of the history of Being after the **turning**. It is the **experience** of the transformations of the **relations** between **human beings** and **Being**. This originally hidden process determines history. Being emits the **truth of Being**. With the Greek experience of '**alètheia**' as the **unconcealment** of Being, the era of **philosophy** begins. The original thinkers, **Anaximander**, **Heraclitus** and **Parmenides**, named the unconcealment of Being but could not think 'alètheia' as the **clearing** of Being in its **ontological difference** to the **being** of **entities**. This was not a failure on their part. It was the **destiny** of Being itself.

The history of **metaphysics** begins with **Plato** and **Aristotle**. 'Alètheia' becomes **truth** as correctness and Being becomes the **beingness** of entities, which is grounded in **God** as the highest entity.

Metaphysics has an onto-theo-logical **structure** and is determined by the **forgetfulness of being**. The history of metaphysics finds its completion in the absolute idealism of **Georg Wilhelm Friedrich Hegel** and its end in **Friedrich Nietzsche**'s reversal of **Platonism**. The present age of **nihilism** is determined by the **will to will** and **technology**. Being emits itself as **enframing** into the clearing and withdraws itself as such into **concealment**. Heidegger tries to overcome metaphysics in an attempt to think the **essence** of metaphysics and in a meditative reflection on the hidden **possibility** of the other **beginning**. He finds traces of this other beginning in early Greek **thinking**, mythology, and **poetry**. The other beginning is also announced in the poetry of **Friedrich Hölderlin** who named the **gods** that have fled. In his *Contributions to Philosophy* Heidegger prepares for the coming of the last God. He will make a turning in the **appropriation** of Being possible and inaugurate a new era in the history of Being.

HISTORY OF THE CONCEPT OF TIME. PROLEGOMENA (*Prolegomena zur Geschichte des Zeitbegriffs*). This Summer Semester 1925 lecture course on the history of the concept of **time** with the subtitle *Prolegomena to a **Phenomenology of History and Nature*** is the penultimate draft of ***Being and Time***. As Heidegger outlines in § 3, it was supposed to have three parts: the first deriving the **concept of time**, the second disclosing the history of the concept of time, and the third elaborating the **horizon** for the **question of being** in general and the **being** of history and nature in particular. In the actual course Heidegger completed only an extended introduction and the first of the three parts.

Heidegger begins his course with a characterization of the **situation** of **philosophy** and **science** in the second half of the 19th century. The decisive event of that time was the breakthrough of **phenomenology** as philosophical research. He discusses and defends against several misunderstandings **Edmund Husserl**'s three essential discoveries: **intentionality**, the **apriori** and **categorial intuition**. He then advances his own critique as to where phenomenology has not done justice to its own call back to the matters themselves and raises the question of their enabling dimension. Heidegger shows how the thematic of **being-there** and **Being** emerges from the phenomenology of Husserl and **Max Scheler**. He discloses its unseen presuppositions, that is, the neglect of the question of the being of intentionality and the neglect of the question of being itself. The course is thus an important step in Heidegger's hermeneutical transformation of phenomenology.

In the main part of the course Heidegger investigates the condition of **possibility** of phenomenology's three essential discoveries. Here we find many themes, like the famous fable of **care**, that he will elaborate upon in *Being and Time*. Intentionality is secondary to being-there's concerned **being-in-the-world**, where it discovers things in their **presence-at-hand** and **readiness-to-hand**. **Understanding** finds its conceptual home and receives its first systematic treatment. It is the primary **ontological** relationship of being-there to the **world** and to itself. **Being-with**, care, **solicitude** and the **with-world** are analyzed and the concept of **involvement** is introduced for the first time.

The most important aspect of the course is Heidegger's **formal indication, to-be**, of the **essence** of being-there. It is remarkable that the **existential** vocabulary is still totally absent from the course. Being-there is the **entity** that I myself have to be and can be in each instance. Being-there qua **time** temporalizes its being.

HÖLDERLIN, FRIEDRICH (1770-1843). Heidegger read Hölderlin's poems when they were first published in an edition by von Hellingrath in 1914. The late hymns especially hit him like an earthquake. He became interested philosophically in Hölderlin's **poetry** when he worked out his conception of the **history of Being** in the thirties. Heidegger's **interpretation** is a dialogue between the thinker who has the task to proclaim **Being** and the poet who has the mission to name the **holy**. Hölderlin felt himself to be a messenger between the **gods** and the **people**. Hölderlin is the poet of the poet because he puts into **words** for the first time the **essence** of poetry. He is also the poet of the **future**. Not only did he name the gods that have fled, but he also grounded the **possibility** of a new **beginning** in the history of Being. The naming of the holy makes a **turning** in the **appropriation** of Being possible and thus makes room for the coming of the last **God** by calling to him. Hölderlin stands on the razor's edge. His poetry is the moment when the old gods have fled and the new God has not yet been revealed. Because the essence of **language** is poetry, Hölderlin was also important for Heidegger's **philosophy** of language. *See also* Hölderlin and the Essence of Poetry; Hölderlin's hymn 'The Ister'; Origin of the Work of Art, The; Poetically Man Dwells; What Are Poets For?

HÖLDERLIN AND THE ESSENCE OF POETRY (*Hölderlin und das Wesen der Dichtung*). In this beautiful essay written in 1936, Heidegger gives an **interpretation** of five pointers taken from **Friedrich**

Hölderlin's writings in order to disclose the **essence** of **poetry**. Heidegger chooses Hölderlin for his interpretation, because he is the poet of the poet. Poetry is the most innocent of occupations. The domain of this occupation is **language**, hence we can only grasp the essence of poetry when we comprehend the essence of language. Language has the task of making **entities** manifest in their **being** and preserving them in **unconcealment**. It is the most dangerous thing of **being-there**'s possessions because it makes our **existence** in the **clearing** possible. Only where there is language is there **world**; only where world predominates is there history. Language has at its disposal and grants the supreme **possibility** of human existence.

The being of being-there is founded in language and the essence of language is conversation. We are a single conversation and that means we can listen to one another. The unity of the one conversation is grounded in the essential **word**, which is related to the one and the same. This unity can only become manifest in the light of something permanent and enduring, that is, **time**. Since language became actual as conversation, the **gods** have acquired names and a world has appeared. The poet names the gods and all **things** and thus makes possible the appearance of a world. Poetry is the institution (*Stiftung*) of being by means of the word.

The institution of being is both the pure **gift** of **Being** and a process of grounding by being-there. In this process of letting things be by naming them in their being, the poet illuminates the entire clearing wherein the gift of Being is bestowed. The poet has been cast out into the **between**, between the gods and the **people**. In this between is decided who we are and where we settle and inhabit our existence.

Hölderlin is the poet in the time of **need** because our time finds itself in the no-longer of the gods who have fled and the not-yet of the coming **God**.

HÖLDERLIN'S HYMN 'THE ISTER' (*Hölderlins Hymne 'Der Ister'*). This Summer Semester 1942 lecture course is the last one Heidegger devoted to **Friedrich Hölderlin**. It is an **interpretation** of the hymn *The Ister* (The Danube) and consists of three parts. In the first part Heidegger exposes the **essence** of the stream. Hölderlin determines the essence of the stream by the tension between being-at-home and wandering. The poet cares for the homecoming of the **people**. To the essence of homecoming belongs the wandering in foreign parts.

The second part is an interpretation of wandering in a double dialogue between Hölderlin and Sophocles, on the one hand, and Heidegger and the Greeks, on the other. As Sophocles showed in his tragedy *Antigone*, **human being** is the most homeless of all **entities**. The hearth is the place where human beings are at home. According to Heidegger we must understand the hearth to be **Being** itself.

The third part is a further exposition of being homeless and home-coming in which Heidegger shows that what Hölderlin has named in the stream is the essence of the demigods. The **spirit** of the stream is the poetic spirit.

HOLY, THE (*das Heilige*).   It is the task of the poet to name **Being** itself as the holy. Being is the holy, because it is both wholesome (*heil*) and unapproachable. The holy is **awe**-some and unsettling insofar as it dislodges by its **coming to presence** all **experience** from the ordinary patterns of everyday **life**. The holy is also the eternal heart of **entities**, since Being is the innermost **origin** of their **presence** and original **time**. In this respect the **essence** of **nature** is holy. The holy is the condition of **possibility** of the divine. Being is that by which the **gods** are and that by which they are holy. The holy is the **openness** of the **fourfold** into which Being calls forth the **mortals** and the **divinities**.

HOMELAND (*Heimat*).   The homeland is the place where a **people** can grow roots and **dwell** authentically. It makes the **autochthony** of a people's **being-there** possible and is closely related to its **language**.

HOMESICKNESS (*Heimweh*).   Homesickness is a fundamental **mood** that leads to **philosophy**. If it is the fundamental mood of the philosopher, then only those who are nowhere at home can become philosophers. But what does being at home everywhere mean? It means being every time and above all in the **whole** that is the **world**. Philosophers are not yet in the world but under way towards the world. In this not-yet and the unrest of being under way, the finitude of our **existence** shows itself. Finitude is the fundamental **way of being** of **being-there**. As finite **entities** we have to take care of our finitude. Finitude is only in the true individualization in which **human beings** concentrate themselves on their being-there. In this solitude we are near the **essence** of all **things**, which is the world. In this **nearness** philosophy begins. *See also* Fundamental Concepts Of Metaphysics: World, Finitude, Solitude, The.

HORIZON (*Horizont*).   In **Edmund Husserl**'s **phenomenology** the horizon is the background of relations from which the object of inten-

tional **lived experience** is given. A horizon is a meaningful prefiguration (*Vorzeichnung*). In Heidegger's early lecture courses horizon
makes several appearances as the horizon of significance of the **world**,
the horizon of **historiology**, and the distressful horizon of the expectation of **existence**. The horizon takes center stage in Heidegger's **fundamental ontology**. In *Being and Time* Heidegger shows that **time** is
projected as the potential horizon for any and every **understanding of
Being**. The **formal indication** of being-there is existence. Being-there
stands out in the **clearing** of **Being**. This spatial and temporal **openness** is the prefiguration of the **sense of being**. This prefiguration is a
horizonal unity that is projected by the three '**equiprimordial' ecstases** of being-there's **temporality**. The horizon makes it possible that
the outward **movement** of being-there's **transcendence** is reflected.
The outermost **possibility** of **death** takes being-there beyond the secure confines of the everyday **world** and throws it back upon itself. As
a movement of transcendence every ecstasis has its own horizon. The
horizon of the **future** is death, that of the **past** is **thrownness**, and that
of the **present** the world. To every ecstasis belongs a whither to which
one is carried away. This whither is the **horizonal schema**.
  After the **turning** the need for a horizon disappears, because being-
there no longer projects the sense of being against the temporal horizon of existence. Being-there is now the 'there' of Being, that is, the
clearing as the **appropriation** of **truth**. The sense of being is emitted
by Being itself. In Heidegger's later philosophy the horizon is mentioned only in the conception of **acquiescence**. The sense of Being is
not the **projection** of being-there; it is the **destiny** of Being itself. In
acquiescence **human beings** let the horizon of their **representations**
be as the **unconcealment** of Being.

HORIZONAL SCHEMA (*horizontales Schema*). In *Being and Time*
Heidegger uses horizonal schemas to explain the different ways in
which **being-there** temporalizes its own **being** in **time**. The horizonal
schema is the whither of the **ecstasis**. The four **ways of being** (authentic and inauthentic **existence, presence-at-hand**, and **readiness-to-
hand**) each have three horizonal schemas that correspond with the
three dimensions of time: **past, present**, and **future**. *See also* Authenticity; Inauthenticity.

HOUSE OF BEING, THE (*das Haus des Seins*). In his famous *Letter
on Humanism* Heidegger refers to the **essence** of **language** as the
house of **Being**, that is, the **dwelling** place of **human beings**.

HUMAN BEING (*der Mensch*). After the **turning, being-there** is no longer the **formal indication** of the **way of being** of humans. It becomes the 'there' or **truth of Being** itself. Human beings exist in the **fourfold**. Here they are the **mortals** who dwell between **earth** and **sky** and before the **divinities**. In their **relation** to **Being** they are the **shepherds of Being** who care for the **being** of **entities**.

HUMANISM (*Humanismus*). In his *Letter on Humanism* Heidegger describes humanism as the liberating of **human beings** into the dignity that is proper to their **essence**. The fundamental conception of human being in humanism is 'animal rationale'. This is the reason why humanism shares the same **fate** as **metaphysics** and cannot cure the homelessness of modern man. Humanism thinks human being from its animality and not to its humanity. Heidegger claims **Jean-Paul Sartre** calcified metaphysics further in the **forgetfulness of being** with his reversal of the dichotomy of **essence** and **existence**. We should therefore try to interpret human being purely out of its **relation** to **Being**.

HUSSERL, EDMUND (1859-1938). As a student Heidegger was influenced by **phenomenology** years before Husserl assumed the chair of **philosophy** at the Albert Ludwigs University in **Freiburg** in 1916. Husserl helped Heidegger with the publication of his qualifying dissertation on Duns Scotus and, by the end of 1917, looked forward to the occasions of 'sumphilosophein' with his favorite coworker. During the years 1917-1920 Heidegger constantly learned in his association with Husserl. During this period his influence is as strong as **Aristotle**'s is.

In Heidegger's phenomenology of religious **experience**, terminology drawn from Husserl's *Ideen I* (1913) abounds. Yet Heidegger shows a growing sense of the hermeneutical rationality of all **lived experience**. He begins to set over against Husserl's pure ego of empty potentiality a historical ego fulfilling itself in historical **situations**. This marks the beginning of his step-by-step transformation of Husserl's transcendental phenomenology into a hermeneutic phenomenology.

Heidegger publicly criticizes Husserl's phenomenology in his Winter Semester 1922/23 seminar on *Ideen I* and his Summer Semester 1923 course *Ontology: The Hermeneutics of Facticity*. Heidegger shows that a **phenomenon** is not merely an object, but more basically a way of access and apprehension. We can only get to the matters themselves in a **destruction** of the **tradition**.

The first lecture course at **Marburg** in the winter of 1923/24, *Introduction to Phenomenological Research*, continues this historical critique by a comparison of Husserl with **René Descartes**, who infected Husserl with a concern for known knowledge that led to an ideal of certainty and evidence. Thus it was decided in advance that consciousness ought to be the main theme of phenomenology. The Summer Semester 1925 lecture course *History of the Concept of Time. Prolegomena* contains Heidegger's most sustained and detailed critique of Husserl. He indicts his mentor for the double **ontological** negligence of the **being** of **intentionality** and the question of the **sense of being** itself. The primacy of **perception** and its overt bodily **presence** in Husserl's method is reduced back to the more immediate presence of **equipment**, which is founded upon the nonobjective presence of **concern** and its **environment**.

Heidegger dedicated *Being and Time* to Husserl for incisive personal guidance and free access to unpublished investigations during their Freiburg years. The dedication page, along with the rough manuscript of *Being and Time*, was presented to Husserl on his birthday in April 1926. The shock of alienation was immediate when Husserl finally got a good look at the long-awaited book. Their differences became even more explicit during their collaboration on a joint statement defining phenomenology for the *Encyclopaedia Britannica*, which ended in failure.

In 1928 Heidegger's edition of Husserl's lectures on inner time-consciousness appears. Heidegger returns as Husserl's successor to Freiburg in late 1928, but there will be no philosophical interchange between them. On April 8, 1929, on the festive occasion of Husserl's 70th birthday, Heidegger formally presents the Festschrift to Husserl with a short speech. The Festschrift is a testimony that Husserl's students wanted to follow his leadership, not a proof that they had succeeded in being followers. Later that year Husserl studies Heidegger's writings and rejects them both in method and contents. In his *Nachwort zu meinen Ideen* he publicly denounces the new philosophy of **existence**. In a letter to Alexander Pfänder in 1931 Husserl bares his soul over the entire course of his relationship with Heidegger, one of the most difficult ordeals of his life. Because of illness Heidegger was conspicuously absent from Husserl's funeral in 1938. In his later auto-biographical essays Heidegger acknowledges his lasting debt to Husserl's principle of phenomenology for his own path of thinking. *See also* Four seminars.

- I -

I, THE (*das Ich*). Heidegger repeats time and again that the I can be understood neither as subject nor as **substance**. The I is not a **thing**; it is an intentional **structure**. As such it is both situated and historical. In *Being and Time* Heidegger uses the **formal indication** of **mineness** to disclose the individual character of **being-there**. *See also* Intentionality; Situation-I, the.

IDEA OF PHILOSOPHY AND THE PROBLEM OF WORLD-VIEWS, THE (*Die Idee der Philosophie und das Weltanschauungsproblem*). This war-emergency semester 1919 lecture course is Heidegger's first teaching assignment after World War I. Its title reflects the goal of **Edmund Husserl**'s program expressed in his *Logos* essay to further **philosophy** as a rigorous **science**. In this course Heidegger develops for the first time his idea of philosophy as an original, and therefore nontheoretical, science. Philosophy is neither a theoretical science nor a **worldview**. It is the plunge into **life** itself in its **authenticity**.

In the first part Heidegger denies with Husserl that philosophy has anything to do with a worldview. He offers his students a **destruction** of the critical-teleological method of neo-Kantian **value-philosophy**. In the second phenomenological part he rejects the neo-Kantian starting point of philosophy in the fact of knowledge and replaces it with the primal fact of life and **experience**. As the original science, philosophy begins with the original **leap** from the **primal something**. The only way to get at this original sphere is by pure dedication to the subject matter, that is, the **lived experience** of life itself. This environmental experience is the condition of **possibility** of the neo-Kantian experience of pure **givenness**, which is nonobjective and impersonal. In a discussion of **Paul Natorp**'s objections to **phenomenology**, Heidegger transforms Husserl's principle of all principles, that is, the primacy of originary giving and so of **intuition**, into a non-theoretical and hermeneutic principle, that is, the primacy of **understanding**. This transformation is the hermeneutical breakthrough in phenomenology. The primal something of philosophy is not a fact but the **relation** as such. It is not an object at all but the intentional moment of out-toward. We can only experience these intentional **structures** in our **factual life experience**. Philosophy itself becomes a distinct possibility of life, which uses **formal indications** to disclose the orienting comportment

.of life itself. Life is meaningful and expresses itself in and through its self-experience and spontaneous self-understanding.

IDLE TALK (*Gerede*). Idle talk is Heidegger's description of a positive **phenomenon** that constitutes **being-there**'s everyday **understanding** and **interpretation**. Being-there is delivered over to the **interpretedness** occurring within the averageness and publicity of the 'they'. Idle talk is the **possibility** of understanding everything without previously making the matter that we talk about our own. In this sense idle talk closes off the access to the matters themselves.

IN-BEING. *see* BEING-IN

IN-ORDER-TO, THE (*das Umzu*). The in-order-to belongs to the essential **structure** of **equipment**. In the in-order-to lies a reference of something to something. Dealings with equipment subordinate themselves to the manifold assignments of the in-order-to within a totality of equipment. The in-order-to of each piece of equipment is discovered in **circumspection**. In Heidegger's analysis of **temporality** the in-order-to is also the **horizonal schema** of the **present**.

INAUTHENTICITY (*Uneigentlichkeit*). As **ways of being, authenticity** and inauthenticity are grounded in the **mineness** of **being-there**. All **existentials** of being-there are determined by the tension between authenticity and inauthenticity. Being-there exists always either in one of these **modes** or in the indifference to both. The ground of inauthenticity is possible authenticity. It characterizes a way of being into which being-there can divert itself and has for the most part always diverted itself. Inauthenticity does not signify a lesser degree of **being** than authenticity. Being-there can also in its fullest concretion be characterized by inauthenticity.

INNERTIMENESS (*Innerzeitlichkeit*). Heidegger uses the technical term innertimeness in *Being and Time* to identify **time** as the time of innerworldly **being**. Every **entity** is in time. Innertimeness is the **origin** of the common conception of time as a succession of **nows**.

INSTANCE (*Inständigkeit*) Heidegger first uses instance or instantiality in his existential **analysis** of **being-there**. The **essence** of being-there is **existence**, that is, a standing-out *in* the **clearing** of the 'there' of **Being**. Instance is the 'there' where being-there exists.

In his later **philosophy** instance is reached when **human beings** achieve **authenticity** as the culmination of thought in **acquiescence**. The essence of authentic thinking is the **resoluteness** of the **being** of **truth** in its essence. Only when the thinker perseveres in his resoluteness may he be said to repose in himself as what he is. This state of repose is what Heidegger now calls instance.

INTENTIONALITY (*Intentionalität*).   Intentionality is one of the fundamental breakthroughs in **Edmund Husserl's phenomenology**. Husserl took from **Franz Brentano** the insight that the defining characteristic of consciousness is its intentionality. Husserl distinguishes between the **meaning** of a conscious act from the object it is about. Heidegger transformed Husserl's conception of the intentionality of consciousness into a hermeneutic conception of the intentionality of **being-there**. The **essence** of being-there lies in its **existence** or being-out-toward, that is, an intentional **structure**. In *Being and Time* Heidegger distinguishes between three different notions of intentionality and its relationship to the **world**: 1. The intentionality and world of theoretical **intuition**, 2. The intentionality and world of practical **concern** and **circumspection**, and 3. The primordial intentionality and **worldhood** of being-there's **understanding**, in which the first two are grounded. For being-there it always worlds (*weltet*). Heidegger's **philosophy** is an ongoing attempt to describe and analyze the structure of the appropriating event that it worlds for me. The starting point of phenomenology is neither a **fact** nor a principle, but the pure **facticity** of the 'it worlds', or as he will later describe it, the **appropriation** of the **truth of Being**.

INTERPRETATION (*Auslegung; Interpretation*).   Heidegger uses the term interpretation in two different senses. In the larger sense interpretation, *Interpretation*, is basically the making explicit of our **understanding** of something. Since every understanding is historical, every interpretation is at the same time a **destruction** of the **tradition** from which we understand something. In this sense Heidegger's interpretation of the **sense of being** is also at the same time a destruction of the history of **ontology**.

In the stricter sense interpretation, *Auslegung* (interpretative exposition) is the development of the **possibilities** of **being-there's projections**. In every interpretation the understanding appropriates understandingly that which is understood by it and thus becomes itself. Interpretation is the working out of possibilities projected implicitly in understanding. This means that it is possible to give an *Interpretation* of an *Auslegung* but not the other way around.

INTERPRETEDNESS (*Ausgelegtheit*). Interpretedness is the **formal indication** of the everyday **interpretation** of human life as it is promoted by the '**they**', and thus in ordinary **language**.

INTRODUCTION TO METAPHYSICS (*Einführung in die Metaphysik*). This Summer Semester 1935 lecture course is a more radical development of the **question of being** than Heidegger has worked out in *Being and Time*. The course consists of four parts.

In the first part Heidegger interprets the fundamental question, why is there something rather than **nothing**?, as the greatest, deepest, and most original question. It asks about **entities** as such and as a **whole**, or as it was called in **Greek philosophy**, '**physis**'. Heidegger wants to introduce his students to this fundamental question. For logical and scientific **thinking**, the nothing of the second part of the question is strange and alienating. The first part of the question, why is there something?, questions the everyday fact that **entities** are, and thus opens up the domain of **Being**. The fundamental question of **metaphysics** concerning entities and the nothing thus leads to the more **basic question**, 'How does it stand with Being?' The question of being determines the historical **fate** of the Occident and is concerned with historical events like the flight of the **gods**, the destruction of the **earth**, and the standardization of **human beings**.

In the second part Heidegger discusses the grammar and etymology of the **word** Being. The infinitive **mode** refers to an abstraction of its **meaning** from all particular **relations**. Being is an empty word that has many meanings.

In the third part Heidegger addresses the question of the **understanding of being**. Does the emptiness of the word Being not hide the **possibility** of a multiplicity of **meanings**?

The fourth part is a discussion of the contexts Being and Becoming, Being and Appearance, Being and **Thinking**, and Being and the Ought. In harmony with Greek **philosophy** and **poetry**, he tries to make a fundamental **experience** of Being possible. The question about the **essence** of Being is at the same time the question about the essence of **being-there**, because being-there is the **site** for the disclosure of Being. Because the essence of being-there is temporal, **time** was the perspective governing the disclosure of Being in the **beginning** of Western philosophy. This perspective as such remained hidden. *Being* *and Time* was a first attempt to make this perspective explicit and point in a different direction than metaphysics.

INTRODUCTION TO PHENOMENOLOGICAL RESEARCH (*Einführung in die phänomenologische Forschung*). This Winter Semester 1923/24 lecture course is the first of Heidegger's courses in **Marburg**. It is both an introduction to phenomenological research and a critique of **Edmund Husserl's** **phenomenology** of consciousness. Guided by the matters themselves Heidegger develops his conception of a phenomenology of **being-there**. The course consists of a clarification of the expression phenomenology and a discussion of the initial breakthrough to phenomenological research in Husserl's *Logical Investigations* and its ensuing course in modern **philosophy**.

The first part of the course begins with a clarification of the expression phenomenology through an **interpretation** of 'phainomenon' and 'logos' in **Aristotle's** writings. Heidegger shows that Aristotle is concerned with the **being** of the **world** and **life** as **being-in-the-world**. Modern philosophy, on the other hand, is guided by the **care** of certain and clear knowledge. The ideal of mathematical strictness makes it impossible for **entities** to show themselves in their being. In an interpretation of Husserl's essay, *Philosophy as Rigorous Science*, Heidegger shows that his conception of phenomenology was still dominated by the **care** of certain and clear knowledge and the **concern** for already known knowledge. The concern for certainty and clarity marks the beginning of modern philosophy with **René Descartes**.

In the second part of the course Heidegger gives an extensive interpretation of the 'res cogitans' in the philosophy of Descartes, which is guided by the question of the **sense** of the **truth** of knowledge. Descartes determines not only truth as certainty, but also retains scholastic **ontology**. To understand Descartes Heidegger must also give an explication of truth and being in the philosophy of Thomas Aquinas.

In the third part Heidegger shows how Descartes failed to ask the question of the being of the 'res cogitans', because his research was dominated by the concern for certain knowledge. Husserl took over from Descartes the ideal of certain and clear knowledge and could therefore not disclose being-there in its being. Heidegger's course is not only a **destruction** of phenomenological research but also a return to the matters themselves, that is, being-there.

INTRODUCTION TO PHILOSOPHY (*Einleitung in die Philosophie*). Heidegger gave this Winter Semester 1928/29 lecture course as **Ed-**

mund Husserl's successor at the University of **Freiburg**. It marks the beginning of the **turning** on his path of thinking, because Heidegger abandons Husserl's project of transforming **philosophy** into a rigorous **science**. Philosophy is not a science, not out of lack but rather out of excess, since it springs from the ever superabundant and ebullient **appropriation** of **being-there**.

At the beginning of the course Heidegger divides his introduction to philosophy into three parts: philosophy and science, philosophy and **worldview**, and philosophy and history. The second part became so extensive that Heidegger could not discuss the third.

In the first part of the course Heidegger develops the difference between philosophy and science out of the **essence** of **truth**. The positivism of science and its truth are grounded in the essential condition of being-there, that is, **transcendence**. Transcendence is the disclosing of **entities** in their **being**. This disclosure can only happen if being-there lets entities be as they are.

The second part is a discussion of the connection between philosophy and worldview on the basis of the fundamental determinations of being-there: **being-in-the-world**, transcendence, and **understanding of being**. Because being-there has been delivered over to the superior power of entities, it is insecure and without a hold. From this insecurity and being without a hold spring two fundamental **possibilities** of worldview: worldview as security (**religion**) and worldview as hold (philosophy). Philosophy is in an outstanding way of worldview as hold: the letting happen and forming of transcendence as **freedom**.

INTRODUCTION TO THE PHENOMENOLOGY OF RELIGION (*Einleitung in die Phänomenologie der Religion*).   This Winter Semester 1920/21 lecture course is divided into two parts, an introductory methodological part and a second part devoted to the phenomenological explication of religious **phenomena**. The second part, focused on the **interpretation** of Paul's eschatological epistles, has become famous. Just before the Christmas break, Heidegger broke off his methodological explanations as a result of objections from students who had complained to the dean of the philosophical faculty over the lack of religious content in the course.

The first part is centered upon the self-understanding of **philosophy**. It springs from **factual life experience** that is at once the experiencing activity and that which is receptively experienced. Experiencing and the experienced are interlaced. Factual life experience tends toward the determination of objects and the objective regulation of **life**. By making factual life experience the central phenomenon of philosophy, Heidegger raises the possibility of reversing this decadent tendency. After a **destruction** of Ernst Troeltsch's philosophy of **religion** Heidegger clarifies the core phenomenon of the historical, which permeates the **meanings** connecting the three key terms of the course title. There are three ways in which the **present** seeks to protect itself from history: 1. The Platonic way, a radical renunciation of the historical, 2. The exact opposite, a radical surrender to history (Oswald Spengler), and 3. A compromise between these two extremes (**Wilhelm Dilthey**, Georg Simmel, **Heinrich Rickert** and Wilhelm Windelband). Heidegger shows that we can only discover the historical in factual life experience through phenomenological explication. The direction of this explication is prefigured by **formal indication**.

The second part is a phenomenological explication of primitive Christian life experience in conjunction with Paul's epistles. Through an interpretation of Paul's epistle to the Galatians Heidegger obtains access to the **lifeworld** of primitive **Christianity**. Christian life is actually factual life experience itself and lives **temporality** as such.

The central phenomenon of Christian life experience is apostolic proclamation, which takes us to the heart of Paul's **self-world** in its vital relation to the **environment** and **with-world** of the first congregations. In his interpretation of Paul's epistles to the Thessalonians Heidegger focuses his attention on the temporality of Christian religiosity, which is dominated by the deciding **moment**, 'kairos', of the Second Coming of Christ.

INTUITION (*Anschauung*). Heidegger agrees with **Edmund Husserl** that the principle of all principles of **phenomenology** is intuition. This intuition, however, is not some theoretical comportment but an **understanding** or hermeneutic intuition. Heidegger transforms Husserl's conception of a phenomenology of pure consciousness into a hermeneutic phenomenology. The hermeneutic intuition understands the **world** prior to any theorizing and the **facticity** of this understanding is the starting point of Heidegger's **philosophy**. *See also* Hermeneutics.

INVOLVEMENT (*Bewandtnis*). Heidegger adopted **Emil Lask**'s alternative term for form in his qualifying dissertation to indicate how a matter is to be viewed. In his Summer Semester 1925 lecture course *History of the Concept of Time. Prolegomena*, involvement replaces **meaningfulness** to specify the orientation to be taken in relation to the other in accord with the other's involvement with the **world**. In the

Winter Semester 1925/26 course *Logic: The Question of Truth*, the **meaning** of involvement is restricted to define the state of functionality, compliance, and readiness of **entities** that are ready-to-hand. In *Being and Time*, it becomes the very **being** of the ready-to-hand, the handy.

- **J** -

JASPERS, KARL (1883-1969). Jaspers and Heidegger met for the first time at a birthday party for **Edmund Husserl** in 1919. Their shared love of **Sören Kierkegaard** and Heidegger's review of Jaspers' *Psychology of Worldviews* would bring them together in the "loving struggle" of friendship. Their long philosophical discussions at Jaspers' house, where Heidegger stayed as often as possible, led them to join forces in the struggle against the **philosophy** of the university professors and form a battle community. The end of World War I signified the end of 19th century culture and philosophy. Heidegger and Jaspers both saw the necessity of a university reform, which would in turn lead to a political revolution. In his famous talk on the calling of **science**, Max Weber had made clear that science had no answer to offer to the most important questions of human life: what should we do; how should we live?

The philosophical starting point of Heidegger and Jaspers was **existence** or personal **life**. From this point they set off in different directions. Heidegger followed Husserl and his project of philosophy as a rigorous science. He developed a new concept of science that made a scientific answer to our most important and intimate questions possible. **Phenomenology** could provide insight into the **facticity** of our lives, since **meaningfulness** is given with the bare **fact** of our existence. Jaspers, on the other hand, followed Kierkegaard and tried to illuminate existence by way of the **limit situations**. He had the feeling that Husserl's concept of phenomenology as a rigorous science denied the possibility of philosophy in the sense that it was meaningful to him. The philosophical conversations of Heidegger and Jaspers would never reach the ideal of loving struggle Jaspers had hoped for. It would, however, take them a long time to bring their philosophical differences to light. Their dialogue would gradually lapse into separate monologues, because they hardly ever studied each other's writings.

In the light of his later critique of Heidegger, it is noteworthy that Jaspers agreed with much of the content of Heidegger's rectoral address. In 1933 they were both convinced of the need for radical renewal and both were fascinated by the *Führer* principle. The present situation had opened up extraordinary **possibilities** that would never return again, although Jaspers, contrary to Heidegger, also saw the extreme danger. Heidegger stayed with Jaspers for the last time from June 30 until July 1. Their correspondence broke off with Heidegger's four-page letter of May 16. When Jaspers was removed from office in 1937, Heidegger failed him badly and the gulf that opened up between them could never be closed again. They continued to send each other their publications until the outbreak of World War II. In 1939 all contact between the former friends broke off.

In 1945 Heidegger asked Professor Oehlkers, a member of the de-Nazification committee, to ask Jaspers about his supposed anti-Semitism. In reply Jaspers wrote a negative report that would ultimately lead to Heidegger's forced retirement without license to teach.

In 1949 Jaspers wrote to Heidegger in an effort to resume communication between them. "There was something between us which bound us together. I cannot believe it has been extinguished. The time seems ripe, so I turn myself to you in the hope that you will join me in the wish to exchange a word." Heidegger answered: "that you have written is to me a great joy." He went on to explain that he stopped his visits in 1933 because he was ashamed and not because Jaspers' wife was Jewish. Their attempts to resume their friendship were doomed to fail. Heidegger simply could not explain his involvement with **National Socialism** to Jaspers' satisfaction, and seemed incapable of assuming full responsibility for his actions and words under the Nazi regime. Heidegger rejected Jaspers' notion of collective guilt. He was no war criminal and therefore he saw no need for a public discussion of his **rectorate** and acts during the Nazi period.

JOINING (*Fug*). see ARRANGEMENT

JUDGMENT (*Urteil*). The doctrine of judgment runs like a continuous thread through Heidegger's lecture courses. It was the topic of his 1914 dissertation in which he supported **Edmund Husserl**'s rejection of **psychologism**. In his early lecture courses in **Freiburg** Heidegger worked out a **destruction** of the traditional doctrine of judgment as the place of **truth**. He showed that the famous definition of truth as the correspondence between the intellect and the object ('veritas est adequatio intellectus et rei') is a misunderstanding of **Aristotle**'s doctrine of truth. The truth of judgment signifies that it uncovers the **entity** as it is in itself. It lets the entity be seen in its uncoveredness. The being true of judgment is being-uncovering, but this in turn is **onto-logically** possible only on the basis of **being-in-the-world**. Being-true is a **way of being** for **being-there**. The **disclosedness** of being-there is the condition of possibility of truth.

In Heidegger's **philosophy** after *Being and Time*, the emphasis shifts from the disclosedness of being-there to the **clearing of Being**. He distinguishes now between the original Greek **understanding** of truth as **unconcealment** ('alètheia') that was expressed in the fundamental **sayings** of **Anaximander**, **Parmenides** and **Heraclitus**, on the one hand, and **Plato** and Aristotle's logical understanding of truth as correctness, on the other. Aristotle's doctrine of truth becomes now the origin of the correspondence theory of truth. *See also* On the Essence of Truth; Plato's Doctrine of Truth.

JÜNGER, ERNST (1895-1998). Heidegger developed his concept of **technology** in constant dialogue with Jünger's writings, especially *The Worker: Dominion and Gestalt* and *Total Mobilization*. He found in these writings a discussion of the **essence** of **technology** and **nihilism**, on the one hand, and a fundamental **understanding** of **Friedrich Nietzsche**'s **metaphysics** of the **will**, on the other. Jünger's writings strongly influenced Heidegger's **interpretation** of **National Social-ism**. Throughout the 1930s he discussed Jünger's writings with circles of like-minded associates. Heidegger and Jünger became personal friends. After the end of World War II Heidegger encouraged Jünger to reprint *The Worker*. Heidegger's most extensive commentary on Jünger is the essay *The Question of Being*.

- K -

KAIROS.   In the **factual life experience** of primitive **Christianity** 'kairos' refers to the **moment** of the Second Coming of Christ. The whole community lives in the expectation of this decisive moment in history. Nobody knows when this moment will occur, although it is certain that it will come. Heidegger contrasts this nonobjective **experi-ence** of **time** with the scientific conception of time as a series of **nows**.

In his reading of **Aristotle** Heidegger finds both experiences of time. In his *Nicomachean Ethics 6*, Aristotle shows that our temporally par-ticular **situation** admits of no absolute and once-and-for-all norm. As each situation is new, we must think anew and act anew. The right middle of passion and action is hard to find and easy to miss. This is why it is hard to be good. The end of action varies according to the 'kairos' or the proper moment. In action we seek the 'kairos', that is, feeling and acting at the right time, for the right purpose and in the right manner.

In *Physics 4*, Aristotle develops another **understanding** of time as a series of nows. This objective understanding of time would determine the history of the concept of time until **Edmund Husserl**. In *Being and Time* the moment of insight (*Augenblick*) and decision constitutes a Kierkegaardian elaboration of the 'kairos'. Heidegger identifies later the term *Augenblick* as **Sören Kierkegaard**'s most prescient insight.

KANT, IMMANUEL (1724-1804). The neo-Kantian **Heinrich Rickert** introduced Heidegger to Kant's **philosophy** when he was still a student at the University of **Freiburg**. Kant's influence on his thought remained marginal until the Winter Semester 1925/26 lecture course *Logic: The Question of Truth* and his seminar on Kant's *Critique of Pure Reason*. In the doctrine of **schematism** of the productive imagination Kant had discovered the rudimentary connection of our most incipient **understanding of being** with **time** and glimpsed a different **sense** of time. The productive imagination is the capacity of finite **human beings**, which puts them in touch with the dynamics of their **existence**. Although Kant shrank back from this fusion of **being** and time, he became the leading figure in Heidegger's phenomenological **destruction** of the history of **ontology**. It is not surprising that *Being and Time* receives a Kantian overlay and impetus.

Heidegger's **interpretation** of Kant culminates in his famous book *Kant and the Problem of Metaphysics*. After his abandonment of the project of *Being and Time* Kant lost his central place in Heidegger's thought. Although **Friedrich Hölderlin** and **Friedrich Nietzsche** would take his place, Heidegger would return time and again to Kant's **philosophy**. *See also* Kant's Critique of Pure Reason and the Task of a Laying of the Ground for Metaphysics; Kant's Thesis about Being; On Odebrecht's and Cassirer's Critique of the Kantbook; On the Essence of Human Freedom. Introduction to Philosophy; Phenomenological Interpretation of Kant's 'Critique of Pure Reason'; What Is a Thing?

KANT AND THE PROBLEM OF METAPHYSICS *(Kant und das Problem der Metaphysik)*. Heidegger presented the essentials of his reading of **Immanuel Kant** for the first time during his Winter Semester 1927/28 lecture course *Phenomenological Interpretation of Kant's 'Critique of Pure Reason'*. His book on Kant is of great importance for the development of Heidegger's own thought because it takes up and extends several themes suggested in **Being and Time**. We can consider the book as a version of the promised **destruction** of Kant's **schematism** and doctrine of **time** in the never-published second part of *Being and Time*.

The starting point of Heidegger's **interpretation** is his claim that Kant's central problem is the **possibility** of **metaphysics**. The *Critique of Pure Reason* is an attempt to provide metaphysics with its foundation. Heidegger rejects the influential neo-Kantian reading of the first *Critique* as a theory of knowledge. Kant's problem is **fundamental ontology** as an **ontological** analytic of the finite **essence** of **human being**, which is to prepare the **ground** for the metaphysics that belongs to human nature. Heidegger's book consists of four parts.

In the first part, *The starting point for the laying of the ground for metaphysics*, Heidegger asks the question: why did the problem of the laying of the ground for metaphysics become a critique of pure reason? For Kant, metaphysics is the fundamental science of **entities** as such and as a **whole**. Through his Copernican revolution the question concerning the possibility of **ontic** knowledge is reduced to the question concerning the possibility of **ontology** itself. This means we have to ask how it is possible that our a priori knowledge of entities is connected with the **transcendence** of pure reason to the entities themselves. When we ask about the essence of this transcendence of our **understanding of being**, we philosophize in a **transcendental** way.

The second part, *Carrying out the laying of the ground for metaphysics*, is a discussion of Kant's elucidation of the essence of the finitude of human knowledge as receptive **intuition** in contrast to the creating infinite intuition of **God**. Finite intuition depends on pure understanding (*Verstand*). Heidegger interprets Kant's transcendental imagination as **temporality** and claims that it is the common root of the two stems of knowledge: intuition and understanding (*Verstand*). When intuition and understanding (*Verstand*) are joined together by the imagination, ontological knowledge becomes possible. It refers to a pure **horizon** within which entities can present themselves and be represented by **being-there**.

The third part, *The laying of the ground for metaphysics in its originality*, is an extensive interpretation of Kant's doctrine of transcendental imagination. Kant shrank back from this unknown root of the essential constitution of being-there in favor of the understanding (*Verstand*). As a result he was unable to think the original temporality of transcendental imagination. He failed to recognize **time** as the enabling ground of the finitude of human **subjectivity** as a whole.

The fourth part, *The laying of the ground for metaphysics in retrieval*, is a **retrieval** of the hidden possibilities of Kant's laying of the ground for metaphysics. Heidegger shows that pure human reason is determined not only by finitude, but also by being-there's **care** of being able to be finite. The question concerning human finitude arises from the task of the laying of the ground for metaphysics. The metaphysics of being-there asks the necessary question for the laying of the ground for metaphysics: what does it mean to be human? Heidegger's interpretation of the temporality of being-there should make it possible to understand **Being** against the horizon of time.

KANT'S CRITIQUE OF PURE REASON AND THE TASK OF A LAYING OF THE GROUND FOR METAPHYSICS (*Kants Kritik der reinen Vernunft und die Aufgabe einer Grundlegung der Metaphysik*). This text is a summary of Heidegger's 1929 course at the second Davos Hochschule from March 17 until April 16, 1929. The course consisted of three lectures, which correspond with the first three parts of his book ***Kant and the Problem of Metaphysics***.

Heidegger shows that **Immanuel Kant**, in laying a **ground** for **metaphysics**, was forced to introduce a third basic source of the mind, the **transcendental** power of imagination, to supplement the other two stems of the mind, sensibility and understanding (*Verstand*). This third source is the root of the other two. Kant himself shrinks back from this discovery. Heidegger wants to go further and sees the necessity of a **destruction** of metaphysics. The ground of the **possibility** of metaphysics is **being-there** and therefore the **existential analysis** of being-there is at the same time the laying of a ground for metaphysics.

KANT'S THESIS ABOUT BEING (*Kants These über das Sein*). In this 1961 lecture Heidegger shows once again that **Being** is worthy of thought and remains within the **horizon** of **human beings**. The topic of the lecture is **Immanuel Kant's** famous thesis that **being** obviously is not a real predicate but merely the positing of a thing in itself (*Ding an sich*). This thesis contains two **assertions**. The first is a negative one, which denies to being the character of a real predicate. The second assertion is positive and characterizes being as merely the positing. In his lecture Heidegger follows Kant's episodic elucidations of his thesis about being. Although it is not a first principle, Kant effects a decisive turn in the history of **metaphysics**. The **question of being** takes a double form in metaphysics: 1. What are **entities**, in general, as entities?, and 2. Which entity is the highest and in what way? The

onto-theo-logical constitution of metaphysics results from the way the being of entities manifests itself. Being manifests itself as **ground**. In Kant's thesis, being is determined as positing, that is, 'positio', which means to lie at the **ground**.

Kant says that **existence** is the absolute positing of a thing. Existence is such a simple concept that we can say nothing by way of unfolding it. Heidegger remarks that Kant thinks of existence and being in relation to the capacities of our intellectual understanding (*Verstand*). Our positing of a thing in itself as object is only possible if something is given to our positing through sensory intuition. Positing has the character of proposition whereby something is placed before us as something. The 'is' of the copula intends the objective unity of apperception. Being and unity belong together. This originally synthetic unity or **transcendental** apperception makes possible the being of entities.

Heidegger points out that Kant never questions his guiding thread that it is possible for being and its **modes** to be determined from their **relation** to the intellectual understanding. 'Being and Thinking' is the main title for the **interpretation** of the being of entities. For Kant **thinking** means representational thinking that posits and judges.

In the section on the postulates of empirical thought in general in the *Critique of Pure Reason*, Kant determines being in its **sense** of being possible, being actual and being necessary, as a transcendental predicate. Because being in its modalities is thought of as a predicate, being is still a positing. Thought determines the modalities of being and the positing. These determinations are discovered in a reflection (*Reflexion*) on thought. Being is positing; thinking is reflection. Kant thus elucidates the relation between positing and reflection (*Reflexion*). Heidegger now asks what the 'and' in 'Being and Thinking' means. According to the famous **saying** of **Parmenides**, being and **thinking** are the same or identical. In **Greek philosophy** being is that which grants **presence**. Being is present as presencing. Here the concealed relation between being and **time** comes to light. Thus it becomes clear that the guiding title of metaphysics, 'Being and Thinking', does not really pose the question of being.

KÄSTNER, ERHART (1904-1974). Kästner attended Heidegger's 1950 lecture on the **thing** in Munich. They soon became close friends and met each other regularly. They shared a love of **poetry** and Greece. Kästner got Heidegger elected as a member of the Prussian Academy of the Fine Arts in 1957. He also helped to arrange Heidegger's trip to Greece in 1962 and later convinced him to grant an interview to *Der Spiegel*, which was published posthumously.

KEEPING SILENT (*schweigen*). In *Being and Time*, **discourse** is the articulation of the **meaningfulness** of being. Discourse involves communication and it makes use of **language** as its tool, but it is not necessarily a matter of speaking. We can sometimes express our **understanding** of something most effectively by keeping silent. Silence belongs to the **essence** of discourse because it enables us to listen to and grasp the understanding we communicate to each other.

KIERKEGAARD, SÖREN (1813-1855). Kierkegaard is one of the hidden influences on Heidegger's early thought. It is remarkable that Heidegger wrote so little on Kierkegaard. **Karl Jaspers'** *Psychology of Worldviews* first awakened his interest in the Danish philosopher. In *Being and Time* Kierkegaard is one of Heidegger's sources for the **phenomenology** of **anxiety** and **fear** as **moods**, on the one hand, and of the **moment** as an **ecstasis** of **temporality**, on the other.

KREBS, ENGELBERT GUSTAV HANS (1881-1950). Heidegger and Krebs met in mid-July 1913 and became friends. Krebs profited from Heidegger's knowledge of modern **logic**, while his friend could benefit from the wealth of his studies in medieval **philosophy** and **mysticism**. Because he was not familiar with the area, **Heinrich Rickert** asked Krebs to write an evaluation of Heidegger's dissertation, *Duns Scotus' Doctrine of Categories and Meaning*. His response to Heidegger's work was very positive. In his function as a Roman Catholic priest, Krebs officiated at the marriage ceremony of Martin Heidegger and Elfride Petri. Their relationship became more distant when Heidegger broke with Catholicism in 1919 and ended in 1923 when he moved to **Marburg**.

- L -

LANGUAGE (*Sprache*). In *Being and Time* Heidegger discusses language within the framework of his **existential analysis** of **being-there**. Being-there has language. The **human being** is the **entity** that speaks. Heidegger rejects the traditional theory of language according to which we must understand language in terms of **expression**, symbolic form or **assertion** as ways of making known our **lived experiences**. This theory understands language as the expression of **mean-**

ings that are given independent of and prior to language. According to Heidegger **discourse** is the **existential-ontological** foundation of language. It is the articulation of intelligibility of **being-in-the-world**. The totality of meanings is put into **words**. Discourse gets expressed in language. **Hearing** and **keeping silent** are **possibilities** belonging to discursive speech. Hearing is the existential openness for the **being-with** of others. Keeping silent is the counterpart to **idle talk** that has lost its relation to the **being** of the entities it talks about.

After the **turning** Heidegger reverses the relation between being-there and language. He no longer grounds language **ontologically** in discourse. Language is in **essence** not the expression of a living entity. It is the clearing-concealing advent of **Being** itself and as such the **house of Being**. In its home human beings **dwell**. The human being must first let himself be claimed again by Being before he speaks and take the risk that under this **claim** he will seldom have much to say. Language speaks originally and human beings speak when they respond to its address. Language achieves its completion in **poetry**. In poetry it invites **things** to gather to themselves **sky** and **earth, mortals** and **divinities**, and thus let **world** be. *See also* Dialogue on Language, A; Language; Language in the Poem; Nature of Language, The; Way to Language, The; Words.

LANGUAGE (*Die Sprache*). In this 1950 lecture Heidegger attempts to give an account of the nature of **language**. He rejects the dominant view that language is an activity of **human beings** in which they express their feelings and thoughts. The **essence** of language is that it speaks. (*Die Sprache spricht.*) To understand the essence of language we must bring it to its place of **being**, that is, our own gathering into the **appropriation**. Language spoken purely is **poetry**. Therefore Heidegger approaches language through a poem of Georg Trakl: *A Winter Evening*.

Language speaks, but what is 'to speak'? A poem speaks when it names **entities** in their being. This naming calls and thus brings closer what it calls. The call brings the **presence** of what was previously uncalled into a **nearness**. Yet, in calling it here, the call has already called out to what it calls. The calling calls into itself and therefore always calls here into presence and there into **absence**. When language calls, it bids **things** to come into a presence sheltered in absence. Bidding is inviting and invites things to gather to themselves **sky** and **earth, mortals** and **divinities**. Things called in this way let the **fourfold** stay with them. This gathering is the thinging of things, that is, the unfolding of **world**, in which things abide. Language bids things to come to world and world to come to things. The two **modes** of bidding are different but not separated. World and things traverse a middle in which they are one. This intimacy is a difference (*Unterschied*). The intimacy of world and thing is present in the separation of the **between**, that is, the difference. The intimacy of the difference is the unifying element of the 'diaphora'. It carries out world in its worlding and things in their thinging. The difference of world and thing discloses and appropriates things into bearing a world and world into the granting of things. In the bidding that calls thing and world, what is really called is the difference.

The difference keeps world and thing in repose. To keep in repose is to still. It is in the double stilling of the difference that stillness takes place. Language speaks as the peal (*Geheiß*) of stillness. Human beings are in their **nature** given to **speech** as the peal of stillness. Only because human beings belong within the peal of stillness are mortals able to speak. Thus the speech of mortals is also a calling that names and a bidding that bids thing and world to come. In its purest form mortal speech is spoken in the poem. Human beings speak in that they respond to language. Responding is a speaking that listens to the stillness of the difference.

LANGUAGE IN THE POEM (*Die Sprache im Gedicht*). In this 1953 essay Heidegger discusses Georg Trakl's poetic work. This discussion is no more than a **thinking** about the **location** that gathers his poetic **saying** into his poetic work. Like every great poet Trakl creates his **poetry** out of one single poem, which remains unspoken. Every poem speaks from the **whole** of this single poem and says it, but yet it can never say it all. Heidegger's discussion of Trakl's poetry is a dialogue of thinking with poetry that aims to call forth the **nature** of **language**, so that **mortals** may learn again to live in language. In a discussion of selected stanzas Heidegger discovers the location of Trakl's poetic work: apartness (*Abgeschiedenheit*). The language of his poetry answers to the homecoming of unborn mankind into the quiet **beginning** of its stiller nature. This language sings the song of the homecoming in apartness that from the lateness of decomposition comes to rest in the earliness of the more still, and still impending, **beginning**. Trakl is the poet of the yet-concealed evening land.

LASK, EMIL (1875-1915). The importance of Lask for the young Heidegger can scarcely be exaggerated, even though it would be a transitory influence. Lask was one of **Heinrich Rickert**'s most famous students, whose works Heidegger first came to know through Rickert's seminars. Lask was important to Heidegger for two reasons: 1. He tried to listen to the Greek thinkers in his mediation between Rickert and **Edmund Husserl**. 2. Lask played a unique role in appropriating the *Logical Investigations*, because he took up Husserl's positive contributions in the six investigations of the second volume. In his *Logik der Philosophie* Lask was strongly influenced by the sections of the Sixth Investigation on sense intuition and **categorial intuition**, while his *Lehre vom Urteil* was influenced by the sections of the investigation on evidence and **truth**. Lask sought to overcome the limitations of **Immanuel Kant**'s transcendental **logic** by giving it an **ontological** grounding in the realm of transcendental intelligible **validity**. He asserted the autonomy of the **sense**, which is performed in acts of **judgment** and opened Heidegger's eyes to the crucial role of categorial intuition of **beingness** in Husserl's **phenomenology**.

LEAP (*Sprung*). Heidegger already mentions **Natorp**'s wordplay on the **origin** as primal leap (*Ursprung*) in his War Emergency Semester 1919 lecture course, *The Idea of Philosophy and the Problem of Worldviews*, before using the metaphor of the leap in *Being and Time*. In **curiosity** the **making present** leaps away from the **thing** that is present to what is coming next. In **solicitude**, **being-there** can leap in for the other and take away its **care**. It can also leap ahead of the other in its '**existentiell**' **can-be** in order to give its care back to him authentically.

In the *Contributions to Philosophy* Heidegger uses the **formal indication** of **appropriation** to identify the very source and primal leap (*Ur-Sprung*) of the dynamic relationship between **Being** and being-there. In the third arrangement, *Leap (Der Sprung)*, he makes clear that the other **beginning** of **thinking** is accessible only through a leap of thought into the **truth of Being** itself.

LEEWAY (*Spielraum*). The **being** of **being-there** is spatial. Being-there can only be spatial as **care**. It does not fill up space like **things** do; it takes in space literally. By taking in space in its **existence**, being-there **makes room** for its own leeway. The leeway, that is, the space to play or the space of **freedom**, is a **projection** of our **understanding** and discloses our **way of being**. It determines the **possibilities** of our **being-in-the-world**.

LEIBNIZ, GOTTFRIED WILHELM (1646-1716). Heidegger's **interpretation** of Leibniz was very consequential for his exposition of the modern **metaphysics** of **subjectivity**. In his lecture course *The Metaphysical Foundations of Logic*, Heidegger discussed Leibniz's definition of **substance** as force and of the latter as **representation**. The monad is determined by representation in its double meaning of 'perceptio' and 'appetitus'. The 'perceptio' signifies any interior spontaneous expression or representation of the universe. The 'appetitus' is the tendency of the monad to pass from one perception to the other in quest of a more and more adequate perception of the universe. Both are types of presentation or proposing: 'perceptio' represents the universe; 'appetitus' proposes the perfection of **life** toward which the monad strives. Leibniz thus anticipated both **Friedrich Nietzsche**'s philosophy of the **will to power** (force) and the modern **philosophy** of **worldviews** that regards the world as a representation of the subject. *See also* Metaphysics as History of Being; Principle of Reason, The.

LETTER ON HUMANISM (*Brief über den Humanismus*). Heidegger wrote this letter in the fall of 1946 in reply to three questions posed by the French philosopher Jean Beaufret: 1. How can we restore **meaning** to the concept of **humanism**? 2. How can we determine the relation of **ontology** to a possible ethics? 3. How can we preserve the element of adventure that all research contains without simply turning **philosophy** into an adventuress? Although he only discusses the first question at length, this letter is an important path mark in Heidegger's way of thinking. In it he rethinks some of the main points of *Being and Time* in the light of the **turning** and tries to move beyond **metaphysics**.

Heidegger rejects the term humanism since it remains tied to the metaphysical conception of **human being** as rational animal. This conception fails to take into account the **relation** of our **essence** to **Being**. Heidegger defines the **existence** of human being as **instance**, that is, standing in the light of Being. The difference between his thinking and **Jean-Paul Sartre**'s **existentialism** is that while Sartre is dealing with a level where there are principally human beings, Heidegger is dealing with the level where there is principally Being.

Being-there exists in the 'there' of Being as the **clearing**. The 'there' is thrown by Being. The nature of human being is to be the 'there' of Being. The being of the 'there' has the **structure** of existence, that is, taking a stance within the **truth of Being**. The existentials, **projection, throwness, fallenness, care** and **historicality** determine being-there. Since in the **unconcealment** of **entities** Being refuses itself at the same time, Being remains hidden as **destiny**. **Errancy** belongs to the **essence** of **truth**. This also means that the **forgetfulness of being** in the history of metaphysics is due primarily to Being itself. Only when we heed the destiny of Being is there a chance of salvation. This **thinking** of Being has to take into account that Being conceals itself in revealing itself as the being of entities, since Being is not an entity. This negating moment in Being is the essence of the **nothing**. The thinking of Being must meditate the nothing and go the way of **language**, because language is the **house of Being**. The coming to pass of 'alètheia' among entities is entrusted to being-there. Being-there should guard truth, serve as watchman, and be the **shepherd of Being**.

Thinking lets Being be when it unfolds the **relation** between Being and being-there. Like language, thinking is a response to the **address of Being**. Language meets the exigencies of its own essence when it becomes a **saying** of Being. When this happens, being-there is **dwelling** in the house of Being. All true and essential thinking is a saying of Being. Thinking as such is bound to the advent of Being, to Being as advent.

LETTING BE (*Gelassenheit*). *see* ACQUIESCENCE

LIFE (*Leben*). Life is one of the early **formal indications** of the life-long topic of Heidegger's **philosophy**: **Being**. In his 1919 lecture course *The Idea of Philosophy and the Problem of Worldviews*, he defines **phenomenology** as the investigation of life itself. **Intentionality** and **meaningfulness** determine the **facticity** of life. In its **being**, life has an **understanding of being**. Heidegger will later replace the formal indication of life with the historical and/or **situation-I, factual life experience**, facticity, **being-in-the-world**, and finally **being-there**.

LIFE PHILOSOPHY (*Lebensphilosophie*). Life philosophy is the late 19th-century philosophical movement that was inspired by **Sören Kierkegaard** and **Friedrich Nietzsche**. Henri Bergson and **Wilhelm Dilthey** became its main representatives. The starting point of life philosophy is that **life** expresses and understands itself immediately in **lived experiences**, which can be understood in **hermeneutics** (Dilthey) or biology (Bergson). According to Dilthey **historicality** determines human life. His influence on Heidegger's early thought was very profound and far-reaching.

LIFEWORLD (*Lebenswelt*). Since **life** is determined by its **being** out-toward or **intentionality**, it always finds itself in a **world**. In his early lecture courses in **Freiburg** Heidegger calls the different worlds in which we always already find ourselves lifeworlds. He differentiates among scientific, aesthetic, ethical and religious lifeworlds, which motivate our behavior in different ways. We can only understand life in its **facticity** from its specific lifeworld. The teleological dispersal of **values** constituted by the plurality of lifeworlds must eventually be returned to their archeological **origin** in the **self-world**, which is at once the with-world-around-us.

LIMIT SITUATION (*Grenzsituation*). **Karl Jaspers** introduced this concept in his groundbreaking book *Psychology of Worldviews*, which would inaugurate the German **philosophy** of **existence**. Limit situations are those decisive **situations** which are tied to what the **human being** as such is, and are inevitably given with finite **being-there**. They all pose ultimate incompatibilities, which make it impossible for us to see our finite situation as a **whole**. Thus the limit situation of **death** contradicts **life**, chance contradicts necessity, war contradicts reciprocity, and **guilt** contradicts innocence. As finite beings we must come to grips with the limit situations of our life. The way we react to and try to find stability in relation to the limit situations conditions who we are. We can either look death right in the eye or try to hide from it. As Jaspers remarks, the contradictions of the limit situations remain as antinomies at the limit of our knowledge in the face of in-finities. This means that our consciousness of limits must at the same time be our consciousness of the infinite whole of life. The **experience** of the antinomy of life is at once the experience of its unity. Limit situations make the experience of the **transcendence** of our being-there possible, since we can only experience a limit as limit when we transcend the limit. Here our possible existence becomes real exis-tence. Heidegger welcomed Jaspers' attempt to illuminate the whole of existence from the limit situations. He would have to adapt and modify the notion of the limit situation for use in his **phenomenology** of **fac-ticity**, since he rejects Jaspers' Kantian methodology and concept of existence. In his Summer Semester 1919 courses Heidegger replaces the limit situation with the **situation-I**, which would develop into the concept of situation in *Being and Time*.

LIVED EXPERIENCE (*Erlebnis*). Human life is lived experience. The basic **structure** of lived experience is **intentionality**. In his early lecture courses at the University of **Freiburg** Heidegger takes over from **Wilhelm Dilthey** and **Edmund Husserl** the term lived experience and uses it as the **formal indication of facticity**. The meaningful structures of lived experience are developed by life **situations** in which the totality of life expresses itself. Lived experiences are through and through expressed in a definite articulation by an **understanding** we have of them as we simply live in them without regarding them thematically.

LOCATION (*Ort*). According to the famous definition, the primordial location of **truth** is in the **judgment**. As a **formal indication** of space, location refers to specific ways of **being-there**'s **being-in**. Being-there's **existential** 'spatiality' determines its location and is itself grounded in **being-in-the-world**. Location is also a keyword in Heidegger's later work.

LOGIC (*Logik*). Logic is one of the most important topics in Heidegger's **philosophy**. He devoted many writings, courses, and lectures to logical problems. Logic, the **science** of the ways in which **being** is addressed and articulated, is closely related to **ontology**, the science of being. This means that logic is not the science of the laws of **thinking**; it is the philosophical logic of **origins**. Already as a student Heidegger stated that the task of original logic is to produce the fundamental concepts which articulate the incipient **ground** of all **reality** as well as its particular domains as the starting basis for further scientific research in those domains. He would later transform this doctrine of science into a **hermeneutics** of **facticity** and then into an **existential analysis** of **being-there**. His hermeneutically **ontological** logic operates at the interface of being and **language**. The correspondence or identity of being ('**physis**') and language ('**logos**') is expressed in the copula of **judgment**. In his **destruction** of the history of ontology Heidegger discovers that the **truth** of judgment presupposes the **unconcealment** ('**alètheia**') of **Being**. In the philosophical sayings of **Anaximander**, **Parmenides**, and **Heraclitus** the unconcealment of Being is named 'logos'. Why this **relation** between Being and 'logos' was forgotten in the **history of Being** is one of the main questions of Heidegger's later philosophy. 'Logos' became judgment, unconcealment became truth as the correspondence between the intellect and the object, and Being was reduced to the 'is' of the copula. Logic is, in other words, a **destiny** of Being.

LOGIC: THE QUESTION OF TRUTH (*Logik. Die Frage nach der Wahrheit*). This Winter Semester 1925/26 lecture course is a milestone on the way to *Being and Time*. It moves toward the interface where **language** is born. Heidegger wants to develop a philosophical **logic** that can discover **existentials** and their hermeneutically indicative sentences. In the first part of the course he rehearses his own prior steps toward such a logic. After a discussion of **Edmund Husserl**'s critique of **psychologism**, he criticizes the neo-Kantian **sense** of judicial **truth** as **validity**. To get to the **essence** of truth it is necessary to return to **Aristotle**'s prejudicative truth of 'nous' or simple apprehension. This truth of **intuition** binds Aristotle and Husserl together in a juxtaposition of Greek and German **thinking**.

Husserl's principle of all principles is intuition, that is, the giving and having of an **entity** in its bodily **presence**. Heidegger shows that underlying intuition there is a more fundamental **understanding** of that intuition which at once understands itself. The primary form of simple apprehension is a having of something as something in the ways we can use it. We discover **entities** first as pieces of **equipment**, which are given in their **in-order-to**. The 'as' of primary understanding is the original articulation of my **getting around** and dealings with the **world**. In this way we acquire the habits of our habitat that constitute our most immediate having. The 'as' of primary understanding makes it possible for us to explicate in **assertions** the **structure** of our **being**. The 'as' of primary understanding can thus become the hermeneutic 'as'. Assertion is a demonstrative letting see or uncovering. Heidegger can now distinguish between worldly assertions which let entities see in their being and categorial assertions or existentials which indicate the being of **being-there**.

After the Christmas break, Heidegger abandons the original outline of his course. Instead of Aristotle's question of truth he discusses **Immanuel Kant**'s doctrine of **schematism**. This **interpretation** of Kant would ultimately result in his later book, *Kant and the Problem of Metaphysics*. Heidegger shows that the original self-affection of the mind is **time**. Time gives itself unthematically as the constant precursory encounter that lets entities be. It lets entities be seen and makes our apprehension of entities possible. The **making present** of an entity as something is a comportment of being-there, for being-there is itself time. The present or **now** as making present is a basic **possibility** of the being of being-there, that is, **existence**. Here at the end of the course Heidegger introduces the **existential** vocabulary that would dominate *Being and Time*.

LOGOS. 'Logos' is one of the fundamental **words** of **Greek philoso-phy**. It names the process that gathers **entities** into **unconcealment** and thus lets them be. As the **structure** of the unconcealment of enti-ties, 'logos' is at the same time the **saying** of **Being**. When human **language** and **thinking** correspond to and commit themselves to this original saying, **truth** comes to pass. The **destiny** of 'logos' is the coming to pass of the history of **metaphysics** in which the original **meaning** of 'logos' is forgotten. 'Logos' is the **nearness** of Being. *See also* Logic; Logos (Heraclitus, Fragment B 50).

LOGOS (HERACLITUS, FRAGMENT B 50) (*Logos [Heraklit, Fragment 50]*). This careful reading of **Heraclitus'** Fragment B 50 is a formal study of '**logos**'. Heidegger tries to explain how 'logos' passed from the original **meaning** of gathering to mean **language**. We must understand 'logos' in terms of 'legein'. Heidegger claims that the original meaning of 'legein', which means to speak or to say, is to lay down or to lay before. 'Logos' is the original **saying** of **Being** that makes human language possible. In the gathering of 'logos' a perma-nence holds sway by reason of which what is gathered together is preserved and guarded as a **whole**. The genuine meaning of 'legein' is letting-lie-forth-as-a-collection. The lying forth is at the same time a coming into **unconcealment** and thus the **appropriation** of **truth**. The process of truth that comes to pass in 'legein' is the **coming to pres-ence** of **entities**. Through 'legein' **being-there** lets entities be.

'Logos' is the absolutely original cause out of which the gathering process proceeds. Heraclitus' formula "hen - panta" describes the way in which 'logos' functions. 'Logos' is the one ('hen') that unifies all entities ('panta') in themselves, insofar as it gathers them into them-selves and lets them lie forth in unconcealment themselves. In the way it gathers all entities into **being**, 'logos' is the **destiny** of Being. It lays the **ground** for entities and at the same time comes to pass as ground in and through the entities that it grounds. In 'logos' Being reveals itself as ground.

The place where the process of 'logos' takes place is the 'there' of being and is as such the **clearing** where being-there exists. The origi-nal gathering process of 'logos' as unconcealment makes possible the gathering process of human **thinking** as the process of truth. When our 'legein' corresponds with the 'legein' of the original 'logos', truth comes to pass. Truth is the letting be of 'logos' and thinking is the thinking of 'logos'.

LÖWITH, KARL (1897-1973).   The wounded war veteran Karl Löwith met Heidegger for the first time in 1919 when he became his student in **Freiburg**. He followed him later to **Marburg**, where he would become the first student to write a qualifying dissertation under Heidegger's supervision. They became close friends. When Löwith was forced to flee Germany in 1933, Heidegger wrote letters of recommendation. Heidegger's involvement with **National Socialism** led to a break in their friendship. After World War II Löwith became one of Heidegger's severest critics. He returned to Germany and accepted a chair of philosophy at the University of Heidelberg. The former friends would occasionally meet and try to be civil to each other.

- M -

MAKE PRESENT (*gegenwärtigen*).   In *Being and Time* the primary **ecstasis** for **fallenness** is making present. It has its **existential** meaning in the **present**. Yet as a **mode** of **temporality** making present also remains included in the **future** and the **having been**. When **being-there** makes an **entity** present, it can become absorbed in the **being** of entities and its own **getting around** them. Being-there thus forgets the **possibilities** of its own being and falls into the **readiness-to-hand** and the **presence-at-hand** with which it concerns itself. In **resoluteness** being-there can bring itself back from fallenness in the **moment** of vision, which is the ecstasis of **authentic** present as a way of temporalizing being-there's **existence**. *See also* Time.

MAKE ROOM (*einräumen*).   Making room is an **existential** of **being-in-the-world**. It lets **entities** within the **world** be encountered by giving them **space**. This making room for entities consists in freeing the entities whose **way of being** is **readiness-to-hand** for their **spatiality**. Space is in the world insofar as space has been disclosed by **being-there** in its making room.

MARBURG.   Heidegger taught as a professor of **philosophy** at the Philipps-Universität of Marburg from Winter Semester 1923/24 until Summer Semester 1928. The years in Marburg were among the most creative of his life. Here he conceived *Being and Time* and fell in love with **Hannah Arendt**. His friendship with **Rudolf Bultmann** led also to some intense collaboration and joint seminars.

MARTIN HEIDEGGER IN CONVERSATION (*Martin Heidegger im Gespräch*). This text is the transcript of Richard Wisser's interview with Heidegger on September 17, 1969. It was aired on television on September 24 as a tribute to Heidegger in honor of his 80th birthday. In the interview Heidegger denies that it is the task of **philosophy** to change society. Since the **essence** of **being-there** is its relation to **Being**, his meditations on the **forgetfulness of being** in **metaphysics** are also a rethinking of man's place in the **world**. As a part of this **ontological** meditation Heidegger tries to disclose the difference between philosophy and **science**. Science is a consequence of **technology**. The essence of technology is **enframing**. Since the triumph of technology implies the end of philosophy, his later work is an attempt to formulate the task of **thinking** after the completion of metaphysics.

MEANING (*Bedeutung*). Meaning for Heidegger is not something that one imposes on an object, and it is neither a distinctive object of **perception** nor an intermediary between the subject and the object. Heidegger thus rejects the traditional notion of meaning. What we understand is not the meaning of a **word** but the **entity** itself in its **being**. We grasp entities as entities in their webs of **relations** with other entities and not as aggregates of perceptual qualities. Meaning involves the holistic way in which something can become intelligible as something in a web of relations. Meaning is prior to **language** and **discourse**. Entities in their being say something to us silently. Since entities can only have meaning within certain interpretative contexts or **meaningfulness**, they require **being-there** as the **clearing** of being within which they can present themselves as they are.

MEANINGFULNESS (*Bedeutsamkeit*). In ***Being and Time*** meaningfulness makes up the **structure** of the **world** as that in which **beingthere** as such always already is. It is the relational totality of **meanings** in which **entities** present themselves. Being-there in its familiarity with meaningfulness is the **ontological** condition of possibility of discovering entities, which are encountered in a world with **involvement** as their kind of **being**. Meaningfulness makes it possible for entities to make themselves known as they are in themselves. It is an existential state of being-there and constitutes the **worldhood** of the world. On the basis of meaningfulness the world is disclosed as such. Meaningfulness thus makes it possible for being-there, as the entity that understands and interprets, to disclose meanings upon which the being of **words** and **language** is founded.

MEMORIAL ADDRESS (*Gelassenheit*). In this **memorial address** at the commemoration of the 175th anniversary of the birthday of the **Meßkirch** composer Conradin Kreutzer, Heidegger discusses the distress of modern times. **Being-there** has lost its foundation and roots. He distinguishes metaphysical thought and **reflection** as the explication of **sense**. Modern man is fleeing from reflection. The triumph of **technology** threatens the **essence** of **human being**, because it makes our **dwelling** impossible. The only solution is **acquiescence** as the necessary attitude of simultaneous acceptance and rejection of technology. In acquiescence we let things be as they are and open ourselves up to the **mystery** of **Being**. This attitude might enable us to escape the danger of homelessness that threatens us in the age of technology and **nihilism**. Acquiescence may enable us to grow roots in the **ground** of our home and make the **autochthony** of our dwelling possible.

MEßKIRCH. In this small town in central southern Germany, Heidegger was born and raised. The town is dominated by the Church of Saint Martin, the patron saint of the city, where Heidegger served as an altar boy. The other important building is the castle with its beautiful park where the **pathway** begins. On May 28, 1976, Heidegger was buried at the small cemetery of Meßkirch.

METAPHYSICAL FOUNDATIONS OF LOGIC, THE (*Metaphysische Anfangsgründe der Logik im Ausgang von Leibniz*). This Summer Semester 1928 lecture course, given under the title *Logic*, was the last Heidegger taught at the University of **Marburg**. During this course he delivered a memorial for **Max Scheler** on May 21, 1928. The course pursues the metaphysical foundations of **logic** in light of the **question of being**. It belongs to the transitional phase in Heidegger's thought from the **existential analysis** of **being-there** in *Being and Time* to the **overcoming** of **metaphysics** in his later thought.

In the introduction Heidegger describes traditional logic as the **science** of determining **thinking**, which expresses itself in **assertions**, and contrasts it with what he calls a philosophical logic. **Plato** and **Aristotle** transformed the latter into the former. Heidegger's course thus becomes an attempt to develop a philosophical logic through a **destruction** of traditional logic.

In the first main part, *Dismantling Leibniz's Doctrine of Judgment Down to Basic Metaphysical Problems*, Heidegger attempts to uncover the metaphysical foundations of logic through an **interpretation** of

Gottfried Wilhelm Leibniz's metaphysics with regard to the function metaphysics has as the **ground** for his logic. He focuses his attention on Leibniz's definition of **substance** as force and of the latter as representation. Leibniz thus anticipated both **Friedrich Nietzsche**'s **philosophy** of the **will to power** (force) and the modern philosophy of **worldviews** that regards the world as a **representation** of the subject.

The second main part, *The Metaphysics of the Principle of Reason as the Foundational Problem of Logic*, is both a confrontation with the philosophy of Scheler and an introduction to *Being and Time*. Heidegger converts **fundamental ontology** into a **metontology**, which is the result of the overturning of the **essence** of **ontology**. Metontology has for its proper theme the **being** of **entities** as a **whole** (*das Seiende im Ganzen*) and is also the domain of the metaphysics of **existence**. It is only possible on the basis and in the perspective of the radical **onto-logical** problematic. This problematic demands an interpretation of being-there on the basis of **temporality** and, from this interpretation, an elucidation of the intrinsic **possibility** of our **understanding of being**. Fundamental ontology is the whole of **founding** and developing ontology. The **existential analysis** of **being-there** and the analysis of the Temporality of Being make this founding possible. The temporal analysis of Being turns at the same time into metontology. In their unity, fundamental ontology and metontology constitute the complete concept of metaphysics.

The introduction to the problem of **time** leads to an extensive discussion of **transcendence** and **intentionality**. They are both attempts to think the subject-object-relation. In their last long conversation, Heidegger and Scheler agreed on four points: 1. The problem of the subject-object-relation needs to be raised completely afresh. 2. It is not a question of epistemology. 3. The problem has central import for the possibility of metaphysics. 4. The moment is here to develop metaphysics from the ground up.

Heidegger would later develop the detailed investigations of the concept of **world** in conjunction with the problem of ground into his treatise *On the Essence of Ground*.

METAPHYSICS (*Metaphysik*). Heidegger's relation to metaphysics is ambiguous. In his first major publication, ***Duns Scotus' Doctrine of Categories and Meaning***, he wrote that **philosophy** cannot for long do without its authentic optic, metaphysics. In his early lecture courses he attempts to develop an authentic metaphysics through a **destruction** of the history of **ontology**. *Being and Time* is more skeptical of a renewal of metaphysics, although it is an attempt to develop a **fundamental ontology**. A new metaphysics presupposes an explicit restating of the **question of being**. In his writings *Kant and the Problem of Metaphysics*, *On the Essence of Ground*, and *What Is Metaphysics?* Heidegger agrees with **Immanuel Kant** that everyone takes an interest in metaphysics. It belongs to our nature. Heidegger now calls fundamental ontology a metaphysics of **being-there**. After the **turning**, Heidegger rejects the term metaphysics for his own philosophy. In his *Introduction to Metaphysics* he uses the term in an ambiguous way. Metaphysics is the attempt to inquire about **entities** in general and as a whole, and yet it also conceals **Being** as such.

For Heidegger philosophy from **Plato** to **Friedrich Nietzsche** is in its **essence** metaphysics. The **guiding question** of metaphysics is what is **being**? Since we cannot answer the **question of being** directly, **Aristotle** reformulated this question as what is the being of entities? With this transformation Being itself was forgotten. The **forgetfulness of being** is a **destiny** of Being. Metaphysics is determined by its onto-theo-logical constitution. As ontology metaphysics names **beingness** as the fundamental quality, which makes an entity what it is and that it is. As **theology** metaphysics reduces the being of entities to **God** as the highest entity from which all the other entities receive their being. **Georg Wilhelm Friedrich Hegel**'s system is the completion of metaphysics and Nietzsche's reversal of **Platonism** its end. Our age is the age of **nihilism** and the triumph of **technology** and as such also the time of the complete abandonment of Being.

In his later work Heidegger tries to overcome metaphysics through a detailed reading of the pre-metaphysical thinkers **Anaximander**, **Parmenides**, and **Heraclitus**. He listens also to the announcement of a new **beginning** in **Friedrich Hölderlin**'s **poetry**. In a dialogue with the cultures of the Far East he tries to develop a nonmetaphysical **thinking** that does not talk about Being, but is a **saying** of Being.

METAPHYSICS AS HISTORY OF BEING (*Die Metaphysik als Geschichte des Seyns*).   This 1941 essay was published in the second volume of Heidegger's **interpretation** of **Friedrich Nietzsche**. It is the presentation of the decisive moments in the history of **metaphysics**, which begins with the distinction between 'essentia', what an **entity** is, and 'existentia', that an entity is. This distinction is an **appropriation** in the **history of Being**. Heidegger reduces the distinction between 'essentia' and 'existentia' to its Greek **origin**. He shows how the Aristotelian concept of 'energeia' became **reality** or the work of causes. He also explains the transformation of **truth** into certitude and of 'hupokeimenon' into subject.

The second part is an interpretation of the relation between reality and **subjectivity** in the **philosophy** of **Gottfried Wilhelm Leibniz**. For Leibniz every entity as an entity is either a subject or a monad. The monad is determined by **representation** in its double meaning of 'perceptio' and 'appetitus'. The 'perceptio' signifies any interior spontaneous expression or representation of the universe. The 'appetitus' is the tendency of the monad to pass from one perception to the other in quest of a more and more adequate perception of the universe. Both are types of presentation or proposing: 'perceptio' represents the universe; 'appetitus' proposes the perfection of **life** toward which the monad strives. In his 24 metaphysical theses Leibniz says that there is a reason in nature why something exists rather than **nothing**. This **ground** is **God** as the necessary entity, which causes the **being** of all other entities.

In the third part Heidegger explains the difference between subjectivity and **subjectity**. Since **René Descartes** grounded the **being** of **entities** in the self-certain subject, every entity has become either an object or a subject as that which objectifies. Heidegger calls this subject reference of all being subjectity, which constitutes both the **objectivity** of objects and the subjectivity of subjects.

The fourth and final part contains the 24 metaphysical theses of Leibniz, which Heidegger considers to be the highlight of his metaphysics.

METONTOLOGY (*Metontologie*).   In his Summer Semester 1928 lecture course, *The Metaphysical Foundations of Logic*, Heidegger converts **fundamental ontology** into a metontology, which is the result of the overturning of the **essence** of **ontology**. Metontology has for its proper theme the **being** of **entities** as a **whole** (*das Seiende im Ganzen*) and is also the domain of the **metaphysics** of **existence**. It is only possible on the basis and in the perspective of the radical **ontological** problematic. This problematic demands an **interpretation** of **being-there** on the basis of **temporality** and, from this interpretation, an elucidation of the intrinsic **possibility** of our **understanding of being**. Fundamental ontology is the whole of **founding** and developing ontology. This founding is made possible by the **existential analysis** of being-there and the analysis of the **Temporality** of **Being**. The temporal analysis of Being turns at the same time into metontology. In their unity, fundamental ontology and metontology constitute the complete concept of metaphysics. Heidegger would later reject this interpretation of the positive **possibilities** of metaphysics.

MINDFULNESS (*Besinnung*). *see* REFLECTION

MINENESS (*Jemeinigkeit*). Heidegger's meditations in his early lecture courses in **Freiburg** on phronetic insight ('phronèsis') into the particular ultimate of what is to be done here and now, and the place of the particular in **ontology**, form the background of the introduction of **being-there** in Summer Semester 1923. As a technical term, it indicates the particular **while** (*Weile*) that each of us is and has. The term is displaced by mineness in *Being and Time*. The **being** of being-there is in each case mine. This is the reason why being-there can never be taken **ontologically** as an instance of some genus of **entities** as **things** that are present-at-hand. Because being-there has in each case mineness, we must always use a personal pronoun when we address it, I am, you are, in the entities we are. Entities, whose being is in each case mine, comport themselves towards their own being. For being-there its being is an issue. Being-there is in each case mine to be. We choose whom we want to be or not to be. Mineness thus is the condition of **possibility** of **authenticity** and **inauthenticity**.

The mineness of being-there expresses itself also in the **existentials** 'being-towards-death' and 'having-a-conscience'. Insofar as **death** is, it is in each case mine. The mineness of death implies that no one can take the other's dying away from him or her. **Conscience** is also, in its basis and its **essence**, in each case mine. The **call of conscience** is an appeal to our most unique **can-be** that comes from that entity which in each case I myself am.

MODE (*Modus*). **Entities** can actualize their different **ways of being** in different modes. **Authenticity** and **inauthenticity** are, for example, the two modes of **being-there**'s **existence**.

MOIRA (PARMENIDES VIII, 34-41) (*Moira [Parmenides VIII, 34-41]*). This essay belongs to Heidegger's lecture course *What Is Called Thinking?* of Winter Semester 1951/52 and Summer Semester 1952, but was not read at the time. It is a careful **reflection** on the relation between **thinking** and **being** by way of an **interpretation** of selected fragments from the famous poem of **Parmenides**. According to fragment III thinking and being are the same. The task of thinking is to take under its **care** the being of **entities** ('noein') and to let it lie forth ('legein') in **unconcealment** ('**alètheia**'). Thinking must accept being as the unifying ('hen') element ('logos') in the coming forth ('physis') of entities. The mysterious **word** 'to auto', the same, is the process of 'alètheia' which constitutes the **history of Being**. It allows both being and thinking to arise. This imparting ('moira') of the belonging together of being and thinking in their ambivalence is the **destiny** of **Being** itself. In the unconcealment of the ambivalence of thinking and being, Being itself remained concealed and unthought.

MOMENT (*Augenblick*). Heidegger underlined already in 1917 the importance of the moment in his reading of Friedrich Schleiermacher. In his early lecture courses on **Aristotle** he uses the term as a translation of '**kairos**'. Phronetic insight is regarded as the way in which the full moment is held in troth. In *Being and Time* the moment becomes the **ecstasis** of that **present** which is held in authentic **temporality** and which thus is authentic itself. Heidegger now underscores the visual sense of *Augenblick* as moment of *insight*. This shift is probably due to his reading of **Sören Kierkegaard**. The moment of vision means the resolute rapture with which **being-there** is carried away to whatever **possibilities** are encountered in its **situation**. In the moment of vision being-there is held in **resoluteness**. The moment of vision also discloses the primordial **limit situation** of **being-towards-death**.

MOOD (*Stimmung*). To **being-there** belongs the **thrownness** of its **existence**. It always finds itself in a certain **disposedness** that makes it possible for being-there to find itself in a certain mood or **attunement**. By mood Heidegger means the **sense** of how we find ourselves to be. Moods belong to the **ontic** constitution of being-there. In *Being and Time* moods first disclose being-there in its thrownness in the manner of an evasive turning away. They not only disclose the 'there' of being-there, but also close it off. A mood assails us and arises out of our **being-in-the-world**. Every mood discloses our being-in-the-world as a **whole** and makes it possible to direct ourselves towards something.

In his later work the term fundamental mood displaces disposedness. In the postscript to the famous lecture, *What Is Metaphysics?*, **anxiety** is the fundamental mood determined by the **nothing**. In his Winter Semester 1929/30 lecture course, *The Fundamental Concepts of Metaphysics*, Heidegger describes deep **boredom** as the fundamental mood of his time. In the *Contributions to Philosophy* he prefers the term attunement as a **formal indication** of fundamental moods, because it captures the fact that **Being** tunes our **being**. Here he distinguishes between the attunement of the Greek **beginning** of **philoso-phy**, astonishment, and the attunement of the new beginning, re-servedness.

MORTALS, THE (*die Sterblichen*).   In his later **philosophy** Heidegger calls **human beings** the mortals because they can die. Only humans die, and they die continuously as long as they dwell on **earth**, under the **sky**, before the **divinities**. Earth and sky, divinities and mortals, are joined together in the oneness of the **fourfold**.

MOVEMENT (*Bewegung*).   In the **beginning** of **Greek philosophy** **Being** was named '**physis**' or self-emergence and thus **revealment**. The central **phenomenon** of 'physis' is 'kinèsis' or movement. This is the reason why the **ontology** of **Aristotle** became physics or an inves-tigation into the **being** of movement and its causes. The **destruction** of physics is a topic to which Heidegger would return time and again in his lecture courses. The dynamic character of Aristotle's **philosophy** is preserved in Heidegger's own **thinking**, which is always under way.

Aristotle's definition of **time**, as that which is counted in the move-ment which we encounter within the **horizon** of the earlier and the later, determined our understanding of time as a stream of **nows**. In *Being and Time* Heidegger attempted to rethink time in the light of the **temporality** of **being-there**.

MY WAY TO PHENOMENOLOGY (*Mein Weg in die Phänomenolo-gie*).   This autobiographical essay written in 1963 as a contribution to the Festschrift for Max Niemeyer in honor of his 80th birthday de-scribes Heidegger's way into **phenomenology**. **Franz Brentano**'s dissertation, **Carl Braig**'s treatise on **being**, and **Edmund Husserl**'s *Logical Investigations* were very important for his philosophical de-velopment. He also refers to the writings of **Emil Lask**. From 1919 on he learned much from Husserl as his assistant. His rethinking of **Aris-totle** would lead to his lifelong topic of the **question of being**. The first edition of *Being and Time* was published by Max Niemeyer, who in 1953 also published the *Introduction to Metaphysics*.

MYSTERY (*Geheimnis*).   Why **Being** reveals itself to us in the **being** of **entities** and yet at the same time withholds itself as such in **con-cealment** is a mystery for Heidegger. In his **memorial address** he calls the comportment which enables us to keep open to the **sense** hidden in **technology**, as a **destiny** of Being, the **openness** to the mystery. This openness and releasement (*Gelassenheit*) toward **things** belong together. They grant us the **possibility** of **dwelling** in a **world** without being imperiled by technology. The **gift** of our **understanding of being** is the mystery of Being.

MYSTICISM (*Mystik*). The importance of mysticism for the development of Heidegger's thought becomes evident in his early book ***Duns Scotus' Doctrine of Categories and Meaning***. In this work he tries to show that the same perennial problems are operative in medieval and modern **philosophy**. The inner **existence** of the medieval **lifeworld** is anchored in the transcendent primal **relation** of the soul to **God**. This is why scholasticism and mysticism in **essence** belong together for the medieval **worldview**. Heidegger's interest in mysticism was strengthened by his religious crisis of 1914-1919 that ends with his break with the system of Catholicism.

In his early lecture courses in **Freiburg** the mystic **experience** is a paradigm for the **phenomenology** of **factual life experience**, because it is determined by **affliction**. Mystic experiences can never be described theoretically without **unliving** the experience. The **phenomenon** of mysticism is determined by the **actualization sense** and thus shows that **human beings** are **entities** for which their **being** is an issue. We care about our being.

Heidegger often uses mystic metaphors and concepts in his later philosophy. The best known example is his use of the term *Gelassenheit* (**acquiescence**) that he borrowed from Meister Eckhart. This mystic vocabulary does not imply that his later thought is in its essence a form of mysticism.

- N -

NATIONAL SOCIALISM (*Nationalsozialismus*). Heidegger's involvement with National Socialism is motivated by political and philosophical deliberations. The untenable situation of the Weimar Republic and the bankruptcy of the old university system in the early 1930s demanded a solution. Like many Germans Heidegger saw in the rise of National Socialism the unique **possibility** of a new **beginning**. His concept of the **history of Being** enabled him to interpret the National Socialist revolution as a first and necessary step toward the overcoming of **technology** and **nihilism**. In his view humanity could be saved from the technological nihilism of both capitalism and communism only if **human beings** would be granted another encounter with **Being** that was as powerful as the beginning granted to the Greeks. Only a **people** that resolutely submitted themselves to the greatness of their **fate** could make such an encounter possible. The most extreme **need** of their fate could bring the German people to turn away from nihilism and achieve the **authenticity** and **autochthony** of their **being-there.** Heidegger mistakenly took the political revolution of the Nazis for the beginning of the spiritual mission of the German people. This is the reason why he supported National Socialism and became the rector of the University of **Freiburg** in 1933. After his resignation in 1934 he began to criticize Nazism for its betrayal of the inner **truth** and greatness of the national (German) socialist movement. However, he would never unambiguously renounce his own authentic version of National Socialism and he also **kept silent** almost completely about the Holocaust. *See also* Rectorate; Rectorate 1933/34: Facts and Thoughts; Self-assertion of the German University, The.

NATORP, Paul (1854-1924). Natorp is one of the main influences on Heidegger's early life and thought. He was Hermann Cohen's successor as the main representative of the **Marburg** school of **neo-Kantianism.** Contrary to most of his contemporaries, he was well aware of the importance of **metaphysics** for **philosophy** and of **Edmund Husserl's phenomenology.** He wrote one of the first reviews of Husserl's *Ideas.* Natorp was also an important scholar of ancient philosophy. Heidegger studied many of his writings carefully. The **destruction** of Natorp's general theory of psychology is a recurring theme in his early lecture courses in **Freiburg.** Heidegger's ideas on the development of the German spirit out of the **theology** of Meister Eckhart and Martin Luther into German idealism were very similar to Natorp's. In 1923 Natorp was responsible for Heidegger's appointment as a professor of philosophy at the University of Marburg. They were kindred spirits who could **keep silent** on their many walks through Marburg.

NATURE (*Natur*). Heidegger's **philosophy** of nature is based upon his reading of **Greek philosophy.** Natural **entities** ('physei on') have the tendency to reveal themselves in **unconcealment.** They thus become accessible and intelligible even if their accessibility and intelligibility are shot through with **untruth** and finitude. As **Aristotle** has shown in his *Nicomachean Ethics* VI, there are different ways in which we can **understand** the **being** of entities. In *Being and Time* Heidegger makes clear that the first and most basic way in which we disclose entities is instrumental. We understand the being of entities as **readiness-to-hand** and the entities themselves as **equipment**. When we objectify entities and thus separate them from both their relations to our comportment and their **involvement** with a **whole**, natural **science** becomes possible. This objectifying procedure reduces the being of entities to **presence-at-hand** and conceals the essential fullness of nature.

After the **turning** Heidegger develops his conception of the **history of Being**. He now realizes that modern **technology** is not the final result of **metaphysics** but the condition of its **possibility**. The Greek **understanding of being** was already technological in its **essence**.

Heidegger's later philosophy is an attempt to preserve nature as a whole of **meaning** that lets entities become manifest in their being. With his conception of the **fourfold** he attempts to revive a cosmological understanding of nature and return entities to their natural **locations**. His poetic view of nature was influenced strongly by **Friedrich Hölderlin** and early Greek **thinking**.

NATURE OF LANGUAGE, THE (*Das Wesen der Sprache*). In these three lectures on the **essence** of **language** in the 'studium generale' at the University of **Freiburg** of Winter Semester 1957/58, Heidegger brings us face-to-face with an **experience** of language. To undergo such an experience means to let ourselves be properly concerned by the **claim** of language. We must enter into and submit to language. This experience with language is something other than gathering information about language as a tool of communication. In an experience with language, language itself brings itself to language. In everyday language it holds itself back and so enables us to speak a language.

To undergo an experience with language Heidegger gives an **interpretation** of Stefan George's poem *Words*. In this poem we experience the **word** as that which gives **things** their **being**. Because the being of **entities** dwells in the word, language is the **house of Being**. The topic of the lectures, the essence of language, refers to the speaking of this essence itself. This implies a turn through which it becomes possible to hold on to that which is spoken in the poetic experience of language.

The essence of language is a way that moves everything. This **movement** of language is the **saying** of the **fourfold** that takes place in the stillness of the **play of time-space**. Saying means the lightning-concealing-releasing offer of **world**. As the being of language, saying swings back into the **presence** of **nearness**. Saying moves the regions of the world's **fourfold** into their nearness. This soundless gathering call is the ringing of stillness, that is, the language of the essence.

NEARNESS (*Nähe*). The correlation between nearness and **farness** allows Heidegger a wordplay of which he never tires in his later work. **Being** is near to **being-there**, because it is that by which **entities** that are near are. In this respect Being is the **origin** of all nearness and is thus nearer to being-there than any entity could ever be. For being-there Being is far, simply because it is not an entity and can never be conceptualized by being-there. Being conceals itself behind the entities to which it gives **presence** in the **clearing**.

NEED (*Not*). Heidegger speaks of need in two different ways. In *On the Essence of Truth* he explains that **being-there** must submit to a double influence: the oppression of **errancy** and the domination of the **mystery**. From this results a tension in being-there in the form of a need that arises out of the constraint imposed upon it by errancy and mystery. The full **essence** of **truth**, which includes within itself the **untruth** of errancy and of mystery, retains being-there in need. Being-there needs to think the **truth of Being**.

In his SS 1935 lecture course *Introduction to Metaphysics* Heidegger says that **Being** itself needs being-there as the 'there' of its **being**. The 'there' as the sphere of **openness** is the necessity of Being. The need of Being is that it needs being-there in order to be.

NEGATIVITY (*Nichtigkeit*). *see* NULLITY

NEO-KANTIANISM (*Neukantianismus*). Neo-Kantianism is one of Germany's most important philosophical movements of the late 19th and early 20th centuries. Wilhelm Windelband, **Heinrich Rickert** and **Emil Lask** were the main representatives of the Southwest German school. They tried to supplement **Immanuel Kant**'s theory of knowledge with a **value-philosophy** and a methodology for the humanities. They divided **reality** into two different realms: the theoretical realm of the facts of natural **science** and the practical realm of **values**, which were studied in the humanities.

Hermann Cohen, **Paul Natorp** and **Ernst Cassirer** belonged to the rival School of **Marburg**. This school used Kant's theory of knowledge to explain the **possibility** of science and thus reduced his philosophy to an epistemology.

NIETZSCHE, FRIEDRICH (1844-1900). Heidegger started reading Nietzsche as a student around 1910. His great confrontation with the philosopher with the hammer took place in the 1930s. Nietzsche became the pivotal figure in the **history of Being**. He was the first to discover that **entities** count for **nothing** in **metaphysics**. He also disclosed that the **being** of entities is grounded in the **will to power** while being itself is **presence** as the **eternal recurrence of the same**. Since **Georg Wilhelm Friedrich Hegel**'s system is the completion of metaphysics as **Platonism** and Nietzsche turned Hegel upside down, his philosophy is the final **truth** of the first **possibility** of metaphysics. Nietzsche's attempts to overcome metaphysics in his revaluation of all **values** resulted in the final consummation of **nihilism**. His **philosophy** is thus both the final completion of the history of metaphysics and the beginning of the dominance of **technology**. *See also* Eternal Recurrence of the Same, The; Eternal Recurrence of the Same and the Will to Power, The; Nietzsche's Metaphysics; Nihilism as Determined by the History of Metaphysics; Value-philosophy; Who Is Nietzsche's Zarathustra?; Will to Power as Art, The; Will to Power as Knowledge, The; Word of Nietzsche: God Is Dead, The.

NIETZSCHE'S METAPHYSICS (*Nietzsches Metaphysik*). This text, written in 1940, was originally announced as a lecture course for Winter Semester 1941/42. Heidegger replaced it at the last moment with the course on **Friedrich Hölderlin**'s hymn *Remembrance*. The starting point of his **interpretation** is that **Friedrich Nietzsche**'s **philosophy** is a unified **metaphysics**, since he thinks **entities** as a **whole** in their **truth**. His attempt to clarify the hidden unity of Nietzsche's thought is grounded in the fundamental **experience** of *Being and Time* that the **truth of Being** as **Being** has remained unthought in the history of philosophy. It is a discussion of the five fundamental expressions of Nietzsche's metaphysics: **will to power, nihilism, the eternal recurrence of the same**, the overman, and justice.

The **being** of entities is grounded in the will to power. Nihilism is the awareness of the emptiness of **values** and of the fact that the being of entities counts for **nothing**. The eternal recurrence of the same names the **presence** of Being. The overman thinks the **essence** of **human being** as the reversal of **subjectivity**. Justice is the supreme representative of **life** itself.

The essay closes with a series of questions concerning the **ground** and **origin** of metaphysics. Behind these questions lies Heidegger's conviction that Nietzsche's philosophy is the consummation of metaphysics as its final truth.

NIHILATION (*das Nichten*).   Since **Being** is not an **entity, being-there** can only grasp it as that, which is not a thing. The **nothing** is the nihilating element in Being itself that makes the **presence** of entities and being-there possible. This nihilation is the **abyss** of the **ontological difference**.

NIHILISM (*Nihilismus*).   For Heidegger nihilism and **metaphysics** are one. Nihilism is the fundamental hidden **movement** within the history of metaphysics. Metaphysics is nihilistic in a double sense: 1. **Friedrich Nietzsche** discovered that in metaphysics, **entities** count for **nothing** and are therefore unable to ground the **sense of being**. 2. What remained hidden for Nietzsche is that in metaphysics, **Being** itself withdraws itself. Metaphysics is the **forgetfulness of being**.

Nietzsche's **philosophy** as an attempt to overcome nihilism is in reality the final completion of metaphysics as nihilism. After Nietzsche nihilism became the normal condition of **being-there**'s **existence** and reaches its final consummation in the dominance of **technology**.

To overcome nihilism we must attempt to turn into its **essence**. This **turning** is the first step on our way to leaving nihilism behind. We must learn to deny the **will** and listen to the **address of Being**. *See also* Nihilism as Determined by the History of Metaphysics.

NIHILISM AS DETERMINED BY THE HISTORY OF METAPHYSICS (*Die seinsgeschichtliche Bestimmung des Nihilismus*).   This essay, written between 1944 and 1946, begins with the question whether **nihilism** as such is overcome in **Friedrich Nietzsche**'s **metaphysics**. Nietzsche insists that the **being of entities** is the **will to power** in the **mode** of the **eternal recurrence of the same**. Since he leaves no room for the **nothing**, it seems that nihilism is overcome. And yet, he misses the **essence** of nihilism, that is, the history in which there is nothing to **Being** itself. He insists Being is a **value**, but if Being is a value, there is nothing to it. In this sense his **philosophy** is the completion of the metaphysics.

The essence of metaphysics is onto-theo-logical and therefore we could call Nietzsche's thought negative **onto-theo-logy**. He neglects to think **unconcealment** as the **truth of Being**. The **relation** of Being to **being-there** becomes the crucial problem for Heidegger. The **forgetfulness of being** is the **gift** of Being itself. The full essence of nihilism is itself something essentially differentiated. To overcome nihilism, thinking must encounter the **mystery** of Being. In this encounter it can experience the withdrawal of Being. In the **need** and danger of the present age, we can only prepare for a new **beginning**.

NOTHING (*Nichts*). In *Being and Time* the nothing is experienced in the fundamental **mood** of **anxiety**. The nothing is that in the face of which we are anxious. In his inaugural lecture *What Is Metaphysics?* Heidegger develops a **phenomenology** of the nothing. In anxiety we experience the slipping away of all **entities** into nothingness. The nothing itself negates the **being** of entities and thus frees **being-there** from its **fallenness**. Since being-there always already exists in the nothing, entities as such can become manifest in their being. In the being of entities the **nihilation** of the nothing happens. In his later philosophy Heidegger describes the nothing as the nihilation in **Being** itself that makes the **presence** of entities and being-there possible. It is the **abyss** of the **ontological difference** that makes the **clearing** as the **essence** of the **truth of Being** possible.

NOTHINGNESS (*Nichts*). *see* NOTHING

NOW, THE (*das Jetzt*). In our ordinary understanding of **time** as a pure sequence of nows without beginning and without end, the ecstatical character of primordial **temporality** has been leveled off. The now belongs to time as **innertimeness**. It is that in which something arises, passes away or is present-at-hand. Every now is now no longer or is now not yet.

NULLITY (*Nichtigkeit*). In **anxiety** the nullity is unveiled, by which **being-there** is determined in its **ground** as finite **being**. **Death** is the nullity that comes towards being-there as its most unique and utmost **possibility**, that is, the possible impossibility of its **existence**. *See also* Nothing.

- O -

OBJECTIVITY (*Objektivität*). **Being-there** determines the **being** of **entities** within its **world** as **readiness-to-hand**. Each entity is a piece of **equipment** within the whole of its **involvement**. As ready-to-hand the being of an entity is determined by its **relation** to being-there. Being-there has the **possibility** to step back from the entities within its world and thematize them as they are objectively in themselves. It frees the entities it encounters within the **world** in such a way that it can throw them over against itself and objectify them. Entities thus become the objects of the **representations** of subjects. Theoretical knowledge objectifies entities and reduces the being of being-there to **subjectivity**. The objectivity of the object is grounded in the subjectivity of being-there, since it is a **projection** of being-there and therefore presupposes its **transcendence**. In the age of **technology** and **nihilism** the objectivity of objects is finally reduced to **standing-reserve**.

OBLIVION (*Vergessenheit*). *see* FORGOTTENNESS

ON ODEBRECHT'S AND CASSIRER'S CRITIQUE OF THE KANTBOOK (*Zu Odebrechts und Cassirers Kritik des Kantbuches*). Heidegger's handwritten notes on the reviews of the Kantbook by Rudolf Odebrecht and **Ernst Cassirer** center on their **interpretation** of the basic question of **Immanuel Kant**'s **philosophy** about the **essence** and grounding of the finitude of human knowledge.

ON THE ESSENCE AND CONCEPT OF PHYSIS. ARISTOTLE, PHYSICS B, 1 (*Vom Wesen und Begriff der Physis. Aristoteles, Physik B, 1*). In this essay, written in 1939 and published in 1960, Heidegger claims that **Aristotle**'s *Physics* is the hidden and therefore never adequately studied foundational book of **philosophy**. Aristotle uses the **word 'physis'** in two fundamental **meanings**. It designates the **being** ('**ousia**') of **entities** as a **whole**, and the being of entities which have in themselves the source of their **movement**. Aristotle's *Physics* is the transition between original Greek **thinking** and **metaphysics**.

In *Physics* B we learn that 'physis' is the principle, 'archè', of movement. The goal of this movement is the 'telos' of the entity. Movement ceases when an entity reaches its end and for this reason repose is the culmination of movement. When entities reach their end, they present themselves in **unconcealment**. 'Physis' as the principle of movement determines the being, 'ousia', of entities.

Aristotle explains the movement of entities as the interplay between form, 'morphè', and matter, 'hulè'. Form poses an entity in its appearance, 'eidos', as it is. This process always involves a privation, 'sterèsis', since the coming to **presence** of an entity (like a fruit) is at the same time the disappearance of what it was before (the blossom).

Form is the **essence** of 'physis' as principle and principle is the essence of 'physis' as form.

'Physis' is the name **Heraclitus** gave to the unconcealment, ('**alètheia**'), of **Being**. Entities **come to presence** out of **concealment**. In Aristotle's conception of 'physis' the negativity inherent in **truth** disappears. Truth is no longer unconcealment, but resides now in the **assertion** and consists in the correspondence of the intellect and its object. *See also* Greek philosophy.

ON THE ESSENCE OF GROUND (*Vom Wesen des Grundes*). In his 1929 essay, written for the Festschrift in honor of **Edmund Husserl's** 70th birthday, Heidegger thinks the **ontological difference** as the **nothing** between **entities** and **Being**. He begins by showing that the problem of the **ground** is essentially one of **truth**. The principle of the ground, that is, every entity has a ground, is grounded in the truth of **judgments**. This truth is in turn grounded in the **ontological** truth as the manifestation of entities in their **being**. **Ontic** truth is grounded in ontological truth as the unveiling of the being of entities. Ontic and ontological truth presuppose the ontological difference. This difference can only be understood by an entity that discloses the being of entities and thus transcends entities to their being. Ontological difference is thus grounded in the **transcendence** of **being-there**. Being-there transcends entities towards the **world**. The transcendence of being-there is its **being-in-the-world**.

Transcendence is the **essence** of the ground as the **coming to presence** of ground. This unified process of grounding consists of three elements: 1. Grounding as laying-claim (*Stiften*), that is, being-there's **projection** of the 'for-the-sake-of-which' as world. 2. Grounding as taking-ground (*Boden-nehmen*). Being-there transcends entities towards their Being, but this is only possible when being-there is among entities. As **disposedness** being-there is attuned by the entities in its world. Being-there can only transcend entities among which it exists in its world, and by which it is also attuned. To transcendence belongs the taking-ground in the being of entities. 3. Grounding as **founding**. Freedom as transcendence is freedom in relation to the ground or founding. Founding makes it possible for being-there to encounter entities by making them manifest in and as themselves. The essence of the ground is the triplex strewing of the grounding process that arises in transcendence as the projection of the world, the taking-ground among the being of entities, and the ontological founding of entities.

ON THE ESSENCE OF HUMAN FREEDOM. INTRODUCTION TO PHILOSOPHY (*Vom Wesen der menschlichen Freiheit. Einleitung in die Philosophie*). This Summer Semester 1930 lecture course on the **essence** of human **freedom** is an introduction to **philosophy** that still belongs to the period of *Being and Time*.

In the first part Heidegger shows how the question about the essence of human freedom is of central importance to the **guiding question** of **metaphysics**: what is the **being** of **entities**? Metaphysics asks about the being of entities as a **whole**. Since we are also a part of this whole, the guiding question concerns us as entities. Metaphysics understands the being of entities as constant **presence**. Presence refers to the **present** and **presentness**. This means metaphysics understands being in the light of **time**. The guiding question is thus transformed into the question what is the **ground** of being *and* time. What is the essence of time and how can we understand time as the ground of being? This is the **basic question** of philosophy. To answer this question we must ask about the essence of **human being**. How do time and **being-there** belong together? The **understanding of being** is the ground of the essence of human being and presupposes human freedom. The guiding question of metaphysics is grounded in the question about the essence of freedom.

In the second part Heidegger discusses the problem of human freedom by way of a concrete **interpretation** of **Immanuel Kant**'s **understanding** of **transcendental** and practical freedom. He shows that in Kant's view freedom and causality belong together. Freedom is the **possibility** to start a causal series. The problem of freedom does not belong to practical philosophy as a special discipline. It is an **ontological** problem, since causality is grounded in freedom and not the other way around.

The final part takes up the problem of practical freedom within an ontological dimension. Heidegger shows that freedom is the condition of possibility of the manifestation of the being of entities. Our understanding of being is grounded in freedom.

ON THE ESSENCE OF TRUTH (*Vom Wesen der Wahrheit*). This essay published in 1943 contains the text of a lecture conceived in 1930 and delivered on different occasions under the same title. The function of the lecture is to analyze the **essence** of **truth**. Since the original meaning of truth is **unconcealment**, 'alètheia', Heidegger has to bring to light not only the essence of truth but also its nonessence (*Unwesen*).

In the first half of the essay Heidegger discusses truth. The traditional definition of truth is the correspondence of the intellect and its object, 'adequatio intellectus et rei'. The measure of truth lies in the correctness of the accordance of an **assertion**, 'logos', with an object. But what makes this accordance possible? Before we are able to make an assertion about an **entity**, we must have discovered its **being**. We can only encounter entities in the **open**, that is, the 'there' of **being-there**. Through its **existence** being-there stands out in the open. The **openness** of being-there's comportment makes the **presence** of entities possible.

Heidegger calls being-there's openness toward the open and the being of entities **freedom**. The essence of truth is grounded in being-there's freedom. Freedom is the essence of truth as the **revealment** of entities through which an openness essentially unfolds. The **possibility** of freedom is grounded in the existence of being-there. The openness of the open is grounded in being-there. The essence of freedom is letting entities be.

What is the essence of **untruth**? The revealment of an entity as such is at the same time the **concealment** of entities as a whole. Because concealment is the nonessence of truth, it also conceals itself. The concealment of being as a whole in the unconcealment of entities is a **mystery** that being-there has forgotten. This is the **forgetfulness of being**. Since being-there has forgotten the mystery, it wanders in **errancy** among entities of which the genuine **sense** lies in **forgottenness**. Freedom is the essence of truth and consists in the letting be of entities. Being-there is subjected to the domination of the mystery and the oppression of errancy. From this double subjection springs the **need** of being-there. Being-there needs to let entities be. When being-there takes this up in its original essence, its **resoluteness** toward the mystery is under way into errancy as such. Now the intertwining of the essence of truth and the truth of essence reveals itself. The glimpse into the mystery is a questioning that thinks the **question of being**.

ON THE HISTORY OF THE PHILOSOPHICAL CHAIR SINCE 1866 (*Zur Geschichte des philosophischen Lehrstuhles seit 1866*). This short text was published in the Festschrift *Die Philipps-Universität zu Marburg 1527-1927* in 1927. In it Heidegger presents the origin, development, effect, and reconstitution of the **neo-Kantianism** of the **Marburg** school. Heidegger gives a brief outline of the work of its main representatives: Hermann Cohen, **Paul Natorp**, Nicolai Hartmann, and **Ernst Cassirer**.

ON THE QUESTION OF BEING (*Zur Seinsfrage*). This 1955 essay presents the unaltered, slightly expanded text of Heidegger's contribution, *Concerning the Line*, to a Festschrift in honor of **Ernst Jünger**. In this text he discusses all the main themes of his late **philosophy**. The alteration of the title is meant to indicate that the discussion of the **essence** of **nihilism** stems from an explication of **Being** as such. What is Being? This is not the metaphysical question about the **being** of **entities**, but a regressive **step back** into the **ground** of **metaphysics**.

In the essay Heidegger comments on a text by Jünger, *Across the Line*. This line is the empty **nothing** where nihilism reigns. Jünger wants to push the **movement** of nihilism beyond this critical point and thus make "a new turning of Being" possible. Heidegger's essay, on the other hand, concerns only the line and does not attempt to cross it. Heidegger criticizes Jünger for moving too quickly. We first must find the **location** of this line. From this location the provenance of the essence of nihilism and its consummation emerge.

With the consummation of nihilism begins the final phase of nihilism, that is, the reign of **enframing**. If we want to reflect on the essence of nihilism, we must first lay out a path that leads to a discussion of the essence of Being. On this path alone can the question concerning the nothing be discussed. In order to be able to follow this path we must relinquish the **language** of metaphysics. If a turning belongs to being as Jünger thinks, than Being itself must become the **turning**. But then we must cross out ~~being~~ in order to distinguish it from the being with which metaphysics concerns itself. This crossing out is the location where the four regions of the **fourfold** are being gathered. In the phase of the consummation of nihilism, Being as such remains absent and thus conceals itself. The **forgetfulness of being** shelters its unrevealed essence. **Unconcealment**, 'alètheia', resides in the **concealment** of presencing. The task of **commemorative thinking** is to attend to this concealment and thoughtfully recollect what is granted by **appropriation**.

ONTIC (*ontisch*). An ontic **interpretation** is concerned with an **entity** as an entity. It does not ask the question about the **being** of an entity and the **structure** of its being. A botanical classification of plants is, for example, an ontic interpretation. When we try to determine the way of being of plants in its difference to the **way of being** of animals, we give an **ontological** interpretation of the being of plants and not of plants as such. *See also* Ontology.

ONTOLOGICAL (*ontologisch*). An ontological **interpretation** is concerned with the **being of entities**. It does not ask the **ontic** question about the entity as such. *See also* Ontology.

ONTOLOGICAL DIFFERENCE (*ontologische Differenz*). The ontological difference is the difference between **Being** as such and the **being of entities**. Being is not an entity. The ontological difference not only separates Being and entities, but also unites them. This process is what Heidegger calls **appropriation**. In their difference Being and entities as a **whole** belong together.

ONTOLOGY (*Ontologie*). Ontology is the **science** of the **being of entities**. It inquires into the being of entities in general and tries to ground the being of entities as a **whole** in the being of a highest entity. This double line of questioning determines the **onto-theo-logical constitution of metaphysics**.

ONTOLOGY: THE HERMENEUTICS OF FACTICITY (*Ontologie. Hermeneutik der Faktizität*). This Summer Semester 1923 lecture course is an important step on the way to *Being and Time*. As the title indicates, Heidegger develops his **ontology** as a **hermeneutics of facticity**. Facticity is the **being** of our own **being-there**. Here Heidegger uses being-there for the first time as a **formal indication** of the central **phenomenon** of **phenomenology**. It indicates the **particular whileness** which each of us is and has. After a historical overview of the history of hermeneutics, Heidegger interprets hermeneutics not as a **science** of **interpretation**, but as explicating communication. Its goal is the self-**understanding** of being-there. Since interpretation is an outstanding **possibility** of the being of factual **life** itself, hermeneutics is an essential possibility of facticity. In order to keep the term being-there **ontologically** neutral we must deconstruct the traditional concepts of **human being** such as rational animal and person. **Existence** is being-there's most unique and most intense possibility. It is being-there's ability to hold itself awake and be alert to itself in its ultimate possibility. After a discussion of the contemporary state of **philosophy**, Heidegger comes to his phenomenological analysis of being-there.

The being of being-there is determined as being in a **world**. In order to characterize the everyday world and to develop the formal indication of being-there as **being-in-the-world**, Heidegger formulates the trio of questions, which we also find in *Being and Time*: 1. What does a world mean? 2. What does in a world imply? 3. How does being in a world appear? Only the first question is worked out in any detail in the course. We encounter world in three different ways as **environment**, **with-world**, and **self-world**. Environment is a meaningful context that discloses the being of **entities** as **equipment**. Our everyday **openness** towards entities is made possible by the fundamental phenomenon of **care**. Because in the **everydayness** of our lives we are first and foremost concerned with entities, the potential **authenticity** of our being-there is at the same time concealed. Heidegger calls this potential authenticity **discovery**. In *Being and Time* the **meaning** of **disclosedness** and discovery will be reversed.

ONTO-THEO-LOGICAL CONSTITUTION OF METAPHYSICS, THE (*Die onto-theo-logische Verfassung der Metaphysik*). This 1957 lecture concludes the Winter Semester 1956/57 seminar on **Georg Wilhelm Fried-rich Hegel**'s *Science of Logic*. Its topic is the relation between **Being** and **thinking**. For Heidegger, Hegel's **logic** is a treatise on thinking. For Hegel thinking means absolute thinking that thinks itself. Since the matter of thinking is historical, every philosopher has his own place within the history of **philosophy**. This means we must also consider Hegel's own place in the history of philosophy. For Hegel the matter of thinking is the concept, for Heidegger the difference as **ontological difference**. Where Hegel tries to sublate all that has been thought before, Heidegger attempts to step back into the domain of that which has remained unthought.

Hegel's philosophy belongs to **metaphysics**. In the *Science of Logic* the onto-theo-logical **structure** of metaphysics comes to light as foundational thought. Hegel is concerned with the **founding** of **entities**, that is, **ontology**. In this founding he determines **being** as the **ground** of entities as a **whole**, that is, **theology**. Because metaphysics is essentially **onto-theo-logy**, it cannot think the difference between Being and the being of entities. This difference is sublated in the concept of **God** as 'causa sui' in whom the being of all entities is grounded. When we take a regressive **step back** to take a closer look at this identity, the ontological difference finally reveals itself as that which is worthy of thought.

ONTO-THEO-LOGY (*Onto-theo-logie*).   Since **metaphysics** represents **entities** as entities, it is itself the **truth** of entities in their universality and in the highest entity. It is **ontology**, the **science** of the **being** of entities in general, and **theology**, the science of the highest entity in which the being of all other entities is grounded. This onto-theo-logical

structure of metaphysics is the **essence** of **philosophy**. Philosophy is onto-theo-logy and thus the reason why **Being** as such remained forgotten in the history of metaphysics.

OPEN, THE (*das Offene*). The open is a **formal indication** of **being-there** as the 'there' of **Being**. It opens up the open **space** within which being-there can encounter **entities**. *See also* Clearing; Instance; Truth of Being, the.

OPENNESS (*Offenständigkeit*). Openness is a comportment of **being-there** through which it stands out in the **open**. It is grounded in being-there's **existence**. This openness of its **instance** makes it possible for being-there to encounter entities.

ORIGIN (*Ursprung*). The origin is the source from which something springs. It makes it possible for an **entity** to rise up ('**physis**') as what it is and how it is. **Art** is for instance the origin of the work of art and the source of its **essence**.

ORIGIN OF THE WORK OF ART, THE (*Der Ursprung des Kunst-werkes*). This essay contains the text of a lecture Heidegger delivered on different occasions in 1935 and 1936. The aim of the lecture is to arrive at the immediate and full **reality** of the work of art in order to discover the **essence** of **art** within it.

In the first part, *Thing and Work*, Heidegger works out the essential difference between a **thing** and a work of art. What is a thing? The concepts with which **philosophy** tries to understand things as things derive their **meaning** from the **being** of **equipment**. Equipment resembles the work of art insofar as it is the product of human work. When we compare van Gogh's painting that depicts a pair of shoes with the shoes themselves, their difference becomes clear. Reliability determines the being of the shoes as equipment. The shoes are there when we need them and we can rely on them to perform their function. When we wear our shoes, we understand what they are. Van Gogh's painting reveals the **beingness** of shoes. It lets us know what shoes in **truth** are. The work of art opens up the being of **entities**. This opening up is the **revealment** of the **truth of Being** and happens in the work of art. In the work of art truth sets itself to work. So Heidegger comes to the next question: what is truth as the setting-itself-to-work?

In the second part, *The Work and the Truth*, Heidegger first discusses the work-being of the work. A work, like a Greek temple, works in the sense that it sets up a **world** and at the same time sets this world back again on **earth**, which itself thus emerges as native ground. This setting up of a world is making **space** for the worlding of world, that is, the liberation of the **open** and the establishment of its **structure**. The work of art lets the earth be an earth and thus makes the **autochthony** of the **dwelling** of **human beings** possible. We can now ask what truth is. Truth is the essence of the true, that is, the **unconcealment** of entities. Truth happens as the primal conflict between revealing (world) and concealing (earth). Art and truth are joined since beauty is one of the ways in which truth occurs as unconcealment. But how does truth happen in the work of art?

Heidegger tries to answer this question in the third part, *Truth and Art*. The happening of truth is the struggle of the conflict between world and earth. Truth happens only by establishing itself in this struggle and clearing the open. It sets itself into work and establishes itself in the work of art as the struggle of earth and world. All art as the letting happen of the advent of the truth of what is, is, as such, essentially **poetry**. Poetry is the **saying** of world and earth, the saying of the arena of their struggle, and thus the place of all **nearness** and **farness** of the **gods**. The essence of poetry is the grounding of truth and may be considered from three points of view as a **gift**, a **founding**, and a **beginning**.

OUSIA.   In ordinary Greek 'ousia' means possessions, household goods, real estate (*Anwesen*). In Heidegger's **interpretation of Greek philosophy**, 'ousia' names the **beingness of entities** as constant **presence** (*Anwesenheit*). Entities are when they are present in **unconcealment**, '**alètheia**'. According to Heidegger the Greek **understanding of being** is oriented toward only one dimension of **time**, the **present**, after the model of entities present at hand.

OVERCOMING (*Überwindung*).   Overcoming is the **formal indication** of what the early Heidegger used to refer to as **destruction**. Since **metaphysics** by reason of its onto-theo-logical **structure** cannot meditate **Being** as **appropriation**, we must pass beyond it into another kind of **thinking**, that is, **commemorative thinking**. This overcoming of metaphysics is a **step back** into the **ground** from which it sprang.

OVERCOMING METAPHYSICS (*Überwindung der Metaphysik*). This essay contains a collection of notes that date from 1936 to 1946. Part of it was published as a contribution to a Festschrift in honor of

Emil Preetorius in 1951. In these notes Heidegger reflects on the **possibility** of the **overcoming** of **metaphysics**. The completion of metaphysics is the decline of the **truth of Being** and the **beginning** of the reign of **technology** and **nihilism**. **Friedrich Nietzsche** understands in his **philosophy** not only the **being** of **entities** as the **will** to will, but he thinks the belonging together of **Being** and **human beings**. His thought is the transition between metaphysics and the new beginning in the **history of Being**. The task of **thinking** is to treasure the **mystery** of Being. In this sense human beings are the **shepherds of Being** and can attempt to stop the desecration of the **earth**.

- P -

PARMENIDES (540-480 BC). Parmenides, **Anaximander**, and **Heraclitus** are the original thinkers in Heidegger's **history of Being**. They speak to us from the earliest **beginning** of **philosophy**. This beginning is not only the **origin** of the **forgetfulness of being**; it also contains the **possibility** of another beginning of thought as **commemorative thinking**. Heidegger tries to understand the pre-metaphysical thought of the early Greek thinkers from a post-metaphysical standpoint. The **saying** of Parmenides that **Being** and apprehending are the same has become the **fate** of Western philosophy. Parmenides has named 'alètheia' as the **unconcealment** of Being. In the **revealment** of the **being** of **entities**, Being as such withdraws itself into **concealment**. In the poem of Parmenides the being of entities is disclosed as constant **presence**. *See also* Moira (Parmenides VIII, 34-41); Parmenides; Principle of Identity, The; What Is Called Thinking?

PARMENIDES (*Parmenides*). This Winter Semester 1942/43 lecture course was originally announced under the title *Parmenides and Heraclitus*. It contains a long meditation on 'alètheia' by way of an **interpretation** of the famous poem of Parmenides.

Heidegger approaches 'alètheia' from four different directions. 'Alètheia' means **unconcealment**. We can read unconcealment as un-*concealment* and as *un*-concealment.

1. When we read un-*concealment*, 'alètheia' names the **appropriation** of **concealment**.

2. When we read *un*-concealment, it becomes clear that the Greeks discovered in the **essence** of **truth** the negation of concealment.

3. The third indication is the relation between 'alètheia' and 'lèthè', **forgottenness**. Since truth has to be wrested from unconcealment, it

always risks falling back into forgottenness. Parmenides named the unconcealment of **Being** and yet this simple **truth** would soon be forgotten.

4. The fourth indication names the relation between unconcealment and **clearing**. 'Alètheia' clears the **open** and within this free **region**, **entities** can **come to presence** in the way they look, 'eidos'. When we free ourselves from the **presence** of entities, we may spring into the **abyss** and commemorate Being as such. We can then become aware of the **ontological difference**.

The saying of Parmenides says the **beginning** of the still-concealed essence of the **truth of Being**. It names the belonging together of **human beings** and 'alètheia'.

PARTICULAR WHILENESS (*Jeweiligkeit*). In his Summer Semester 1923 lecture course, **Ontology: The Hermeneutics of Facticity**, Heidegger introduces particular whileness as a **formal indication** of the 'there' of **being-there**. It indicates the particular **while** which each of us is and has. The 'there' of being-there is a brief space of **time** in which we have to decide what is to be done now and here in our **life**. Heidegger developed his **interpretation** of particular whileness in the light of his study of the Aristotelian conception of 'tóde ti' (this-here) and 'phronèsis' (phronetic insight). In **Being and Time** particular whileness is displaced by **mineness**.

PAST (*Vergangenheit*). The past is one of the dimensions of **time** as we understand it first and foremost in our everyday life. An **entity** is past when it is no longer present at hand. **Being-there** is never past, but always a **having been**. In correspondence with the past as the dimension of past times are having been and **forgottenness** as two **ecstases** of **temporality**.

PATHWAY, THE (*Der Feldweg*). In this short essay written in 1949 as a contribution to a Festschrift for Conradin Kreutzer, Heidegger describes the pathway which he often followed from the gate at the court garden in **Meßkirch** to the oak wood and back again. It is both an autobiographical essay and a **reflection** on the **claim** of his **origin**.

PATTERN OF ARRANGEMENT (*Fuge*). The pattern of arrangement is the harmonic and dynamic **structure** which not only binds all **entities** together in their **being**, but also assigns to each entity its proper place within the whole of **Being**. In the pattern of arrangement, **time** manifests itself as the allocated **while** of each entity's being. Heidegger developed this conception originally in his **interpretation** of the fragments of **Anaximander** and **Heraclitus**. It is also a **formal indication** of **appropriation** as the gathering process of the **unconcealment** of Being. **Earth** and **sky**, the **divinities** and the **mortals**, are also joined in the pattern of arrangement of the **fourfold**.

PEOPLE (*Volk*). The **essence** of a people is determined by its **language**. Each people lives in its own **house of Being** and discloses **Being** in its own, historically unique way. Since the essence of language is **poetry**, the poets found the **being** of a people. Each people has its own **fate**, which is destined by Being. During his involvement with **National Socialism** from 1933 until 1934, Heidegger thought the *Führer* as the political leader of the German people could decide their fate. Hitler could reassemble the German people in the essence and **autochthony** of their **being-there** and the National Socialist revolution could force them to achieve the **authenticity** of their **existence**.

In the **history of Being** the Greeks are the people of the first **beginning** of **philosophy**. The Germans are the people of the other beginning of **commemorative thinking**. The great poets Homer, Aeschylus, Euripides, and Sophocles founded the essence of the Greek people. It is remarkable that the great poets of the German people, like **Friedrich Hölderlin** and **Rainer Maria Rilke**, have not founded their essence, but only foretold the still future **possibility** of their essence. This implies that the Holocaust did not taint the essence of the German people.

PERCEPTION (*Wahrnehmung*). Heidegger rejects the primacy of perception of **Edmund Husserl**'s **phenomenology**. When we exemplify phenomenological **intuition** through sense perception, we objectify and thus **unlive** the **lived experiences** of **intentionality**. Heidegger suggests that the first level of phenomenological intuition is in the sheer **understanding** of the meaningful contexts in which the totality of **life** expresses itself. In *Being and Time* he proclaims that intuition, perception, and seeing as ways of access to **entities** and their **being** are derivatives of **existential understanding**.

PETRI, ELFRIDE. *see* HEIDEGGER-PETRI, ELFRIDE

PHENOMENOLOGICAL INTERPRETATION OF KANT'S 'CRITIQUE OF PURE REASON' (*Phänomenologische Interpretation von Kants 'Kritik der reinen Vernunft'*). This Winter Semester 1927/28 lecture course focuses on the transcendental aesthetic and the first book of the transcendental analytic. It is a more precise and detailed section-by-section **interpretation** of **Immanuel Kant**'s text than the book *Kant and the Problem of Metaphysics*. Heidegger explains to the last detail the significance of each concept in terms of its content and also considers other parallel passages in Kant's work.

In the introduction, *The 'Critique of Pure Reason' as Laying the Foundation for Metaphysics as Science*, Heidegger determines the relation between positive **science, ontology**, and **fundamental ontology**. Each science has for its object a specific realm of **being**. These objectifications of **entities** are made possible by **being-there**'s pre-ontological **understanding of being**. Heidegger exemplifies the formation of objectification by the genesis of the modern mathematical sciences. Such an objectification, as for example **nature**, needs to be established by ontology as an objectification of an entity in its being. The problem of the *Critique of Pure Reason* is the problem of laying the foundation of **metaphysics** as a science of supersensible entities in close connection with the question concerning the condition of **possibility** of entities in general. All founding **ontological** knowledge is a knowledge, which is independent of **experience** and is pure. Kant's central question is, how are synthetic **judgments** a priori possible? Laying the foundation of metaphysics as science is for Kant not only the laying of a foundation of ontology; it is at the same time a critique of pure reason as a limiting of its possible knowledge a priori.

The greater part of the lecture course is a phenomenological interpretation of the *Critique of Pure Reason*. Heidegger would not get to an explicit interpretation of the **schematism** of the concepts of pure reason. He only dealt with it in principle. He shows that synthetic knowledge a priori is possible on the basis of the original synthetic unity of the productive power of imagination, which in turn is made possible by **temporality**. Temporality is the basic **structure** of being-there. Its **existential** constitution enables being-there to have a pure understanding of being and of the determinations of being. The possibility of being-there to comport itself simultaneously toward other entities and toward other being-there is grounded in its temporality.

PHENOMENOLOGICAL INTERPRETATIONS TO ARISTOTLE: INTRODUCTION TO PHENOMENOLOGICAL RESEARCH (*Phänomenologische Interpretationen zu Aristoteles. Einführung in die phänomenologische Forschung*). This Winter Semester 1921/22 lecture course is an introduction to the **interpretation** of **Aristotle**, which

Heidegger will develop in the next semester. This phenomenological interpretation was also the title of a book on which Heidegger worked from 1922 through 1924. The lecture course is basically a **destruction** of his earlier work and leads to a new explication of **life**.

The brief first part on the reception of Aristotle remarks on the **need** for a fundamental clarification of philosophizing to its history on the level of factual life itself, on the then-fashionable reception of Aristotle as a naive epistemologist, and on the problem of the 'Greekification' of **Christianity**.

In the second part, *What Is Philosophy?*, Heidegger defines **philosophy** as a phenomenological **ontology** and develops the intrinsically historical character of **ontological** research. Ultimately there is no difference between the ontological and the historical. Philosophizing takes place within a **hermeneutic situation** that determines the way in which we have philosophy. Since philosophy is not a thing but a fundamental having of the **situation** of our lives, it demands **resolution**. We can have philosophy in a genuine way. This kind of having involves an addressing *of* the object and is always grounded in a prior **claim** of already being had. Philosophy is a way of comportment or **intentionality**. The triple sense of intentionality, **content sense, actualization sense**, and **relational sense**, is refined, and a fourth sense is added, the **temporalizing sense**, which comprehends the other three. Temporalization determines the temporalizing sense. We can have philosophy in the full-fledged sense that concerns my own **existence** or as an object of **curiosity**. The **authenticity** of philosophy is in the full stretch of the actualization sense itself, pursuant to the temporalizing sense of always being under way. Philosophizing as a fundamental knowing is nothing other than the radical actualization of the **historicality** of life's **facticity**.

The third part is an ontological revision of Heidegger's **categories** of life and centers upon demonstrating the inherently historical character of the facticity of life. The primary ontological category of life is **care**, which is indigenous to life itself. Heidegger begins to rethink his analysis of the **environment** in terms of using and making rather than seeing. Ruination, or **fallenness** as it will be called later, is the dominant tendency of life.

PHENOMENOLOGICAL INTERPRETATIONS WITH RESPECT TO ARISTOTLE: INDICATION OF THE HERMENEUTIC SITUATION (*Phänomenologische Interpretationen zu Aristoteles: Anzeige der hermeneutischen Situation*). Heidegger wrote this famous text as a private communication to **Paul Natorp** in connection with his possible appointment as professor at the University of **Marburg**. In it he founds and develops the **hermeneutic situation** in which **Aristotle**'s texts are to be interpreted.

The first part is a kind of research report summarizing his work of the previous three years. Heidegger also breaks new ground and finds a solution to the problem of fusing the historical with the systematic approach in **phenomenology**. He outlines the double-pronged program of a **fundamental ontology** and a **destruction** of the history of **ontology**. The averageness of the public 'they' and **fallenness** are juxtaposed with the **possibility** of a more original seizure of my own **death** in order to define an **ontological** way of access to the **temporality** and **historicality** of human **being-there**. Heidegger designates **existence** as the counter-movement against falling. Here existence has the **meaning** of **life**'s most unique and authentic **possibility**.

In the second part Heidegger discusses the problem of an original **retrieval** of **Greek philosophy** rooted in '**alètheia**', '**logos**', and '**physis**'. He also gives an **interpretation** of *Nicomachean Ethics VI* that centers on the different ways in which the soul trues (*wahrnimmt*). '**Phronèsis**' is the interpretative insight into a concrete **situation** of action coupled with resolute decision and **truth** as counter-movement to **concealment**.

PHENOMENOLOGY (*Phänomenologie*). According to Heidegger phenomenology is not a philosophical movement, but an outstanding **possibility** of **thinking**. During his early study of **Edmund Husserl**'s *Logical Investigations* and their later collaboration in **Freiburg**, he learned the essentials of this method. We can distinguish three phases in his relation to phenomenology.

In the first phase of his early lecture courses from 1919 until the publication of *Being and Time*, Heidegger brings phenomenology and **hermeneutics** together in hermeneutic phenomenology. Since the primal **phenomena** are not readily accessible to **intuition** in a spontaneous self-showing but are concealed, they are in need of the labor of **destruction**. Heidegger therefore replaces Husserl's empiric **structure** of **intentionality** as intuitive fulfillment of empty signification with the more basic structural process of explication of implicit **meaning**. **Care**, **interpretation**, and **understanding** replace **intentionality**, **intuition**, and signifying intending as the fundamental concepts of phenomenology. The central phenomenon of Heidegger's hermeneutic phenomenology of **facticity** is **life**, which in its **being** is concerned with this very being. Life is rooted in **care** and always implicitly interprets itself in **concern, solicitude,** and **affliction.** Since life in its facticity finds itself always in a historical **situation,** the interpretation of the **temporality** of care as the **essence** of life itself becomes the fundamental task of phenomenology.

In the second phase from ***Being and Time*** until the **turning,** phenomenology is the method of **fundamental ontology.** The **question of being** is worked out in a twofold way: the **existential analysis** of **being-there** and a destruction of the history of **ontology.** The task of phenomenology is to let the being of **entities** as that which shows itself be seen from itself in the very way it shows itself from itself. Since the being of entities shows itself in being-there's **understanding of being,** this understanding must be interpreted in an **existential analysis** of being-there. The understanding of being is the temporal-historical circular **movement** of being to being. This movement is the source that gives meaning to being-there's **existence.** Phenomenology takes its departure from the hermeneutics of being-there, which, as an analysis of existence, has made fast the guiding line for all philosophical inquiry at the point where it arises and to which it returns.

The third phase begins with the turning. In his later work Heidegger no longer uses the **word** phenomenology to describe his own thinking. He attempts now to move through phenomenology and **philosophy** to thinking, which still bears a certain resemblance to phenomenology.

PHENOMENOLOGY AND THEOLOGY (*Phänomenologie und Theologie*). Heidegger delivered this lecture on two occasions in 1927 and 1928. **Philosophy,** as the 'ontological' **science** of universal **being** itself, differs absolutely from **theology,** which is the **ontic** science of **God** as a particular **entity.** Theology is a positive science because it deals with a posited entity, which makes it more like chemistry than philosophy. The 'positum' of Christian theology is Christianness (*Christlichkeit*), that is, the factual **mode** of existing of a believing Christian. Christian **existence** is determined by the history that is set in motion by the cross, the crucified, and Christ on the cross. The task of theology is to seek the **Word** that is able to make us believe and to safeguard us in our **faith.** This means that theologians must learn to listen again to the Word of God through a **destruction** of Christian theology. They must attempt to bring the **existential** rebirth that comes by faith to conceptual form. Theology is the science of existing in faith, that is, of existing historically as a Christian.

Theology is founded on faith, which does not need philosophy, but theology as the science of faith does. What it means to be a Christian can only be lived and experienced in faith. The cross and sin as **existentiell** determinations of the ontological **structure** of **guilt** can be conceptualized with the help of philosophy. Sin depends on guilt. Theology can thus receive the direction of its inquiry from **ontology**.

The lecture is also Heidegger's farewell to theology as a matter of personal concern. He now calls faith the existentiell enemy of philosophy. To each other they appear to be mere foolishness. *See also* Christianity.

PHENOMENON (*Phänomen*). Heidegger's hermeneutical transformation of **Edmund Husserl's** **phenomenology** frees it from its one-sided orientation towards **perception** and theoretical knowledge and leads to an **ontological** reinterpretation of the phenomenon. The phenomenon belongs no longer to consciousness. For Heidegger, it is a manifestation of **Being**. We must distinguish between the phenomenon as that which shows itself and the appearance as that which does not appear itself, but announces itself through the appearance of something else. The phenomenon is a distinctive way in which something can be encountered. And yet, a phenomenon can also be concealed. There are three ways in which phenomena can be covered up: 1. A phenomenon can simply be undiscovered. 2. A phenomenon can be buried over after it has been discovered. 3. A phenomenon can be disguised as something else and appear as that which it is not.

It is therefore one of the main tasks of phenomenology to reveal phenomena and bring their **being** and **structures** to light. Since Being always shows itself in the being of **entities**, it conceals itself as such. The **unconcealment** of Being is the forgotten phenomenon at the heart of phenomenology that Heidegger discovered in his **thinking**.

PHILOSOPHY (*Philosophie*). In *Being and Time* Heidegger defines philosophy as universal phenomenological **ontology**. **Phenomenology** is the method of ontology. Because **being-there** is the **horizon** and foundation of ontology, phenomenology becomes **hermeneutics**. Heidegger follows **Edmund Husserl's** motto "back to the matters themselves" and understands phenomenology as an outstanding **possibility** of **thinking**. His hermeneutic phenomenology is an attempt to think the **essence** of phenomenology in a more originary way, so as to fit it back into the place that is properly its own within philosophy.

In his conception of the **history of Being** Heidegger identifies philosophy and **metaphysics**. The **onto-theo-logical constitution of metaphysics** is the **origin** of the **forgetfulness of being**. The history of philosophy begins with **Plato** and **Aristotle**'s metaphysical transformation of the first **beginning** of Greek thinking and is completed in **Friedrich Nietzsche**'s metaphysics of the **will**. The end of philosophy is the reign of **technology** and **nihilism**. Since this end has exhausted all the **possibilities** of metaphysics, the possibility of another beginning reveals itself. In his later thought Heidegger rejects philosophy in favor of another kind of thinking, which tries to commemorate the **address of Being**.

PHYSIS. 'Physis' is the Greek **word** for **nature** and has the same double **meaning**. The nature of an **entity** is its **essence**, while nature can also refer to the **being** of entities as a **whole**, which shows itself from itself. The essence of 'physis' is **movement**, 'kinèsis'. We find both these meanings of 'physis' in the *Physics* of **Aristotle**.

Prior to the Aristotelian use of the word 'physis', **Heraclitus** named **Being** 'physis', as that which loves to conceal itself. **Parmenides** identified 'physis' and '**alètheia**'. 'Physis' names the process of the **unconcealment** of Being. This original meaning of 'physis' would be forgotten in the history of **metaphysics**.

PIETY (*Frömmigkeit*). In his lecture *The Question Concerning Technology* Heidegger calls questioning the piety of **thinking**. As he explains in *The Nature of Language*, piety is meant here in its ancient sense: obedient and submissive to what thinking is called to think. Questioning is in its **essence** not the asking of questions but a listening to the **address of Being**. When thinking submits itself to the address of Being, its questioning becomes piety. Thinking itself then becomes **commemorative thinking**.

PLATO (428-348 BC). The history of **philosophy** begins with Plato as the pivotal figure who transforms the early Greek **thinking** of **Being** into **metaphysics**. He conceives Being no longer as '**physis**' but as idea, 'eidos', that is, the form in which **entities** show themselves. His new **understanding of being** leads also to a transformation in the process of '**alètheia**'. The early Greek thinkers understood 'alètheia' as the **unconcealment** of Being. Plato transforms 'alètheia' into **truth**, that is, the correctness of the correspondence between idea and entity. For Plato philosophy is no longer a **saying** of Being; it has become the determination of the **beingness** of entities as idea and the **founding** of the **being** of entities in the idea of the good as highest entity. *See also* Greek philosophy; Plato: The Sophist; Platonism; Plato's Doctrine of Truth.

PLATO: THE SOPHIST (*Platon: Sophistes*). In this Winter Semester 1924/25 lecture course, originally delivered under the title *Interpretation of Platonic Dialogues (Sophist, Philebus)*, Heidegger discusses the fundamental problem of **concealment**. Why did the Greeks name falsity, 'pseudos', positively and **truth** privatively, **'alètheia'**, as if something were lacking in a **phenomenon** which nevertheless rightfully belongs to it? According to the Greeks, **human beings** from the **beginning** had to struggle for and win the **unconcealment** of the **world**. In the struggle between the Greek philosophers and the Sophists, it becomes clear that **philosophy** not only has to overcome the concealment of **entities** in order to get to the matter itself. Philosophy must also do battle with the concealing **idle talk** of everyday life that is repeated by the Sophists. Heidegger will give an **interpretation** of the *Sophist*, because **Plato** discusses in this dialogue the difference between **being** and non-being, truth, and appearance and the philosopher and the Sophist. The hermeneutic principle of his interpretation is the old principle of always proceeding from the clear to the obscure. Heidegger presumes that **Aristotle** understood his teacher better than Plato understood himself.

In the introductory part of the course Heidegger gives a thoroughgoing exegesis of *Nicomachean Ethics 6*. His intent is to make clear what the Greeks meant when they raised the **question of being**. In Aristotle's treatise the five **movements** in which human beings disclose **entities** are investigated: 'technè', 'epistèmè', 'phronèsis', 'sophia', and 'nous'. 'Technè' is skilled know-how. 'Epistème' is **science**. 'Phronèsis' is circumspective insight into one's own **situation** of action. 'Sophia' is wisdom or the pure beholding of the eternal and highest entity. 'Nous' is a pure beholding without **'logos'**. Of the estimative faculties 'phronèsis' is the highest, of the scientific faculties 'sophia'. The praxis of **being-there** is the principle and goal of 'phronèsis'. In a remarkable passage Heidegger claims that Aristotle has come upon the phenomenon of **conscience**. 'Phronèsis' is nothing but the conscience already set in motion in order to make action transparent. 'Sophia' is the best habit, because its object is eternal.

The main part of the course is a meticulous exegesis of Plato's *Sophist*. Here Heidegger comes to the question he will repeat in the opening lines of *Being and Time*: "Since we found ourselves at an impasse from what you say, you will have to explain to us what you mean when you use the **word** 'being'." The question, what does the word being mean?, is the central concern of the entire dialogue. The battle of the Titans over 'ousia' historically fought by the early Greek thinkers for the middle ground between matter and idea, the one and the many, being and becoming, is the **origin** of **ontological** research. Plato followed the inclination to transcend the **ontic** toward the ontological. He discovered the difference between being and entities. The milieu for ontological research must be prepared by the concrete elaboration of the very placing of the question of being. This consists of an analysis into: 1. What is asked for, that is, the **sense of being**; 2. What is asked about, that is, **Being**; and 3. What is interrogated, that is, the entity whose **structure** is to guide us toward what is asked for. What entity is truly adequate to the sense of being? From this perspective the Greeks themselves left the question of the sense of being unasked. For them it was self-evident that Being means **presence**. Heidegger will show in *Being and Time* that the question of the sense of being can be answered only through an interpretation of the being of being-there. *See also* Greek philosophy; Plato's Doctrine of Truth.

PLATONISM (*Platonismus*) In Heidegger's **history of Being, philosophy** from **Plato** until **Friedrich Nietzsche** and **metaphysics** is one. As Whitehead once said: "The history of philosophy is a collection of notes in the margin of Plato." For Heidegger, philosophy is metaphysics and in its **coming to presence**, Platonism. Since it is also determined by the **forgetfulness of being**, the history of Platonism is at the same time nihilistic. In Platonism **Being** counts for **nothing**. Its long tale is therefore in its **essence** the history of **nihilism**. *See also* Greek philosophy.

PLATO'S DOCTRINE OF TRUTH (*Platons Lehre von der Wahrheit*). This 1940 essay was published in 1942 and is based upon the Winter Semester 1930/31 lecture course on the **essence** of **truth**. It is an **interpretation** of **Plato**'s famous metaphor of the cave in which Heidegger shows how Plato transformed the early Greek **understanding** of **Being** as 'physis' and of 'alètheia' as **unconcealment** into a doctrine of ideas and **truth** as correctness. The **beingness** of an **entity** is its idea, 'eidos', that is, the way in which it shows itself and **comes to presence**. The privileged relation between apprehending, 'noein', and idea in Plato's **philosophy** is at the **origin** of the explication of 'logos' as reason. Since the essence of an entity is its idea as constant **presence**, 'alètheia' becomes the correctness of the correspondence between **thinking** and its object. This correctness is expressed in **assertions** and thus **judgment** becomes the primary place of truth. *See also* Greek philosophy.

PLAY OF TIME-SPACE (*Zeitspielraum*). **Time** simultaneously times the **having been**, the **present**, and the **future**. Time in its timing removes us into its threefold simultaneity, while holding open for us the **openness** of **space**. Space spaces and thus throws open **locations**. This **movement** of space and time is the play of stillness that Heidegger calls the play of time-space. Timing and spacing are the same play that moves the **fourfold**. Their interplay is the never-ending process of generating the fourfold's **nearness**.

POETICALLY MAN DWELLS (*dichterisch wohnet der Mensch*). In this lecture delivered on October 6, 1951, Heidegger dialogues with **Friedrich Hölderlin**. It is a meditation on the **relation** between **thinking** and **language** and completes the earlier lecture *Building Dwelling Thinking* in which thinking received only incidental treatment. Since **poetry** is the **essence** of language, poetizing and thinking belong together.

Dwelling designates the fundamental **structure** of **being-there** as it sojourns in **nearness** to **entities**. As Hölderlin says in the poem that Heidegger interprets, man dwells between heaven and **earth**. This **between** is a dimension that admits of measure. Since man dwells in this dimension, it is his task to do the measuring. Only insofar as man measures out his **dwelling** can he be in accordance with his essence. But what is this measuring process?

The fundamental sense of measure lies in taking a measure. The measure is an appearance of **Being** itself. In Hölderlin's poem, Being appears in the guise of an unknown **god**. The **mystery** of Being is the process of **unconcealment**. The **ontological difference** and the ensuing **forgetfulness of being** together conceal the measure of man's dwelling. Man can only take this measure by letting it come to him in **acquiescence**. Man measures out the dimension between earth and heaven wherein he dwells. Thinking lets man dwell in nearness to entities. This kind of dwelling is authentic **building**. Since the taking of the measure of man's dwelling takes place in language as a response to the **address of Being**, Heidegger calls this measure-taking poetizing.

POETRY (*Dichtung*). Since all **art** is the setting-into-work of **truth**, it is in its **essence** poetry. Poetry is the **saying** of the **unconcealment** of **entities** and the illumination of the self-revealing **concealment** of **Being**. The light of this illumination joins its shining to and into the work of art. Beauty is the way in which truth shines as unconcealment.

The voice of poetry bids all that is - **world** and **things, earth** and **sky, divinities** and **mortals** - to gather into the simplicity (*Einfalt*) of their intimate belonging together. Poetry is thus the 'founding and giving' or institution (*Stiftung*) of the unconcealment of Being and so the **origin** of the **history** of a **people**. **Friedrich Hölderlin** is the poet of the poet because he poetizes the essence of poetry in his work.

Language spoken purely is also poetry and lets the world be as the **location** for the **building, dwelling,** and **thinking** of **human beings.**

POSSIBILITY (*Möglichkeit*). Heidegger's whole path of **thinking** is one continuing attempt to disclose **being** as possibility. The being of **entities** is never fixed. Entities are not dead and motionless objects. Their being is always a having the possibility to change and develop. Even **equipment** has the possibilities of its different uses. **Being-there** is its own **can-be** and has the fundamental possibilities or **modes** of the **authenticity** and **inauthenticity** of its own **existence**. **Being** itself as Being is **appropriation** and has the possibility to emit a new **beginning** in the **history of Being.**

POTENTIALITY-FOR-BEING. *see* CAN-BE

PRECONCEPTION (*Vorgriff*). *see* FORE-CONCEPTION

PREPOSSESSION (*Vorhabe*). *see* FORE-HAVING

PRESENCE (*Anwesenheit*). The Greeks disclosed the **sense of being** as presence. The **being** of an **entity** is its being **present** in **unconcealment, 'alètheia'.** Entities can only be encountered by **being-there** if they **come to presence** in unconcealment. In presence in the sense of being present, the relation between **Being** *and* **Time** comes to light. It shows also that the Greeks understood being from only one dimension of time. The highest entity is the entity that is constantly present. In the being of the highest entity, the being of all other entities is founded.

An entity can be present only if there is an open space or **clearing** in which it can present itself. The presence of entities presupposes the **absence** of Being as such. The interplay of the presence of entities and the absence of Being is what Heidegger calls **appropriation**. The **truth of Being** is the unconcealment of entities. In their presence entities can reveal themselves as something they are not but only appear to be. The essence of truth is the interplay of **concealment** and **revealment**.

PRESENCE-AT-HAND (*Vorhandenheit*).   Presence-at-hand is the kind of **being** that is discovered when we encounter **entities** within in the **world** purely in the way they look. This theoretical stance disregards the referential totality of practical and personal concerns that make up the everyday world. This disregard leads to an objectification of entities as that which stands against a subject. When entities are present at hand, they appear as objects for a knowing subject. Of objects we can have objective knowledge, that is, a knowledge which is valid for all subjects. *See also* Readiness-to-hand.

PRESENCING (*anwesen*). *see* PRESENCE

PRESENT (*Gegenwart*).   In our everyday life we understand the present as one of the three dimensions of **time**. It is the **now** that separates the **past** and the **future**. In Heidegger's **phenomenology** of time the present is one of the three **ecstases** of **temporality**. The authentic **mode** of the present is the **moment**, the inauthentic mode to **make present**.

PRESENTNESS (*Präsenz*).   In Heidegger's Winter Semester 1925/26 lecture course *Logic: The Question of Truth*, presentness comprehends both **being** as **presence** and **truth** as **making present**. In the Summer Semester 1927 lecture course *The Basic Problems of Phenomenology*, presentness is the **horizonal schema** of making present. It is the condition of **possibility** of **transcendence** as the **projection** of a **horizon** within which an **entity** can be present and made present.

PRIMAL SOMETHING (*Ur-etwas*).   In his War Emergency Semester 1919 course *The Idea of Philosophy and the Problem of Worldviews* Heidegger described the primal something as the condition of **possibility** of **lived experience**. It refers to the dimension of 'it's giving' (*es gibt*); 'it holds' (*es gilt*); 'it ought' (*es soll*); it's valuing (*es wertet*); and 'it's worlding' (*es weltet*). This pre-theoretical **region** is the matter itself of **phenomenology**. The primal something is **life** as not yet differentiated and not yet worldly. This not-yet is the index for the highest potentiality of life. The primal something has a motivated tendency and tending motivation to world out into particular **lifeworlds**. The primal something is no **thing** at all, but **intentionality** as such. Our life can only be lived experience, because life itself is the **appropriation** of **meaningfulness**. As life we can immediately **understand** the meaningfulness of life. It's giving or making **sense** to us. Phenomenology can therefore no longer be the intuitive **science** of **Edmund Husserl**. Heidegger transforms it into **hermeneutics**, that is, the explanation of our **understanding** of the **sense of being**. The hermeneutical breakthrough of the primal something only comes to full fruition in the 1930s after the project of **Being and Time** had failed. That it's giving the sense of being, the appropriation, is the wonder of all wonders of Heidegger's thought.

PRINCIPLE OF IDENTITY, THE (*Der Satz der Identität*). Heidegger delivered this lecture on June 27, 1957, at the University of **Freiburg**. It is a careful meditation on the principle of identity that looks back at the essential **origin** of **metaphysics** and looks ahead into the domain of **technology** and **nihilism** as the end of metaphysics. The principle of identity expresses the highest law of **thinking** in the formula: A = A. In this formula the **essence** of identity remains unthought. With **Plato** Heidegger tries to clarify the sense of the relation of identity. A = A does not mean that each self is the same. Its sense is that each self is for itself the same. The relation of identity is a mediation and synthesis. The principle of identity neither asserts that two terms are identical nor names the empty self-identity of each **entity**. It expresses the mediation in the **being** of each entity and is therefore not only a principle of thinking but also of being. The mediation of being and thinking finds its completion in the **philosophy** of the German idealists.

What does the identity of being and thinking mean? Heidegger elucidates this essential relation in an **interpretation** of the poem of **Parmenides**. **Human beings** and **Being** belong together and have been delivered up to each other. In the age of technology and nihilism the constellation of human beings and Being is dominated by **enframing**. **Appropriation** is the **abyss** of the belonging together of human beings and Being. In our time this belonging together has been forgotten. A return to the **origin** of the principle of identity may make another **beginning** in the **history of Being** possible.

PRINCIPLE OF REASON, THE (*Der Satz vom Grund*). This Winter Semester 1955/56 lecture course is the last one Heidegger gave at the

University of **Freiburg**. It is a **retrieval** of the fundamental question of **metaphysics** and brings this question to light in the questionability of its **ground**. The principle of reason, **nothing** is without reason, asserts that our **understanding** looks always and everywhere for the reason why something is. Human **representation** searches everywhere for a **founding**. The **phenomenon** that is brought to light in the principle of reason is older than the explicit formulation of this principle as principle by **Gottfried Wilhelm Leibniz**. He stated that each **entity** has its reason. Although it is impossible to verify the principle of reason empirically, it asserts something that is necessary. It is the fundamental principle of all other fundamental principles, like the **principle of identity** and the principle of contradiction.

The principle of reason presupposes that we know what a reason is. After an **interpretation** of the different ways in which reason has been thought, Heidegger plays the principle of reason off against the poetic **experience** of Angelus Silesius that the rose is without why. **Human beings** and the rose are not without reason, but like the rose, human beings can be without always looking for the cause of entities. The principle of reason says that to the **being** of entities belongs something like a reason or cause. Yet we must differentiate between **Being** and reason. Reason does not reach Being as such. Being is the **abyss** (*Abgrund*) and as such without reason. When we recollect this **truth**, we can read the principle of reason in a different way. Instead of *nothing* is *without* reason, we can also read, nothing *is* without *reason*. The emphasis lies now on the relation between Being *and* reason.

During the incubation period of the principle of reason, the **destiny** of Being changed several times, although Being as such remained concealed. Being withdraws from the **unconcealment** of entities and can therefore never be explained by an entity. Being has no reason. Human beings stand in the **open** of the **projection** of Being and have the **possibility** to respond to the being of entities. In this way thinking opens itself for the destiny of Being and may move beyond metaphysics. Metaphysics thinks Being as reason or ground and forgets that if Being itself is grounding, Being itself can have no ground. Thinking can only reach Being if it is prepared to jump into the ungrounded abyss of its being without why. Or to use a word of **Heraclitus**, Being is the **mystery** of play. This other kind of **commemorative thinking** may free human beings from the frenzy and madness of **calculative thinking** and **technology**.

PRINCIPLE OF REASON, THE (*Der Satz vom Grund*). Heidegger delivered this lecture on two occasions in 1956. It is more or less a summary of the 1955/56 lecture course *The Principle of Reason*.

PRINCIPLES OF THINKING, THE (*Die Grundsätze des Denkens*). Under the title *The Principles of Thinking*, Heidegger delivered a cycle of five lectures in Summer Semester 1957 at the University of **Freiburg**. The first lecture was published under the same title in a Festschrift in honor of Victor von Gebsattel in 1958. The third and most famous lecture of the cycle was *The Principle of Identity*.

The principles of **thinking**, like the principle of identity and the principle of contradiction, organize the activity of thinking. As principles they can be formalized in formulas like $A = A$. Since they are the fundamental principles of thinking, they cannot be proven in thinking itself. Every proof would presuppose the **validity** of these principles. Heidegger's attempt to reflect upon these principles as principles seems therefore doomed from the start.

However, as Heidegger sees it, this problem dissolves automatically when we realize what happened in the history of **philosophy** some 150 years ago. The **essence** of thinking becomes dialectical and reaches its completion in **Georg Wilhelm Friedrich Hegel**'s *Science of Logic*. In the realm of dialectics it is revealed that thinking must necessarily think itself. This dialectical process is at the same time the basic **movement** in the **whole** of the **objectivity** of all objects. What does this mean for Heidegger's **reflection** (*Besinnung*) upon the **sense** of the principles of thinking?

In his *Science of Logic* Hegel has shown that ordinary thinking does not obey the principles of thinking. Contradiction is the root of all movement and **life**. It is a fundamental traction of **reality**. Heidegger's elucidation of the title of his cycle of lectures brings us to a **way** of thinking that reflects upon thinking itself. The title indicates a thinking of thinking. The genitive in the title is an objective genitive, since the principles of thinking are posited by thinking itself. They are not the object of thinking, and in thinking, the subject of the positing of the principles announces itself. As **Immanuel Kant** has shown, all thinking is in its essence an 'I think'. The '**I**' in 'I think' must be one and the same. Since thinking is the subject of the principles of thinking, the genitive in the title of the lecture must be a subjective genitive. But as Heidegger had remarked before, it is also an objective genitive. Is it the one or the other, or is it both the one and the other? The elucidation of title thus leaves us in the dark.

What the title indicates is a commemoration of thinking. Thinking determines the **historicality** of **being-there**. This implies that every attempt to reflect upon thinking is related to our history. In the later lectures Heidegger wants to let his listeners experience thinking in such a way that they will be able to recognize another kind of thinking. This different kind of thinking has left its trace in the **beginning** of thinking and is in its **having been** our **future**.

PROJECTION (*Entwurf*). Projection is the **existential** constitution of **understanding**. It projects the **being** of **being-there** both upon its **for-the-sake-of-which** and upon **meaningfulness**. The character of understanding as projection constitutes **being-in-the-world** with regard to the **disclosedness** of its 'there' as a 'there' of a **can-be**. The projection opens up the **leeway** for the **possibilities** of being-there's can-be. Projecting has nothing to do with comporting oneself towards a plan that has been thought out beforehand.

In projection the understanding does not grasp thematically that upon which it projects, but throws before itself the possibility as possibility and lets it be as such. The projection of being-there's most unique can-be has been delivered over to the fact of its **thrownness** in the 'there'.

PSYCHOLOGISM (*Psychologismus*). Psychologism is a reductionist attempt to explain the laws of **logic** in terms of material laws of **thinking**. It fails to understand the essential difference between psychical act and logical sense, that is, between **being** and **validity**. At the end of the 19th century many psychologist theories of logic were developed. Since logic is the **science** of thinking and thinking a capacity of the mind, psychologism led to the conviction that **philosophy** should be founded upon psychology. **Edmund Husserl** refuted psychologism in his *Logical Investigations*.

PUBLICNESS (*Öffentlichkeit*). Publicness determines the **disclosedness** of the '**they**'. **Being-there** is thrown into publicness and thus falls away from the authentic **possibilities** of its most unique **can-be**. Because being-there understands the possibilities of its own authentic **existence** in the way everybody does, it projects these possibilities upon the general view that is therefore nobody's view. In the **ambiguity** of this **projection** upon publicness, being-there's most unique can-be remains concealed. The disclosedness of the 'they' or 'anyone' is determined by **idle talk**. Being-there falls prey to the idle talk of the 'they' and leaps, curious, from novelty to novelty. It never tarries with the **entities** it encounters and always forgets the authentic possibilities of its own existence.

Throughout his life Heidegger remained very critical and suspicious of the public domain. Public life can never be authentic. He preferred to work in the solitude of his wood cabin in **Todtnauberg**.

- Q -

QUADRATE, THE (*das Geviert*). *see* FOURFOLD, THE

QUESTION CONCERNING TECHNOLOGY, THE (*Die Frage nach der Technik*). Heidegger delivered this lecture on November 18, 1955, in Munich. It is the enlarged version of his 1950 lecture, *Das Gestell* (*Enframing*). In the lecture he gives an exposition of the **essence** of **technology**. According to ancient doctrine the essence of a **thing** is considered to be what a thing is. Everyone knows the two statements that answer the question concerning the essence of technology: 1. Technology is a means to an end. 2. Technology is a human activity. Heidegger shows that this instrumental **understanding** of technology is founded upon the **representation** of causality that was developed in **Greek philosophy**. According to **Aristotle**, a cause is that to which something else is indebted for its **being**. **Being** is **presencing**. The cause induces an **entity** to come forth into **presence**. This bringing forth into presence is 'poièsis'. 'Poièsis' determines not only human activity but also the **way of being** of **nature**, 'physis', since 'physis' is the bringing forth of something out of itself. The **word** technology stems from the Greek 'technè', which is the name for both the activities and skills of the craftsman and the arts of the mind and the fine **arts**. It belongs to 'poièsis' and is therefore a way of **revealment**. In 'technè' **truth** is appropriated.

Modern technology is determined by challenging. In natural **science** we force nature to answer our questions. In this way of revealment, that which is revealed is disclosed as **standing-reserve** or stock of materials and products that are ready to be used by **human beings**. Technology gathers entities into **enframing**. Enframing is the essence of technology. In the danger of enframing and the desecration of the **earth**, the saving power also grows. This famous **saying** of **Friedrich Hölderlin** indicates the **possibility** of looking for other ways of revealment besides technology. This **reflection** upon the **sense** of technology discovers the **nearness** of technology to 'poièsis'. Technology is not the work of the devil. In its essence the liberating appeal of revealment holds sway and discloses its nearness to art.

The more questioningly we ponder the essence of technology, the more mysterious the essence of art becomes. The closer we come to the danger of technology, the more questioning we become. And as Heidegger says in his closing statement, questioning is the **piety** of **thinking**.

QUESTION OF BEING (*Seinsfrage*).   The question of being is the question what is **being**? It is both the **guiding question** of **metaphysics** and the **basic question** of Heidegger's **thinking**. The metaphysical question, what is an **entity** as entity?, can be worked out in two different ways that constitute the onto-theo-logical **structure** of metaphysics: 1. What is **beingness**? and 2. What entity is the **ground** of being? Heidegger raised the question of being anew in *Being and Time* and showed in his **destruction** of the history of **ontology** that **Being** as such had remained forgotten in the guiding question of metaphysics. His path of thinking is an attempt to answer the basic question of thinking: what is Being as such, or what is **appropriation**?

- R -

READINESS-TO-HAND (*Zuhandenheit*).   Readiness-to-hand is the way in which **entities** as they are in themselves are defined ontologico-categorially. It determines the **way of being** of **equipment**, which is disclosed in **being-there**'s **circumspection**. We can only discover what equipment is in its **in-order-to** by putting it to use. *See also* Presence-at-hand.

REALITY (*Wirklichkeit*).   Higher than reality stands **possibility**. For Heidegger the most fateful development in the history of the **forgetfulness of being** is the orientation toward **being** as reality. When we think the being of **entities** as reality, we reduce the **world** to a sum total of independent **things** (*res*). Each thing stands in itself independent of other things. The **origin** of this development lies in **Greek philosophy**. The **philosophy** of **René Descartes** is its outcome. Since **thinking** and extension are two different realities, the **existence** of the outside world becomes a major problem. The theoretical stance of **science** reduces the world to a collection of objects that are present only for observing subjects insofar as those subjects manage to make contact with them. This theoretical view of the being of entities as reality may be justified in science, but we must realize that there are also other ways in which being is given to us. If we take into consideration only the being of objects, we will never be able to understand our own being. We are not initially worldless subjects who somehow establish contact with the outside world; we are **being-in-the-world**. Only because we are always already in a world can we disclose the being of entities as reality.

RECOLLECTION (*andenken*). *see* COMMEMORATIVE THINKING

RECOLLECTION IN METAPHYSICS (*Die Erinnerung in die Metaphysik*). In this short text, written in 1941, Heidegger develops further some of the insights of his lecture courses on **Friedrich Nietzsche** and **nihilism**. Recollection in the **history of Being** thinks history as the arrival of the issue of the **essence** of **truth** in which **Being** appropriates itself. This recollection makes possible the **commemorative thinking** of the **truth of Being** insofar as it remembers that the essence of truth is the truth of essence. Being and truth belong together. Their intertwining in the **beginning** of the history of Being is still pregnant with a coming **possibility**.

Recollection in **metaphysics** is a necessary epoch in the history of Being, which gives us the task to think how Being determines the **unconcealment** of **entities** and how the **address of Being** attunes **thinking**. Recollection in metaphysics trusts **human beings** to discover that the essence of human being is admitted in the truth of Being.

RECTORATE (*Rektorat*). Heidegger would later call his rectorate from April 21, 1933, until April 23, 1934, the biggest mistake of his life. On April 21, 1933, the professors of the University of **Freiburg** elected Heidegger rector almost unanimously with the exception of their Jewish colleagues who were banned from voting. He was nominated for the election by the resigning rector, Professor Wilhelm von Möllendorff, whose position as a Social Democrat had become untenable. Heidegger supported Hitler and lent his name and efforts to the National Socialist revolution as rector. He became for a short time an outspoken propagandist for Hitler's policies. During his rectorate the 'cleansing laws' were applied to the Freiburg University student body and thus ended financial support for anyone who fit the description of non-Aryan in Nazi law. The *Führer* principle was established at the university on October 1, 1933, thereby making Heidegger the virtual dictator of the campus. It is therefore remarkable, and an often-overlooked fact, that he appointed only non-party members (including his predecessor von Möllendorff) as dean of the different departments. He tried to reform the university in conformity with his own ideas that Karl Jaspers shared to a large extent.

The rectorate is at the heart of Heidegger's involvement with **National Socialism**. On November 3, 1933, he told the assembled students that "the *Führer* himself and he alone *is* the German reality and its law, today and for the future". A week later he took to the radio to urge ratification of Hitler's withdrawal from the League of Nations. In reply to requests by the Baden Ministry of Culture Heidegger wrote negative reports on Professor Hermann Staudinger and Eduard Baumgarten in 1933. He knew Baumgarten, a nephew of Max Weber, personally. In 1930 Werner Brock and not Baumgarten had become his private assistant on philosophical merit. In 1938 he prevented his student Max Müller from getting an academic position by informing the administration of the Freiburg University that he was unfavorably disposed to the Nazi regime. On the other hand, he helped former students and friends like **Karl Löwith**, **Elisabeth Blochmann**, Helene Weiss, and Werner Brock to settle abroad, and as rector he tried to avoid the forced retirement of his colleagues Eduard Fraenkel and Georg von Hevesy in 1933. Fraenkel was fired, but von Hevesy could stay on.

At the end of February 1934 Heidegger told the Baden minister of culture, Otto Wacker, that he wanted to resign as rector because he did not want to replace von Möllendorff and Erik Wolf as deans. Wacker asked Heidegger to keep his resignation secret until a successor could be found. After two failed attempts, the minister found Professor Eduard Kern willing to take over. While in the meantime Professor Adolf Lampe had been negotiating behind his back with the Ministry of Culture, Heidegger forced the issue and resigned officially as rector on April 23, 1934. He announced the news to the deans of the different departments on the same day. They resigned as well out of solidarity! Heidegger's attempt to reform the university had been frustrated by both the party apparatus and his colleagues. *See also* Rectorate 1933/34: Facts and Thoughts; Self-assertion of the German University, The.

RECTORATE 1933/34: FACTS AND THOUGHTS (*Das Rektorat 1933/34: Tatsache und Gedanken*). In this short text, written in 1945, Heidegger renders an account for his **rectorate** in 1933/34 and his relation to **National Socialism**. He claims that he was elected rector in

April 1933 by the unanimous vote of the plenum of the university. He had no contact with the relevant government and party agencies, was himself not a member of the party, nor had he been active politically in any way. It was uncertain whether those at the center of political power would listen to him and whether the university would actively join him to discover and shape its own **essence** in a more primordial manner.

He saw in National Socialism the **possibility** of an inner recollection and renewal of the German **people** and a path that would allow them to discover their historical vocation in the Western world. In Heidegger's view it was the task of the university to contribute to this inner self-collection of the German people. For this reason he saw in the rectorate an opportunity to lead all capable forces back to this process of **reflection** and renewal. In this manner he hoped also to counter the advance of unsuitable persons and the threatening hegemony of the party apparatus and party doctrine. Because of differences with the minister of culture concerning the conception of the university and its place in society, Heidegger resigned from office in 1934.

REFLECTION (*Besinnung*). Reflection (*Besinnung*) is the explication of **sense** and as such the **essence** of **commemorative thought**. It is opposed to **calculative thinking** and **representation** and so should not be confused with a subject's reflection (*Reflexion*) on an object. It is a recollecting thinking on that which is worthy of thought. Reflection lets itself be determined by the matter of thought. In its essence it is a venturing after **sense**. In philosophical reflection we meditate upon the **sense of being**. Reflection is not an attempt to determine and dominate **entities**, but strives to let them be what they are. Reflection is a calm, self-possessed surrender to that which is worthy of questioning, that is, the **mystery** of **Being**. In this sense it is the **piety** of thinking.

REGION (*Gegend*). The region is the whither, which makes it possible for **equipment** to belong somewhere and which we circumspectively keep in view ahead of us in **concern**. Within a region **entities** can have their place, and when they have found their place, we can measure the **space** between them. For every region some kind of **involvement** is decisive. The **discovery** of regions is codetermined by the totality of its involvements for which the ready-to-hand is freed.

RELATION (*Bezug*). In the **unconcealment** of the **being** of **entities**, **Being** withdraws itself as such and draws **being-there** with it. This condition of being drawn (*Zug*) into the being of entities is the relation Heidegger calls **existence** as standing out. Its relation to Being makes it possible for being-there to reveal entities in their being. Being-there's relation to Being and to entities is two-dimensional and determines **commemorative thinking**. Commemorative thinking recollects entities in the **truth of Being** and commemorates Being as such in the being of entities.

RELATIONAL SENSE (*Bezugssinn*). As Heidegger showed in his Winter Semester 1919/20 course on the basic problems of **phenomenology**, **life** derives from certain motives and proceeds according to certain tendencies. Life is a sequence of motives and tendencies that are not always conscious. We always live in an **environment**, a circle of tasks, and life conditions, where we are with others.

The relation of motive to tendency is the relational sense of life in which it always already lives itself without having itself. We can either live our lives as if our lives do not concern us personally or we can live our own lives. From 1922 onward Heidegger determines **care** as the basic relational sense of the factual **movement** of life. *See also* Actualization sense; Content sense; Temporalizing sense.

RELEASE (*Gelassenheit*). *see* ACQUIESCENCE

RELIGION (*Religion*). Religion, that is, the binding of one's own **existence** to a higher **entity**, is an outstanding **possibility** of human **being-there**. We can distinguish three periods in Heidegger's relation to religion.

The first period of his youth ends with Heidegger's break with the system of Catholicism in 1919. His Roman Catholic background was an important element in his philosophical development. As he would later say, his theological provenance first put him on the path of **thinking**.

The second period centers on his **phenomenology** of religion and lasts from 1919 until the early 1930s. During this time Heidegger understood the **facticity** of his own life as that of a logician of Christian **theology**. To come to an authentic **understanding** of our own **existence**, we must repeat our Greek-Christian **tradition**. This **retrieval** of our **past** took the shape of a **destruction** of **Greek philosophy** and a repetition of primitive **Christianity**.

Heidegger's conception of the **history of Being** is at the **origin** of the third period. The dominant factor in the facticity of modern **life** is no

longer Christian theology but **nihilism**. In **Friedrich Hölderlin**'s poems on the **gods** that have fled and the terrible **word** of **Friedrich
Nietzsche**, "God is dead", the **absence** of **Being** comes to light. Heidegger's later **philosophy** is also a search for a new religion as a new
binding together of **mortals** and **divinities** in the **fourfold** and of being-there and Being in the **mystery**. *See also* Introduction to the Phenomenology of Religion; Phenomenology and Theology.

REMEMBRANCE OF THE POET (*Heimkunft / An die Verwandten*).
Heidegger delivered this lecture on two occasions in 1943. It is a
meditation on the **essence** of **poetry** and describes the poet as a wan-
derer returning home. The poet returns to the **homeland**, that is, the
nearness to the **origin**. Poetizing is a process in which **Being** in the
guise of the **holy** addresses the poet and he responds by putting this
address into **words**. The address is the **mystery** of the self-revealing-
concealing of the holy. When the poet abides near the **source** from
which the holy springs, he guards and preserves it as mystery.

The response of the poet is a commemoration where Being comes
through what is as **having been** and is **made present** in words when
the poet accedes to the **address of Being**. In the poems that Heidegger
interprets, the **attunement** of the poet is joy. Joy in poetizing consists
in knowing that in every joyous **entity** that already is encountered, the
joyous hails the poet insofar as it holds itself in reserve. The poet needs
the help of his kinsmen, that is, the thinkers, to guard the full import of
his words and help the **people** to comprehend it. The homecoming of
the poet is the **future** of the historical **destiny** of the German people.

REPETITION (*Wiederholung*). *see* RETRIEVAL

REPRESENTATION (*Vorstellung*). Representative **thinking** is one of
the characteristic features of modern **philosophy**. In modern philosophy from **René Descartes** to **Friedrich Nietzsche**, every **entity** is an
object for a subject by which it is represented. As representations entities are dominated by and submitted to the control of the subject. An
entity can only be an entity insofar as a subject perceives it. The relation between entity and **Being** is thus lost. **Truth** is no longer the **unconcealment** of entities in their being, but the certitude of our representations.

RESOLUTENESS (*Entschlossenheit*). Resoluteness is an outstanding
mode of **being-there**'s **disclosedness**. It is the **authenticity** of **care**

and makes it possible for being-there to exist authentically. It frees us from the everywhere and nowhere of **curiosity** and gathers us in the unique **situation** of our **existence**. By its '**ontological**' **essence** it is the particular resoluteness of a particular factual being-there at a particular time. The receptive **openness** of resoluteness exists only as a closing **resolution**, which understandingly projects its own authentic **existence**. Resoluteness is the **existentiell** attestation of owned **can-be**, that is, the **actualization sense** of existence. It is a concrete **understanding** of a concrete situation of our existence in which our can-be is summoned by the **call of conscience**. *See also* Moment.

RESOLUTION (*Entschluß*). Resolution is the closing decision of **resoluteness**, which understandingly projects itself. It decides what we have to be and do in this particular **situation**. The resolution of a situation, as it is understood in resoluteness, is the disclosing **projection** and determination of what is possible for us at the time.

RETAIN (*behalten*). **Forgottenness** is the condition of **possibility** of **being-there**'s retaining of **entities** encountered in the **world** by the concernful **making present**, which **awaits**. Retaining belongs to the ecstatic unity of **temporality**. **Circumspection** is grounded in a retention of the **involvement** of the **equipment** with which being-there concerns itself in awaiting the **toward-which** of this equipment.

RETRIEVAL (*Wiederholung*). Heidegger uses the concept of retrieval in two different ways. In *Being and Time* retrieval belongs to the **temporality** of **being-there**. It is the authentic way of **having been** as **ecstasis**. Retrieval is handing down explicitly, that is, going back into the **possibilities** of the being-there that has been there. The authentic retrieval of an **existential** possibility is grounded in anticipatory **resoluteness**. By retrieval being-there makes its own history manifest. In this second sense retrieval is also **destruction**. The destruction of the history of **ontology** is the retrieval of its original possibility. Here retrieval is a repetition of its **beginning** in order to transform it into a new beginning. Heidegger speaks in this sense about a retrieval of **metaphysics**.

REVEAL (*entbergen*). *see* REVEALMENT

REVEALMENT (*Entborgenheit*). Heidegger interprets the Greek concept of **truth**, 'alètheia', as **unconcealment**. Truth as revealment of the **being** of **entities** must be wrested from **concealment**. By virtue of its **existence** and **openness**, **being-there** can reveal entities in their being. However, when it reveals an entity in what and how it is, it conceals at the same time entities as a **whole**. In Heidegger's later work the emphasis shifts from being-there to **Being** as such. The **truth of Being** is the **appropriation** of its self-revealing concealing and its self-concealing revealing. The unconcealment of entities is now destined by Being and no longer in the power of being-there.

RICKERT, HEINRICH (1863-1936). Rickert was one of the main representatives of the Southwest German school of **neo-Kantianism**. He developed a **value-philosophy** to supplement **Immanuel Kant's** theory of knowledge. He held the chair of **philosophy** at the University of **Freiburg** when Heidegger was a student. Heidegger wrote his qualifying dissertation, ***Duns Scotus' Doctrine of Categories and Meaning***, under Rickert's directorship. He acknowledged his indebtedness to Rickert for helping him see and understand the problems of modern **logic**. He also introduced Heidegger to the work of **Emil Lask** whose influence on his early thought can hardly be exaggerated. In his first lecture courses in Freiburg after World War I, Heidegger would deconstruct Rickert's value-philosophy.

RILKE, RAINER MARIA (1875-1926). For Heidegger, Rilke is the poet par excellence of **metaphysics** in its consummation, since he expressed in his **poetry** the **being** of **entities** as a universal **will** whose **essence** is simply to be itself as will. He recognized the danger of **nihilism** and **technology**. His attempt to overcome the danger of technology as the unholy implies that he is at least under way toward a naming of the **holy** and in this sense he is, like **Friedrich Hölderlin**, a poet for our destitute time. *See also* What Are Poets For?

RUINANCE (*Ruinanz*). In his Winter Semester 1921/22 lecture course ***Phenomenological Interpretations to Aristotle: Introduction to Phenomenological Research***, Heidegger used the term ruinance as a **formal indication** of the **fallenness** of factual life. It indicates the pull toward taking things lightly and making things easy that is built into **facticity**. In its actualization, ruinance takes· away **time**. In ruination we no longer have time to care about our own **life**.

- S -

SARTRE, JEAN-PAUL (1905-1980). The French existentialist writer and philosopher was strongly influenced by **Edmund Husserl** and Heidegger. In his main work, *Being and Nothingness*, traces of his reading of Heidegger's **phenomenology** of **anxiety**, **existence**, and nothingness abound. His reading of *Being and Time* was one of the most fruitful misunderstandings in the history of **philosophy**. He mistook Heidegger's attempt to develop a **fundamental ontology** by way of an **existential analysis** of **being-there** for an **existentiell** anthropology. In his famous essay *Existentialism Is a Humanism*, he claimed wrongly that he and Heidegger belonged to the atheistic wing of **existentialism**, whereas **Karl Jaspers** and Gabriel Marcel formed the religious wing.

SAYING (*Sage*). Heidegger uses saying in two different ways. In its more traditional **meaning**, saying refers to the cultural **tradition** of a **people** that has been handed down in its sayings. The sayings of a people are its proverbs, anecdotes and oral traditions, on the one hand, and the tacit **interpretations** embodied in its customs, rituals and festivals, on the other. **Poetry** and **thinking** draw on this background and transform the sayings into a configuration that articulates for a people its **understanding** of **reality**. They transform the people's saying so that now every living word fights the battle and puts up for decision what is **holy** and what is unholy, what is great and what is small, what is brave and what is cowardly.

The second meaning of saying (*sagen*) is speaking silently. The **meaningfulness** of the **world** speaks silently to **being-there**. **Human beings** are **hearing** this silent speaking in their understanding. As Heidegger says in his later writings on **language**, hearing always precedes the speaking of human beings. This hearing is a listening to the saying in which **presence** is realized. Language makes **entities** present in their **being**. In this sense language itself speaks. We hear the speaking of language. The play of the reciprocity of the four **regions** of the **fourfold** is the saying by which human beings are addressed and to which they respond. The saying of language is the condition of **possibility** of human **speech**, but without the hearing of human beings the saying of language would remain mute.

SAYING (*Spruch*). The saying of the original thinkers, **Anaximander**, **Heraclitus**, and **Parmenides**, means the whole of their **thinking** as it has been expressed in words. It is the one thought that expresses the **beginning** of thinking.

SCHELER, MAX (1874-1928). Scheler was a rather independent member of **Edmund Husserl**'s school of **phenomenology**. He perceived new **possibilities** of phenomenology. Heidegger met Scheler for the first time in 1924 when he delivered a lecture on **Aristotle** and **truth** in Cologne. This was the start of an intensive discussion that ended abruptly with Scheler's death. They asked the same fundamental questions: who are **human beings** and what is their place within the **whole** of being? They were both very critical of contemporary **philosophy** and tried to break the primacy of theoretical consciousness in philosophy. The problem of **intentionality** needed to be developed in a different way in order to make a new **metaphysics** possible. Their fundamental difference was that according to Scheler, the human being is the naysayer, while Heidegger claimed he was the why-questioner. As Heidegger said in his *In Memoriam Max Scheler* during his Winter Semester 1928/29 lecture course, *The Metaphysical Foundations of Logic*, Scheler was the strongest force in contemporary philosophy. With his death a path of philosophy once again fell back into darkness.

SCHELLING, FRIEDRICH WILHELM JOSEPH (1775-1854). For Heidegger, Schelling is the mediator between **Georg Wilhelm Friedrich Hegel**'s **philosophy** of absolute **spirit** and **Friedrich Nietzsche**'s **metaphysics** of the **will**. In his most profound work, his 1809 essay on the **essence** of human **freedom**, Schelling elevated the will to a first principle. Willing is primal **being**. Nietzsche would later transform Schelling's will of love into the **will to power** that governs and rules modern **technology**. *See also* Schelling's Treatise on Human Freedom.

SCHELLING'S TREATISE ON HUMAN FREEDOM (*Schellings Abhandlung über das Wesen der menschlichen Freiheit*). Heidegger published this book in 1971. It contains the text of his Summer Semester 1936 lecture course on **Friedrich Wilhelm Joseph Schelling**'s treatise on human **freedom** and some notes from his Schelling seminars in the early 1940s.

After a short introduction on Schelling's life and work and the background of his **philosophy**, Heidegger gives a section-by-section **interpretation** of Schelling's essay. This interpretation is part of his attempts to overcome **metaphysics**. In the history of the **forgetfulness of being**, Schelling's philosophy is the transition between **Georg Wil-**

helm Friedrich **Hegel**'s system of absolute knowing and **Friedrich Nietzsche**'s metaphysics of the **will to power**. The inaugural thesis of Schelling's essay is that willing is primal **being**.

Heidegger's interpretation centers on two problems: 1. Schelling's core distinction between **ground** and **existence**, and 2. The **possibility** of philosophy as system.

The starting point of Schelling's treatise is the **fact** of human freedom. In his essay he attempts to develop a system of freedom. As Heidegger points out, there are no pure facts. Every fact needs an interpretative context or system. Schelling's system is nothing other than the exposition of this fact of human freedom. It presupposes **Immanuel Kant**'s joining of the two modalities, **possibility** and necessity, in his formal concept of freedom as self-determination on the basis of its own law of **essence**. Yet, this does not comprehend the fact of human freedom in its **facticity**. This third modality comes into view only when the fact of evil is taken into account. Schelling therefore defines freedom as the capacity for good and evil. Evil is the revolt that perverts the ground of the essential **will** into the reverse of **God**'s. Because the act that determines all of man's being occurs beyond or above all **time**, freedom is necessity and necessity is freedom.

According to Schelling we must distinguish between the ground and the existence of an **entity**. The ground of an entity is its foundation; its existence is its self-emergence as self-revelation. The root of this core distinction is the will. The becoming of the will is the unifying division and dividing unification. This process is the systematic unfolding of **subjectivity**. The center of Schelling's system is human freedom. The **whole** of entities is joined together by the basic relation of human freedom. In God the ground of existence is joined inseparably with the existence of the ground. In **human beings** this original accord is separable, allowing for the discord of evil. Here is the rift that threatens the system. As Heidegger sees it, the fatal flaw which makes the conjuncture of archaic being as system impossible is Schelling's positing of the ground in opposition to existence. In his ***Contributions to Philosophy*** Heidegger developed another kind of textuality to avoid this flaw. He did not write a systematic work but a conjuncture of aphorisms.

In his seminar notes Heidegger works out in further detail some parts of his lecture course.

SCHEMA (*Schema*). *see* HORIZONAL SCHEMA

SCHEMATISM (*Schematismus*). In *Being and Time* schematism is the doctrine of the horizontal schematizing of **being-there**'s **temporality**. It provides the specific directive ways to be for the various **entities** that are. In his Summer Semester 1927 lecture course *The Basic Problems of Phenomenology*, Heidegger would attempt for the last time to work out a satisfactory doctrine of horizonal schematizing.

SCIENCE (*Wissenschaft*). The essential difference between **philosophy** and science is that philosophy tries to understand the **being** of **entities** as a **whole**, while science tries to discover what an entity is in itself. Science wants to know how things work. Because science discovers how things work, it is the **origin** of **technology**. In order to be able to study an entity as such, science must objectify it and transform it into an object of research. As objects entities can be controlled and measured. They become available as **standing-reserve**. In its **essence**, science is **calculative thinking** because it always takes the measure of its object. This is why Heidegger can claim that science does not think (in an authentic way). *See also* Thinking.

SCIENCE AND REFLECTION (*Wissenschaft und Besinnung*). Heidegger delivered this lecture on August 4, 1953. It is a meditation on the difference between **science** and **reflection**. Science is a decisive way in which all that is presents itself to us. It is the theory of the real. In this statement the **essence** of science comes to light. What does the real mean and what does theory mean?

The real is the working, the worked. It is that which brings forth into **presence**. The real presents itself as a stance in **unconcealment**. It stands over against and is therefore the object. In the modern age the **being** of **entities** is objectness (*Gegenständigkeit*). As an object for a subject the real becomes a **representation**.

The word theory stems from the Greek 'theorein', which means the beholding that watches over **truth**. Theory understood in the modern way lives out of the former and has become observation. In observation we pursue our object and try to entrap it in order to secure it. Theory makes secure at any given time a **region** of the real as its object-area. In the age of **technology**, the objectness of the real is secured as **standing-reserve**. Since each science objectifies **reality** in its own specific way, science as such can never represent objectness itself. This means that science can never arrive at its own essence. We need to pay heed to this inconspicuous state of affairs. Precisely this state of affairs is worthy of questioning.

Reflection is the kind of **thinking** that travels in the direction toward that which is worthy of questioning. The essence of reflection is to venture after sense by way of a self-possessed surrender to that which is worthy of questioning, that is, the **truth of Being**.

SELF, THE (*das Selbst*). The self for Heidegger is neither a **substance** nor a subject but the intentional movement of **existence**. The self is reflective and yet at the same time being directed toward and directing itself toward. Existence formally indicates a having to be without a final having. The self is ever under way. It is a being toward the end. The end of **death** understood as the extreme **possibility** of the impossibility of **being-in-the-world** can only be had if the self is destroyed. The self finds itself in existence; it is not mine and at the same time it is all mine as a possibility to own up to or disown. In its ordinary daily **life** the self falls away from the most unique possibility of its **can-be**. The **call of conscience** frees the self from its **fallenness** and brings it into the **situation** of its own existence. In **resolution** the self can become what it has to be. The self is what it cares for, its possibilities, tasks, and choices.

SELF-ASSERTION OF THE GERMAN UNIVERSITY, THE (*Die Selbstbehauptung der deutschen Universität*). Heidegger delivered his rectoral address on May 27, 1933, on the occasion of the ceremonial transfer of the rector's office. In his opening statement Heidegger outlines his thoughts on the **essence** of the German university and its historical mission. The assumption of the **rectorate** is the commitment to the spiritual leadership of the university. His following of teachers and students can grow strong only in a true and joint rootedness in the essence of the German university. This essence can gain power only when the leaders themselves are led by the spiritual mission that forces the **fate** of the German **people** to bear the stamp of their history. The university should help the German people to fulfill their historical mission, that is, the **retrieval** of the awakening of **Greek philosophy**. This **beginning** still *is*; it does not lie in the **past** but stands before the German people. Greek philosophy is the source from which all **sciences** have sprung.

The National Socialist revolution is the great awakening of the German people. The university teachers must take the lead and advance to the most extreme posts of danger amid the constant uncertainty of the **world**. The essential **will** to knowledge requires that the people be subjected to the greatest inner and outer danger in order to enjoy their true spiritual world, that is, the **truth of Being**. This world is grounded in the forces of soil and blood as the power of the inmost agitation and greatest shattering of their **being-there**. The German students are on the march. The academic freedom of the old university will be replaced by a new series of obligations: the labor service, the military service, and the service in knowledge. Teachers and students must form a fighting community in service to the people in their state. All capacities of the heart and the body must be unfolded through struggle, intensified in struggle and preserved as struggle. Heidegger closes his address with a quotation from **Plato**: everything great stands in the storm and thus indicates that the project of a renewal of both the university and the being-there of the German people is threatened from all sides.

SELF-WORLD (*Selbstwelt*). In his early lecture courses in **Freiburg** and **Marburg** until Summer Semester 1925, Heidegger uses the self-world as a **formal indication** of the way in which I first have myself tacitly in and through that **world**. He juxtaposes the self-world to the **environment** and the **with-world**. In *Being and Time* the self-world will be displaced by **mineness**.

SENSE (*Sinn*). Sense is an **existential** of **being-there** and must be conceived from the **disclosedness** that belongs to **understanding**. It is the 'toward-which' and 'upon-which' of a **projection** in terms of which an **entity** becomes intelligible as entity. Sense gets its **structure** from a **fore-having**, a **foresight** and a **fore-conception**.

SENSE OF BEING, THE (*der Sinn von sein*). In *Being and Time* Heidegger takes up the Greek **question of being**: what is the **sense of being**? What does it mean to be? This fundamental question must be made transparent. The question of being is **being-there**'s **mode** of being. Heidegger must therefore first give a proper explication of being-there with regard to its being before answering the question about the sense of being. The **understanding** of the sense of being belongs to the essential constitution of being-there. In everything it says, thinks and does, being-there implicitly understands its sense of being. But how can we make this understanding explicit? Is there a way from primordial **time** to the sense of being? As **Aristotle** remarked, being has many senses. On Heidegger's path of thinking, many senses of being are discovered, like **existence**, **readiness-to-hand**, **presence**, and **appropriation**. Since the sense of being is the **destiny** of **Being** itself and Being has its own history, there can be no final answer to the question about the sense of being.

SHEPHERD OF BEING (*Hirt des Seins*). The **relation** of **human beings** to **Being** determines their **way of being**. When they care for the **being** of **entities**, human beings are the shepherds of Being. The coming to pass of '**alètheia**' is entrusted to their **care**. In their **thinking** they should commemorate the **appropriation** of Being and treasure its **mystery**.

SIGNIFICANCE (*Bedeutsamkeit*). *see* MEANINGFULNESS

SIGNIFICATION (*Bedeutung*). *see* MEANING

SILENCE (*Stille*). *see* KEEPING SILENT

SITE (*Stätte*). **Things** like a bridge may gather the **fourfold** in such a way that they grant them a site. The site of a bridge presupposes its **location**. This location is not already there before the bridge is. Before the bridge stands, there are many places along the river where a bridge may be built. The place where the bridge is built proves to be a location. The bridge does not come to a location to stand in it; the location comes into **being** only by virtue of the bridge. The bridge allows a site for the fourfold. This site determines the localities and ways by which a **space** is provided for. Within this space the bridge brings stream, banks, and land in each other's neighborhood.

SITUATION (*Situation*). In his early lecture courses Heidegger uses the term situation to formally indicate the fundamental event that defines me in my motivations. The event of situation happens to me, I make it my own, and it relates to me. **Factual life experience** is an ever-changing coherence of situations.
   In *Being and Time* Heidegger introduces situation in connection with **resoluteness**. The 'there' of **being-there** is grounded either in **disclosedness** or in resoluteness. The **location** of being-there is disclosed in disclosedness and its situation in resoluteness. In **fallenness** being-there's situation is closed off. Resoluteness puts itself into a situation and takes action. The **resolution** of the situation is the **authenticity** of being-there's **existence** in which it realizes the most unique **possibilities** of its own **can-be**. In resolution we resolve the problem of what we have to do in this situation by taking action. The

problem of meeting a beggar in the street can, for instance, be resolved by the giving of alms.

SITUATION-I, THE (*das Situations-Ich*). For Heidegger **the I** is never a pure ego but always situated in a certain context. I always already have myself as involved in certain **situations**. *See also* Self-world.

SKETCHES FOR A HISTORY OF BEING AS METAPHYSICS (*Entwürfe zur Geschichte des Seins als Metaphysik*). In these sketches from 1941 Heidegger reflects on several elements and steps in the **history of Being** as **metaphysics**. **Plato** brought 'alètheia' under the yoke of the idea. Thinking as the **saying** of the **unconcealment** of **Being** became **representation**. In modern **philosophy** the **being** of **entities** was understood as **objectivity** and founded upon their representation by subjects. Being as such became **reality** and reality is the self-positing of consciousness. **Friedrich Nietzsche** discovered that this self-positing is a manifestation of the **will to power** that subjected the being of all entities to itself. The completion of metaphysics in modern **technology** installs the being of entities in the **absence** of Being.

Heidegger reflects also on the history of the concept of **existence** and the difference between the concepts of **Friedrich Wilhelm Joseph Schelling** and **Sören Kierkegaard**, on the one hand, and Heidegger's own concept of existence, on the other. For Heidegger existence is an ecstatic standing in the **clearing** of the 'there' of **being-there**.

SKY (*Himmel*). The **mortals** are **dwelling** on the **earth** under the **sky** in the oneness of the **fourfold**. The sky is not only the vaulting path of the sun and the course of the moon; it is also the clemency and inclemency of the weather, the change of the seasons, the light of day and the gloom of night.

SOLICITUDE (*Fürsorge*). Solicitude is the form of **care** that concerns the other **being-there**. It determines the **being-with** of being-there and has two extreme **possibilities**. It can take away the care from the other and put itself in his position in **concern**. It takes over for the other that with which he is to concern himself. The other is dominated and becomes dependent upon the one that takes away his care.

The other kind of solicitude does not leap in for the other but ahead of him to liberate him for his own **'existentiell' can-be**. This kind of solicitude pertains to authentic care and helps the other become transparent to himself in his care and to become free for it.

SOMETHING IN GENERAL (*Ur-Etwas*). *see* PRIMAL SOMETHING

SOURCE (*Ursprung*). *see* ORIGIN

SPACE (*Raum*). According to Heidegger **world** is prior to space. Space becomes accessible only if the **environment** is deprived of its **worldhood**. Yet space is also constitutive for the world. The **spatiality** of **being-there** is the condition of **possibility** of space. Because being-there is **being-in-the-world**, it makes room for the **being** of **entities**. Every entity has its place within the **whole** of **meaningfulness** that constitutes the world. When entities have found their place, we can abstract from the spatial **involvements** that determine their place. Their places get reduced to a multiplicity of positions for random **things**. They are now in space and we can measure the distance between. Things in space are only determined by their extension and their position within the whole of extension. In **science** we abstract from extension to algebraic relations. These relations make room for the possibility of the purely mathematical construction of manifolds with an arbitrary number of dimensions. The space provided for in this manner is the one space of mathematical science within which everything is.

SPATIALITY (*Räumlichkeit*). In *Being and Time* Heidegger describes the spatiality of **being-there** in terms of de-distancy (*Entfernung*) and directionality (*Ausrichtung*), which are both **modes** of **being-in-the-world**. De-distancy is a constitutive state of the **being** of being-there that makes **farness** disappear by bringing something close in circumspective **concern**. As de-distanary **being-in**, being-there has the character of directionality. Every bringing close has already taken in advance a direction towards a **region** out of which what is de-distanced brings itself close, so that one can come across it with regard to its place. Circumspective concern is the de-distancy that gives directionality.

The spatiality of **entities** that are **ontologically** determined by **readiness-to-hand** is determined by their **nearness**. This nearness regulates itself in terms of circumspective concern. **Equipment** has its place with the totality of its **involvements**.

SPEECH (*Sprache*). Since the Greeks, **language** has been represented in terms of **speech**. Speaking is defined as a kind of human activity. Heidegger abandons this approach, because he wants to **understand** the manner in which language has **being**. He wants to experience language *as* language. Language first shows itself as our way of speaking. Speaking must have speakers who are present in the way of speaking. They **dwell** together in speech. They speak about that which concerns them. Everything spoken stems from the unspoken. In the **nature of language**, speech and what is spoken reveal themselves as that by which and within which something is given voice and language, that is, makes an appearance insofar as something is said. Heidegger insists that **saying** and speaking are not the same. Speaking qua saying belongs to the design (*Aufriß*) of the being of language. The **essence** of language is saying as showing. Every showing by way of language presupposes the prior **presence** of that which is shown. In this sense speaking is of itself a **hearing**. Language speaks by saying. Speaking as the hearing of language lets saying be said to it.

SPIEGEL-INTERVIEW, THE (*Das Spiegel Gespräch*). On February 7, 1966, *Der Spiegel* published an article on Alexander Schwan's book, *Political Philosophy in the Thought of Martin Heidegger*, in which Heidegger was falsely accused. As rector he would have forbidden **Edmund Husserl** to enter the library of the university and he would also have refused to visit **Karl Jaspers** at his home after 1933, because his wife was Jewish. At the instigation of **Erhart Kästner**, Heidegger accorded *Der Spiegel* an interview in order to defend himself against these serious accusations. Rudolf Augstein interviewed Heidegger in **Freiburg** on September 23, 1966, after *Der Spiegel* had complied with the demand that the interview be published posthumously. The interview would finally be published in 1976 under the title *Only a God Can Save us*.

In the interview Heidegger answered questions about his involvement with **National Socialism**, his **rectorate** in 1933/34, and his relationship with Jaspers and Husserl. He explained that at the time he had thought the National Socialist revolution would make possible a renewal of the whole **being-there** of the German **people**. This renewal should have led to an overcoming of **technology** and inaugurated a new era in the **history of Being**. Heidegger claimed he had accepted the position of rector in 1933 to defend the purity of the revolution and to block the promotion of unsuitable persons. In the latter part of the interview he clarified his conception of technology and reflected upon the **essence** of **thinking** and its relation to **art**.

SPIRIT (*Geist*). Spirit is one of the fundamental concepts of **metaphysics** that Heidegger deconstructs in his **destruction** of the history of **ontology**. In *Being and Time* he warns that we should not understand the **being** of humans as a unity of spirit, soul, and body. The **substance** of human beings is not spirit as a synthesis of body and soul. He puts spirit consistently in quotation marks, because it belongs to the inadequate anthropology of **Christianity**.

It is remarkable that Heidegger uses the concept of spirit without reservations in his rectoral address, *The Self-Assertion of the German University*. He speaks of the spiritual mission of the German **people**. Spiritual is here the opposite of political. The revolution of **National Socialism** is not so much a political turning point as a spiritual renewal of the German people.

STANDING-RESERVE (*Bestand*). Standing-reserve designates the way in which everything is brought to **presence** by the challenging revealing of modern **technology**. When **entities** are revealed in this way, they have their own standing in the sense that they stand ready to be used by **human beings**. A tree is no longer a living plant; it becomes a potential quantity of paper for newspapers, which in turn transform the paper into printed opinions that are standing ready to be swallowed by the public. As standing-reserve, entities become a stock of materials and items that are immediately and completely available for the consumption of human beings.

STATE OF MIND (*Befindlichkeit*). *see* DISPOSEDNESS

STEP BACK (*Schritt zurück*). In his inaugural lecture, *What Is Metaphysics?*, Heidegger introduced the step back as the **formal indication** of a possible way to overcome **metaphysics**. The step back is a step back into the **ground** in which the tree of **metaphysics** has its roots. The step back should enable us to discover the incipient *(das Anfängliche)* in the **beginning** of the history of **philosophy**. This beginning may harbor another **possibility** for **thinking** at the end of the history of philosophy. The step back is thus at the same time a step forward into the beginning of **commemorative thinking**.

STOCK (*Bestand*). *see* STANDING-RESERVE

STRUCTURE (*Struktur*). Structure is one of the most important elements in Heidegger's **phenomenology**. The central phenomenon of his thought is **intentionality** as a way of human comportment. Every comportment has its own structure and Heidegger attempts time and again to lay bare the structure of comportment. The **essence** of **being-there** is **existence**, that is, a standing out in the **clearing** of the 'there' of being-there. This outstanding **instance** has its own structure. In his **existential analysis** of being-there Heidegger uncovers the structure of human existence.

His later **philosophy** is also to a large extent an analysis of structures, for example, the structure of the **fourfold** or the structure of **appropriation**. In this sense Heidegger is a structuralist. He always defines the essence of an **entity** as the unfolding of its structure. These structures are actualized and temporalized in different ways. Since every structure can unfold itself in different ways, Heidegger can only point to them with **formal indications**. It is impossible to give an essential definition of a structure that would be universally valid.

SUBJECTITY (*Subjektität*). Since **René Descartes** grounded the **being** of **entities** in the self-certain subject, every entity is either an object or that which objectifies. Heidegger calls this subject reference of all being subjectity.

SUBJECTIVITY (*Subjektivität*). The **way of being** of **human beings** was reduced to subjectivity when **René Descartes** grounded the **being** of **entities** in a self-certain subject. As subjects, human beings are interchangeable and no longer have their own unique **possibilities** of **existence**. When subjectivity reigns, everything is either the object of the **representation** of a subject or a subject that represents the **world** as a picture. The modern age is the age of subjectivity and therefore also the **age of the world picture**.

SUBSTANCE (*Substanz*). Substance is the basic concept of traditional **ontology**. The substance of an **entity** is the quality that makes it what it is and underlies the changing of its attributes. In his **destruction** of the history of ontology Heidegger shows that substance as a translation of 'ousia' is misleading, since 'ousia' is a having (possession) of oneself in a certain way and not an unmovable foundation to which attributes are attached. In *Being and Time* Heidegger plays the meaning of 'ousia' off against the concept of substance, when he defines the 'substance' of **human beings** as **existence**. Existence is a having of myself in my own unique **situation** with its own **possibilities** of my **can-be**.

- T -

TECHNOLOGY (*Technik*). The reign of technology is the final result of the history of **metaphysics**. It is the manifestation of the **will to power** that wants to subject everything to its own control. One of the problems of technology is that it seems to slip from human control. It is not so much the doing of **human beings** as the **destiny** of **Being**. In its **essence** technology is **enframing**. It reduces the **being** of all entities to **standing-reserve**. The greatest danger of technology is that it may lead to the acceptance of **calculative thinking** as the only way of **thinking**. And yet we should not reject technology as the work of the devil, but learn to live with it in **acquiescence**. Heidegger also points to the **nearness** of technology, 'technè', to **art**, 'poièsis'. In the essence of technology the saving power also grows, since it contains a liberating appeal as a way of **revealment** of the being of **entities**. Precisely because technology is determined by challenging, we may come to the insight that it is only a way of revealment and that therefore there must be other ways of revealment. In **commemorative thought** and **reflection** we may ponder the **mystery** of the **absence** of Being and overcome technology. *See also* Question Concerning Technology, The; Turning, The.

TEMPORALITY (*Zeitlichkeit*). Heidegger acknowledged **Edmund Husserl's** original phenomenological **time** and Henri Bergson's distinction of concrete duration from objective cosmic time as proximate sources of his concept of temporality. Temporality is the **sense of being** of **being-there** and the **ontological** basis for being-there's **existentiality**.

Heidegger broached original temporality as the ultimate **meaning** and order of **factual life experience** in his Winter Semester 1919/20 lecture course on the basic problems of **phenomenology**. **Lived experience** has its motivated tendencies and rhythms that articulate the immediacy of the individual human **situation**. The **temporalizing sense** unifies the threefold way in which **intentionality** unfolds itself according to its **actualization sense**, **content sense**, and **relational sense**. Because time has its **moment** of fullness as the outcome of its ripening process, Heidegger can distinguish between authentic and inauthentic temporality. This distinction enables Heidegger to explain the kairological temporality of **Christianity**. The 'kairos' is the moment of the critical junction at the fullness of time, which decides between owned and disowned temporality. Original temporality is the source from which all other levels of time derive.

In *Being and Time*, time is developed from **care** as the fundamental **structure** of being-there's **existence**. Being-there stands out in the 'there' of its **being**, which is constituted by **thrownness, being-in-the-world**, and **being-towards-death**. In its standing out, being-there can be authentic or inauthentic. Each of the different ways in which it actualizes its existence can in turn be temporalized in different ways. Ecstatic temporality clears the 'there' of being-there originally. In *Being and Time* Heidegger develops four theses with regard to being-there's temporality: 1. Temporality makes possible the structure of care, 2. It is essentially ecstatical, 3. It temporalizes itself primarily out of the **future**, and 4. It is finite. To the three dimensions of objective time, **past**, **present**, and future, correspond the three **ecstases** of temporality, **having been**, present, and **futurity**.

TEMPORALITY (*Temporalität*).   In *Being and Time* the ecstatic **temporality** of **being-there** projects the horizonal Temporality of **Being**. Heidegger would later discover that this **projection** presupposes the temporal openness or **clearing** of Being itself. In other words, the temporality of being-there mirrors the Temporality of Being. Being-there does not project, but only mirrors the Temporality of Being. Since we can discover in the temporality of being-there only the 'mirror image' of the Temporality of Being, Being as such remains concealed. This is why Heidegger could not finish *Being and Time*. The way does not lead from being-there's temporality to the **sense of being**, but instead the way leads from the **unconcealment** of Being to being-there's temporality. The temporality of being-there as the 'mirror image' of the Temporality of Being is what Heidegger would later name the **appropriation** of the **truth of Being**.

TEMPORALIZING SENSE (*Zeitigungssinn*).   The temporalizing sense unifies the three experiential vectors of **situations**: the **actualization sense, content sense**, and **relational sense**. With the temporalizing sense Heidegger is able to distinguish between the **authenticity** and **inauthenticity** of our **resolution** of the different situations that constitute our **life**.

TENSORS (*Temporalien*). In his Winter Semester 1925/26 lecture course, *Logic: The Question of Truth*, Heidegger introduces the term tensors as **formal indications** of **phenomena**, which are characterized *through* **time** in contrast with the temporary (*zeitliche*) characters of phenomena, which take place *in* time. In the last hour of the course Heidegger renames tensors **existentials**.

THEOLOGICAL DISCUSSION OF 'THE PROBLEM OF A NONOBJECTIFYING THINKING AND SPEAKING IN TODAY'S THEOLOGY' - SOME POINTERS TO ITS MAJOR ASPECTS (*Einige Hinweise auf Hauptgesichtspunkte für das theologische Gespräch über 'Das Problem eines nichtobjektivierenden Denkens und Sprechens in der heutigen Theologie'*). Heidegger wrote this letter for a theological discussion that took place at Drew University in New Jersey in 1964. Heidegger sees three themes that are worth questioning in regard to the problem of the meeting.

1. **Theology** as a **mode** of **thinking** and speaking must discuss Christian **faith** and what is believed therein. With this kept in view, one can inquire into how thinking and speaking can correspond to the proper **sense** and **claim** of faith.

2. Prior to this discussion it should be made clear what objectifying thinking and speaking is. Heidegger offers five pointers in the form of questions for the treatment of this problem: a. What does objectifying mean? b. What does thinking mean? c. What does speaking mean? d. Is all thinking in itself a speaking and all speaking in itself a thinking? e. In what sense are thinking and speaking objectifying and in what sense are they not?

3. One must decide to what extent the problem of a nonobjectifying thinking and speaking is a genuine problem at all.

When these problems are discussed, it will become clear that the positive task for theology implies that it cannot be a **science**.

THEOLOGY (*Theologie*). For Heidegger theology is a positive **science**, because its object is **God** as a particular **entity**. The 'positum' of Christian theology is Christianness (*Christlichkeit*), that is, the factual **mode** of existing as a believing Christian. Christian **existence** is determined by the history that is set in motion by the cross, the crucified, and Christ on the cross. The task of theology is to seek the **Word** that is able to make us believe and to safeguard us in our **faith**.

Theology is founded on faith, which does not need **philosophy**, although theology as the **science** of faith does. What it means to be a

Christian can only be lived and experienced in faith. The cross and sin as **existentiell** determinations of the ontological **structure** of **guilt** can be conceptualized with the help of philosophy. Sin depends on guilt. Theology can thus receive the direction of its inquiry from **ontology**. *See also* Christianity; Phenomenology and Theology; Religion; Theological Discussion of 'The Problem of a Nonobjectifying Thinking and Speaking in Today's Theology' - Some Pointers to Its Major Aspects; Youthful Theological Writings.

THEORY OF JUDGMENT ACCORDING TO PSYCHOLOGISM, THE (*Die Lehre vom Urteil im Psychologismus*). Heidegger's inaugural dissertation, *The Theory of Judgment According to Psychologism: A Critical and Positive Contribution to Logic*, was published in 1913. It consists of two parts.

In the first part he criticizes four psychologistic theories, which respectively see **judgment** in terms of a genesis from apperceptive mental activity (Wilhelm Wundt) as consisting of component acts (Heinrich Maier), as a basic class of psychic **phenomena (Franz Brentano)**, and as something fulfilled through the action of the psychical subject that is demanded by the object (Theodor Lipps). Heidegger's main criticism is that the very questioning in **psychologism** has already from the start turned away from the logical content of judgment to the psychical act of judging. It is therefore not a theory of **logic** but a psychology. Its failure to **understand** is a genuine nonunderstanding. Psychologism omits the essential distinction between the noetic act and the pure noematic logical **sense** to which the act is intentionally directed. Heidegger's critique is to a large extent a **retrieval** of **Edmund Husserl**'s **destruction** of psychologism in the first book of his *Logical Investigations*.

The second, much shorter, part is an outline of a pure logical theory of judgment. Heidegger explains that there are four distinct and irreducible kinds of **reality**: the realm of the physical, the realm of the psychical, the realm of metaphysical **entities**, and the realm of logical sense. Since the realm of sense is not to be confused with the other realms, we must not say that it exists or that it is, but rather that it validates, it has **validity**. The **being-there** of logical sense has an irreducible **givenness** that cannot be explained through anything else. We can only show and describe sense through evidential acts of nonsensory **categorial intuition**.

Heidegger concludes his dissertation with the claim that his investigation provides the basis for a pure logic, which would include **ontol-**

ogy in the form of a doctrine of **categories** that articulate **being** into its manifold senses.

THERE-BEING (*Dasein*). *see* BEING-THERE

THEY, THE (*das Man*). In *Being and Time* the 'they' is an **existential** and a primordial **phenomenon** that belongs to **being-there**'s positive **structure**. The 'they' is what being-there is in its **everydayness**. The 'they' takes the burden of its **existence** away from being-there since it was always they who did it and so it was no one in particular.

At first, being-there is not its authentic **self**, but has already been dispersed in the 'they' and must first find itself. Authentically **being** oneself does not rest upon an exceptional condition of the subject that has been detached from the 'they'; it is rather an **existentiell** modification of the 'they'. Distantiality, averageness, and leveling down, as **ways of being** of the 'they', constitute **publicness**. Publicness controls every way in which the **world** and being-there get interpreted, and yet it never gets to the heart of the matter. It determines the familiarity of the being of **entities** and thus covers up their **discovery**.

THING (*Ding*). The **essence** of a thing is its thinging, that is, its bringing into nearness of the **fourfold**. A thing gathers the four, **earth** and **sky**, **divinities** and **mortals**, into the light of their mutual belonging. In its thinging, the thing gathers and unites the fourfold and thus also things the **world**. Things appear as things out of the ringing of the world's mirror-play. *See also* Thing, The.

THING, THE (*Das Ding*). Heidegger delivered this lecture in 1949 and 1950 in Bremen and Bühlerhöhe as part of a cycle of four lectures under the title *Insight Into That Which Is*, and in a slightly expanded version in Munich in 1950.

The starting point of the lecture is the fact that today all distances in **space** and **time** are shrinking. Yet, the abolition of distance does not bring about **nearness**. What is nearness? **Things** are near to us, but do we know what a thing is?

In a phenomenological description of a jug, Heidegger shows that the jug's jug-character consists in the poured **gift** of the pouring out. In the drink of this gift, **earth** and **sky** both dwell. The gift of the pouring out can be a drink for **mortals** or a consecration for the **divinities**. In the jugness of the jug, mortals and divinities dwell. In the gift of the outpouring dwells the simple singlefoldness of the **fourfold**.

A thing stays earth and sky, divinities and mortals. This staying **appropriation** stays the fourfold in the sense that it brings the four into the light of their mutual belonging. Thing means gathering into nearness. Thinging the thing stays the united four, earth and sky, divinities and mortals, in the simple onefold of their self-unified fourfold. The four mirror each other. The appropriating mirror-play of the single onefold of earth and sky, divinities and mortals, is the **world**. The world **presences** by worlding. Since the thing stays the fourfold, it also things the world. Things appear as things out of the ringing of the world's mirror-play. **Human beings** attend in their **dwelling** to the world by responding to the **address of Being** in their **thinking**.

THINKER AS POET, THE (*Aus der Erfahrung des Denkens*). These poems and aphorisms were written in the cabin in **Todtnauberg** in 1947 and published in 1954. Heidegger originally jotted them down as a form of therapy after his nervous breakdown at the end of 1946. They are impressions from the **experience** of **thinking**. They are both an attempt to answer the **address of Being** and an exploration of the **nearness** of thinking and **poetry**.

THINKING (*denken*).   We can distinguish two distinct periods in Heidegger's thought on thinking. Before the **turning**, he has very little to say about thinking. In *Being and Time* he diligently avoids using the word. He translates 'noein' not as thinking but as apprehending, that is, the simple awareness of something present-at-hand in its sheer **presence-at-hand**. As Heidegger sees it, apprehending became the guiding thread for the **interpretation** of **Being** in **Greek philosophy**. Being is that which shows itself in the pure receptivity of apprehending. In his **retrieval** of the **question of being** Heidegger overcomes this position by showing that apprehending presupposes **being-there**'s caring **being-in-the-world**. This means that thinking and **representation** can only be secondary **modes** of **understanding**. Theoretical knowledge is only possible on the basis of a modification of **circumspection**.

After the turning, thinking in a positive sense becomes of the utmost importance to Heidegger. The original thinkers, **Anaximander**, **Heraclitus**, and **Parmenides**, revealed in their **sayings** the belonging together of Being and thinking. This belonging together was forgotten in the course of the history of Greek philosophy, because Being withdrew itself ever more into the **being** of **entities**. At the end of this process, which is the **beginning** of **metaphysics**, thinking was no longer the

saying of Being; it had become the representation of entities. '**Alètheia**' as the **unconcealment** of Being was transformed into **truth** as the correspondence between thinking and its object in **judgment**. In the **philosophy** of **Plato** and **Aristotle** there were still traces of the original **experience** of the belonging together of thinking and Being. At the beginning of modern philosophy **René Descartes** reduced thinking to the representation of objects by self-certain subjects. This inaugurated the triumph of **technology** and **calculative thinking**.

In his later philosophy Heidegger tries to overcome traditional **logic**. The misuse of thinking should be overcome by a more original and other kind of thinking. This other kind of thinking belongs to Being and is close to **poetry**. The saying of Being of the thinker and the naming of the **holy** of the poet belong together in the essential and fundamental thinking-poetizing experience of Being. Thinking is an **appropriation** of Being, which claims **human beings** for the **truth of Being**. To overcome metaphysics we need to take a **step back** out of **philosophy** into original thinking.

Heidegger describes this original thinking as **commemorative thinking** and **reflection**. It is basically a co-responding, which, appealed to by the **address of Being**, answers within itself to that appeal. This thinking is a kind of thanking for the **gift** of Being. *See also* Introduction to Metaphysics; What Is Called Thinking?

THROWNNESS (*Geworfenheit*). Thrownness belongs to the **facticity** of **being-there**. It is neither a fact that is finished nor a fact that is settled. Being-there's facticity is such that as long as it is what it is, being-there remains in the throw and is drawn into the turbulence of the **inauthenticity** of the 'they'. Thrownness, in which facticity lets itself be seen phenomenally, belongs to being-there, for which in its **being** that very being is an issue. Being-there exists factually. It is thrown into **projection**. Projection is the co-original correlate to thrownness.

TIME (*Zeit*). **Being** and Time names the central matter of Heidegger's entire path of thinking. Is Being the condition of **possibility** of time, or is time the condition of possibility of Being, or do Being and time belong together in **appropriation** as the **play of time-space**? That there exists an essential relation between Being and time becomes manifest in the Greek **interpretation** of Being as 'ousia'. 'Ousia' means, in an **ontological**-temporal way, **presence**. The **being** of enti-

ties is understood with regard to the **present** as a definite **mode** of time.

The distinction between original time and objective time is essential to Heidegger's **concept of time**. Objective time is the time of the **world** and the clock. This is the **innertimeness** of all entities within the world. Every entity is within time. Innertimeness is the **origin** of the common concept of time as a stream of **nows** of which each one is earlier than a later now and later than an earlier now. Original time is grounded in the **temporality** of **being-there**.

In *Being and Time*, time is developed from **care** as the fundamental **structure** of being-there's **existence**. Being-there stands out in the 'there' of its being, which is constituted by **thrownness, being-in-the-world**, and **being-towards-death**. In its standing out being-there can be authentic or inauthentic. Each of the different ways in which it actualizes its existence can in turn be temporalized in different ways. Ecstatic temporality clears the 'there' of being-there originally. In *Being and Time* Heidegger develops four theses with regard to being-there's temporality: 1. Temporality makes possible the structure of care, 2. It is essentially ecstatical, 3. It temporalizes itself primarily out of the **future**, and 4. It is finite. To the three dimensions of objective time, **past**, present, and future, correspond the three **ecstases** of temporality, **having been**, present, and **futurity**.

Heidegger can now claim that time is the **horizon** for all **understanding of being** and for every way of interpreting it. We need to explicate time as the horizon for the understanding of being in terms of temporality as the being of being-there, which understands being. The ecstatic temporality of being-there projects the horizonal **Temporality** of Being. Heidegger would later discover that this **projection** presupposes the temporal openness or **clearing** of Being itself. In other words, the temporality of being-there mirrors the Temporality of Being. Being-there does not project, but only mirrors the Temporality of Being. Since we can discover in the temporality of being-there only the mirror image of the Temporality of Being, Being as such remains concealed. In his late lecture *Time and Being*, Heidegger therefore tells us that the attempt in *Being and Time* to derive the 'there' of being-there from temporality was untenable. The ecstatic-horizonal temporality of being-there is not the most proper attribute of time that must be sought in answer to the **question of being**.

In his later **thinking** Heidegger substitutes the clearing of the self-concealing of presence for time. Now Being itself is determined through the **open**, which is projected by time. The projection or temporalizing of time is only possible if thinking takes the clearing of the self-concealment of presence into its care. Time simultaneously times the having-been, the present, and the future and in its timing removes us into its threefold simultaneity, while holding open for us the **openness** of **space**. Space spaces and thus throws open **locations**. This **movement** of space and time is the play of stillness that Heidegger calls the play of time-space. Timing and spacing, as the same interplay, gather and unite the **fourfold**. Their interplay is the never-ending process of generating the fourfold's **nearness**. This process is at the origin of the **history of Being**.

Heidegger's final word on time seems to be that it gives Being through time and time through Being. They let each other be as the **mystery** of appropriation.

TIME AND BEING (*Zeit und Sein*). Heidegger delivered this lecture in **Freiburg** on January 31, 1962. His first remark is that his lecture will not be immediately understandable, because it is a meditation (*Besinnung*) on **Being** as such and not a treatise on the **being** of **entities**. We will need to linger, or while (*verweilen*) a long time, in the **presence** of what is being said in order to understand its **sense**.

Why does the title of the lecture bring **time** and Being together? Heidegger shows first that in the history of **philosophy**, being means presence. Like the **past** and the **future**, presence is a characteristic of time. Being as presence is determined by time. We say, for instance, that everything has its time. This means that every entity comes and goes at the right time and in between whiles during its allotted time. But is Being a **thing**? Being is not a thing and therefore nothing temporary. And yet, it is determined as presence by time. What about time? Time itself is neither a thing nor temporary and yet it gives time constantly. Although time and Being are not entities, they determine each other.

In a second movement of thought Heidegger remarks that time and Being are both matters of **thinking**. It gives time and it gives being. Being itself gives the **coming to presence** of entities in **revealment**. At the **beginning** of **Greek philosophy** Being was thought not as that which gives, but as its **gift**, that is, the being of entities. The gift of Being is its **destiny** and has its own history. Time is characterized from the **present** and being present means presence. Time is as **now**. In time we are in the presence of entities. Heidegger calls this the **open**, that is, time-space. In time-space the future, **having been**, and the present arrive in the presence and in this way they can reach each other in the

clearing of the **open**. The unity of the three dimensions of time is grounded in their reaching each other, which brings them near to each other. Time gives this **nearness** and enables us to be with entities and each other.

It gives Being as emitting and as the destiny of presence in its epochal changes. It gives time as the clearing reaching of the four-dimensional realm of the open. Heidegger next asks what this 'It' is that 'It' gives. Does time give Being and Being time? Time and Being belong together and this belonging together is the **appropriation**. The 'It' that gives time and Being is the appropriating event of time and Being in which time and Being come into their own. Heidegger ends his lecture with the remark that the elucidation of appropriation is no longer the matter of his lecture.

TO-BE (*Zu-sein*). Heidegger uses to-be as a **formal indication** of the characters of the **being** of **being-there** in his Winter Semester 1924/25 and Summer Semester 1925 lecture courses. 'Having to be' determines the **ways of being** of being-there as **possibilities**. To-be recurs in *Being and Time*, but is by and large displaced by **existence**.

TODTNAUBERG. In this little hamlet deep in the Black Forest, about 30 kilometers from **Freiburg**, **Elfride Petri-Heidegger** had a cabin built for her husband in 1922. In the famous *Hütte* Heidegger could work in solitude and tranquillity. He spent as much time as he could in Todtnauberg. Here he wrote most of his works and received close friends like **Hans-Georg Gadamer** and noteworthy guests like Paul Celan and René Char.

TOWARD-WHICH, THE (*das Worauf, das Woraufhin*). The 'toward-which' is first explicitly mentioned in Winter Semester 1920/21 as the **formal indication** of any object. In Winter Semester 1921/22 it is identified with the **content sense** of **intentionality**. In his *Phenomenological Interpretations with Respect to Aristotle: Indication of the Hermeneutic Situation*, Heidegger uses the 'toward-which' in a more general sense as the 'according-to-which' something is interpreted as something. **Time** itself emerges as the ordering 'toward-which' in Heidegger's **interpretation** of **Immanuel Kant**'s doctrine of **schematism** in Winter Semester 1925/26.

In *Being and Time* Heidegger defines **sense** as the 'toward-which' (*das Woraufhin*) of **being-there**'s **projection**, which is structured by the triple fore-**structure** of its **hermeneutic situation**. This triple fore-structure is constituted by the 'wherein' (*das Worin*) of the **world**'s **meaningfulness**, the 'toward-which' of the '**for-the-sake-of-which**' of being-there's **existence**, and the 'through-which' (*das Wodurch*) of the **interpretation**. This a priori framework of projection is the very sense and **temporality** of being-there.

TRADITION (*Tradition, Überlieferung*). Because of its **historicality**, **being-there** has grown both into and in a traditional way of interpreting **being**. By this traditional **understanding of being** the **possibilities** of being-there's **existence** are disclosed and regulated. This tradition may remain hidden from being-there and be considered as something only of the **past**. But being-there can discover tradition, preserve it, and study it explicitly. The **destruction** of tradition is not a critique of the past, which would be useless, since it would not change anything, but of our present **understanding** of the past, that is, its **having been**.

In the large sense tradition (*Tradition*) is our culture with its distinct ways of revealing the **being** of **entities** and disclosing our being-there. In a more restricted sense, tradition (*Überlieferung*) refers to the **sayings** of a **people** that have been handed down from **generation** to generation.

TRANQUILLITY (*Ruhe*). In *Being and Time* Heidegger explains that **idle talk** and **ambiguity** develop the supposition that **being-there**'s **disclosedness**, which is so available and so prevalent, guarantees to being-there that all of its **possibilities** of **being** will be secure. This supposition of the 'they' that one is leading a full and genuine **life** brings being-there a certain measure of tranquillity. The tranquillity in inauthentic **existence** does not come to rest, but only aggravates the **fallenness** of being-there.

In Heidegger's later work tranquillity refers to the repose of **thinking** in '**logos**'. 'Legein' has also the **meaning** of laying-oneself-down-to-rest. This resting in the 'logos' as the belonging together of **Being** and **human beings** is the tranquillity of **commemorative thinking**.

TRANSCENDENCE (*Transzendenz*). Heidegger uses transcendence in two different ways. In *Being and Time* he calls **Being** the transcendence pure and simple, because Being and its **structure** lie beyond every **entity** and every possible attribute which an entity may possess.

From his Summer Semester 1927 lecture course *The Basic Problems of Phenomenology* on, transcendence becomes the **formal indication** of the condition of possibility of **intentionality**. It replaces **existence**.

Being-there's transcendence is its **being** beyond itself in the midst of entities in the **clearing** of Being.

TRANSCENDENTAL (*transzendental*). **Immanuel Kant** introduced the term transcendental in his *Critique of Pure Reason*. It refers to the conditions of **possibility** of **metaphysics** as **science**. In *Being and Time* Heidegger uses the term transcendental for the **disclosedness** of **being** as **transcendence**. The phenomenological **truth**, that is, the disclosedness of being, is transcendental truth. Knowledge of being as transcendence is transcendental truth.

TRUTH (*Wahrheit*). According to Heidegger, the original **meaning** of truth is **unconcealment, 'alètheia'**. Truth is the belonging together of **Being** and **thinking**. This belonging together is **language, 'logos'**. Language is the **house of Being**. From this basic **structure** Heidegger derives two different concepts of truth: **ontic** truth of **entities** and **ontological** truth of Being as such. Being reveals itself in the **presence** of entities and at the same time withdraws into the **being** of entities and thus conceals itself.

The original thinkers, **Anaximander, Heraclitus**, and **Parmenides**, experienced the unconcealment of Being. In their **sayings,** however, they failed to ask about truth as truth. In the **philosophy** of **Plato** and Aristotle, truth as unconcealment was transformed into truth as the presence of entities. Truth thus became the correspondence between thinking and its objects and finds its locus in **judgment**. Philosophy becomes **logic** and is only concerned with the being of entities. This is the **beginning** of the **forgetfulness of being**.

In his essay *On the Essence of Truth* Heidegger tries to overcome this ontic concept of truth. Before we are able to judge what an entity as entity is, we must first have discovered its being. This **discovery** can only take place in the **open** or the 'there' of **being-there**. The ontic truth of judgment presupposes the ontological truth of the discovery of the being of entities.

Since the original meaning of truth is unconcealment, **untruth** belongs to the **essence** of truth. In every **revealment, concealment** holds sway as well. This implies that on the way to truth we may wander into **errancy**. The finitude of human being-there is expressed in the belonging together of truth and errancy.

TRUTH OF BEING, THE (*die Wahrheit des Seins*). The truth of Being is the process of the self-revealing-concealing of **Being**, that is, the

unconcealment of Being. In the history of **philosophy**, Being reveals itself in the **presence** of **entities** and at the same time withdraws into the **being** of entities. As a process, the truth of Being has its own history. Being reveals and conceals itself in different ways at different times. The history of these **appropriations** of the truth of Being is the **history of Being**.

TURNING (*Kehre*). In Heidegger's work the turning has two different meanings, although they are linked.

1. Heidegger uses the term turning to describe the fundamental change on his path of thinking in the early 1930s when he transformed his 'existential-ontological' phenomenology into a **reflection** upon the **history of Being**. In the first period he tries to understand the **sense of being** of **Being** itself from the sense of being of **being-there**. In the second period he turns this around. He now tries to disclose Being as such immediately and show how it determines the **being** of **human beings**. We should not interpret the turning as an alteration of standpoint. The **thinking** of the turning resulted from the fact that he stays with that which is worthy of thought: 'Being *and* **Time**'. In the turning, that which is worthy of thought is reversed and becomes 'Time *and* Being'. The turning is in play within the matter of thinking itself. One of the consequences of the turning in Heidegger's thought is that he drops the title **phenomenology** for his thinking. In his later work he took a **step back** from **philosophy** and tried to overcome **metaphysics** in a more original kind of **commemorative thinking**.

2. The turning refers also to an **appropriation** in the history of Being. In the danger of **technology** as the completion of the history of the **forgetfulness of being**, the **truth of Being** will suddenly turn into truthless Being. This will be the **beginning** of the overcoming of metaphysics, **nihilism**, and technology, on the one hand, and a new **destiny** of Being, on the other. *See also* Turning, The.

TURNING, THE (*Die Kehre*). Heidegger delivered this lecture in 1949 and 1950 in Bremen and Bühlerhöhe as part of a cycle of four lectures under the title *Insight into That Which Is*. In this final lecture of the cycle Heidegger describes the **coming to presence** of **enframing** as the danger, although it does not therewith announce itself as the danger. Enframing is the **essence** of **technology**, which hides itself in its **presence** in **forgottenness**. The real hidden danger of enframing is that **Being** endangers the **possibility** of its **truth**. Enframing is the **destiny** of Being. Technology can only be overcome if Being comes to presence in another way. **Human beings** can never overcome technology by themselves, because Being itself is its essence. Since Being is the essence of technology, human beings can surmount technology only if they discover the as-yet hidden **truth of Being**, and thus prepare for a new destiny of Being. This can only happen if human beings first establish themselves in the **space** proper to their essence and take up their **dwelling** there.

As Heidegger explains, we should first learn how to think before we will be able to ponder the essence of Being as that which is worthy of questioning. **Language** is the primal dimension within which our essence can correspond to Being and its **claim** that human beings belong to Being. Through **thinking** we first learn to dwell in the realm where will come to pass the surmounting of technology.

The danger of the coming to presence of enframing conceals the possibility of a **turning**, in which the **forgottenness** belonging to the coming to presence of Being will turn of itself. With this turning, the truth of the coming to presence of Being will turn into whatever is. In this sense Heidegger can refer to the **words** sung by **Friedrich Hölderlin**: "But where there is danger, the saving power also grows."

The turning of the danger will come to pass suddenly. In this turning, the **clearing** belonging to the essence of Being will suddenly clear itself and light up. In the lightning of the turning, the truth of Being will flash. When forgottenness turns around, the in-flashing of **world** comes into the injurious neglect of the **thing**. This in-flashing is what Heidegger calls **appropriation**. The sudden flash of the truth of Being into truthless Being is, as the title of the lecture cycle indicates, insight into that which is.

TWOFOLD, THE (*Die Zwiespalt*). The **essence** of **Being** is the twofold of Being and **entities**. Being is the uniform **ground** out of which entities come to presence in the **clearing** as the **coming to presence** of **Being**. This double **presence** is the twofold that constitutes the 'there' of **being-there**.

- U -

UNCANNINESS (*Unheimlichkeit*). *see* WEIRDNESS

UNCONCEALMENT (*Unverborgenheit*). Unconcealment is the **word** Heidegger uses to translate the Greek word for **truth**, 'alètheia'. It is the self-revealing-concealing process of **Being**. In the history of

philosophy, Being reveals itself in the **presence** of **entities** while at the same time it withdraws into the **being** of entities and thus conceals itself as such. *See also* Truth of Being, the.

UNCOVER (*entdecken*). In its **understanding**, **Being-there** uncovers **entities** within-the-world, which have **readiness-to-hand** as their **way of being**. This is only possible because being-there is in its **being-in-the-world** familiar with **meaningfulness**. The discovery of entities presupposes the **disclosedness** of the **world**. Only when the being of an entity within the world has been discovered can it be uncovered in its pure **presence-at-hand**. The discovery of entities is the foundation for the primordial **phenomenon** of **truth**.

UNDERSTANDING (*Verstehen*). For Heidegger understanding is our most basic ability to live and cope skillfully with our **world**, with each other, and with ourselves. Understanding formally indicates the familiarity of **life** with itself. The **intentionality**, **existence**, or **transcendence** of **being-there** indicates precisely that it is always implicitly or explicitly an **understanding of being**. Understanding is the **existential** being of being-there's own **can-be** in such a way that this **being** discloses in itself what its being is capable of. The **structure** of understanding is **projection** and understanding always has a **mood**. Understanding gives the **possibility** of **interpretation**.

Understanding projects **sense** implicitly or explicitly in three different ways, which correspond to being-there's **existence, being-in-the-world**, and **being-with**. 1. Understanding projects the being of being-there upon its **for-the-sake-of-which**. 2. It projects the being of being-there upon the **meaningfulness** of the **worldhood** of its world. It holds the relations that constitute the world as world in a prior **disclosedness** of the world. 3. Understanding projects the being of being-there upon the disclosedness of its being-with the other being-there. Being-there's understanding of being already includes its empathy with others.

Since understanding has its own **possibilities**, it can be authentic or inauthentic. Authentic understanding of being-there's existence discloses being-there in its anticipating **resoluteness**, its wanting to have a **conscience** and its having an outstanding **guilt**. In its inauthenticity understanding falls prey to **fallenness**; it flees from **death** and closes off the possibility of resoluteness.

In Heidegger's later work understanding is displaced by **language** as the **appropriation** of the belonging together of **Being** and **human being**.

UNDERSTANDING OF BEING (*Seinsverständnis*). **Being-there** has in all its different **ways of being** always an implicit understanding of being. When we say that something is, we already understand it as something. To be means in a fundamental sense to be already understood as. This does not need to be an explicit **understanding**; most of the time we do not think about **being**, but show in our dealings with **entities** that we have already understood their being. This implicit understanding of being can be made explicit through **interpretation**. Because in our everyday life we understand being as the being of entities, **Being** as such remains forgotten. In the history of **philosophy**, **ontology** has always been an interpretation of our **ontic** understanding of being. In *Being and Time* Heidegger provides for the first time an interpretation of our **ontological** understanding of Being.

UNLIVING (*entleben*). Heidegger developed his formally indicative **hermeneutics** in order to overcome a fundamental problem of **phenomenology**. As **Paul Natorp** points out, every description of the **lived experiences** of **life** objectifies the lived experience and so "stills the stream" of life. This unliving of lived experience is, Natorp maintains, the result of phenomenological description. This is the reason why Heidegger formally indicates the different **phenomena** of **being-there** and insists that we must experience them in our own life by reliving the lived experience as such.

UNTRUTH (*Unwahrheit*). Since the original **meaning** of **truth** is unconcealment, untruth belongs to the **essence** of truth. In every **revealment, concealment** holds sway as well. This implies that on the way to truth we may wander in **errancy**. The finitude of human **being-there** is expressed in the belonging together of truth and errancy. *See also* On the Essence of Truth.

UNWORLDING (*Entweltlichung*). When the **world** as a totality of **equipment** ready-to-hand is reduced to a context of extended things, which are just present-at-hand, it is deprived of its **worldhood**. This deprivation of worldhood is what Heidegger calls unworlding. In unworlding the world is objectified into the pure extendedness of **space**.

UTTERANCE (*Sage*). *see* SAYING

- V -

VALIDITY (*Geltung*). Rudolf Hermann Lotze introduced the term validity in his *Logic*. It became a central concept in the Southwest German school of **neo-Kantianism** of Wilhelm Windelband, **Heinrich Rickert** and **Emil Lask**. In his early writings Heidegger borrowed the term from Lask and called it a felicitous German expression. Validity means basically three things in his student writings.

1. Validity means the 'form' of ideality possessed by the **sense** of a **judgment**, which does not exist in **space** and **time**. Next to an 'it is' there is an '*es gilt*', it validates, it has validity, it holds, it is effective.

2. Validity also means the validity of predicative sense of a judgment for the logical subject of the judgment. "The book cover is yellow" means that "being-yellow has validity for the book cover." The copula "is" means nothing more than the predicative meaning-content (being yellow) has validity for the meaning-content in the subject position (book cover). The **sense of being** of the copula "is" in the judgment not only means the validity of one meaning-content for another, but also entails the validity of these meaning-contents for the sensible **entity** about which the judgment is made.

3. Validity finally means the universal and normative bindingness of the ideal sense of judgments on all judging agents. Valid sense functions as a norm for psychical acts of thought. Heidegger wanted to develop a pure **logic** as a phenomenological **ontology** of the **existence** of the categorial sense of the **being** of entities, which is valid in the triple sense of ideality, validity-for, and bindingness.

After his **destruction** of **value-philosophy** in his early lecture courses, Heidegger would denounce validity as a word idol in *Being and Time*.

VALUE (*Wert*). In the **value-philosophy** of the neo-Kantian school of Wilhelm Windelband, **Heinrich Rickert**, and **Emil Lask**, a sharp distinction is made between facts and values. The **sense of being** of facts is **existence** and that of values is **validity**. The realm of values is studied and understood in the humanities. The realm of facts is studied and explained in the natural **sciences**.

Values also play a very important part in **Friedrich Nietzsche**'s **metaphysics** of the **will to power** and a revaluation of all values. Nietzsche understands value as an aspect of the conditions of constancy and surpassing evolution with a view to the complex **structures** of **life** that have a relative duration within the process of becoming.

The will to power poses all values, for all values are nothing more than the self-posed conditions of its own unfolding. In this sense the metaphysics of the will to power is a **philosophy** of values. The death of **God** has made all traditional 'Christian' values worthless. To fill the void left by the death of God, Nietzsche wants to revaluate all values. This is, as Heidegger sees it, precisely the reason why his philosophy remains the end of the history of metaphysics, despite his attempt to overcome **Platonism.**

VALUE-PHILOSOPHY (*Wertphilosophie*). The Southwest German school of **neo-Kantianism** developed a value-philosophy to supplement **Immanuel Kant**'s theory of epistemology. **Heinrich Rickert** and Wilhelm Windelband made a sharp distinction between facts and **values.** The **sense of being** of facts is **existence**; that of values is **validity.** Values are independent of our **judgment** and reside in a transcendent realm of validity. As a student Heidegger accepted the central doctrines of Rickert's and especially **Emil Lask**'s value-philosophy. In his early lecture courses in **Freiburg** he would deconstruct value-philosophy and show its limits.

As Heidegger sees it, **Friedrich Nietzsche**'s **metaphysics** of the **will to power** is also a **philosophy** of values. In his moral **interpretation** of **Platonism**, Nietzsche identifies **Plato**'s ideas and values. The history of **nihilism** is the long story of the devaluation of these values. To overcome nihilism Nietzsche proposes a revaluation of all values. Heidegger argues that Nietzsche's overcoming of metaphysics is in fact its final completion, because he only puts Platonism upside down.

VOICE OF BEING, THE (*die Stimme des Seins*). In his later writings Heidegger sometimes speaks of the voice of Being. In **language** as the **coming to presence** of the belonging together of **Being** and **human beings**, the voice of Being calls silently. It hails the poet and addresses the thinker. The voice of Being calls the tune of their **attunement**. In the naming of Being as the **holy** by the poet and the **saying** of the **truth of Being** by the thinker, the voice of Being is expressed in **words.**

- **W** -

WAY (*Weg*). According to Heidegger the lasting element in **thinking** is the way. Ways of thinking hold within them the mysterious quality that we can walk them forward and backward, although only the way back will lead us forward in thinking. Heidegger's entire path of thinking is a collection of ways, and not of works, on which we are invited to follow him. Sometimes we lose ourselves on the **forest trails** and sometimes we come to a **clearing**.

WAY OF BEING (*Seinsweise*). To the **essence** of an **entity** belongs a specific way of being. As **Aristotle** had already noted, **being** is said in many ways. Heidegger distinguishes between the way of being of **objects**, i.e., **equipment**, **readiness-to-hand**, and **presence-at-hand** and the way of being of **being-there**, i.e., authentic and inauthentic **existence**. The distinction between different ways of being is important for Heidegger's attempt to overcome the subject-object dichotomy in his early work until ***Being and Time***.

WAY TO LANGUAGE, THE (*Der Weg zur Sprache*). Heidegger delivered this lecture on two occasions in 1959 as part of a lecture cycle on **language** and information at the Bavarian Academy of the Fine Arts in Munich and at the Academy of the Arts in Berlin. In the introduction Heidegger describes language as the foundation of human being. The way to language is the attempt to speak about **speech** qua speech. When language shows itself clearly, this definition will become a soundless echo, which lets us hear something of the proper character of language.

Since the Greeks, language has been represented in terms of speech. Speaking is one kind of human activity. Heidegger abandons this approach, because he wants to understand the manner in which language has **being**. He wants to experience language *as* language. Language first shows itself as our way of speaking. Speaking must have speakers who are present in the way of speaking. They are **dwelling** together in speech. They speak about that which concerns them. Everything spoken stems from the unspoken. The **nature of language** exhibits a great diversity of elements and relations. Heidegger looks for the unity of language. In the **nature** of language, speech and what is spoken reveal themselves as that by which and within which something is given voice and language, that is, makes an appearance insofar as something is said. Heidegger insists that **saying** and speaking are not the same.

Speaking qua saying belongs to the design (*Aufriß*) of the being of language. The **essence** of language is saying as showing. Every showing by way of language presupposes the prior **presence** of that which is shown. In this sense speaking is of itself a **hearing**. Language speaks by saying. Speaking as the hearing of language lets saying be said to it. Saying sets all present **entities** free into their given presence and brings all absent entities into their **absence**. It is the gathering that joins together all present and absent entities in the in-itself manifold showing and lets all that is shown abide in itself. Heidegger names this moving force in the showing of saying 'owning'. Owning is what brings all present and absent **entities** each into their own, where they show themselves in what they are and where they abide according to their kind.

Heidegger can now name this process of owning **appropriation**. It yields the opening of the **clearing** in which present entities can **come to presence** and from which absent entities can depart. In saying, appropriation appropriates. In this sense we may call language the **house of Being**. As Novalis has said, language is a monologue. It is language alone that speaks authentically and language speaks lonesomely.

WEIRDNESS (*Unheimlichkeit*). In *Being and Time* Heidegger describes how **anxiety** individualizes **being-there** and makes it feel weird. Weirdness is the fundamental **mood** in which being-there is no longer at home in its **world**. When being-there flees for weirdness, it really flees from its own **being-towards-death**. Because weirdness frees being-there from its **fallenness** to the 'they' and the world, it opens up the silent **nothing** in which being-there may **hear** the **call of its conscience**. Weirdness is closely related to being-there's finitude, mortality, and the nothingness at the heart of its **existence**. Only **human beings** can experience the weirdness of their **being-in-the-world**.

WHAT ARE POETS FOR? (*Wozu Dichter?*). Heidegger delivered this lecture in 1946 in commemoration of the 20th anniversary of **Rainer Maria Rilke**'s death. In the introduction Heidegger takes up the fundamental question raised by **Friedrich Hölderlin** in his elegy *Bread and Wine*: what are poets for in a destitute time? A destitute time is the **time** of the **world**'s night, which is determined by the absence of the **gods**. It is the darkness of **nihilism** that spreads itself all over the world. This destitution is a **destiny** of **Being**. In this darkness Hölderlin still found traces of the fugitive gods. Dionysus, the wine god, guards in the vine and the fruit the belonging together of **earth** and **sky**, of **divinities** and **mortals**. The **fourfold** is the **site** where traces of the fugitive gods still remain for godless **human beings**. Poets remain in the trace of the fugitive gods and trace the way toward the **turning** in the **history of Being**. This turning can only come about in the **holy** and Hölderlin therefore names the holy in his **poetry**. The world's night is at the same time the holy night. Heidegger shows that the destituteness of what is destitute in time is the extreme **forgetfulness of being**. In a dialogue with poetry, **thinking** can discover what remained unspoken. To which poet should thinking turn in order to experience the **mystery**? Could Rilke be a poet in destitute times?

The main part of this lecture is a careful meditation on the **essence** of Rilke's poetry. For Heidegger, he is the poet par excellence of **metaphysics** in its consummation, since he expressed in his poetry the **being** of **entities** as a universal **will** whose **nature** is simply to be itself as will. Rilke uses nature in the sense of the 'natura' of **Gottfried Wilhelm Leibniz**. The will **comes to presence** as a will to willing. In his poetry Rilke tries to overcome this will and that makes him a poet for our destitute time.

For Rilke, being is a sort of gravitational force that draws all entities into their true selves and gives them weight as entities. At the same time, it gathers all entities into a single sphere. For Rilke, the metaphor of the sphere suggests the many-sidedness of being as a conglomerate whole. For Heidegger, on the other hand, being is a sphere in the sense of the One of **Parmenides**, which he interprets as the **clearing** that reveals entities in their being and wherein they can come to presence in their **presence**.

Rilke's most significant **word** for being is the **open**. Being is the open insofar as it admits of no enclosures within itself. Being, conceived as the open, is another form of being as universal will. For Heidegger, the open has another **meaning**. It is that which renders entities open, hence accessible one to another and capable of encountering each other.

According to Rilke, human beings are different from other entities because they are self-conscious. This power of consciousness is founded on the principle of **René Descartes** that the essence of consciousness is **representation**. Entities can only have a presence through the presence of representation and for consciousness. The being of entities and human beings is thus reduced to **standing-reserve** for **calculative thinking**. This implies also that human beings depart from the open and close it off.

Rilke's attempt to overcome nihilism contains a basic difficulty. On the one hand, human beings must overcome the subject-object dichotomy which is the **ground** of **technology**; on the other hand, they cannot abandon their conscious nature, and that implies also representation. Rilke suggests a reversal of our departure from the open as an antidote to technology and nihilism. In this reversal consciousness should recollect the immanence of the objects of representation into a presence within the realm of the heart. This is a renewal of Blaise Pascal's **logic** of the heart and as such an alternative to the method of Descartes. Rilke attempts to accomplish this reversal by means of **language**. In the language of the heart, language yields to what is to be said. The poet must receive what is to be said as coming from the source of being, and having accepted it, he must let it unfold into its fullness. According to Heidegger, Rilke still conceives of language as a tool of human beings. In this respect he remained locked in **subjectivity**. The essence of language resides for Heidegger in its possessing human beings before human beings 'have' language or are possessive of speech. Language speaks and human beings can speak only if they **hear** the **saying** of language.

Rilke recognized the danger of technology. His attempt to overcome the danger of technology as the unholy implies that he is at least under way toward a naming of the holy. In this sense he is a poet for our destitute time.

WHAT IS A THING? (*Die Frage nach dem Ding. Zu Kants Lehre von den transzendentalen Grundsätzen*). This book brings the text of Heidegger's Winter Semester 1935/36 lecture course, originally delivered under the title *Basic Questions of Metaphysics*. It contains an **interpretation** of **Immanuel Kant**'s doctrine of the system of all principles of the pure understanding (*Verstand*) in his *Critique of Pure Reason*. In his course Heidegger revises some aspects of his earlier interpretation of Kant in his book *Kant and the Problem of Metaphysics*.

In the first part of the course Heidegger develops the guiding question of the course: what is a **thing**? He distinguishes between the philosophical question, on the one hand, and the everyday and scientific question, on the other. The difference between these kinds of questions is that in everyday life and in **science**, we ask what particular **entities** are: what is a jug or what is an atom? In **philosophy**, we inquire about the thingness of things, that is, the quality that makes a thing a thing. The first determinations of the thingness of things that Heidegger discusses are **space** and **time**. Things are in each instance 'this here', which seems to be both an objective determination, since all things are in space and time, and a subjective determination, since this particular thing is next to me. At this point Heidegger brings **Georg Wilhelm Friedrich Hegel**'s dialectics of sense-certainty into play. The thing as a particular entity determined by its spatial and temporal relations is described in the **metaphysics** of **Aristotle** as the carrier of qualities. This interpretation of the thingness of things is the foundation of the correspondence theory of **truth**. The primary **location** of truth is in the **assertion**. Aristotle's **ontology** is a historical answer to the **guiding question** of metaphysics, which springs from the **historicality** of **being-there**. A thing is the carrier of properties and the corresponding truth has its location in the assertion, the **judgment**, which is a relation of subject and predicate. What has not been decided is whether the **essence** of judgment and truth determine themselves from the essence of a thing, or the other way around. Or, is there a common **ground** of both? As Heidegger points out, that which determines (*bedingt*) the essence or thingness of a thing (*Ding*) can no longer itself be a thing. It must be an unconditioned (*Unbedingtes*). The essence of the unconditioned is co-determined by what has been established as a thing and as condition. If a thing is the 'ens creatum', the unconditioned is **God** in the sense of the Old Testament. If the unconditioned is a not-I, the unconditioned is the absolute **I** of German idealism.

In the second part of the course Heidegger analyzes Kant's way of asking the question what is a thing. In an introduction he discusses first the historical background of Kant's question along three lines: the problem of **categories**, the development from 'logos' via 'ratio' to reason, and the rise of Newtonian science. The beginning of modernity is the radicalization of mathematics by **René Descartes**, which leads to the self-certain 'cogito' as the ground of all **being**. From Descartes the question of the thing was transmitted to Kant by **Gottfried Wilhelm Leibniz** and Christian Wolff.

The second section is an extensive interpretation of the question of the thing in Kant's *Critique of Pure Reason*. As Heidegger sees it, the system of the principles of the pure understanding is the inner heart and foundation of the whole work. Since Kant defines the object of experience as **nature**, the thing is a natural thing or appearance in contrast to the thing-in-itself. Heidegger's interpretation centers on the highest principle of all analytic judgments, on Kant's essential definition of the judgment, on the highest principle of all synthetic judgments, and on the systematic **representation** of all the synthetic principles of the pure understanding.

In his main work, Kant is confronted time and again with the fact that we encounter objects that we ourselves did not make in **openness** and that we let this encounter happen. For Heidegger it is of the utmost importance to reflect upon the **between**, between **human beings** and things. The question, what is a thing?, thus leads us to the question, what is being human? Kant discovers that **thinking** depends upon **intuition**, but he fails to ask explicitly about the **open** as that which is manifest before we encounter the objects of **experience**.

WHAT IS CALLED THINKING? (*Was heißt Denken?*). In this Winter Semester 1951/52 and Summer Semester 1952 lecture course, Heidegger develops the **question of being** in a dialogue with pre-Socratic **philosophy** and **Friedrich Nietzsche's** **metaphysics** of the **will**. In the first part, Heidegger diagnoses the **coming to presence** of our **time**. The most thought-provoking in our thought-provoking time is that we are still not **thinking**. The cause of our failure to think is not that we do not reach out sufficiently and turn to what is to be thought, but rather that what must be thought turns away from us. It withdraws from us and refuses its arrival. We can only learn to think what must be thought if we unlearn at the same time what thinking has traditionally become, that is, **science**. As **Friedrich Hölderlin** said in his poetry: "We are a sign that is not read." The conclusion of Heidegger's diagnosis is that we are not yet on the way to thinking.

In a second movement of thought, Heidegger points to the essential relation between thinking and history, which is grounded in the **historicality** of **human beings**. Since the **philosophy** of Arthur Schopenhauer, human beings have **worldviews**. They experience the **world** as will and **representation**. Today our worldview is determined by science. As long as science determines our thinking, we will not be able to think what is thought-provoking. This is the reason why Nietzsche tries to overcome man as he so far has been. The **spirit** of revenge characterizes the type of the last man. According to Nietzsche, we must liberate ourselves from this spirit. The morality of Nietzsche's philosophy is founded upon his metaphysics, which is in turn determined by his revulsion against his own time. The will wants only its own eternity. In this willing of itself, the **essence** of **technology** comes to light.

In the second part of the course Heidegger asks the question, what is thinking?, in a different way: what calls us to think? When we ask this question, we are looking both to what it is that gives to us the **gift** of this endowment and to ourselves, whose **nature** lies in being gifted with this endowment. What calls to us to think in **poetry** and thinking is **language**. Language speaks and addresses us. Heidegger can now explicate thinking as thanking and a commemoration of the **coming to presence** of human beings. What gives us to think is **Being**, which is at once the 'food for thought'. The explication of the **relation** between thinking and Being belongs to **logic**. But as Heidegger points out, logic has been determined by the **saying** of **Parmenides**. "One should both say and think that Being is." What Parmenides has given us to think is the **experience** of the **presence** of what is **present**, that is, the **being** of **entities**. Thinking is thanking only when it recollects the 'one' in thought. This is the **twofold** of Being and entities. This duality is what gives food for thought. And what is so given is, as Heidegger remarks at the end of the course, the gift of what is most worthy of thought.

WHAT IS METAPHYSICS? (*Was ist Metaphysik?*). Heidegger delivered his inaugural lecture on July 24, 1929, in the assembly hall of the University of **Freiburg**. It was published the same year. In his lecture Heidegger takes up a particular metaphysical question, 'Why are there **entities** at all and not rather **nothing**?', and foregoes an extensive explication of the **essence** of **metaphysics**.

In the first part of the lecture Heidegger distinguishes sharply between **science** and metaphysics. In metaphysics each question is itself always the **whole**. This implies that the questioner as such is also there within the question and thus placed in question. Metaphysics must be posed as a whole and from the essential position of the **being-there** that questions. Although there are many different fields of inquiry in science, we always approach what is essential in all **things**. In the pursuit of science **human beings** irrupt into the whole of entities in such a way that this irruption breaks open and shows what entities are in their **being**. Science studies entities and nothing else. In science the questioner remains outside his objective field of study and does not question himself. Science wishes to know nothing of the nothing. And yet, when it tries to express its essence, that is, the study of entities and nothing else, it calls upon the nothing for help. In this duplicitous state of affairs a question has already unfolded: how is it with the nothing?

Heidegger elaborates the question of the nothing in the second part of his lecture. The nothing is not an entity, and so we come face-to-face with the problem of how we can encounter the nothing. Heidegger defines the nothing as the complete negation of the totality of entities and can then ask how entities as a whole can be given to us. Being-there finds itself in the midst of entities as a whole. Although we concern ourselves first and foremost in our **everydayness** with particular entities, entities as a whole may become manifest in certain **moods**, for example, deep **boredom**. Heidegger describes how entities conceal from us the nothing precisely when we come face-to-face with them as a whole. Is there an **attunement** in which we may be brought before the nothing itself? Heidegger can now point to **anxiety** as the mood that makes the nothing manifest.

In the third part Heidegger answers the question of how it is with the nothing. The nothing reveals itself in anxiety but not as an entity. In anxiety, human beings shrink back before the nothing. This wholly repelling gesture toward entities that are slipping away as a whole in anxiety is the essence of the nothing: **nihilation**. The nothing itself nihilates. Nihilation manifests entities in their full. In the clear night of the nothing of anxiety, the original **openness** of entities as such arises: that they are entities and not nothing. The encounter between being-there and entities is made possible by the original manifestation of the nothing. Being-there is being held out into the nothing. Only because the nothing is manifest in the **ground** of being-there can the strangeness of entities overwhelm us and evoke wonder. Only on the ground of wonder does the 'why' loom before us. Only then can we inquire into the ground and question entities. It is only because we can question and ground things that we ourselves are put in question.

In 1943 Heidegger added a postscript to the fourth edition of his inaugural lecture, where he explains that the question 'What is metaphysics?' questions beyond metaphysics. It springs from a **thinking** that has already entered into the overcoming of metaphysics. Heidegger then goes on to discuss some of the central themes of his later thought. Modern science, **calculative thinking**, and **technology** are manifestations of the **will to power**. Metaphysics is determined by the **forgetfulness of being**. Heidegger opposes a more originary kind of **commemorative thinking** to metaphysics. This other kind of thinking is the echo of **Being**'s gift: the **appropriation** of the being of entities. It is obedient to the **voice of Being** and seeks from Being the **word** through which the **truth of Being** may come to **language**. The thinking of Being cares for our use of language. The task of the thinker is the **saying** of Being, while the poet must name the **holy** in his **poetry**.

In 1949 Heidegger placed an introduction at the beginning of the fifth edition. It is a careful meditation on the metaphor of **René Descartes** in which he describes **philosophy** as a tree. The roots are metaphysics, the trunk of the tree is physics, and the branches that issue from the trunk are all the other sciences. Heidegger uses the metaphor to introduce his **step back** into the ground of metaphysics. Although metaphysics speaks continually of Being, it fails to ask the **question of being**. It does not ask this question because it thinks Being only by representing entities as entities. The essence of metaphysics is **onto-theo-logy**. Metaphysics has become the barrier that refuses human beings the primordial **relation** of Being to their **coming to presence** as human beings. All philosophy has fallen into the forgetfulness of being. If we want to overcome metaphysics, we must attempt to think the truth of Being itself. This commemorative thinking attempts to ask the **basic question** of thinking: what is the ground of metaphysics, that is, what is Being as such?

WHAT IS PHILOSOPHY? (*Was ist das, die Philosophie?*). Heidegger delivered this lecture in August 1955 in Cerisy-la-Salle in France. With the question 'What is **philosophy**?', we touch upon the topic of the lecture, that is, an introduction to philosophy. When we ask this question, we talk about philosophy, but as long as we talk about it, we remain outside of it and do not philosophize in any real sense.

Heidegger claims that the **word** philosophy appeared for the first time in **Heraclitus** and there as an adjective rather than as a noun. 'Philosophos' describes the man who 'philei to sophon', that is, loves the wise. The philosophical man responds to the **address of Being**. The original **meaning** of love is to be in harmony with the wise '**logos**'. Wise means for Heraclitus 'hen panta', that is, one is all. According to Heidegger this means **Being** is **being**, the meaning of which he interprets as Being's gathering of all **entities** into their being. For us this may seem a trivial truth; for the Greeks it was the wonder of all wonders. Astonishment is the fundamental **mood** of **Greek philosophy**.

During the era of sophistry both the address and response took different forms. The **mystery** of Being revealed itself to the true thinker as threatened by the charlatanism of the Sophists. In this situation **Plato** and **Aristotle** try to salvage Being from this fallen condition. They search for wisdom beyond the level of **everydayness**. Philosophy thus becomes an erotic search for wisdom instead of an attempt to be in harmony with the 'logos'. Aristotle transforms the original **thinking** of Being of Heraclitus and **Parmenides** into **metaphysics**. The search for wisdom becomes an inquiry into the first **grounds** and principles of the being of entities. The **guiding question** of metaphysics is, what is **beingness**? Philosophy is a **saying** of what being is in the **sense** of beingness. Aristotle's conception of philosophy is an authentic response to the address of Being, since it makes explicit the **relation** between Being and **human beings** in a specific historic way.

Christianity transformed the original Greek **understanding** of philosophy and therewith also its fundamental mood. The mood of modern philosophy since **René Descartes** is doubt. This is the reason why he searched for the certitude of the being of entities. He founded this certitude upon the self-certain subject. The consummation of metaphysics is **technology**. For this reason we must return to the original Greek **experience** of thinking as the saying of the harmony between Being and human beings. This responding to the address of Being serves **language**. The essence of language holds sway in both thinking and **poetry**. Both have been determined by the Greek experience of 'logos'. Heidegger therefore states that we can learn what philosophy is only in a dialogue with the Greek thinkers.

WHILE (*Weile*). In his early lecture courses Heidegger speaks of the **particular whileness** of the **being-there** of **human beings**. This term is dropped in *Being and Time* and displaced by **mineness**. In his later work the while is a temporal determination of **entities** other than human beings whose **existence** is determined by their **temporality**. Every **entity** has its particular while, that is, the allotted **time** of its **presence**. The **essence** of an entity is its **coming to presence** and whiling in its presence before it passes away. The while comes to presence in the **arrangement** of the **being** of entities. The while of an entity is correlated to the **moment** of vision of being-there's **resoluteness**.

WHO IS NIETZSCHE'S ZARATHUSTRA? (*Wer ist Nietzsches Zarathustra?*). Heidegger delivered this lecture on May 8, 1953, in Bremen. It was published in 1954.

Who is **Nietzsche**'s **Zarathustra**? It seems this question can easily be answered since Nietzsche wrote a book that bears the title *Thus Spoke Zarathustra*. In the subtitle he states that it is a book for everyone and no one. As Heidegger sees it, everyone means every **human being** insofar as he becomes in himself a matter worthy of thought. No one refers to the curious readers who imbibe freely of the striking aphorisms in the book. What does the title really tells us? First of all, it gives us the clue that Zarathustra is a speaker in the sense of a spokesman. He speaks on behalf of the circle of **life** and suffering and the coherence of the **will to power**. He teaches the doctrine of the **eternal recurrence of the same** and the overman. Heidegger's lecture is a meditation on these themes.

At the beginning and end of the lecture stands the emblem of Zarathustra's animals. The eagle and the serpent are totems of Zarathustra, the thinker of the eternal recurrence, and talismans for Heidegger, who thinks the belonging together of **Being** and human beings. The teaching of the eternal recurrence is marked by dismay for this, Nietzsche's most abysmal thought. Heidegger interprets the overman as that human being who goes beyond prior humanity solely in order to lead that humanity for the first time to its **essence**. While Nietzsche prepares human beings to assume the dominion of the **earth**, Heidegger seeks to save the earth. In his **interpretation** of the eternal recurrence Heidegger shows that Nietzsche's concept of **time** remains metaphysical. Eternal recurrence is an eternity of recurring **nows**.

The overman is a transition or a bridge between prior humanity and its **future**. Zarathustra calls this bridge redemption from the spirit of revenge as man's ill **will** toward time and its 'it was'. Nietzsche diagnoses such a revenge at the heart of all **tradition**. His understanding of revenge is metaphysical since it determines man's relation to **entities**. Heidegger's next step is to ask, what may grant redemption from the revulsion against time? Nietzsche wills that transience last forever, which is only possible as an eternal recurrence of the same. Heidegger can now bring **Friedrich Wilhelm Joseph Schelling**'s definition of primal **being** as willing into play. In traditional **metaphysics** primal being is eternity. Instead of leading to the overman and liberation from revenge, Zarathustra's doctrine of the eternal recurrence stamps being upon becoming. Nietzsche only inverted the Platonic hierarchy and retained the distinction between true being and becoming. Heidegger therefore concludes that Zarathustra remains a spokesman for the consummation of metaphysics.

WHOLE, THE (*die Ganzheit*).   For Heidegger the whole means a totality. **World** used as **ontic** concept signifies the whole of those **entities** which are present-at-hand within the world. In **metaphysics** we inquire about entities as a whole, that is, the totality of all entities, which is revealed in **anxiety**.

WHY DO I STAY IN THE PROVINCES? (*Schöpferisches Landschaft: Warum bleiben wir in der Provinz?*).   Heidegger wrote this short text in 1993 after he had rejected the philosophy chair of the University of Berlin. It was aired on the radio in 1933 and 1934 and published in 1934. Heidegger explains that his philosophical work is closely related to the work of the farmers in the Black Forest. It could not thrive in the madness of a great city like Berlin. At the end of the text Heidegger recounts how he asked his neighbor in **Todtnauberg**, a 75-year-old farmer, whether he should go to Berlin. The farmer **kept**

silent and only shook his head almost imperceptibly, which meant an absolute no.

WILL, THE (*der Wille*). In Heidegger's **history of Being, Friedrich Wilhelm Joseph Schelling** inaugurates the final phase when he identifies modern **subjectivity** and the will. Willing is primal **being**. The **value** of all **entities** depends now upon the will. For Schelling the will is still essentially the will of a benevolent **God**, although the **freedom** of the will of **human beings** was a capacity for good and evil.

Friedrich Nietzsche takes the next step and shows that the will is in its **essence** a **will to power**. This will no longer strives for anything other than itself, and certainly not for **truth**, beauty or the good. It only wants to increase its own power.

The **coming to presence** of nihilism is the will. This is the reason why Heidegger tries to deny the will in a **mood** of **acquiescence** in his attempt to overcome **metaphysics**. The failure of his **rectorate** and his involvement with **National Socialism** had taught him that every attempt to willfully overcome the will increases only the hold of the will over human beings. To overcome the will we must learn to stop willing.

WILL TO POWER, THE (*der Wille zur Macht*). In his **metaphysics** of the will to power, **Friedrich Nietzsche** describes the **essence** of all **entities** as will to power. The will to power is the only principle of value estimation, which means that wherever the will to power manifests itself as the fundamental **way of being** of entities, the **value** of every entity is estimated in terms of its increasing or decreasing the will to power. The being of all entities is grounded in the will to power as highest entity. Heidegger sees in Nietzsche's doctrine of the will to power the culmination of the history of metaphysics as **nihilism**. The most extreme expression of the will to power, as the will that only wants itself, is contemporary **technology**.

WILL TO POWER AS ART, THE (*Der Wille zur Macht als Kunst*). This Winter Semester 1936/37 lecture course, published in *Nietzsche I*, belongs to Heidegger's encounter with **Friedrich Nietzsche** as a setting apart from one another (*Auseinandersetzung*). The course consists of three parts that are joined together by two transitions.

The first part introduces the theme of Nietzsche as a metaphysician and interprets the **essence** of the **will to power** in his thought. The will to power defines the **beingness** of **entities**. In this sense his thought is still directed by the **guiding question** of **philosophy**: what is an entity as entity? What is beingness, '**ousia**'? For Heidegger the most fundamental work of Nietzsche is his collection of notes for his major work entitled *The Will to Power*, which was never written. In this collection there are three dominant themes: the will to power, the **eternal recurrence of the same**, and the revaluation of all **values**. They are closely related and form a unity. For Nietzsche all **being** is becoming, all becoming is willing, and all willing is an **expression** of the will to power. In Heidegger's **interpretation**, the will to power is the being of becoming. The will to power only wants its own becoming. This neverending becoming of the will to power is an eternal recurrence of the same. What is the link between the eternal recurrence and the revaluation of values?

In the history of philosophy, true being is distinguished from becoming. Since all values are dependent on true being, Nietzsche's claim that true being is not that which does not change but instead becoming, all values become groundless. This inner process of **nihilism** leads to the necessity of a revaluation of all values. In a discussion of the **will** in metaphysics prior to Nietzsche, Heidegger comes to the conclusion that the essence of the will to power involves a moving beyond oneself and, as such, the original opening unto entities.

In the first transition, *The Grounding Question and the Guiding Question of Philosophy*, Heidegger distinguishes between the guiding question and the **basic question** of philosophy. In both questions the 'is' seeks an overture upon entities as a **whole** by which we might determine what they in **truth**, or in essence, are. For Nietzsche entities are in truth will to power. Truth and will to power, as the opening up of entities in their being, converge in **art**. In the culmination of the history of philosophy **thinking** and art are rejoined.

The second part of the lecture course is an interpretation of Nietzsche's five statements on art. 1. Art is the most perspicuous and familiar configuration of the will to power. The truth of entities is that they are will to power. The artist discloses entities as they are in truth. 2. Therefore, art must be grasped in terms of the artist. Nietzsche's physiology of art focuses on the **phenomenon** of artistic rapture. Rapture as an expression of the will to power is both the force that engenders form and the fundamental condition of the enhancement of **life**. Form constitutes the actuality of art in the grand style. 4. Art is the most potent stimulant of life and as such the counter-movement to nihilism. 5. As a counter-movement to nihilism, art is worth more than truth. These four statements are grounded in the middle one: 3. Art is the basic occurrence of the being of all entities. Insofar as they are, entities are self-creating, created. As the basic occurrence of the being of entities, art is truth in the sense of **unconcealment** or 'alètheia'.

In the second transition of the course, *The Raging Discordance Between Truth and Art*, Heidegger tries to understand why Nietzsche stands in holy dread before this discordance. He distinguishes between truth as the truth of true **assertions** and truth as the essence of the true, that is, the universal that is always valid, hence immutable, eternal, and transcending **time**. Nietzsche moves the true from the realm of knowledge to the domain of art. But he does not pose the question concerning the essence of truth and the truth of essence, that is, the problem of unconcealment.

In the third part Heidegger asks why truth for Nietzsche is not knowledge but art. He first elaborates the meaning of the true as an object of knowledge in an interpretation of **Platonism** and positivism. For the former the standard is the supersensible idea; for the latter, the sensible fact. In this sense positivism is inverted Platonism. Since Nietzsche describes his thought as inverted Platonism, must we conclude that it is nothing other than positivism? According to Heidegger, Nietzsche's insight into nihilism as the fundamental **appropriation** in Western history, on the one hand, and his recognition of art as the essential counter-movement to nihilism, on the other, distinguishes his thought from positivism. Heidegger next turns to **Plato**'s interpretation of truth and art. Because art shares in beauty, it is a way of letting entities appear. Yet, Plato denies that art is truth. Truth belongs to the knowledge of the ideas. When Nietzsche removes the true from knowledge to art, he overturns Platonism and exposes the hidden discordance between truth and art. He eradicates the **horizon**, which during the long fable of **metaphysics** separated the true from the sensory **world**. Truth in a metaphysical sense is a fixation of an apparition, clings to a perspective that leads to nihilism and is therefore destructive of life. Nietzsche rescues the sensory, celebrates all perspectives, and enhances life as a counter-movement to nihilism. Yet, he failed to ask the question of truth as such. The truth of entities presupposes the **truth of Being**. How may the thinker and the artist respond to this truth? With this question Heidegger ends his course.

WILL TO POWER AS KNOWLEDGE, THE (*Der Wille zur Macht als Erkenntnis*). This Summer Semester 1939 lecture course, published in *Nietzsche II*, is Heidegger's third course on **Friedrich Nietzsche**'s **philosophy**. It is an elaboration of Nietzsche's progress toward the question of the **essence** of **truth**. In Heidegger's **interpretation** his view of truth as error is the extreme metaphysical transformation of truth as correctness.

Heidegger opens his course with the claim that in Nietzsche's philosophy we confront the consummation of **metaphysics** in which is decided what **entities** as a **whole** are. For Nietzsche the **beingness** of entities is **will to power**, which is also the principle of a revaluation of all **values**. This new valuation should establish the conditions and perspectives for self-preserving, self-enhancing **life**. In this revaluation the question of knowledge and truth is addressed, since truth and knowledge are values. For the philosophical tradition, truth is the correctness of **assertions** about entities; for Nietzsche, truth is illusion. And yet, this illusion is essential to life. For Heidegger, Nietzsche's thought is a metaphysics of life and as such the consummation of metaphysics as the **science** of 'physis'. Nietzsche reduces the **categories** of **logic** to schemata devised by and for the preservation of **human beings**. His understanding of the value of truth as holding-to-be-true marks the end of the two-world theory of Platonism. Heidegger points out that even if life is becoming and not eternal **being**, Nietzsche retains still the concept of correctness, since he claims the truth of Platonism is incorrect and an illusion.

All valuation interprets the being of entities as a whole as chaos. For Nietzsche every human being is a body that somehow is alive. In chaos human beings try to secure stability and permanence. Accordance with each other and reckoning of entities brings about the much-needed stability. This stability is no longer founded upon the eternal ideas; it is brought about by the holding-to-be-true of certain truths that are conditions of the possibility of human life. Heidegger can now take up the theme with which his lecture course on the **will to power as art** had concluded: Nietzsche's overturning of **Plato**'s distinction between the true and the apparent **world**. Is Nietzsche's overcoming of metaphysics a liberation from Platonic thought or did he merely invert Platonic **structures**?

Heidegger pursues two paths to the extreme **moment** and uttermost transformation of correctness in Nietzsche's thought. The first path inquires whether Nietzsche's holding-to-be-true as the commanding perspective of knowledge can save itself from a collapse into mere arbitrariness. The other path shows that **art** and knowledge are fixations of horizons and, as such, forms for securing permanence and assimilation to chaos. The raging discordance between truth and art is thus brought to an end. They are now a transfiguration that commands and poetizes, establishes and fixates, different **horizons** of perspective. Truth and art aim at justice, which is a **mode** of **thinking** that constructs, excludes, and annihilates. Justice is the supreme representative of life. Heidegger next asks whether such justice can provide a standard for the commanding and poetizing element in cognition. This seems doubtful since the will to power does not strive for preservation, but enhancement. Nietzsche secures the permanence of becoming by means of **Being** as an eternal recurrence of the will to power. This eternal recurrence is its never-ending **presence**. Nietzsche's philosophy of the **will** expresses the final truth of **beingness** and is in this sense the consummation of metaphysics. Yet, as Heidegger sees it, he still remained blind to the question of the essence of truth, that is, the self-revealing-concealing of Being. As the last **word** of metaphysics his philosophy is bound up with **appropriation** and the coming **destiny** of another **beginning** for **thinking**.

WITH-WORLD (*Mitwelt*). Heidegger juxtaposed the with-world to the **environment** and the **self-world** in his early **phenomenology** of the **world**. In *Being and Time* he describes **being-there** as **being-with**. Being-there is never alone, but finds itself always already with others. Its **being-in-the-world** is co-determined by this being-with. The world is always already the world that I share with others. The other is there in this book as the gift of a friend. The other is here in the nightgown on the chair, because it was she who wore it. This shared world is the with-world.

WORD (*Wort*). In his reflection upon the **essence** of **language**, Heidegger agrees with Stefan George's **saying** in his poem *Words* that where words are lacking, no **thing** may be. The word first bestows **presence**, that is, **being**, in which things can appear as things. In this sense the word lets a thing be as a thing. Heidegger therefore names the word the bethinging (*Bedingnis*) of a thing. This bethinging power of the word is a **mystery**.

WORD OF NIETZSCHE: 'GOD IS DEAD', THE (*Nietzsches Wort 'Gott ist tot'*). Heidegger delivered this lecture, published in 1950 in *Holzwege*, on several occasions in 1943. It is basically a summary of his **interpretation** in his five lecture courses on **Friedrich Nietzsche** from 1936 until 1940. They were later published in his famous two-volume book, *Nietzsche*. In this lecture Heidegger understands

Nietzsche's thought as the culmination of **metaphysics** from the perspective of the **history of Being**.

The starting point of Heidegger's interpretation is an explication of Nietzsche's **word** '**God** is dead'. For Nietzsche, God is the Christian God understood in a non-Christian way as the symbol of the supersensible **world** of ideas and **values**. As the highest **entity** God is the final **ground** of the **being** of all other entities. **Plato**'s supersensible world of ideas is separated from the merely apparent world of the senses and ordinary **life**. When Nietzsche claims that God is dead, he is really saying that the metaphysical world has lost its vitality. It has become a fable. We can no longer find our bearings in this world. It has become meaningless and means nothing at all. Nietzsche experiences the **nothing** at the heart of the metaphysical world and explains it as **nihilism**. Nihilism designates the basic **movement** in the history of Europe, which Heidegger identifies with the history of metaphysics.

Since the traditional interpretation of the **beingness** of entities has become meaningless, entities have also lost their value. This is the reason why Nietzsche proclaims the devaluation of all values, on the one hand, and proposes a revaluation of all values, on the other.

For Nietzsche, all being is becoming, all becoming is willing, and all willing is an expression of the **will to power**. Nietzsche interprets the beingness of entities as will to power. This **will** only wants its own becoming and this never-ending becoming is an **eternal recurrence of the same**. With the will to power Nietzsche has also found his principle of valuation. What is valuable is that which enhances the will to power.

For Heidegger, the **essence** of nihilism lies in its taking the truth of entities as such as **Being**. To overcome metaphysics we must take a **step back** into its ground: the **appropriation** of Being. Nietzsche interprets the **coming to presence** of entities as will to power and their **existence** as an eternal recurrence of the same. His thought is therefore still guided by the two fundamental **categories** of metaphysics, 'existentia' and 'essentia'. As Heidegger sees it, Nietzsche did not overcome metaphysics. His philosophy is the culmination of metaphysics, because he failed to ask the question of the essence of truth and the truth of essence, that is, the **truth of Being**.

WORDS (*Das Wort*). Heidegger delivered this lecture on different occasions in 1958 and 1959. It is a meditation on the **essence** of **language** by way of an **interpretation** of Stefan George's poem *Words*.

The starting point of Heidegger's interpretation is **Friedrich Höl-derlin's experience** of the fugitive **gods**. Since the gods have fled, the **word** as it once was is withheld. In the **saying** of the poets the gods no longer approach. This saying is the place of the intimacy of the strife between **human beings** and gods. Since the Greeks, the saying of these poetic words has long since lapsed into silence. This kind of saying must remain an enigma to us. Heidegger does not dare to attempt to bid the gods to return. He limits himself to an explication of the enigma of the word as it is told by **poetry** - in the poem *Words* by Stefan George.

In this poem George is saying that where words are lacking, no **thing** may be. It is only the word at our disposal which endows the thing with **being**. In his interpretation of the poem Heidegger tries to answer three questions: 1. What are words that they have such power? 2. What are things that they need words in order to be? and 3. What does being mean, that it appears as an endowment, which is dedicated to the thing from the word?

The poet names **entities** in his poetry. Names are words that portray. They present what already is to representational **thinking**. The word first bestows **presence**, that is, being in which things can appear as things. In this sense the word allows a thing to be as a thing. Heidegger therefore names the word the bethinging (*Bedingnis*) of a thing. This bethinging power of the word is a **mystery**. The mysterious **coming to presence** of the word explains why the poet must renounce explaining what bethinging is. He may only name it in his poetic saying. As mystery the word remains remote, but as experienced mystery, it dwells in **nearness**.

Heidegger next discovers that there is no word for the mystery of the word. Hence it must remain a mystery. The poet is not granted a word for the being of the word. There is no saying that could bring the being of language to language. The poet teaches us what is worthy of the thinking of poetic being. When we let ourselves be told what is worthy of thought, we are thinking. Poetry and thinking belong together. The saying of words is the gathering which first brings what comes to presence to its presence. The Greek word for saying is '**logos**', which is also the name of **Being**, that is, the coming to presence of entities. Saying and being, word and thing, belong together. This belonging together is what is worthy of thought and what is named as mystery in poetry.

WORKER, THE (*der Arbeiter*). Heidegger sees in the worker an unfortunate form of human **nature** that was brought about by the **will to power**. **Ernst Jünger's** book, *Der Arbeiter*, opened his eyes to the suprametaphysical **meaning** of the modern **world**. The form of the worker is only a form of **subjectivity** whose **essence** consists in the certitude of **calculative thinking**. As an **expression** of the will to power, it is the last form of the **truth** of **entities** as a **whole**. The worker and the limitless subjectivity of man's dominion over the **earth** consist in the **appropriation** of Being as the power to make. The worker is the extreme counterpart of the **shepherd of Being** as the other **possibility** of **human being**.

WORLD (*Welt*). World has two different **meanings** in Heidegger's work. Until the **turning**, world is not the sum total of **entities**, but a pre-objective, pre-theoretical context of meaning already given in **being-there's** implicit **understanding** of **meaningfulness**. In his early lecture courses Heidegger distinguishes among **environment**, **with-world**, and **self-world**, where the last disappears in *Being and Time*. The world is our **hermeneutic situation**, that is, the overall context of mutually implicated referential contexts, from the use of **equipment** to social life and from **tradition** to **language**, in terms of which everything gets explicated as meaningful to and for **human being**.

In the later Heidegger, the world reappears on the level of **being** as its opening, **clearing**, and **play of time-space**. Language as the **house of Being** is its worlding. The work of art is the contest between the world that it opens and the sheltering **earth** from which it rises. The inauguration of world is also glimpsed in the thinging of the **thing** that gathers earth and **sky**, **divinities** and **mortals**, into the **fourfold**.

WORLD-AROUND (*Umwelt*). *see* ENVIRONMENT

WORLDHOOD (*Weltlichkeit*). The worldhood of the **world** is the referential totality that constitutes **meaningfulness**.

WORLDVIEW (*Weltanschauung*). A worldview is the totality of the fundamental **values** and views of human **life** that are accepted in a certain culture or era as the **expression** of the **meaning** of life. The **life philosophy** of the late 19th century attempted to develop such world-views. In a similar vein the neo-Kantians developed elaborate systems of all **values** of human **being** in their **value-philosophy**. **Karl Jaspers** published a psychology of worldviews that was carefully studied by

Heidegger. A worldview determines the way in which we resolve the antinomies of the **limit situations** of life. In his early years Heidegger agreed with life philosophy that it is the task of **philosophy** to develop a worldview. Under the influence of **Edmund Husserl's** critique of **historicism**, he would later opt for philosophy as a rigorous **science**. In his 1919 lecture course, *The Idea of Philosophy and the Problem of Worldviews*, he denied explicitly that philosophy is or could be a worldview. *See also* Neo-Kantianism.

- X -

XIASMA. The Greek word 'xiasma' refers to the shape of the letter X. It means placing crosswise or in a diagonal arrangement. In this sense Heidegger's **fourfold** is a 'xiasma' since the **sky** corresponds with the **earth** and the **mortals** with the **divinities**. Because in its **coming to presence** in the fourfold, **Being** withdraws itself as such into **concealment**, Heidegger uses the 'xiasma' to cross out ~~Being~~ in his later **philosophy** in order to distinguish it from the traditional concept of **being**. Being hides, as it were, behind the **presence** of the 'xiasma' of the fourfold.

- Y -

YIELDING (*Gönnen*). Yielding is a **formal indication** of the relation between **world** and **things**. World yields things in their thinging, while things give bearing to world.

YOUTHFUL THEOLOGICAL WRITINGS (*Theologische Jugendschriften*). Under this heading are collected the short essay, reviews, and poems Heidegger published in 1910-1915 as a student. The majority were published in the Roman-Catholic journal *Der Akademiker*. Under the influence of **Carl Braig**, Heidegger defends the eternal **truth** of Roman Catholicism against the attacks of modernism. The poems reflect his **existential** crisis after the abandonment of his study of **theology**. In his reviews we find the first glimpses of things to come. It is remarkable that in this small body of writings we already find most of the important themes of his later work: the critique of modernity and **technology**, the attempt to rethink the philosophical **tradition**, the problem of **logic** and **language**, and a reflection on the **essence** of **art**.

- Z -

ZARATHUSTRA. In **Friedrich Nietzsche**'s **philosophy**, Zarathustra preaches the overman only insofar as he preaches the eternal recurrence. He proclaims both at once because they belong together. The overman as the **essence** of **human being** and the eternal recurrence as the **being** of **entities** belong together. At the end of the history of **metaphysics**, Zarathustra's **saying**, that **Being** and human beings belong together, is the **retrieval** of the saying of **Parmenides**, that Being and apprehending are the same.

ZOLLIKON SEMINARS (*Zollikoner Seminare*). This series of seminars started on September 8, 1959, with a lecture by Heidegger at the University of Zurich. **Medard Boss**, who would become a close friend of Heidegger, organized them in 1959, 1964, 1965, 1966 and 1969. They usually took place at his house. What makes them especially interesting is that the participants were students of medicine and psychiatry. They give the reader a glimpse of Heidegger at work. The main topics of the seminars are the **coming to presence** of **human being**, **being** and **time**, the **essence** of **science**, and **being-there** and medicine.

The book also contains Boss' notes on his conversations with Heidegger and a large part of their correspondence.

APPENDIX I: HEIDEGGER'S WRITINGS, LECTURES, COURSES, and SEMINARS

(Author's note: Heidegger's independent publications are printed in bold as are the numbers of the published volumes of the *Gesamtausgabe*.

I have decided to list separately the different texts that were collected in section 3 of GA 60 under the title *Die philosophischen Grundlagen der mittelalterlichen Mystik*, since they were written at different times and for different goals. Heidegger collected these different notes in one file in August 1919 with a view to his planned Winter Semester 1919/20 course on mysticism, which he later cancelled. This file bears the general title "*Phänomenologie des religiösen Lebens*". The notes have partly been dated according to differences in Heidegger's handwriting.

The titles of the seminars in *Zollikon* and *Le Thor* are mine and based upon the subject matter of the different seminars.)

1910a *Per mortem ad vitam* (Gedanken über Jörgensens *Lebenslüge und Lebenswahrheit*). In: Der Akademiker II. Jhg., Nr. 5, März 1910.

1910b Friedrich Wilhelm Förster. *Autorität und Freiheit* [review]. In: Der Akademiker II. Jhg., Nr. 7, Mai, 1910.

1910c Abraham a Sankta Clara. Zur Enthüllung seines Denkmals in Kreenheinstetten am 15. August 1910. In: **GA 13**.

1910d Cüppers, Ad. Jos. *Versiegelte Lippen* [review]. In: Der Akademiker III. Jhg., Nr. 2, Dezember 1910.

1910e Sterbende Pracht [poem]. In: **GA 13**.

1911a Jörgensen, Joh. *Das Reisebuch* [review]. In: Der Akademiker III. Jhg., Nr. 3, Januar 1911.

1911b Zur philosophischen Orientierung für Akademiker. In: Der Akademiker III. Jhg., Nr. 5, März 1911.

1911c Zimmermann, O., S.J. *Das Gottesbedürfnis* [review]. In: Akademische Bonafatius-Korrespondenz 15. Mai 1911.

1911d Auf stillen Pfaden [poem]. In: Der Akademiker III. Jhg., Nr. 6, Juli 1911.

1911e Julinacht [poem]. In: Ott 1993.

1911f Ölbergstunden [poem]. In: **GA 13**.

1911g Wir wollen warten [poem]. In: **GA 13**.

1912a   Religionspsychologie und Unterbewußtsein. In: Der Akademiker IV. Jhg., Nr. 5, März 1912.

1912b   Gredt O.S., Jos. *Elementa Philosophiae Aristotelico-Thomisticae*. Vol. I. Logica et Philosophia Naturalis. Edit. II. [review]. In: Der Akademiker IV. Jhg., Nr. 5, März 1912.

1912c   Das Realitätsproblem in der modernen Philosophie. In: Philosophisches Jahrbuch der Görresgesellschaft 25, 1912; in: **GA 1**.

1912d   Neuere Forschungen über Logik. In: Literarische Rundschau für das katholische Deutschland 38, 1912; in: **GA 1**.

1912e   Brief an Josef Sauer [excerpt of letter]. In: Ott 1993.

1913a   *Die Lehre vom Urteil im Psychologismus. Ein kritisch-positiver Beitrag zur Logik* [inaugural dissertation]. Leipzig 1914. In: **GA 1**.

1913b   *Kants Briefe in Auswahl* [review]. In: Literarische Rundschau für das katholische Deutschland 39, 1913; in: **GA 1**.

1913c   *Bibliothek wertvoller Novellen und Erzählungen* [review]. In: Der Akademiker V. Jhg., Nr. 3, Januar 1913.

1913d   Nikolai von Bubnoff. *Zeitlichkeit und Zeitlosigkeit* [review]. In: Literarische Rundschau für das katholische Deutschland 39, 1913; in: **GA 1**.

1913e   Lebenslauf [curriculum vita]. In: *Die Lehre vom Urteil im Psychologismus* (1913a) and Sheehan 1988.

1914a   Franz Brentano. *Von der Klassifikation der psychischen Phänomene* [review]. In: Literarische Rundschau für das katholische Deutschland 40, 1914; in: **GA 1**.

1914b   Charles Sentroul. *Kant und Aristoteles* [review]. In: Literarische Rundschau für das katholische Deutschland 40, 1914; in: **GA 1**.

1914c   *Kant-Laienbrevier* [review]. In: Literarische Rundschau für das katholische Deutschland 40, 1914; in: **GA 1**.

1914d   Brief an Engelbert Krebs [letter]. In: Ott 1993.

1915a   *Die Kategorien- und Bedeutungslehre des Duns Scotus* [qualifying dissertation]. Tübingen 1916. In: **GA 1**.

1915b   Frage und Urteil [lecture Freiburg in Rickert's seminar]. In: GA 80.

1915c   W. Wundt. Probleme der Völkerpsychologie [review]; in: Philosophisches Jahrbuch 28, 1915.

1915d   Der Zeitbegriff in der Geschichtswissenschaft [test-lecture Freiburg]. In: Zeitschrift für Philosophie und philosophische Kritik, 161, 1916; in: **GA 1**.

1915e   Trost [poem]. In: Heliand März 1915.

1915f   Das Kriegstriduum in Meßkirch; in: Heuberger Volksblatt Jhg. 17, 13. Januar 1915.

1915g   Lebenslauf [curriculum vita]. In: Ott 1993 and Sheehan 1988.

1915/16a   Die Grundlinien der antiken und scholastischen Philosophie [course].

1915/16b   Über Kant, *Prolegomena* [seminar].

1916a   Abendgang auf der Reichenau [poem]. In: **GA 13**.

1916b   Der deutsche Idealismus [course].

1916c   Übungen über Texte aus den logischen Schriften des Aristoteles (with E. Krebs) [seminar].

1916/17   Grundfragen der Logik [course].

1917a   Selbstanzeige: *Die Kategorien- und Bedeutungslehre des Duns Scotus.* In: Kant-Studien 21, 1917; in: **GA 1**.

1917b   Brief an Grabmann [letter]. In: Philosophisches Jahrbuch 87, 1980.

1917c   Über das Wesen der Religion [lecture Freiburg, on Schleiermacher's second speech *On Religion*]; in: **GA 60**, pp 319-322.

1917d   Das religiöse Apriori; in: **GA 60**, pp. 312-315.

1917e   Irrationalität bei Meister Eckhart; in: **GA 60**, pp. 315-318.

1917f   Religiöse Phänomene; in: **GA 60**, p. 312.

1917g   Phänomenologie des religiösen Erlebnisses und der Religion; in: **GA 60**, p. 322-324.

1918a   Zu: den *Sermones Bernardi in canticum canticorum* (Serm. III); in: **GA 60**, pp. 334-336 until line 2.

1918b   Zu: Theresia von Jesu. *Die Seelenburg*; in: **GA 60**, pp. 336-337.

1918c   Zu: Adolf Reinach. *Das Absolute*; in: **GA 60**, pp. 324-327.

1918d   Das Heilige; in: **GA 60**, pp. 332-334.

1918e   Glaube; in: **GA 60**, p. 329.

1918f   Hegels ursprüngliche, früheste Stellung zur Religion - und Konsequenzen; in: **GA 60**. P. 328.

1918g   Zu: Schleiermacher, *Der christliche Glaube* - und Religions-
phänomenologie überhaupt; in: **GA 60**, pp. 330-332.

1918h   Probleme; in: **GA 60**, p. 328.

1919a   Die Idee der Philosophie und das Weltanschauungsproblem
[course]. In: **GA 56/57**.

1919b   Phänomenologie und transzendentale Wertphilosophie [cour-
se]. In: **GA 56/57**.

1919c   Über das Wesen der Universität und des akademischen
Studiums [course]. In: **GA 56/57**.

1919d   Einführung in die Phänomenologie im Anschluß an Descartes,
Meditationes [seminar].

1919e   Brief an Engelbert Krebs [letter]. In: Ott 1993.

1919f   Die philosophischen Grundlagen der mittelalterlichen Mystik;
in: **GA 60**, pp. 303-306.

1919g   Mystik im Mittelalter; in: **GA 60**, pp. 306-307.

1919h   Mystik (Direktiven); in: **GA 60**, p. 308.

1919i   Aufbau (Ansätze); in: **GA 60**, p. 309.

1919j   Glaube und Wissen; in: **GA 60**, p. 310.

1919k   Irrationalismus; in: **GA 60**, p. 311.

1919l   Historische Vorgegebenheit und Wesensfindung; in: **GA 60**,
pp. 311-312.

1919m   Frömmigkeit und Glaube; in: **GA 60**, pp. 329-330.

1919/20a   Grundprobleme der Phänomenologie [course]. **GA 58**.

1919/20b   Übungen im Anschluß an Natorp, *Allgemeine Psychologie*
[seminar].

1919/20c   Die philosophischen Grundlagen der mittelalterlichen Mystik
[course, not taught]. (The notes listed above as 1919f-m
belong to this course.)

1919/20d   Über Oswald Spengler [lecture Wiesbaden].

1920a   Phänomenologie der Anschauung und des Ausdrucks.
Theorie der philosophischen Begriffsbildung [course]. **GA 59**.

1920b   Kolloquium im Anschluß an die Vorlesung [seminar].

1920/21a   Einleitung in die Phänomenologie der Religion [course]. In:
GA 60.

1920/21b   Phänomenologische Übungen für Anfänger im Anschluß an
Descartes, *Meditationes* [seminar].

1921a   Augustinus und der Neuplatonismus [course]. In: **GA 60**.

1921b   Phänomenologische Übungen für Anfänger im Anschluß an
          Aristoteles, *De Anima* [seminar].

1921c   Brief an Karl Löwith [letter]. In: Papenfuss & Pöggeler 1992.

1919-21   Anmerkungen zu Karl Jaspers *'Psychologie der Weltan-
          schauungen'* [review]. In: **GA 9**.

1921/22a Phänomenologische Interpretationen zu Aristoteles. Einfüh-
          rung in die phänomenologische Forschung [course]. **GA 61**.

1921/22b Phänomenologische Übungen für Anfänger im Anschluß an
          Husserl, *Logische Untersuchungen II* [seminar].

1922a   Phänomenologische Interpretationen zu Aristoteles. Ontologie
          und Logik [course]. GA 62.

1922b   Phänomenologische Übungen für Anfänger im Anschluß an
          Husserl, *Logische Untersuchungen II, 2. Untersuchung* [semi-
          nar].

1922c   *Phänomenologische Interpretationen zu Aristoteles. Anzeige
          der hermeneutischen Situation.* In: Dilthey-Jahrbuch 6, 1989.

1922/23a Übungen über: Phänomenologische Interpretationen zu Aris-
          toteles (*Ethica Nicomachea VI; De Anima; Metaphysica VII*)
          [seminar].

1922/23b Phänomenologische Übungen für Anfänger im Anschluß an
          Husserl, *Ideen I* [seminar].

1923a   Ontologie. Hermeneutik der Faktizität [course]. **GA 63**.

1923b   Phänomenologische Übungen für Anfänger im Anschluß an
          Aristoteles, *Ethica Nicomachea* [seminar].

1923c   Kolloquium über die theologischen Grundlagen von Kant,
          Die Religion innerhalb der Grenzen der bloßen Vernunft,
          nach ausgewählte Texten, für Fortgeschrittene (with Ebbing-
          haus) [seminar].

1923d   Übungen über: Phänomenologische Interpretationen zu
          Aristoteles {Fortsetzung} [seminar].

1923e   Aufgaben und Wege der phänomenologischen Forschung
          [lecture Hamburg].

1923/24a Einführung in die phänomenologische Forschung [course].
          GA 17.

1923/24b Phänomenologische Übung für Anfänger: Husserl, *Logische Untersuchungen II. 1. Untersuchung* [seminar].

1923/24c Phänomenologische Übung für Fortgeschrittene: Aristoteles, *Physica B* [seminar].

1924a Grundbegriffe der aristotelischen Philosophie [course]. GA 18.

1924b Fortgeschrittene: Die Hochscholastik und Aristoteles (Thomas, *De ente et essentia*; Cajetan, *De nominum analogia*) [seminar].

1924c *Der Begriff der Zeit* [lecture Marburg]. Tübingen 1989. In: GA 64.

1924d Dasein und Wahrsein nach Aristoteles [lecture Elberfeld-Barmen, Köln, Dortmund]. In: GA 80.

1924e Der Begriff der Zeit [review of *Briefwechsel zwischen Wilhelm Dilthey und Graf Yorck von Wartenburg*]. In: GA 64.

1924f Das Problem der Sünde bei Luther [lecture in Bultmann's seminar]. In: Jaspert 1996.

1924/25a Interpretation platonischer Dialoge (*Sophistès, Philèbos*) [course]. **GA 19**.

1924/25b Übungen zur Ontologie des Mittelalters (Thomas, *De ente et essentia, Summa contra gentiles*) [seminar].

1925a Geschichte des Zeitbegriffs. Prolegomena zur Phänomeno-logie von Geschichte und Natur [course]. **GA 20**.

1925b Anfangsübungen im Anschluß an Descartes, *Meditationes* [seminar].

1925c Wilhelm Diltheys Forschungsarbeit und der gegenwärtige Kampf um eine historische Weltanschauung. 10 Vorträge (Gehalten in Kassel vom 16.IV-21.IV.1925) [lectures Kassel]. In: Dilthey-Jahrbuch 8, 1992/93.

1925/26a Logik [course]. **GA 21**.

1925/26b Anfänger: Phänomenologische Übungen (Kant, *Kritik der reinen Vernunft*) [seminar].

1925/26c Fortgeschrittene: Phänomenologische Übungen (Hegel, *Wis-senschaft der Logik I. Buch*) [seminar].

1926a Grundbegriffe der antiken Philosophie [course]. **GA 22**.

1926b   Übungen über Geschichte und historische Erkenntnis im Anschluß an J.B. Droysen, *Grundriß der Historik* [seminar].
1926c   Vom Wesen der Wahrheit [lecture Marburg].
1926d   Begriff und Entwicklung der phänomenologischen Forschung [lecture Marburg]. In: GA 80.

1926/27a Geschichte der Philosophie von Thomas von Aquin bis Kant [course]. GA. 23.
1926/27b Übungen im Anschluß an die Vorlesung [seminar].

1927a   Die Grundprobleme der Phänomenologie [course]. **GA 24.**
1927b   Fortgeschrittene: Die Ontologie des Aristoteles und Hegels Logik [seminar].
1927c   Luthers *Galater* Kommentar (with Bultmann) [seminar].
1927d   ***Sein und Zeit.*** In: Jahrbuch für Philosophie und phänomenologische Forschung VIII, Halle 1927. **GA 2.**
1927e   Phänomenologie und Theologie [lecture Tübingen]. In: **GA 9.**
1927f   Phänomenologie und Theologie. I. Teil: Die nicht-philosophischen als positive Wissenschaften und die Philosophie als transzendentale Wissenschaft [lecture Tübingen]. In: GA 80.
1927g   Kants Lehre vom Schematismus und die Frage nach dem Sinn des Seins [lecture Köln].
1927h   Zur Geschichte des philosophischen Lehrstuhls seit 1866; in *Die Philipps-Universität zu Marburg 1527-1927.* In: **GA 3.**
1927i   Brief an Karl Löwith [letter]. In: Papenfuss & Pöggeler 1990.

1925-27 Aufzeichnungen zur Temporalität; in: Heidegger Studies 14, 1998.

1927/28a Phänomenologische Interpretation von Kants *Kritik der reinen Vernunft* [course]. **GA 25.**
1927/28b Phänomenologische Übungen für Anfänger über Begriff und Begriffsbildung [seminar].
1927/28c Phänomenologische Übungen für Fortgeschrittene (Schelling, *Über das Wesen der menschlichen Freiheit*) [seminar].

1928a   Logik [course] **GA 26.**
1928b   Vorbemerkungen des Herausgebers; in: Husserl. *Vorlesungen zur Phänomenologie des inneren Zeitbewußtseins*, Jahrbuch für Philosophie und phänomenologische Forschung IX, 1928.

1928c   Phänomenologische Übungen zu Aristoteles, *Physica III* [seminar].

1928d   Theologie und Philosophie [lecture Marburg].

1928e   Zum Thema Kant und die Metaphysik [lecture Riga].

1928f   Gutachten zur Habilitation von Karl Löwith; in: Löwith 1981.

1928g   Ernst Cassirer. *Philosophie der symbolischen Formen. 2. Teil: Das mythische Denken* [review]. In: **GA 3**.

1928h   Andenken an Max Scheler. (In memoriam, for Max Scheler); in: **GA 26**.

1928i   Brief an Matthäus Lang [letter]. In: Ott, 1993.

1928/29a   Einleitung in die Philosophie [course]. **GA 27**.

1928/29b   Phänomenologische Übungen für Anfänger: Kant, *Grundlegung zur Metaphysik der Sitten* [seminar].

1928/29c   Phänomenologische Übungen für Fortgeschrittene: Die ontologischen Grundsätze und das Kategorienproblem [seminar].

1929a   ***Kant und das Problem der Metaphysik***. In: **GA 3**.

1929b   *Vom Wesen des Grundes*; in: *Festschrift für Edmund Husserl zum 70. Geburtstag*. Halle 1929. In: **GA 9**.

1929c   Philosophische Anthropologie und Metaphysik des Daseins [lecture Frankfurt]. In: GA 80.

1929d   Kants *Kritik der reinen Vernunft* und die Aufgabe einer Grundlegung der Metaphysik [lecture Davos]. In: **GA 3**.

1929e   Disputation in einer Arbeitsgemeinschaft zwischen Heidegger und Cassirer. In: **GA 3**.

1929f   Edmund Husserl zum siebzigsten Geburtstag [speech].

1929g   Der deutsche Idealismus und die philosophische Problemlage der Gegenwart [course]. In: **GA 28**.

1929h   Einführung in das akademische Studium [course]. In: **GA 28**.

1929i   Anfänger: Über Idealismus und Realismus im Anschluß an die Hauptvorlesungen (Hegels 'Vorrede' zur *Phänomenologie des Geistes*) [seminar].

1929j   Fortgeschrittene: Vom Wesen des Lebens mit besonderer Berücksichtigung von Aristoteles, *De Anima, De Animalium Motione* und *De Animalium Incessu* [seminar].

1929k   ***Was ist Metaphysik?*** [inaugural lecture Freiburg]. Bonn 1929. In: **GA 9**.

1929l   Die heutige Problemlage der Philosophie [lecture Karlsruhe and Amsterdam]. In: GA 80.

1929m   Brief an Victor Schwoerer [letter]. In: U. Sieg. Die Verjudung des deutschen Geistes, Die Zeit 22.12.1989.

1929/30a Die Grundbegriffe der Metaphysik. Welt - Endlichkeit - Vereinzelung [course]. **GA 29/30**.

1929/30b Unbenutzte Vorarbeiten zur Vorlesung *Die Grundbegriffe der Metaphysik*. In: Heidegger Studies 7, 1991.

1929/30c Für mittlere und höhere Semester: Über Gewißheit und Wahrheit im Anschluß an Descartes und Leibniz [seminar].

1930a   1. Die heutige Problemlage der Philosophie. 2. Hegel und das Problem der Metaphysik [lectures Amsterdam]. In: GA 80.

1930b   Vom Wesen der menschlichen Freiheit. Einleitung in die Philosophie [course]. **GA 31**.

1930c   Anfänger: Ausgewählte Kapitel aus Kants *Kritik der Urteilskraft* [seminar].

1930d   Vom Wesen der Wahrheit [lecture Karlsruhe]. In: *NzH*.

1930e   Vom Wesen der Wahrheit [lecture Bremen]. Revised draft in: **GA 9**.

1930f   Augustinus: Quid est tempus? [lecture Beuron]. In: GA 80.

1930g   Philosophieren und Glauben. Das Wesen der Wahrheit [lecture Marburg].

1930h   Vom Wesen der Wahrheit [lecture Freiburg]. Revised draft in: **GA 9**.

1930i   Vorrede zur japanischen Übersetzung von *Was ist Metaphysik?*

1930/31a Hegels *Phänomenologie des Geistes* [course]. **GA 32**.

1930/31b Augustinus, *Confessiones XI* [seminar].

1930/31c Fortgeschrittene: Platons *Parmenides* [seminar].

1931a   Interpretationen aus der antiken Philosophie [course]. **GA 33**.

1931b   Anfänger: Kant, *Über die Fortschritte der Metaphysik* [seminar].

1931c   Gutachten über Hendrik Josephus Pos; in: J. Aler (red.). *Martin Heidegger 1889-1976. Filosofische Weerklank in de Lage Landen*. Amsterdam 1991.

1931/32a Vom Wesen der Wahrheit [course]. **GA 34**.

1931/32b Übungen über Kants *Kritik der reinen und praktischen Vernunft* (Transzendentale Dialektik) [seminar].

1931/32c Zu Odebrechts und Cassirers Kritik des Kantbuches. In: **GA 3**.

1931/32d Vom Ursprung des Kunstwerkes. In: Heidegger Studies 5, 1989.

1932a Der Anfang der abendländischen Philosophie (Anaximander und Parmenides) [course]. GA 35.

1932b Mittelstufe: Platon, *Phaidros* [seminar].

1932c Der Satz vom Widerspruch [lecture Freiburg].

1932d Vom Wesen der Wahrheit [lecture Dresden]. Revised draft in: **GA 9**.

1933a ***Die Selbstbehauptung der deutschen Universität*** [lecture]. Breslau 1933.

1933b Schöpferische Landschaft: Warum bleiben wir in der Provinz [lecture]. In: **GA 13**.

1933c Schlageter [speech]. In: *NzH*.

1933d Arbeitsdienst (Arbeitsdienst und Universität). In: *NzH*.

1933e Die Universität im neuen Reich [lecture]. In: *NzH*.

1933f Nationalsozialistische Wissensschulung [speech]. In: *NzH*.

1933g Aufruf an die Deutschen Studenten [speech]. In: *MHDR*.

1933h Deutsche Männer und Frauen (Wahlaufruf vom 10.11. 1933). In: *NzH*.

1933i Bekenntnis zu Adolf Hitler und dem nationalsozialistischen Staat. Ansprache bei der Wahlkundgebung der deutschen Wissenschaft am 11. November 1933 [speech]. In: *NzH*.

1933j Der deutsche Student als Arbeiter [speech]. In: *NzH*.

1933k Die Universität im nationalsozialistischen Staat [lecture]. In: *MHDR*.

1933l 'Ruf an die Gebildeten der Welt'. Schreiben Heideggers an die Dekane. In: *MHDR*.

1933m Die Grundfrage der Philosophie [course]. In: GA 36/37.

1933n Oberstufe: Der Satz vom Widerspruch [seminar].

1933o Unterstufe: Der Begriff der Wissenschaft [seminar].

1933p Brief an Carl Schmitt [letter]. In: Telos 72, 1987.

1933q Gutachten über Richard Hönigdwald; in: W. Schmied-Kowarzik. *Richard Hönigswalds Philosophie der Pädagogik*. Würzburg, 1995.

1933/34a Vom Wesen der Wahrheit [course]. In: GA 36/37.
1933/34b Über Wesen und Begriff von Natur, Geschichte und Staat [seminar].

1934a Der Ruf zum Arbeitsdienst [speech]. In: *NzH.*
1934b Mahnwort an das allemanische Volk. In: *NzH.*
1934c Logik [course]. **GA 38.**
1934d Hegels *Jenenser Realphilosophie* [seminar].
1934e Hauptstücke aus Kants *Kritik der reinen Vernunft* [seminar].
1934f Zur Überwindung der Ästhetik. Zu 'Ursprung des Kunstwerks'. In: Heidegger Studies 6, 1990.
1934g Die gegenwärtige Lage und die künftige Aufgabe der deutschen Philosophie [lecture Konstanz].

1934/35a Hölderlins Hymnen *Germanien* und *Der Rhein* [course]. **GA 39.**
1934/35b Unterstufe: Hegel, Über den Staat (with E. Wolf) [seminar].
1934/35c Oberstufe: Hegel, *Phänomenologie des Geistes* [seminar].

1935a Einführung in die Metaphysik [course]. **GA 40.**
1935b Oberstufe: Hegel, *Phänomenologie des Geistes* [seminar].
1935c Der Ursprung des Kunstwerkes [lecture Freiburg]. In: **GA 5.**

1935/36a Grundfragen der Metaphysik; published in 1962 under the title: *Die Frage nach dem Ding. Zu Kants Lehre von den transzendentalen Grundsätzen* [course]. **GA 41.**
1935/36b Mittelstufe: Leibnizens Weltbegriff und der Deutsche Idealismus [seminar].
1935/36c Oberstufe: Hegel, *Phänomenologie des Geistes* [seminar].
1935/36d Die Überwindung der Ästhetik in der Frage nach der Kunst (with Bauch) [colloquium].

1936a Hölderlin und das Wesen der Dichtung [lecture Rome]. In: Das Innere Reich, 1936; in: **GA 4.**
1936b Schelling: *Vom Wesen der menschlichen Freiheit* [course]. Tübingen 1971. **GA 42.**
1936c Oberstufe: Kant, *Kritik der Urteilskraft* [seminar].
1936d Das Dasein und der Einzelne [lecture Zürich]. In: GA 80.
1936e Der Ursprung des Kunstwerkes [lecture Frankfurt am Main]. In: **GA 5.**
1936f Europa und die deutsche Philosophie [lecture Rome]. In: H.-

H. Gander. *Europa und die Philosophie.* Frankfurt am Main 1993 and GA 80.

1936g   Die Unumgänglichkeit des Da-seins ('Die Not') und Die Kunst in ihrer Notwendigkeit ('Die bewirkende Besinnung'). In: Heidegger Studies 8, 1992.

1936/37a   Nietzsche: Der Wille zur Macht [course]. **GA 43.**

1936/37b   Der Wille zur Macht als Kunst. In: **GA 6.1** (*Nietzsche I*).

1936/37c   Unterstufe: Ausgewählte Stücke aus Schillers philosophischen Schriften über die Kunst [seminar].

1937a   ***Hölderlin und das Wesen der Dichtung.*** München 1937. (1936a).

1937b   Wege zur Aussprache. In: *Jahrbuch der Stadt Freiburg,* Band 1. *Allemannenland;* in: **GA 13.**

1937c   Nietzsches metaphysische Grundstellung im abendländischen Denken [course]. **GA 44.**

1937d   Die ewige Wiederkehr des Gleichen. In: **GA 6.1** (*Nietzsche I*).

1937e   Übung: Nietzsches metaphysische Grundstellung [seminar].

1937f   Brief an Jean Wahl [letter]. In: Bulletin de la Société française de Philosophie 37, 1937, p. 193.

1937g   Brief an Karl Löwith [letter]. In: Papenfuss & Pöggeler 1990.

1937h   Prologue de l'auteur; in the French translation of *Was ist Metaphysik?*

1937i   Das Sein (Ereignis); in: Heidegger Studies 15, 1999

1937/38a   Grundfragen der Philosophie. Ausgewählte 'Probleme' der 'Logik' [course]. **GA 45.**

1937/38b   Die metaphysische Grundstellungen des abendländischen Denkens [seminar].

1937/38c   Die Bedrohung der Wissenschaft. In: Papenfuss & Pöggeler 1991.

1936-38   ***Beiträge zur Philosophie. Vom Ereignis.*** In: **GA 65.**

1938   Die Zeit des Weltbildes [lecture Freiburg]. In: **GA 5.**

1938/39a   Einleitung in die Philosophie. Nietzsches *II. Unzeitgemäße Betrachtung* [course]. GA 46.

1938/39b Unterstufe: Die philosophische und wissenschaftliche Begriffsbildung [seminar].

1938/39c *Besinnung*. **GA 66**.

1938/39d Die Negativität. Eine Auseinandersetzung mit Hegel aus
dem Ansatz in der Negativität (1938/39, 1941). In: **GA 68**.

1938/39e Die Überwindung der Metaphysik. In: **GA 67**.

1939a Vom Wesen und Begriff der Φυσις; in: *Il Pensiero*. Vol. III,
N. 2 and 3, Milano-Varese 1958. In: **GA 9**.

1939b Nietzsches Lehre vom Willen zur Macht als Erkenntnis
[course]. **GA 47**.

1939c Nietzsches Lehre vom Willen zur Macht als Erkenntnis. In:
GA 6.1 (*Nietzsche I*).

1939d Die ewige Wiederkunft des Gleichen und der Wille zur
Macht. In: **GA 6.2** (*Nietzsche II*).

1939e Oberstufe: Vom Wesen der Sprache. Die Metaphysik der
Sprache und die Wesung des Wortes. Zu Herders Abhandlung *Über der Ursprung der Sprache* [seminar]. **GA 85**.

1939f Von der Grundbestimmung des Wissens [lecture Freiburg].
In: GA 80.

1939g Koinon. Aus der Geschichte des Seyns. In: **GA 69**.

1939/40a 'Wie wenn am Feiertage . . .' [lecture]. In: **GA 4**.

1939/40b Mittel- und Oberstufe: Hegels Metaphysik der Geschichte
[seminar].

1938-40 Die Geschichte des Seyns. In: **GA 69**.

1940a Nietzsche: Der europäische Nihilismus [course]. **GA 48**.

1940b Der europäische Nihilismus. In: **GA 6.2** (*Nietzsche II*).

1940c Nietzsches Metaphysik. In: **GA 6.2** (*Nietzsche II*).

1940d Über die Φυσις bei Aristoteles [seminar].

1940e Vom Wesen der Wahrheit [seminar].

1940f Der Spruch des Parmenides [lecture Freiburg]. In: GA 80.

1940/41 Fortgeschrittene: Leibniz, *Monadologie* [seminar].

1941a *Winke* [Privatdruck]; in: **GA 13**.

1941b *'Wie wenn am Feiertage . . .'*. Halle 1941 (1939/40a).

1941c Die Metaphysik des deutschen Idealismus. Zur erneuten
Auslegung von Schelling: *Philosophische Untersuchungen*

über das Wesen der menschlichen Freiheit und die damit zusammenhängende Gegenstände (1809) [course]. **GA 49**.

1941d　Übungen über den Anfang der abendländischen Philosophie [seminar].

1941e　Grundbegriffe [course]. **GA 51**.

1941f　Anfänger: Kant, *Prolegomena* [seminar].

1941g　Die Metaphysik als Geschichte des Seins. In: **GA 6.2** (*Nietzsche II*).

1941h　Entwürfe zur Geschichte des Seins als Metaphysik. In: **GA 6.2** (*Nietzsche II*).

1941i　Die Erinnerung in die Metaphysik. In: **GA 6.2** (*Nietzsche II*).

1941j　Ausgewählte Stücke aus den Manuskripten zum Schelling-Seminar SS 1941; in: *Schellings Abhandlung: Über das Wesen der menschlichen Freiheit.*

1941k　Zur Geschichte des Existenzbegriffs [lecture Freiburg]. In: GA 80.

1941l　Über den Anfang. GA 70.

1941/42a　Nietzsches Metaphysik [course, not taught]. **GA 50**.

1941/42b　Hölderlins Hymnen [course]. **GA 52**.

1941/42c　Anfänger: Schiller: *Über die ästhetische Erziehung des Menschen* [seminar].

1941/42d　Fortgeschrittene: Platons *Siebenter Brief* [seminar].

1941/42e　Das Ereignis. GA 71.

1942a　*Platons Lehre von der Wahrheit*; in: Geistige Überlieferung. Das Zweite Jahrbuch, Berlin 1942. In: **GA 9**.

1942b　Hölderlins Hymnen [course]. **GA 53**.

1942c　Anfänger: Die Grundbegriffe der Metaphysik Kants [seminar].

1942d　Fortgeschrittene: Hegel, *Phänomenologie des Geistes* und Aristoteles, *Metaphysik IX, 10* und *VI* [seminar].

1942e　Erläuterung der 'Einleitung' zu Hegels *Phänomenologie des Geistes*. In: **GA 68**.

1942f　Brief an Max Kommerell [letter]. In: M. Kommerell. *Briefe und Aufzeichnungen 1919-1944*. Freiburg 1967.

1942/43a　Hegels Begriff der Erfahrung. In: **GA 5**.

1942/43b　Parmenides und Heraklit [course]. **GA 54**.

1942/43c　Fortgeschrittene: Fortsetzung von 1942d.

1941-43 Auszug aus den Seminar-Notizen 1941-43 [seminars]; in: *Schellings Abhandlung über das Wesen der menschlichen Freiheit.*

1943a **Vom Wesen der Wahrheit** (1930e). Frankfurt am Main 1943. In: **GA 9.**

1943b Nachwort zu: Was ist Metaphysik? In: **GA 9.**

1943c Nietzsches Wort 'Gott ist tot' [lecture]. In: **GA 5.**

1943d Andenken; in: P. Kluckhon (Hg.). *Tübinger Gedenkschrift zum hundertsten Todestag Hölderlins.* Tübingen 1943. In: **GA 4.**

1943e Heimkunft/An die Verwandten [lecture]. In: **GA 4.**

1943f Aletheia (Heraklit, Fragment 16). In: *VA.* GA 7.

1943g **Chorlied aus der Antigone des Sophokles** [Privatdruck]. In **GA 13.**

1943h Der Anfang des abendländischen Denkens (Heraklit) [course]. **GA 55.**

1943i Fortgeschrittene: Hegel, *Phänomenologie des Geistes* [seminar].

1943/44a **Besinnung auf unser Wesen.** Frankfurt am Main 1994 (Jahresgabe der Heidegger-Gesellschaft).

1943/44b **Die Herkunft der Gottheit.** Frankfurt am Main 1997 (Jahresgabe der Martin-Heidegger-Gesellschaft)

1944a **Erläuterungen zu Hölderlins Dichtung.** Frankfurt am Main 1944. **GA 4.**

1944b Vorbemerkung zur Wiederholung der Rede. In: **GA 4.**

1944c Logik. Heraklits Lehre vom Logos [course]. **GA 55.**

1944d Fortgeschrittene: Aristoteles, *Metaphysik IV* [seminar].

1944e Das Wort. Die Bedeutung der Wörter. In: Papenfuss & Pöggeler 1992.

1944f **Die Stege des Anfangs. GA 72.**

1944/45a Zur Erörterung der Gelassenheit. Aus einem Feldweggespräch über das Denken. In: **GA 13.**

1944/45b Einleitung in die Philosophie - Denken und Dichten [course]. **GA 50.**

1944/45c Leibniz, *Die 24 Thesen* [seminar].

1944/45d **Feldweg - Gespräche: 'Αγχιβασίη. Ein Gespräch selbstdritt auf einem Feldweg zwischen einem Forscher, einem**

Gelehrten und einem Weisen; Der Lehrer trifft den Türmer an der Tür zum Turmaufgang; Abendgespräch in einem Kriegsgefangenenlager in Rußland zwischen einem Jüngeren und einem Älteren. **GA 77**.

1941-45a **Das Wesen des Menschen**. Frankfurt am Main 1993 (Jahresgabe der Heidegger-Gesellschaft).

1941-45b **Die Armut**. Frankfurt am Main (Jahresgabe der Heidegger-Gesellschaft).

1945a   Das Rektorat 1933/34. Tatsachen und Gedanken. In: *Die Selbstbehauptung der deutschen Universität/Das Rektorat*.

1945b   Die Armut [lecture]. In: Heidegger Studies 10, 1994.

1945c   Brief an das Akademische Rektorat der Albert-Ludwigs-Universität [letter]. In: K.A. Moehling: *Martin Heidegger and the Nazi Party*. Dissertation Northern Illinois University 1972.

1945d   Brief an Sartre [letter]. In: H. Ott: Martin Heidegger schreibt an Jean-Paul Sartre; in: *Perspektiven der Philosophie. Neues Jahrbuch* 20, 1994.

1945e   Brief an den Vorsitzenden des politischen Bereinigungsausschusses Professor von Dietze [letter]. In: *MHDR*.

1936-46   Überwindung der Metaphysik. In: *VA*. GA 7.

1944-46   Die seinsgeschichtliche Bestimmung des Nihilismus. In: **GA 6.2** (*Nietzsche II*).

1946a   Brief über den Humanismus. In: **GA 9**.

1946b   Wozu Dichter? [lecture]. In: **GA 5**.

1946c   Der Spruch des Anaximander. In: **GA 5**.

1946d   Die Grundfrage nach dem Sein selbst. In: Heidegger Studies 2, 1986.

1947a   **Platons Lehre von der Wahrheit/Brief über den Humanismus**. Bern 1947. In: **GA 9**.

1947b   **Aus der Erfahrung des Denkens** [Privatdruck]. In: **GA 13**.

1946-48   Das Wesen des Nihilismus. In: **GA 67**.

1949a   Der Feldweg. In: *Conradin Kreutzer - Stadt Meßkirch.* Meßkirch 1949; in: **GA 13**.

1949b   Einleitung zu: Was ist Metaphysik?; in: **GA 9**.

1949c   Die Kehre [lecture]. In: *Die Technik und die Kehre.*

1949d   Holzwege ('Dem künftigen Menschen...') [Faksimile]. In: **GA 13**.

1949e   ***Einblick in das was ist. Bremer Vorträge 1949: Das Ding, Das Gestell, Die Gefahr, Die Kehre*** [lectures]. in: **GA 79**.

1950a   *Holzwege*. Frankfurt am Main 1950. **GA 5**.

1950b   Das Ding [lecture München]. In: *Jahrbuch der Bayerischen Akademie der Schönen Künste*, Band I. München 1951; in: *VA.* **GA 7**.

1950c   Die Sprache [lecture Bühlerhöhe]. In: **GA 12**.

1950d   Brief an Ernst Jünger [letter]. Frankfurt am Main 1998 (Jahresgabe der Martin-Heidegger-Gesellschaft).

1950e   Fünf Gedichte: Ohne Titel, Du, Das Mädchen aus der Fremde, Entsprechung, Tod [poems]. In: Arendt/Heidegger.

1950f   Stürze aus entzogenen Gnaden: November 1924, Der Mensch, Der Ruf, Welt, Die Sterblichen, Persona, Das Ereignis, Ohne Titel [poems]. In: Arendt/Heidegger.

1950g   Vier Gedichte: Fünf Jahrfünfte, Märzanfang, Holzwege, Denken [poems]. In: Arendt/Heidegger.

1950h   Zwei Gedichte (Ohne Titel) [poems]. In: Arendt/Heidegger.

1950i   Aus der Sonata sonans: Der Ton, Uns ereignend, Das Licht, Schöne, ΠΥΡ ΑΕΙΖΩΟΝ, Gedacht und Zart, Ohne Titel [poems]. In: Arendt/Heidegger.

1950j   Fünf Gedichte: Sonata sonans, Die Fluh, Das Geheimnis wächst, Der Wieder-Blick, Sprache [poems]. In: Arendt/Heidegger.

1950k   Wellen [poem]. In: Arendt/Heidegger.

1950l   Brief an Herman Zelter [letter]. In: H. Zelter. *Existentielle Kommunikation.* Erlangen 1978.

1951a   Bauen Wohnen Denken [lecture Darmstadt]. In: *VA.* **GA 7**.

1951b   'Dichterisch wohnet der Mensch' [lecture Bühlerhöhe]. In: Akzente. Zeitschrift für Dichtung 1, 1954; in: *VA.* **GA 7**.

1951c   Logos (Heraklit, Fragment 50). In: *VA.* **GA 7**.

1951d   Zu einem Vers von Mörike. Ein Briefwechsel mit Martin Heidegger von Emil Staiger. In: Trivium 9, Zürich 1954; in: **GA 13**.

1951e   Was heißt lesen? In: Welt der Schule 11, Jahrgang 7, 1954; in: **GA 13**.

1951f   Übungen im Lesen: Aristoteles, *Physik II, 1* und *III, 1-3* [seminar].

1951g   Aussprache mit Martin Heidegger in Zürich [seminar]. In: **GA 15**.

1951h   Zu einer Zeichnung von Henri Matisse [poem]. In: Arendt/ Heidegger.

1951/52a   Was heißt Denken? [course]. In: *Was heißt Denken?* GA 8.

1951/52b   Übungen im Lesen: Aristoteles, *Metaphysik I* und *IX, 10* [seminar].

1952a   Moira (Parmenides VIII, 34-41). In: *VA.* GA 7.

1952b   Was heißt Denken? [lecture Bayerische Rundfunk]. In: Merkur 6, 1952; in: *VA.* GA 7.

1952c   Was heißt Denken? [course]. In: *Was heißt Denken?* GA 8.

1952d   Die Sprache im Gedicht [lecture Bühlerhöhe]. In: Merkur 61, 1953; in: **GA 12**.

1953a   ***Einführung in die Metaphysik*** [course 1935]. Tübingen 1953.

1953b   ***Der Feldweg.*** Frankfurt am Main 1953.

1953c   Die Frage nach der Technik [lecture München]. In: *Jahrbuch der Bayerischen Akademie der Schöne Künsten*, Band III. München 1954; in: *VA.* GA 7.

1953d   Wissenschaft und Besinnung [lecture München]. In: *VA.* GA 7.

1953e   Wer ist Nietzsches Zarathustra? [lecture Bremen]. In: *VA.* GA 7.

1953f   Die Sprache im Gedicht. Eine Erörterung von Georg Trakls Gedicht. In: **GA 12**.

1953g   Technik und Kunst - Ge-stell. In: Biemel & Herrmann 1989.

1953h   Ein Brief Martin Heideggers zu seinem Hölderlin-Erläuterungen [letter]. In: Jahrbuch des freien deutschen Hochstifts. Tübingen 1977. In: **GA 4**.

1953i   Ein Brief Martin Heideggers über die *Einführung in die Metaphysik* [letter]. In: Die Zeit, Jhg. 8, Nr. 39. In: **GA 40**.

1953/54   Aus einem Gespräch über die Sprache. In: **GA 12**.

1954a   *Vorträge und Aufsätze.* Pfullingen 1954. GA 7.
1954b   Vom Geheimnis des Glockenturms. In: **GA 13**.
1954c   Für das Langenharder Hebelbuch. In: **GA 13**.
1954d   Johann Peter Hebel [lecture Zähringen]. In: GA 80.

1954/55   *Existenzialismus.* Frankfurt am Main 1995 (Jahresgabe der Martin-Heidegger-Gesellschaft).

1955a   Zur Seinsfrage. In: *Festschrift für Ernst Jünger zum 60. Geburtstag 'Freundschaftliche Begegnungen'*. Frankfurt am Main 1955; in: **GA 9**.
1955b   Gelassenheit [lecture]. In: *Gelassenheit*. Pfullingen 1957, and in: **GA 13**.
1955c   Über die Sixtina. In: M. Putscher: *Raphaels Sixtinische Madonna - Das Werk und seine Wirkung*. Tübingen 1955; in: **GA 13**.
1955d   Die Sprache Johann Peter Hebels. In: Der Lichtgang 5. Jahrgang, Heft 7, Freiburg 1955; in: **GA 13**.
1955e   Begegnungen mit Ortega Y Gasset. In: Clavileno - Revista de la Asociacion International de Hispanismo, Jahrgang 7, Nr. 39; in: **GA 13**.

1955/56a Der Satz vom Grund [course]. In: **GA 10**.
1955/56b Zu Hegels *Logik*: Die Logik des Wesens [seminar].

1956a   *Was ist das, die Philosophie?* Pfullingen 1956. In: GA 11.
1956b   Zusatz (zu: *Der Ursprung des Kunstwerkes*); in: **GA 5**.
1956c   Der Satz vom Grund [lecture]. In: *Der Satz vom Grund.*
1956d   Was ist die Zeit? In: *Die Zeit* 8, 1956; in: **GA 13**.
1956e   Die nachgelassenen Klee-Notizen. In: Heidegger Studies 9, 1993.

1956/57   Zu Hegels *Logik*: Über den Anfang der Wissenschaft [seminar].

1957a   *Der Satz vom Grund.* Pfullingen 1957. **GA 10**.
1957b   *Identität und Differenz.* Pfullingen 1957. GA 11.
1957c   Der Satz der Identität [lecture Freiburg]. In: *ID*. GA 11.
1957d   Die onto-theo-logische Verfassung der Metaphysik [lecture Freiburg]. In: *ID*. GA 11.
1957e   *Hebel - der Hausfreund.* Pfullingen 1957. In: **GA 13**.

1957f   **Grundsätze des Denkens. Freiburger Vorträge 1957** [lectures Freiburg]. In : **GA 79**.

1957g   Über das Prinzip 'Zu den Sachen selbst'. In: Heidegger Studies 11, 1995.

1957/58   Das Wesen der Sprache [lecture Freiburg]. In: **GA 12**.

1958a   Grundsätze des Denkens. In: *Jahrbuch für Psychologie und Psychotherapie* 6, 1958.

1958b   Das Wort [lecture Wien, Konstanz, Amriswil]. In: **GA 12**.

1958c   Hegel und die Griechen [lecture Heidelberg]. In: *Die Gegenwart der Griechen. Festschrift für Hans-Georg Gadamer zum 60. Geburtstag.* Tübingen 1960; in: **GA 9**.

1958d   Die Kunst und das Denken. Protokoll eines Kolloquiums am 18. Mai 1958 (with S. Hisamatsu). In: Buchner 1989.

1958e   Shinichi Hisamatsu - Martin Heidegger: Wechselseitige Spiegelung. Aus einem Gespräch mit Martin Heidegger. In: Buchner 1989.

1959a   **Unterwegs zur Sprache**. Pfullingen 1959. GA 12.

1959b   **Gelassenheit**. Pfullingen 1959.

1959c   Der Weg zur Sprache [lecture München, Berlin]. In: **GA 12**.

1959d   Hölderlins Erde und Himmel [lecture München]. In: **GA 4**.

1959e   Antrittsrede in der Heidelberger Akademie der Wissenschaften [lecture Heidelberg].

1959f   Aufzeichnungen aus der Werkstatt. In: *Neue Zürcher Zeitung* 264, Blatt 10 (Fernausgabe); in: **GA 13**.

1959g   Dank an die Meßkircher Heimat. Ansprache von Professor Martin Heidegger anläßlich seiner Ernennung zum Ehrenbürger der Stadt Meßkirch am 27. September 1959 [speech]. In: Stadt Meßkirch (Hg.): *Meßkirch gestern und heute. Heimatbuch zum 700-jährigen Stadtjubiläum.* Meßkirch 1961.

1959h   Über die Be-stimmung der Künste im gegenwärtigen Zeitalter [lecture Baden-Baden]. In: GA 80.

1959i   Das menschliche Dasein als ein Bereich des Vernehmens [seminar Zollikon]. In: *ZS*. GA 89.

1960a   Sprache und Heimat [lecture Wesselburen]. In: Hebbel-Jahrbuch 1960, Heide in Holstein 1960; in: **GA 13**.

1960b   Kant: Sein ist kein reales Prädikat [seminar Zollikon]. In: *ZS*. GA 89.

1960c	Bild und Wort [Symposion].
1960d	Brief an Heinrich Ochsner [letter]. In: C. Ochwadt & E. Tecklenborg (Hg.). *Das Mass des Verbogenen*. Hannover, 1981.
1961a	*Nietzsche*. Band I-II. Pfullingen. **GA 6.1-6.2**.
1961b	*700 Jahre Meßkirch* (Ansprache zum Heimatabend am 22. Juli 1961). Meßkirch 1961. In: *700 Jahre Stadt Meßkirch. Festansprache zum 700jährigen Meßkircher Stadtjubiläum vom 22. bis 30. Juli 1961 80*. Meßkirch 1962.
1961c	Kants These über das Sein [lecture Kiel]. In: *Existenz und Ordnung. Festschrift für Erik Wolf zum 60. Geburtstag*. Frankfurt am Main 1962; in: **GA 9**.
1962a	*Die Frage nach dem Ding. Zu Kants Lehre von den transzendentalen Grundsätzen* (course WS 1935/36), Tübingen 1962.
1962b	*Die Technik und die Kehre*. Pfullingen 1962.
1962c	Zeit und Sein [lecture]. In: *ZSD*. GA 14.
1962d	Protokoll zu einem Seminar über den Vortrag 'Zeit und Sein'. In: *ZSD*. GA 14.
1962e	Vorwort (zu Richardson 1963).
1962f	Über Igor Strawinsky. In: Melos, Jahrgang 1962, Heft 6/29; in: **GA 13**.
1962g	Max Kommerell [lecture]. In: GA 80.
1962h	*Überlieferte Sprache und technische Sprache* [lecture Comburg]. St. Gallen 1989. In: GA 80.
1962i	Aufenthalte - Griechenlandreise. In: *Aufenthalte*.
1963a	Mein Weg in die Phänomenologie. In: *Hermann Niemeyer zum 80. Geburtstag*. Tübingen 1963; in: *ZSD*. GA 14.
1963b	Seminarprotokolle (Zollikon 1963). In: M. Boss: Triebwelt und Personalisation. In: Fr. Böckle u.a. (Hg.): *Christlicher Glaube in moderner Gesellschaft*. Bd. 6. Freiburg/Basel/Wien 1981.
1963c	Vorwort zur Lesung von Hölderlins Gedichten. In: **GA 4**.
1963d	Für René Char. In: Hommage à Georges Braque; in: Derrière le Miroir, Nr. 144-146, Mai 1964; in: **GA 13**.
1963e	Brief an T. Kojima [letter]. In: Zeitschrift für Literatur, bildende Kunst, Musik und Wissenschaft 1, 1965.

1964a   Das Ende der Philosophie und die Aufgabe des Denkens [lecture]. In: J. Beaufret & Fr. Fédier (Ed.): *Kierkegaard vivant*. Paris 1966; in: *ZSD*. GA 14.

1964b   Aus der letzten Marburger Vorlesung. In: *Festschrift für Bultmann zum 80. Geburtstag*. Tübingen 1964. **GA 9**.

1964c   ***Bemerkungen zur Kunst - Plastik - Raum*** [lecture St. Gallen]. Erker-Verlag St. Gallen 1996. In: GA 80.

1964d   ***Über Abraham a Santa Clara*** [lecture Meßkirch]. Meßkirch 1964.

1964e   Adalbert Stifter *Eisgeschichte*. In: *Wirkendes Wort*. Zürich 1964; in: **GA 13**.

1964f   Einige Hinweise auf Hauptgeschichtspunkte für das theologische Gespräch über 'Das Problem eines nicht-objektivierenden Denkens und Sprechens in der heutigen Theologie' [letter]. In: **GA 9**.

1964g   Der Raum als das Freie und Offene [seminar Zollikon]. In: *ZS*. GA 89.

1964h   Die Frage nach dem Sein der Zeit [seminar Zollikon]. In: *ZS*. GA 89.

1964i   Brief an Manfred Frings [letter]. In: Th. Sheehan (ed.). *Heidegger. The Man and the Thinker*. Chicago: Precedent 1988.

1965a   Das Ende des Denkens in der Gestalt der Philosophie [lecture]. Published as: ***Zur Frage nach der Bestimmung der Sache des Denkens***. St. Gallen 1984.

1965b   Die Frage was die Zeit ist [seminar Zollikon]. In: *ZS*. GA 89.

1965c   Die Frage nach der Zeit [seminar Zollikon]. In: *ZS*. GA 89.

1965d   Das Leibproblem [seminar Zollikon]. In: *ZS*. GA 89.

1965e   Das Leibproblem und das Methodebewußtsein der Wissenschaften [seminar Zollikon]. In: *ZS*. GA 89.

1965f   Die Daseinsanalytik [seminar Zollikon]. In: *ZS*. GA 89.

1966a   Nur noch ein Gott kann uns retten. Spiegel-Gespräch mit Martin Heidegger am 23. September 1966. In: *Der Spiegel* 1976 und Neske & Kettering 1990.

1966b   Parmenides/Heraklit [seminar Le Thor]. In: **GA 15**.

1966c   Wink in das Gewesen. In: *Vittorio Klostermann zum 29.12.1976*. Frankfurt am Main 1976; in: **GA 13**.

1966d   Grundzug des Menschseins [seminar Zollikon]. In: *ZS*. GA 89.

1966e   Letter to Arthur H. Schrynemakers. In: Sallis 1970.
1966f   Letter to Manfred S. Frings. In: Frings 1968.
1966g   Für Eugen Fink zum sechzigsten Geburtstag; in: **GA 29/30**.
1966h   Leserbrief an den *Spiegel* [letter]. In: Der Spiegel, Jhg. 20, Nr. 11.
1966i   Ein Brief an Keikichi Matsuo [letter]. In: Buchner 1989.

1966/67   **Heraklit** (with E. Fink) [seminar].

1967a   ***Wegmarken***. Frankfurt am Main 1967. **GA 9**.
1967b   Die Herkunft der Kunst und die Bestimmung des Denkens [lecture Athens]. In: P. Jaeger & R. Lüthe (Hrsg.): *Distanz und Nähe*. Würzburg 1983; in: *Denkerfahrungen*; and in: GA 80.
1967c   Die Bestimmung der Sache des Denkens [lecture Kiel]. In: GA 80.
1967d   Hans Jantzen dem Freunde zum Andenken; in: *Erinnerung an Hans Jantzen*. Freiburg 1967.

1968a   Das Gedicht [lecture Amriswil]. In: **GA 4**.
1968b   Hegel: *Differenzschrift* [seminar Le Thor]. In: **GA 15**.
1968c   Brief an François Bondy [letter]. In: Critique 24, 1968.
1968d   Zur Frage nach der Bestimmung der Sache des Denkens. Vorwort für die japanische Übersetzung. In: Buchner 1989.

1969a   ***Zur Sache des Denkens***. Tübingen 1969. GA 14.
1969b   ***Die Kunst und der Raum***. St. Gallen 1969. In: **GA 13**.
1969c   Fragen nach dem Aufenthalt des Menschen. In: Neue Züricher Zeitung. Nr. 606, 5. Oktober 1969.
1969d   Dankansprache von Professor Martin Heidegger [speech]. In: Stadt Meßkirch (Hg.): *Ansprachen zum 80. Geburtstag*. Meßkirch 1969.
1969e   Kant: *Der einzig mögliche Beweisgrund zu einer Demonstration des Daseins Gottes* [seminar Le Thor]. In: **GA 15**.
1969f   Martin Heidegger im Gespräch; in: R. Wisser (Hrsg.). *Martin Heidegger im Gespräch*. Freiburg and München 1970, and in: Neske & Kettering 1990.
1969g   Zeichen. In: *Neue Zürcher Zeitung* 579, 21.09.1969; in: **GA 13**.
1969h   Das Räumlichsein des Daseins und das Im-Raume-sein des Gebrauchdinges [seminar Zollikon]. In: *ZS*. GA 89.

1969i	Letter to Albert Borgmann. In: Philosophy East and West 20, 1970.
1969j	Brief an Ernst Jünger [letter]. In: E. Jünger. *Federbälle I-II*. Zürich, 1980.

1970a	*Phänomenologie und Theologie*. Frankfurt am Main 1970. In: **GA 9**.
1970b	Das Wohnen des Menschen. In: *Hesperus. Festschrift für Gustav Hillard Steinbömer zum Geburtstag*. Hamburg 1971; in: **GA 13**.
1970c	*Heraklit* (with E. Fink) (1966/67). Frankfurt am Main 1970.
1970d	Brief an Jan Aler [letter]. In: Zeitschrift für Ästhetik und allgemeine Kunstwissenschaft 18, 1973.
1970e	Zeit [poem]. In: Arendt/Heidegger.

1971a	*Schellings Abhandlung über das Wesen der menschlichen Freiheit (1809)*. Tübingen 1971. **GA 42**.
1971b	*Was heißt Denken?* Tübingen 1971. GA 8.
1971c	Pensivement - Gedachtes. Für René Char in freundschaftlichen Gedenken. In: D. Fourcade (Ed.): *Cahier de l'Herne - René Char*. Paris 1971; in: **GA 13**.
1971d	Cézanne [poem]. In: Arendt/Heidegger.

1961-72	Zwiegespräche mit Medard Boss. In: *ZS*. GA 89.

1972a	*Frühe Schriften*. Frankfurt am Main 1972. **GA 1**.
1972b	Rimbaud. In: Archives des Lettres modernes 160, 1976; in: **GA 13**.
1972c	Sprache. In: Argile, I Hiver 1973; in: **GA 13**.
1972d	Vorwort zu: Frühe Schriften. In: **GA 1**.
1972e	Dank [poem]. In: Arendt/Heidegger.
1972f	Lettre - Préface [letter]. In: H. Mongis. *Heidegger et la Critique de la Notion de Valeur*. The Hague: Nijhoff 1976.

1973a	Husserl: *Logische Untersuchungen VI.2: Sinnlichkeit und Verstand* [seminar Zähringen]. In: **GA 15**.
1973b	Andenken an Marcelle Mathieu. In: *Denkerfahrungen*.

1974a	Der Fehl heiliger Namen. In: Contre toute attente, 2/3, 1981; in: **GA 13**.

1974b   Fridolin Wiplingers letzter Besuch. In: Fr. Wiplinger: *Metaphysik. Grundfragen ihres Ursprungs und ihrer Vollendung.* Freiburg and München 1976; in: **GA 13**.

1974c   *Cézanne.* Frankfurt am Main 1991 (Jahresgabe der Heidegger-Gesellschaft).

1974d   Ein Grusswort für das Symposion in Beirut November 1974 [letter]. In: Extasis. Cahiers de philosophie et de littérature No. 8, Beirut 1981.

1974e   Grußwort anläßlich des Erscheinens von Nr. 500 der Zeitschrift 'Risô'. In: Buchner 1989.

1975a   Erhart Kästner zum Gedächtnis. In: A. Kästner & R. Kästner (Hg.): *Erhart Kästner - Leben und Werk in Daten und Bildern.* Frankfurt am Main 1980; in: **GA 13**.

1975b   Brief an Jean Beaufret [letter]. In: E. de Rubercy & D. le Buhan: *Douze questions à propos de Martin Heidegger.* Paris 1983; and in: Heidegger Studies 3/4, 1987/88.

1975c   Widmung für Gerd Haeffner; in: Haeffner, Gerd. München: *Heideggers Begriff der Metaphysik.* Johannes Berchmanns Verlag, ²1981.

1976a   Grußwort von Martin Heidegger. In: *Stadt Meßkirch - Ehrenbürgerfeier Professor Dr. Bernhard Welte.* Meßkirch 1978; in: **GA 13**.

1976b   *Neuzeitliche Naturwissenschaft und moderne Technik [Grusswort an die Teilnehmer des zehnten Colloquiums vom 14. bis 16. Mai 1976 in Chicago].* Frankfurt am Main 1989 (Jahresgabe der Martin-Heidegger-Gesellschaft).

1983a   *Denkerfahrungen.* Frankfurt am Main 1983. **GA 13**.
1983b   *Die Selbstbehauptung der deutschen Universität / Das Rektorat.* Frankfurt am Main 1983.

1987   *Zollikoner Seminare: Protokolle - Gespräche - Briefe.* Hrsg. von M. Boss, Frankfurt am Main 1987. GA 89.

1989a   *Aufenthalte.* Frankfurt am Main 1989. GA 75.
1989b   *Der Begriff der Zeit.* Tübingen 1989.

APPENDIX II:
GERMAN-ENGLISH GLOSSARY

Abgeschiedenheit	-	apartness
Abgrund	-	abyss, abground
Abwesenheit	-	absence
Affekt	-	affect
Alltäglichkeit	-	everydayness
Als-Struktur	-	as-structure
andenken	-	commemorative thinking
aneignen	-	appropriate
Anfang	-	beginning
Anfängliche, das	-	incipient, the
Angst	-	anxiety
Anklang	-	echo
Anschauung	-	intuition
Anspruch	-	claim
Anwesenheit	-	presence
apophantisches Als	-	apophantic as
Apriori, das	-	a priori, the
Arbeiter	-	worker
Aufriß	-	design
Augenblick	-	moment of vision
Ausdruck	-	expression
Auseinandersetzung	-	setting apart from one another
Ausgelegtheit	-	interpretedness
Auslegung	-	interpretation
Ausrichtung	-	directionality
Aussage	-	assertion
aussein auf	-	being-out-for
bauen	-	building
Bedeutsamkeit	-	meaningfulness

Bedeutung	-	meaning
bedingen	-	determine
Bedingnis	-	bethinging
Befindlichkeit	-	disposedness
Begründung	-	founding
behalten	-	retain
Bekümmerung	-	affliction
Besinnung	-	reflection, mindfulness
besorgen	-	concern
Bestand	-	standing reserve
Betroffenheit	-	affectedness
Bewandtnis	-	involvement
Bewegung	-	movement
Bezug	-	relation
Bezugssinn	-	relational sense
Boden-nehmen	-	taking-ground
Bodenständigkeit	-	autochthony
Brauch	-	use, handling
Christentum	-	Christianity
Christlichkeit	-	Christianness
Dasein	-	being there
denken	-	thinking
Destruktion	-	destruction
Dichtung	-	poetry
Ding	-	thing
Ding an sich	-	thing in itself
Durchschnittlichkeit	-	averageness
Eigen	-	own
Eigentlichkeit	-	authenticity
Einfalt	-	simplicity
einräumen	-	make room
Ekstase	-	ecstasis
Empfängnis	-	acceptance
entbergen	-	reveal
Entbergung	-	revealment
entdecken	-	uncover
Entdecktheit	-	discovery
Entfernung	-	de-distancy

Entgötterung	-	de-godding
entleben	-	unliving
Entschlossenheit	-	resoluteness
Entschluß	-	resolution
Entweltlichung	-	unworlding
Entwurf	-	projection
eräugen	-	to place before the eyes
Eräugnung, der	-	placing before the eyes, the
Erde	-	earth
ereignen	-	to make one's own, proprerize
Ereignis	-	appropriation, enowning
Ereignung	-	propriation
Erfahrung	-	experience
Erklärung	-	explanation
Erlebnis	-	lived experience
Erschlossenheit	-	disclosedness
Es gibt	-	it is giving
Es gilt	-	it holds, it validates, it has validity
Es soll	-	it ought
Es weltet	-	it is worlding
Es wertet	-	it is valuing
Existenz	-	existence
existenzial	-	existential [adjective]
Existenzial	-	existential [noun]
existenziale Analytik	-	existential analysis
Existenzialismus	-	existentialism
Existentialität	-	existentiality
existenziell	-	existentiell
faktische Lebenserfahrung	-	factual life experience
Faktizität	-	facticity
Faktum	-	fact
Ferne	-	farness
formale Anzeige	-	formal indication
Freiheit	-	freedom
Frommigkeit	-	piety
Fug	-	arrangement, fugue, joining
Fuge	-	pattern of arrangement
Fügung	-	arranging
Fundamentalontologie	-	fundamental ontology
Furcht	-	fear

Fürsorge	-	solicitude
Ganzheit	-	whole, the
Gegebenheit	-	givenness
Gegend	-	region
Gegenständigkeit	-	objectness
Gegenständlichkeit	-	objectivity
Gegenwart	-	present
gegenwärtigen	-	make present
Gegnet	-	expanse
Gehaltssinn	-	content sense
Geheimnis	-	mystery
Geheiß	-	peal
Geist	-	spirit
Gelassenheit	-	acquiescence (release, releasement)
Geltung	-	validity
Generation	-	generation
Gerede	-	idle talk
geschehen	-	come to pass
Geschichtlichkeit	-	historicality
Geschick	-	destiny
Gestell	-	enframing
Gestimmtheit	-	attunement
Geviert, das	-	fourfold, the
gewärtigen	-	awaiting
Gewesenheit	-	having been
Gewissen	-	conscience
Gewissensruf	-	call of conscience
Geworfenheit	-	thrownness
Glaube	-	faith
gleichursprünglich	-	equiprimordial
gönnen	-	yield
Gott	-	God
Götter	-	gods
Göttlichen, die	-	divinities, the
Grenssituation	-	limit situation
griechische Philosophie	-	Greek philosophy
Grund	-	ground
Grundfrage	-	basic question
Gründung	-	grounding

Haus des Seins, das	-	house of Being, the
Heil	-	wholesome
Heilige, das	-	holy, the
Heimat	-	homeland
Heimweh	-	homesickness
Held	-	hero
Hermeneutik	-	hermeneutics
hermeneutische Situation	-	hermeneutic situation
hermeneutische Zirkel	-	hermeneutic circle
Himmel	-	sky
Hinsehen	-	inspection
Hirt des Seins	-	shepherd of Being
Historie	-	historology
Historismus	-	historicism
Holzwege	-	forest trails
hören	-	hearing
Horizont	-	horizon
horizontales Schema	-	horizonal schema
Huld	-	grace
Humanismus	-	humanism
Ich, das	-	I, the
In-der-Welt-Sein	-	being-in-the-world
Innerzeitlichkeit	-	innertimeness
In-Sein	-	being-in
Inständigkeit	-	instance, instantiality
Intentionalität	-	intentionality
Interpretation	-	interpretation
Irre	-	errancy
Jemeinigkeit	-	mineness
Jeweiligkeit	-	particular whileness
kategoriale Anschauung	-	categorial intuition
Kategorie	-	category
Kehre	-	turning
Kundschaft	-	announcing of something
Kunst	-	art
Langeweile	-	boredom
leben	-	life

Lebensphilosophie	-	life philosophy
Lebenswelt	-	lifeworld
Leitfrage	-	guiding question
letzte Gott, der	-	last god, the
lichten	-	come-to-light
Lichtung	-	clearing
Logik	-	logic
Man, das	-	they, the
Mensch	-	human being
Metaphysik	-	metaphysics
Metontologie	-	metontology
Mitdasein	-	being-there-with
Mitsein	-	being-with
Mitwelt	-	with-world
Modus	-	mode
Möglichkeit	-	possibility
Mystik	-	mysticism
Nähe	-	nearness
National-Sozialismus	-	National Socialism
Natur	-	nature
Neugier	-	curiosity
Neukantianismus	-	Neo-Kantianism
Nichten, das	-	nihilation
Nichtigkeit	-	nullity
Nichts	-	nothing
Nihilismus	-	nihilism
Not	-	need
Offenbarkeit	-	manifestness
Offene, das	-	the open
Offenständigkeit	-	openness
Öffentlichkeit	-	publicness
ontisch	-	ontic
Ontologie	-	ontology
Ontologisch	-	ontological
ontologische Differenz	-	ontological difference
Onto-theo-logie	-	onto-theo-logy
Ort	-	location

Phänomen	-	phenomenon
Phänomenologie	-	phenomenology
Philosophie	-	philosophy
Platonismus	-	Platonism
Präsenz	-	presentness
Psychologismus	-	psychologism
Raum	-	space
räumen	-	make space
Räumlichkeit	-	spatiality
rechnendes denken	-	calculative thinking
Rede	-	discourse
Reflexion	-	reflection
Reflexionsphilosophie	-	philosophy of reflection
Rektorat	-	rectorate
Religion	-	religion
Ruhe	-	tranquillity
Ruinanz	-	ruinance
Sage	-	saying
Schematismus	-	schematism
Schenkung	-	gift
Scheu	-	awe
Schicksal	-	fate
Schritt zurück	-	step back
Schuld	-	guilt
schweigen	-	keep silent
Seiende	-	entity
Seiende im Ganzen, das	-	being of entities as a whole, the
Seiendheit	-	beingness
sein	-	being
Sein	-	Being
Seinkönnen	-	can-be, potentiality for being
Seinsfrage	-	question of being
Seinsgeschichte	-	history of Being
Seinsvergessenheit	-	forgetfulness of being
Seinsverständnis	-	understanding of being
Seinsweise	-	way of being
Sein-Zu	-	being-out-for
Sein-zum-Tode	-	being-towards-death
Selbst, das	-	self, the

Selbstwelt	-	self-world
Seyn	-	Being, Be-ing, beon
Sinn	-	sense
Sinn des Seins	-	sense of being
Situation	-	situation
Situations-Ich, das	-	Situation-I, the
Sorge	-	care
Spielraum	-	leeway
Sprache	-	language, speech
sprechen	-	speak
Spruch	-	saying
Sprung	-	leap
Stätte	-	site
Sterblichen, die	-	mortals, the
stiften	-	laying claim
Stiftung	-	founding and giving, institution
Stille	-	silence
Stimme des Seins	-	voice of being
Stimmung	-	mood
Struktur	-	structure
Subjektität	-	subjectity
Subjektivität	-	subjectivity
Substanz	-	substance
Technik	-	technology
Temporalien	-	tensors
Temporalität	-	Temporality
Theologie	-	theology
Tod	-	death
Tradition	-	tradition
transzendental	-	transcendental
Transzendenz	-	transcendence
Übereignung	-	surrender
Überlieferung	-	tradition
Übermensch	-	overman (superman)
Überwindung	-	overcoming
Umgang	-	getting around
Umsicht	-	circumspection
Umwelt	-	environment
Umzu, das	-	in-order-to, the

unbedingt	-	unconditioned
Uneigentlichkeit	-	inauthenticity
Unheimlichkeit	-	weirdness
Unterschied	-	difference
Unverborgenheit	-	unconcealment
Unwahrheit	-	untruth
Unwesen	-	nonessence
Ur-Etwas	-	primal something
Ursprung	-	origin
Ur-sprung	-	primal leap
Urteil	-	judgment
Verborgenheit	-	concealment
Vereinzelung	-	individualization
Verfallenheit	-	fallenness
Vergangenheit	-	past
Verhaltenheit	-	reservedness
Verstand	-	understanding
verstehen	-	understand
verweilen	-	to while
Volk	-	people
Vollzug	-	actualization
Vollzugssinn	-	actualization sense
Vorbei, das	-	being gone, the
Vorblick	-	preview
Vorgriff	-	fore-conception
Vorhabe	-	fore-having
Vorhandenheit	-	presence-at-hand
vorlaufen	-	anticipate
Vorsicht	-	foresight
Vorstellung	-	representation
Vorzeichnung	-	prefiguration
währen	-	last, endure
Wahrheit	-	truth
Wahrheit des Seins, die	-	truth of Being, the
wahrnehmen	-	to take as true
Wahrnemung	-	perception
Weg	-	way
Weile	-	while
Welt	-	world

Weltanschauung	-	worldview
welten	-	to world
Weltlichkeit	-	worldhood
Wert	-	value
Wertphilosophie	-	value-philosophy
wesen	-	coming-to-presence
Wesen	-	essence
Wiederholung	-	retrieval
Wille, der	-	will, the
Wille zur Macht, der	-	will to power, the
Wirklichkeit	-	reality
Wissenschaft	-	science
Wofür, das	-	for-which, the
wohnen	-	dwelling
Worauf, das	-	toward-which, the
Woraufhin, das	-	toward-which, the
Wort	-	word
Worumwillen, das	-	for-the-sake-of-which, the
Wozu, das	-	for-which, the
Zeit	-	time
Zeitigungssinn	-	temporalizing sense
zeitlich	-	temporary
Zeitlichkeit	-	temporality
Zeitspielraum	-	play of time-space
Zeug	-	equipment
zueignen	-	assign
Zueignung	-	assigning
Zug	-	condition of being drawn
Zuhandenheit	-	readiness-to-hand
Zukunft	-	future
Zukünftigen	-	ones to come, the
Zukünftigkeit	-	futurity
zu-sein	-	to-be
Zuspiel	-	interplay, playing-forth
Zuspruch des Seins	-	address of Being
Zweideutigkeit	-	ambiguity
Zwiespalt, das	-	twofold, the
Zwischen, das	-	between, the

APPENDIX III:
GREEK-ENGLISH GLOSSARY

(Author's note: In this glossary I give Heidegger's translations of the Greek terms. When his translation is very specific, I give also the usual English translation between brackets.)

Adikia	-	derangement (injustice)
Aisthèsis	-	perception
Alètheia	-	unconcealment (truth)
Alètheuein	-	uncover, trueing (speak the truth)
Apeiron	-	limitless, the
Archè	-	beginning, principle
Auto, to	-	same, the
Chreon	-	handling, use (necessity)
Diaphora	-	difference
Dikè	-	pattern of arrangement (justice)
Dynamis	-	potentiality
Eidos	-	appearance, form in which something shows itself, idea
Energeia	-	actuality (reality)
Eon	-	being, that which is present
Epistèmè	-	theoretical knowledge, science
Genesis	-	coming-forth (generation)
Harmoniè	-	harmony
Hèn	-	unifying element (one, the)

Hulè	-	matter
Hupokeimenon	-	that what lies before (subject)
Idein	-	representative thinking
Kairos	-	moment of insight (moment of the Second Coming of Christ, proper moment)
Kata	-	as
Kinèsis	-	movement
Kosmos	-	ornament (cosmos)
Legein	-	lay down, lay before, let something lay forth (say, speak)
Lèthè	-	concealment, forgottenness (untruth)
Logos	-	speech, announcement, gathering, saying (assertion, concept, language, reason, word)
Logos kata tinos	-	concept of something
Metéta to pan	-	care about entities as a whole
Moira	-	imparting of belonging together (fate)
Morphè	-	form
Noein	-	apprehend, take under its care (perceive, think)
Nous	-	pure beholding without logos (mind)
On	-	entity
Ousia	-	beingness, constant presence (essence, substance)
Pan	-	all, the
Panta	-	all entities
Paschein	-	undergo (suffer)
Poiein	-	act
Poièsis	-	bringing forth into presence (art, creation)
Polemos	-	strife (war)
Pseudos	-	lie, untruth
Pur	-	fire

Sophia	-	wisdom
Sterèsis	-	privation
Sumphilosophein	-	philosophizing together
Technè	-	skilled know-how
Telos	-	goal
Tóde ti	-	something, 'this-here'
Phainomenon	-	that which shows itself (phenomenon)
Philei to sophon	-	loves the wise
Philosophos	-	philosopher
Phronèsis	-	conscience, phronetic insight (prudence)
Phthora	-	concealment (destruction)
Phusei on	-	natural entities
Physis	-	self-revealment, process of unconcealment of Being (nature)
Xiasma	-	diagonal arrangement

BIBLIOGRAPHY

INTRODUCTION

A complete bibliography of works by and about Heidegger would exceed the scope of this dictionary. Hans-Martin Sass's 1982 bibliography contains 185 works by Heidegger and more than 5,300 entries on secondary literature! This bibliography is therefore selective, emphasizing classic studies and recent works in English, German and French. It includes only book-length publications. A satisfactory listing of articles would require a volume of its own. If books have been translated into English, only the English translation is given. The biographical details of the books mentioned in this introduction can be found in the bibliography.

The literary estate of Martin Heidegger is preserved at the Heidegger-Archive of the Deutsches Literaturarchiv in Marbach am Neckar in Germany. This collection contains practically all of the manuscripts of his books, lectures, courses and seminars. Here are also preserved many transcripts of Heidegger's lecture courses and a large part of his correspondence. Many letters from and to Heidegger are preserved in library-archives throughout Germany or still owned by private persons throughout the world. The Herbert-Marcuse-Archiv of the Stadt- und Universitätsbibliothek in Frankfurt am Main and the Hans-Jonas-Archiv at the library of the University of Constance own both a large collection of transcripts of Heidegger's lecture courses as well as his correspondence with Marcuse and Jonas respectively. The largest collection of Heideggeriana in the United States, including transcripts of courses, seminars, and lectures, is to be found at the Helene-Weiss-Archive at the Department of Special Collections of Stanford University Libraries.

Klostermann in Frankfurt publishes the *Gesamtausgabe* (collected edition) of Heidegger's works. Vittorio Klostermann presented the idea of a collected edition to Heidegger in 1973. After much hesitation and some long conversations with his son Hermann, Heidegger accepted Klostermann's proposal in 1974. He worked out the conception of the *Gesamtausgabe* with his personal assistant Friedrich-Wilhelm von Herrmann and his former student and close friend Walter Biemel. He also discussed many questions and problems with his wife Elfride, his brother Fritz, and his son Hermann. Heidegger did not want an editorial board and decided that each editor should be fully responsible for the edition of his volume. He also decided that after his death the executor of his literary estate should grant permission for the printing of his writings and the volumes of the *Gesamtausgabe*. Over the years Professor Von Herrmann has become the most important collaborator of the *Gesamtausgabe*. Since the early 1980s he has checked together with Hartmut Tietjen and Hermann Heidegger the proof pages of all the newly published volumes of the *Gesamtausgabe*.

The three major periodical publications on Heidegger are *Heidegger Studies*, and the *Schriftenreihe* and *Jahresgaben der Martin-Heidegger-Gesellschaft*. *Heidegger Studies* is an annual international publication dedicated to promoting the understanding of Heidegger's thought through the interpretation of his writings. It publishes papers in English, French, and German. Many of the published essays focus on recently published volumes of the *Gesamtausgabe*. It always also includes an unpublished text from Heidegger's *Nachlaß*. Duncker & Humblot in Berlin publish the *Heidegger Studies*.

The Martin-Heidegger-Gesellschaft is an international society dedicated to promoting the understanding of Heidegger's philosophy. Its membership is open to all interested in the work of Martin Heidegger. The society organizes conferences on Heidegger, publishes a book series, *Schriftenreihe der Martin-Heidegger-Gesellschaft*, with Klostermann in Frankfurt am Main, and offers its members every year a small publication with unpublished writings of or about Heidegger. The address is Martin-Heidegger-Gesellschaft, c/o Martin-Heidegger-Gymnasium, Am Feldweg 26, D-88605 Meßkirch.

Besides the bibliographies listed in section IV, scholars may want to consult the following bibliographical essays:

Gerber, Rudolph. Focal Points in Recent Heidegger Scholarship. In: *New Scholasticism* 42, 1968 (pp. 560-577).

Lübbe, Hermann. Bibliographie der Heidegger-Literatur 1917-1955. In: *Zeitschrift für philosophische Forschung* 11, 1957 (pp. 401-452).

Paumen, Jean. Eléments de bibliographie Heideggérienne. In: *Revue internationale de philosophie* 14, 1960 (pp. 263-268).

Pereboom, Dirk. Heidegger Bibliographie 1917-1966. In: *Freiburger Zeitschrift für Philosophie und Theologie* 16, 1969 (pp. 100-161).

The best introduction to the philosophical background of Heidegger's thought is Herbert Schnädelbach's *Philosophy in Germany, 1831-1933*. Readers may also want to consult the well-written book by Michael Großheim, *Von Georg Simmel zu Martin Heidegger. Philosophie zwischen Leben und Existenz*. Of particular interest are also the very readable and enlightening autobiographical works by Karl Jaspers, *Philosophische Autobiographie*, and Hans-Georg Gadamer, *Philosophical Apprenticeships*. Gadamer has also published a wealth of important essays on Heidegger's thought which can now easily be consulted in his collected works (*Gesammelte Werke*) and his classic study *Heidegger's Ways*. Karl Löwith, one of Heidegger's first students, has also written a well-known work on his former teacher: *Heidegger: Denker in dürftiger Zeit: Zur Stellung der Philosophie im 20. Jahrhundert*.

Rüdiger Safranski has written the most comprehensive biography of Heidegger. His *Martin Heidegger. Between Good and Evil* is also one of the best introductions to Heidegger's thought and highly recommended for first-year students. Hugo Ott's *Martin Heidegger: A Political Life* focuses, as the title indicates, on Heidegger's political activities and is written from a Roman Catholic point of view. It is obligatory reading for all those interested in Heidegger's involvement with National Socialism, since almost all the books on this topic are based on the material that Ott has collected in his study. It is therefore regrettable that Ott's book shows some significant shortcomings and contains several untruths and errors. Heinrich W. Petzet's *Encounters & Dialogues with Martin Heidegger* offers the reader a more personal and sympathetic view of Heidegger. Walter Biemel's too short *Martin Heidegger: An Illustrated Study* is still a very readable and worthwhile work. The many photographs in the book make it a must for those interested in Heidegger's life. Ernst Nolte's biography, *Heidegger, Politik und Geschichte im Leben und Denken*, is in some ways a disappointing work because it has surprisingly little to say about the historical background of Heidegger's life and contains little or no new information.

The two major classics on Heidegger's thought are William Richardson's monumental *Heidegger - Through Phenomenology to Thought* and Otto Pöggeler's *Martin Heidegger's Path of Thinking*. Both books were written in collaboration with Heidegger. However, since many of Heidegger's unpublished writings have been published in the meantime, scholars may want to consult also Herman Philipse's *Heidegger's Philosophy of Being. A Critical Interpretation* and Dieter Thomä's impressive and critical *Die Zeit des Selbst und die Zeit danach. Zur Kritik der Textgeschichte Martin Heideggers 1910-1976*. Charles Guignon has edited *The Cambridge Companion to Heidegger*, which is a very practical and enlightening introduction for students to the whole of Heidegger's thought and life. The different essays in this

collection were all written by well-known scholars. Christopher Macann has edited a wonderful collection of the most important essays on
Heidegger that were published in journals since the 1930s. This four-
volume collection, *Martin Heidegger. Critical Assessments*, is one of
the major publications on Heidegger. Unfortunately, it is hardly af-
fordable for private persons.

In recent years the publication of Heidegger's early lecture courses
has led to a wealth of publications on his early thought. The two major
works on this topic were written by American scholars. Theodore
Kisiel's *The Genesis of Martin Heidegger's "Being and Time"* not
only offers the reader an exhaustive chronological overview of Heidegger's early work, but also abstracts of many still unpublished writings, courses, and lectures. John van Buren's massive *The Young Heidegger. Rumor of the Hidden King* is the best thematically organized
book on the early philosophy of Heidegger.

Friedrich-Wilhelm von Herrmann was Martin Heidegger's personal
assistant from 1972 until the latter's death in 1976. He has so far edited
13 volumes of the *Gesamtausgabe*. His commentaries and writings on
Heidegger's works are highly recommended for students and scholars
alike. The best commentary on *Being and Time* is Jean Greisch's massive and impressive study *Ontologie et temporalité. Esquisse d'une
interprétation intégrale de "Sein und Zeit"*. English-speaking readers
may prefer to consult Hubert L. Dreyfus' *Being-in-the-World: A
Commentary on Heidegger's "Being and Time", Division I*. For those
readers who would like to read the rest of the work as well, there is
Michael Gelven's classic *A Commentary on Heidegger's "Being and
Time"*, which is still useful.

Werner Marx has written a famous book on Heidegger and the
history of philosophy, *Heidegger and the Tradition*. Another classic is
Gustav Siewerth's neo-scholastic work, *Das Schicksal der Metaphysik
von Thomas zu Heidegger*. The best studies of Heidegger and ancient
philosophy are Markus J. Brach's scholarly *Heidegger - Platon. Vom
Neukantianismus zur existentiellen Interpretation des "Sophistes"* and
Ted Sadler's *Heidegger and Aristotle: The Question of Being*. There
are remarkably few books on Heidegger and medieval philosophy. The
most interesting work is undoubtedly John D. Caputo's well-balanced
Heidegger and Aquinas: An Essay on Overcoming Metaphysics.

There is a wealth of literature on Heidegger and modern philosophy. Henri Declève's *Heidegger et Kant* is still unsurpassed and one of
the most interesting works on this topic. Students and scholars may
also want to consult Frank Schalow's *The Renewal of the Heidegger -*

Kant Dialogue: Action, Thought, and Responsibility, which is not only exceptionally well written, but also deals with questions of ethics, moral freedom, and its social implications. Annette Sell, a student of Otto Pöggeler, published the most comprehensive book on Heidegger and Hegel, *Martin Heideggers Gang durch Hegels "Phänomenologie des Geistes"*. The best introduction to Heidegger and Nietzsche is the collection of essays edited by Hans-Hetmuth Gander, *"Verwechselt mich vor allem nicht". Heidegger und Nietzsche*. One of the classic and widely read studies of Heidegger and contemporary philosophy is Michael Theunissen's well-balanced *The Other: Studies in the Social Ontology of Husserl, Heidegger, Sartre, and Buber*. Another classic is Ernst Tugendhat's *Der Wahrheitsbegriff bei Husserl and Heidegger*, which is very critical of Heidegger. The most complete study of Heidegger and Wittgenstein is Thomas Rentsch's *Heidegger und Wittgenstein. Existenzial- und Sprachanalysen zu den Grundlagen philosophischer Anthropologie*. Hermann Mörchen, who studied with both Heidegger and Adorno, wrote a fair interpretation of their relationship, *Adorno und Heidegger. Untersuchung einer philosophischen Kommunikationsverweigerung*. Those readers interested in the reception of Heidegger's work in France will find a complete overview of this subject in Tom Rockmore's interesting and critical study, *Heidegger and French Philosophy*.

Lester Embree edited a massive *Encyclopedia of Phenomenology*, which is the reference book on this subject. Of great interest and importance are of course Edmund Husserl's own comments on Heidegger that were edited in his *Notes sur Heidegger* and *Psychological and Transcendental Phenomenology and the Confrontation with Heidegger (1927-1931): The Encyclopaedia Britannica Article, the Amsterdam Lectures*. Herbert Spiegelberg's *The Phenomenological Movement: A Historical Introduction* is a classic and instructive study and still obligatory reading for all those interested in phenomenology. Burt C. Hopkins wrote a well-balanced, but very scholarly, work on Heidegger and Husserl. His *Intentionality in Husserl and Heidegger. The Problem of the Original Method and Phenomenon of Phenomenology* is one of the few works on Heidegger and Husserl that is not written from a Heideggerian perspective and does justice to Husserl's work. It is highly recommended for scholars and graduate students.

Although Heidegger's involvement with National Socialism has become one of the most discussed topics in contemporary philosophy since the publication of Victor Farias's controversial book *Heidegger and Nazism*, we are still waiting for a comprehensive and equitable work on this important issue. Those interested in this topic may want to start with the different collections of essays and sources that have been published in the last few years. Bernd Martin's *Martin Heidegger und das 'Dritte Reich'. Ein Kompendium* limits itself to a presentation of the facts and different points of view. The most comprehensive collection of Heidegger's political writings (and their background since most of the texts in this volume are not by Heidegger) is to be found in Guido Schneeberger's one-sided *Nachlese zu Heidegger*. The most important collection of essays in English is *Martin Heidegger and National Socialism: Questions and Answers*, edited by Günther Neske and Emil Kettering, where readers will also find translations of Heidegger's rectoral address, his *Facts and Thoughts*, his interview with Richard Wisser and the authentic version of the *Spiegel-Interview*. This version differs significantly from the version published in *Der Spiegel*. Tom Rockmore and Joseph Margolis edited the more critical volume, *The Heidegger Case: On Philosophy and Politics*. The classic study on Heidegger and politics is Alexander Schwan's *Politische Philosophie im Denken Heideggers*. The three major works on Martin Heidegger and National Socialism are Tom Rockmore's very critical *On Heidegger's Nazism and Philosophy*, Dominico Losurdo's comprehensive *Die Gemeinschaft, der Tod, das Abendland. Heidegger und die Kriegsideologie*, and Richard Wollin's *The Politics of Being. The Political Thought of Martin Heidegger*. Two of the most important books written in defense of Heidegger are François Fédier's outstanding *Heidegger. Anatomie d'un scandale*, which unfortunately has neither been translated into English nor received the attention it deserves, and Silvio Vietta's *Heideggers Kritik am Nationalsozialismus und an der Technik*. The best introduction to Heidegger and the problem of ethics is Joanna Hodge's very readable book, *Heidegger and Ethics*.

Joseph Kockelmans has written two classic studies on Heidegger and language and art, *On Heidegger and Language* and *Heidegger on Art and Art Works*. The outstanding book on Heidegger's early theory of language is Pol Vandevelde's exhaustive study, *Être et Discours. La question de langage dans l'itinéraire de Heidegger (1927-1938)*. For his later views on language the reader may want to consult Gerald L. Bruns's important study, *Heidegger's Estrangements: Language, Deconstruction, and the Hermeneutic Project*. The best introduction to Heidegger and art is Friedrich-Wilhelm von Herrmann's careful and well-thought-out interpretation of the essay *The Origin of the Work of Art* published in German under the title *Heideggers Philosophie der Kunst. Eine systematische Interpretation der Holzwege-Abhandlung*

"Der Ursprung des Kunstwerkes". Beda Alleman's *Hölderlin und Heidegger* is the first comprehensive study of the relation between the poet and the thinker. In the meantime, it has been surpassed by Suzanne Ziegler's *Heidegger, Hölderlin und die Alètheia. Martin Heideggers Geschichtsdenken in seinen Vorlesungen 1935/35 bis 1944.*

The best book on Heidegger and technology is Michael Zimmermann's *Heidegger's Confrontation with Modernity. Technology, Politics and Art*, which discusses also the larger context and background of Heidegger's thought. Both students and scholars will enjoy reading this very insightful book. Another justly famous work is Günter Seubold's *Heideggers Analyse der neuzeitlichen Technik.* Rainer Bast has written a penetrating but difficult book on Heidegger's understanding of science. His *Der Wissenschaftsbegriff Martin Heideggers in Zusammenhang seiner Philosophie* is recommended for scholars. Students may prefer to consult the collection of essays edited by Joseph Kockelmans, *Heidegger and Science.* In his readable book *Inhabiting the Earth: Heidegger, Environmental Ethics and the Metaphysics of Nature*, Bruce Foltz demonstrates the importance of Heidegger for ecology.

The classic work on Heidegger and theology was written by Annemarie Gethmann-Siefert, *Das Verhältnis von Philosophie und Theologie im Denken Martin Heideggers.* The most recent and exhaustive study is Philippe Capelle's *Philosophie et théologie dans la pensée de Martin Heidegger.* Heidegger's relation to and influence upon Roman Catholic theology is discussed in Richard Schaeffler's, *Heidegger und die katholische Theologie.* Gerhard Noller has edited a very useful collection of texts that presents a historical overview of the discussion of Heidegger in both Catholic and Protestant theology under the title *Heidegger und die Theologie. Beginn und Fortgang der Diskussion.* One of the very few books on Heidegger and Judaism is Marlène Zarader's *La Dette impensée. Heidegger et l'héritage hébraique.*

Heidegger's influence on psychology and psychotherapy is evident in the writings of Ludwig Binswanger and Medard Boss, who were both psychotherapists. Martin Bartels has written the most famous book on Heidegger and Freud, published under the title *Selbstbewußtsein und Unbewußtes. Studien zu Freud und Heidegger.* The most comprehensive study of this topic is Gion Condrau's *Sigmund Freud und Martin Heidegger. Daseinsanalytische Neurosenlehre und Psychotherapie.* He also published a very readable introduction and overview of Heidegger's influence on psychotherapy, *Martin Heidegger's Impact on Psychotherapy.*

Heidegger's influence in Japan has been immense. Hartmut Buchner has edited a beautiful volume on Heidegger and Japan, *Japan und Heidegger. Gedenkschrift der Stadt Meßkirch zum hundertsten Geburtstag Martin Heideggers*, which is highly recommended for everyone interested in this topic. Yoshiko Oshima has written two enlightening and introductory books on Heidegger and Zen, *Zen anders Denken? Zugleich ein Versuch über Zen und Heidegger*, and *Nähe und Ferne. Mit Heidegger Unterwegs zum Zen*. Graham Parkes has edited the best-known collection of essays on this topic under the title *Heidegger and Asian Thought*. Both scholars and students will find this a very useful collection.

To make the bibliography easy to use, it is divided into 16 comprehensive categories. These categories include: (I) Works in German, (II) Works in English, (III) Correspondence, (IV) Bibliography and Reference, (V) Background and Biography, (VI) General, (VII) Commentaries, (VIII) History of Philosophy, (IX) Phenomenology, (X) Ethics, National Socialism, and Politics, (XI) Art, Hermeneutics, and Language, (XII) Science, Philosophy of Nature, and Technology, (XIII) Theology and Religious Studies, (XIV) Psychology and Psychotherapy, (XV) Eastern Philosophy and Religion, and (XVI) Periodicals. Included is a complete list of the *Gesamtausgabe* in category (I) and a list of all English translations known to me in category (II). The number in superscript before the year of publication (^{2}1998) refers to the edition (in this case second edition 1998). If no number is given, it is the first edition.

I. WORKS IN GERMAN

(Author's note: Vittorio Klostermann, Frankfurt am Main, publishes the collected edition of Martin Heidegger's works. The volumes without a year-date have not yet been published.)

1. Gesamtausgabe (Ausgabe letzter Hand)

I. Abteilung: Veröffentlichte Schriften 1910-1976

1   Frühe Schriften (1910-1916), 1978
2   Sein und Zeit (1927), 1977
3   Kant und das Problem der Metaphysik (1929), 1991
4   Erläuterungen zu Hölderlins Dichtung (1936-1968), 1991, ^{2}1996

5   Holzwege (1935-1946), 1977
6.1   Nietzsche I (1936-1939), 1996
6.2   Nietzsche II (1936-1946), 1997
7   Vorträge und Aufsätze (1953)
8   Was heißt Denken? (1951-1952)
9   Wegmarken (1919-1961), 1976, ²1996
10   Der Satz vom Grund (1955-1956), 1997
11   Identität und Differenz (1955-1957)
12   Unterwegs zur Sprache (1950-1959), 1985
13   Aus der Erfahrung des Denkens (1910-1976), 1983
14   Zur Sache des Denkens (1962-1964)
15   Seminare (1951-1973), 1986
16   Reden und andere Zeugnisse eines Lebensweges (1910-1976),
      2000

II. Abteilung Vorlesungen 1919-1944

Marburger Vorlesungen 1923-1928
17   Einführung in die phänomenologische Forschung (Winter Se-
      mester 1923/ 24), 1994
18   Grundbegriffe der aristotelischen Philosophie (Summer Seme-
      ster 1924)
19   Platon: Sophistes (Winter Semester 1924/25), 1992
20   Prolegomena zur Geschichte des Zeitbegriffs (Summer Seme-
      ster 1925), 1979, ³1994
21   Logik. Die Frage nach der Wahrheit (Winter Semester 1925/
      26), 1976, ²1995
22   Grundbegriffe der antiken Philosophie (Summer Semester
      1926), 1993
23   Geschichte der Philosophie von Thomas von Aquin bis Kant
      (Winter Semester 1926/27)
24   Die Grundprobleme der Phänomenologie (Summer Semester
      1927), 1975, ²1989
25   Phänomenologische Interpretation von Kants Kritik der reinen
      Vernunft (Winter Semester 1927/28), 1977, ²1995
26   Metaphysische Anfangsgründe der Logik im Ausgang von
      Leibniz (Summer Semester 1928), 1978, ²1990

Freiburger Vorlesungen 1928-1944
27   Einleitung in die Philosophie (Winter Semester 1928/29), 1996
28   1. Der Deutsche Idealismus (Fichte, Schelling, Hegel) und die

philosophische Problemlage der Gegenwart (Summer Semester 1929)

2. Einführung in das akademische Studium (Summer Semester 1929), 1997

29/30 Die Grundbegriffe der Metaphysik. Welt - Endlichkeit - Einsamkeit (Winter Semester 1929/30), 1983, ²1992

31 Vom Wesen der menschlichen Freiheit. Einleitung in die Philosophie (Summer Semester 1930), 1982, ²1994

32 Hegels Phänomenologie des Geistes (Winter Semester 1930/31), 1980, ²1997

33 Aristoteles. Metaphysik Θ 1-3. Von Wesen und Wirklichkeit der Kraft (Summer Semester 1931), 1981, ²1990

34 Vom Wesen der Wahrheit. Zu Platons Höhlengleichnis und Theätet (Winter Semester 1931/32), 1988, ²1997

35 Der Anfang der abendländischen Philosophie (Anaximander und Parmenides) (Summer Semester 1932)

36/37 Sein und Wahrheit.
1. Die Grundfrage der Philosophie (Summer Semester 1933)
2. Vom Wesen der Wahrheit (Winter Semester 1933/34)

38 Logik als die Frage nach der Sprache (Summer Semester 1934), 1998

39 Hölderlins Hymnen "Germanien" und "Der Rhein" (Winter Semester 1934/35), 1980, ²1989

40 Einführung in die Metaphysik (Summer Semester 1935), 1983

41 Die Frage nach dem Ding. Zu Kants Lehre von den transzendentalen Grundsätze (Winter Semester 1935/36), 1984

42 Schelling: Vom Wesen der menschlichen Freiheit (1809) (Summer Semester 1936), 1988

43 Nietzsche: Der Wille zur Macht als Kunst (Winter Semester 1936/37), 1985

44 Nietzsches metaphysische Grundstellung im abendländischen Denken: Die ewige Wiederkehr des Gleichen (Summer Semester 1937), 1986

45 Grundfragen der Philosophie. Ausgewählte "Probleme" der "Logik" (Winter Semester 1937/38), 1984, ²1992

46 Nietzsches II. Unzeitgemäße Betrachtung (Winter Semester 1938/39)

47 Nietzsches Lehre vom Willen zur Macht als Erkenntnis (Summer Semester 1939), 1989

48 Nietzsche: Der europäische Nihilismus (II. Trimester 1940), 1986

49   Die Metaphysik des deutschen Idealismus. Zur erneuten Auslegung von Schelling: Philosophische Abhandlungen über das
Wesen der menschlichen Freiheit und die damit zusammenhängende Gegenstände (1809) (I. Trimester 1941), 1991

50   1. Nietzsches Metaphysik (für Winter Semester 1941/42 ange-
kündigt, aber nicht vorgetragen)

2. Einleitung in die Philosophie - Denken und Dichten (Winter
Semester 1944/45), 1990

51   Grundbegriffe (Summer Semester 1941), 1981, [2]1991

52   Hölderlins Hymne "Andenken" (Winter Semester 1941/42),
1982, [2]1992

53   Hölderlins Hymne "Der Ister" (Summer Semester 1942), 1984,
[2]1993

54   Parmenides (Winter Semester 1942/43), 1982, [2]1992

55   Heraklit. 1. Der Anfang des abendländischen Denkens (Summer Semester 1943).

2. Logik. Heraklits Lehre vom Logos (Summer Semester 1944),
1979, [3]1994

Frühe Freiburger Vorlesungen 1919-1923

56/57 Zur Bestimmung der Philosophie.

1. Die Idee der Philosophie und das Weltanschauungsproblem
(War Emergency Semester 1919).

2. Phänomenologie und transzendentale Wertphilosophie (Summer Semester 1919)

3. Anhang: Über das Wesen der Universität und des akademischen Studiums (Summer Semester 1919), 1987, [2]1999

58   Grundprobleme der Phänomenologie (Winter Semester 1919/
20), 1992

59   Phänomenologie der Anschauung und des Ausdrucks. Theorie
der philosophischen Begriffsbildung (Summer Semester 1920),
1993

60   Phänomenologie des religiösen Lebens.

1. Einleitung in die Phänomenologie der Religion (Winter Semester 1920/ 21)

2. Augustinus und der Neuplatonismus (Summer Semester
1922)

3. Die philosophischen Grundlagen der mittelalterlichen Mystik
(Ausarbeitungen und Entwürfe zu einer nicht gehaltenen Vorlesung 1918/19), 1995

298 *Bibliography*

61   Phänomenologische Interpretationen zu Aristoteles. Einführung in die phänomenologische Forschung (Winter Semester 1921/22), 1985, [2]1994

62   Phänomenologische Interpretation ausgewählter Abhandlungen des Aristoteles zu Ontologie und Logik (Summer Semester 1922)

63   Ontologie. Hermeneutik der Faktizität (Summer Semester 1923), 1988, [2]1995

III. Abteilung: Unveröffentlichte Abhandlungen - Vorträge - Gedachtes

64   Der Begriff der Zeit. (I. Die Fragestellung Diltheys und Yorcks Grundtendenz - II. Die ursprünglichen Seinscharaktere des Daseins - III. Dasein und Zeitlichkeit - IV. Zeitlichkeit und Geschichtlichkeit.) Anhang: Der Begriff der Zeit (Vortrag Marburg Juli 1924)

65   Beiträge zur Philosophie. (Vom Ereignis) (1936-1938), 1989, [2]1994

66   Besinnung (1938/39), 1997

67   Metaphysik und Nihilismus
      1. Die Überwindung der Metaphysik (1938/39)
      2. Das Wesen des Nihilismus (1946-48), 1999

68   Hegel
      1. Die Negativität (1938/39)
      2. Erläuterung der "Einleitung" zu Hegels "Phänomenologie des Geistes" (1942), 1993

69   Die Geschichte des Seyns.
      1. Die Geschichte des Seyns (1938/40)

      2. Κοινόν. Aus der Geschichte des Seyns (1939), 1998

70   Über den Anfang (1941)

71   Das Ereignis (1941/42)

72   Die Stege des Anfangs (1944)

73   Zum Ereignis-Denken

74   Zum Wesen der Sprache

75   Zu Hölderlin - Griechenlandreisen

76   Zur Metaphysik - Neuzeitlichen Wissenschaft - Technik

77   Feldweg Gespräche (1944/45)
      1. Ἀγχιβασίη. Ein Gespräch selbstdritt auf einem Feldweg zwischen einem Forscher, einem Gelehrten und einem Weisen
      2. Der Lehrer trifft den Türmer an der Tür zum Turmaufgang

2. Separate Works

(Author's note: Here I only list the separate works that are still in print. For a complete list of Heidegger's writings see Appendix I.)

Aufenthalte. Frankfurt: Klostermann, 1989

Aus der Erfahrung des Denkens. Pfullingen: Neske, 1947, [6]1986

Begriff der Zeit, Der. (Vortrag vor der Marburger Theologenschaft Juli 1924.) Edited, with a Postscript, by Hartmut Tietjen. Tübingen: Niemeyer, 1989, [2]1995

Bemerkungen zu Kunst-Plastik-Raum. St. Gallen: Erker, 1995

Denkerfahrungen 1910-1976. Frankfurt: Klostermann, 1983

Diltheys Forschungsarbeit und der gegenwärtige Kampf um eine historische Weltanschauung. 10 Vorträge (Gehalten in Kassel vom 16.IV.21 - IV.1925). Edited by Frithjof Rodi. Dilthey-Jahrbuch 8, 1992-93

Einführung in die Metaphysik. Tübingen: Niemeyer, 1953, [6]1998

Erläuterungen zu Hölderlins Dichtung. Frankfurt: Klostermann, 1944, [6]1996

Feldweg, Der. Frankfurt: Klostermann, 1953, [7]1991

Frage nach dem Ding, Die. Zu Kants Lehre von den transzendentalen Grundsätzen. Tübingen: Niemeyer, 1962, [3]1987

Frühe Schriften. Frankfurt: Klostermann, 1972

Gelassenheit. Pfullingen: Neske, 1959, [10]1992

Heraklit. (with Eugen Fink). Frankfurt: Klostermann, 1970, [2]1996

Holzwege. Frankfurt: Klostermann, 1950, [7]1994

Identität und Differenz. Pfullingen: Neske, 1957, [9]1990

Kant und das Problem der Metaphysik. Frankfurt: Klostermann, 1929, [5]1991

Kunst und der Raum, Die. L'Art et l'espace. St. Gallen: Erker, 1969, [2]1983

Nietzsche: Band I und II. Pfullingen: Neske, 1961, [6]1998

Phänomenologie und Theologie. Frankfurt, Klostermann, 1970

Phänomenologische Interpretationen zu Aristoteles (Anzeige der hermeneutischen Situation). Edited, with a Postscript, by Hans-Ulrich Lessing. Dilthey-Jahrbuch 6, 1989

Platons Lehre von der Wahrheit. Frankfurt: Klostermann, 1947, [4]1997

Satz vom Grund, Der. Pfullingen: Neske, 1957, [6]1986

Schellings Abhandlung über das Wesen der menschlichen Freiheit. Tübingen: Niemeyer, 1971, [2]1995

Sein und Zeit. Tübingen: Niemeyer, 1927, [16]1986

Selbstbehauptung der deutschen Universität, Die. Das Rektorat 1933/34: Tatsachen und Gedanken. Frankfurt: Klostermann, 1983, [2]1990

Technik und die Kehre, Die. Pfullingen: Neske, 1962, [8]1991

Über Abraham a Santa Clara. Meßkirch: Stadt Meßkirch, 1964

Über den Humanismus. Frankfurt: Klostermann, 1947, [9]1991

Überlieferte Sprache und technische Sprache. St. Gallen: Erker, 1989

Unterwegs zur Sprache. Pfullingen: Neske, 1959, [9]1990

Ursprung des Kunstwerkes, Der. Stuttgart: Reclam, 1960, [3]1982

Vier Seminare. Frankfurt: Klostermann, 1977

Vom Wesen der Wahrheit. Frankfurt: Klostermann, 1943, [7]1986

Vom Wesen des Grundes. Frankfurt: Klostermann, 1929, [8]1995

Vorträge und Aufsätze. Pfullingen: Neske, 1954, [6]1990

Was heißt Denken? Tübingen: Niemeyer, 1971, [4]1984

Was heißt Denken? Stuttgart: Reclam, 1992

Was ist das die Philosophie? Pfullingen: Neske, 1956, [10]1992

Was ist Metaphysik? Frankfurt: Klostermann, 1929, [14]1992

Wegmarken. Frankfurt: Klostermann, 1967, [3]1996

Zollikoner Seminare. Frankfurt: Klostermann, 1987, [2]1994

Zur Frage nach der Bestimmung der Sache des Denkens. St. Gallen: Erker, 1984

Zur Sache des Denkens. Tübingen: Niemeyer, 1969, [3]1988

Zur Seinsfrage. Frankfurt: Klostermann, 1956, [4]1997

II. WORKS IN ENGLISH

1. English Translations

(Author's note: The year and letter in parentheses after the titles of the essays refer to the German title in Appendix I.)

Aristotle's Metaphysics Θ 1-3: On the Essence and Actuality of Force. (GA 33). Translated by W. Brogan and P. Warnek. Bloomington: Indiana University Press, 1995

Basic Concepts. (GA 51). Translated by G. Aylesworth. Bloomington: Indiana University Press, 1994

Basic Problems of Phenomenology, The. (GA 24). Translated by A. Hofstadter. Bloomington: Indiana University Press, 1982

Basic Questions of Philosophy. Selected "Problems" of "Logic". (GA 45). Translated by R. Rojcewicz and A. Shuwer. Bloomington: Indiana University Press, 1994

Basic Writings. Edited by David F. Krell. New York: Harper & Row, ²1993
Contains:
1. *Being and Time: Introduction.* Translated by Joan Stambaugh with J.G. Gray and D.F. Krell. (1927d)
2. *What Is Metaphysics?* Translated by D.F. Krell. (1929k)
3. *On the Essence of Truth.* Translated by J. Sallis. (1943a)
4. *The Origin of the Work of Art.* Translated by A. Hofstadter. (1935c)
5. *Letter on "Humanism".* Translated by Fr.A. Capuzzi, and J.G. Gray. (1946a)
6. *Modern Science, Metaphysics and Mathematics.* Translated by W.B. Barton Jr. and V. Deutsch. (1962a, selection)
7. *The Question Concerning Technology.* Translated by W. Lovitt. (1953c)
8. *Building Dwelling Thinking.* Translated by A. Hofstadter. (1951a)
9. *What Calls for Thinking?* Translated by F.D. Wieck and J.G. Gray. (1971b, selection)
10. *The Way to Language.* Translated by D.F. Krell. (1959c)
11. *The End of Philosophy and the Task of Thinking.* Translated by J. Stambaugh. (1964a)

Being and Time. (GA 2). Translated by J. Macquarrie and E. Robinson. New York: Harper & Row, ⁴1978

Being and Time. (GA 2). Translated by J. Stambaugh. Albany: State University of New York Press, 1996

Concept of Time, The. Translated by W. McNeill. Oxford: Blackwell, 1992. (1924c)

Contributions to "Der Akademiker". Translated by J. Protevi. In: New School for Social Research New York. *Graduate Faculty Philosophy Journal.* Vol. 14, No. 2 and Vol. 15, No. 1, 1991
Contains:
1. *Per mortem ad vitam (Thoughts on Johannes Jörgensen's "Lies of Life and Truth of Life").* (1910a)

2. Förster, Fr.W., *"Authority and Freedom: Observations on the Cultural Problem of the Church".* (1910b)
3. Cüppers, Ad. Jos., *"Sealed Lips: The Story of Irish Folk Life in the 19th Century".* (1910d)
4. Jörgensen, Joh., *"Travelogue: Light and Dark Nature and Spirit".* (1911a)
5. *On a Philosophical Orientation for Academics.* (1911b)
6. *Psychology of Religion and the Subconscious.* (1912a)
7. Gredt, Jos. O.S.B., *Elementa Philosophia Aristotelico-Thomisticae. Vol I. Logica, Philosophia Naturalis. Editio. II.* (1912b)
8. *Library of Valuable Novellas and Stories.* (1913c)

Contributions to Philosophy. From Enowning. (GA 65). Translated by P. Emad and K. Maly. Bloomington: Indiana University Press, 1999

Discourse on Thinking. Translated by J.M. Anderson and E.H. Freund. New York: Harper & Row, 1966
Contains:
1. *Memorial Address.* (1955b)
2. *Conversation on a Country Path About Thinking.* (1944/45a)

Discussion Between Ernst Cassirer and Martin Heidegger, A. Translated by Fr. Slade. In: N. Langiulli (ed.), *The Existential Tradition: Selected Writings.* New York: Doubleday, 1971. (1929e)

Early Greek Thinking. Translated by D.F. Krell and Fr.A. Capuzzi. New York: Harper & Row, 1975
Contains:
1. *The Anaximander Fragment.* (1946c)
2. *Logos (Heraclitus, Fragment B 50).* (1951c)
3. *Moira (Parmenides, VIII, 34-41).* (1952a)
4. *Aletheia (Heraclitus, Fragment B 16).* (1943f)

End of Philosophy, The. Translated by J. Stambaugh. New York: Harper & Row, 1973
Contains:
1. *Metaphysics as History of Being.* (1941g)
2. *Sketches for a History of Being as Metaphysics.* (1941h)
3. *Recollection in Metaphysics.* (1941i)
4. *Overcoming Metaphysics.* (1936-46)

Essays in Metaphysics: Identity and Difference. Translated by K.F. Leidecker. New York: Philosophical Library Inc., 1960
Contains:
1. *The Principle of Identity.* (1957c)
2. *The Onto-Theo-Logical Nature of Metaphysics.* (1957d)

Essence of Reasons, The. Translated by T. Malick. Evanston: Northwestern University Press, 1969. (1929b)

Existence and Being. Edited by Stefan Schimanski, and with an Introduction by Werner Brock. Washington, D.C.: Regnery Gateway Company, 1949
Contains:
1. *Remembrance of the Poet.* Translated by D. Scott. (1943e)
2. *Hölderlin and the Essence of Poetry.* Translated by D. Scott. (1936a)
3. *On the Essence of Truth.* Translated by R.F.C. Hull and A. Crick. (1930e & h)
4. *What Is Metaphysics?* Translated by R.F.C. Hull and A. Crick. (1929k)

Fundamental Concepts of Metaphysics: World, Finitude, Solitude, The. (GA 29/30). Translated by W. McNeill and N. Walker. Bloomington: Indiana University Press, 1995

Hegel's Concept of Experience. Translated by J.G. Gray. New York: Harper & Row, 1970. (1942/43a)

Hegel's Phenomenology of Spirit. (GA 32). Translated by P. Emad and K. Maly. Bloomington: Indiana University Press, 1988

Heraclitus Seminar (with Eugen Fink). Translated by Ch.H. Seibert. Evanston: Northwestern University Press, 1993. (1966/67)

History of the Concept of Time. Prolegomena. Translated by Th. Kisiel. Bloomington: Indiana University Press, 1985

Hölderlin's Hymn: "The Ister". (GA 53). Translated by W. McNeill and J. Davis. Bloomington: Indiana University Press, 1997

Identity and Difference. Translated by J. Stambaugh. New York:
Harper & Row, 1969
Contains:
1. *The Principle of Identity.* (1957c)
2. *The Onto-Theo-Logical Constitution of Metaphysics.* (1957d)

Introduction to Metaphysics, An. (GA 40). Translated by R. Manheim.
New Haven: Yale University Press, 1984

Kant and the Problem of Metaphysics. (1929a). Translated by J.S.
Churchill. Bloomington: Indiana University Press, 1962

Kant and the Problem of Metaphysics. (GA 3). Translated by R. Taft.
Bloomington: Indiana University Press, 1997

Martin Heidegger and National Socialism: Questions and Answers.
Edited by Günther Neske and Emil Kettering. Translated by L. Harries. New York: Paragon House, 1990
Contains:
1. *The Self-Assertion of the German University.* (1933a)
2. *The Rectorate 1933/34: Facts and Thoughts.* (1945a)
3. *The Spiegel-Interview.* (1966a)
4. *Martin Heidegger in Conversation.* (1969f)
5. *Greetings to the Symposium in Beirut.* (1974d)

Metaphysical Foundations of Logic, The. (GA 26). Translated by M.
Heim. Bloomington: Indiana University Press, 1984

Nietzsche I: The Will to Power as Art. Edited and Translated, with
Notes and an Analysis, by David F. Krell. New York: Harper &
Row, 1979
Contains:
    The Will to Power as Art. (1936/37b)

Nietzsche II: The Eternal Recurrence of the Same. Edited and Translated, with Notes and an Analysis, by David F. Krell. New York:
Harper & Row, 1984
Contains:
1. *The Eternal Recurrence of the Same.* (1937d)
2. *Who Is Nietzsche's Zarathustra?* (1953e)

Nietzsche III: The Will to Power as Knowledge and Metaphysics. Edited, with Notes and an Analysis, by David F. Krell. Translated by J. Stambaugh, D.F. Krell, and F.A. Capuzzi. New York: Harper & Row, 1984

Contains:

1. *The Will to Power as Knowledge.* (1939c)
2. *The Eternal Recurrence of the Same and the Will to Power.* (1939d)
3. *Nietzsche's Metaphysics.* (1940c)

Nietzsche IV: Nihilism. Edited, with Notes and an Analysis, by David F. Krell. Translated by F.A. Capuzzi. New York: Harper & Row, 1982

Contains:

1. *European Nihilism.* (1940b)
2. *Nihilism as Determined by the History of Being.* (1944-46)

On the Way to Language. Translated by P.D. Hertz. New York: Harper & Row, 1971

Contains:

1. *A Dialogue on Language.* (1953/54)
2. *The Nature of Language.* (1957/58)
3. *The Way to Language.* (1959c)
4. *Words.* Translated by J. Stambaugh. (1958b)
5. *Language in the Poem.* (1952d)

On Time and Being. Translated by J. Stambaugh. New York: Harper & Row, 1972

Contains:

1. *Time and Being.* (1962c)
2. *The End of Philosophy and the Task of Thinking.* (1964a)
3. *My Way to Phenomenology.* (1963a)

Ontology. The Hermeneutics of Facticity. (GA 63). Translated by J. van Buren. Bloomington: Indiana University Press, 1999

Parmenides. (GA 54). Translated by A. Schuwer and R. Rojcewicz. Bloomington: Indiana University Press, 1993

Pathmarks. (GA 9). Edited by William McNeill. Cambridge: Cambridge University Press, 1998

Contains:

1. *Comments on Karl Jaspers's "Psychology of Worldviews".* Translated by J. van Buren. (1919-21)
2. *Phenomenology and Theology.* Translated by J.G. Hart and J.C. Maraldo. (1927e)
3. *From the Last Marburg Lecture Course.* Translated by M. Heim. (1964b)
4. *What Is Metaphysics?* Translated by D.F. Krell. (1929k)
5. *On the Essence of Ground.* Translated by W. McNeill. (1929b)
6. *On the Essence of Truth.* Translated by J. Salis. (1930e & h)
7. *Plato's Doctrine of Truth.* Translated by Th. Sheehan. (1942a)
8. *On the Essence and Concept of in Aristotle's "Physics B, 1".* Translated by Th. Sheehan. (1939a)
9. *Postscript to "What Is Metaphysics?"* Translated by W. McNeill. (1943b)
10. *Letter on "Humanism".* Translated by F.A. Capuzzi. (1946a)
11. *Introduction to "What Is Metaphysics?"* Translated by W. Kaufmann. (1949b)
12. *On the Question of Being.* Translated by W. McNeill. (1955a)
13. *Hegel and the Greeks.* Translated by R. Metcalf. (1958c)
14. *Kant's Thesis about Being.* Translated by T.E. Klein and W.E. Pohl. (1961c)

Pathway, The. Translated by Th. Sheehan. In: Thomas Sheehan (ed.), *Heidegger: The Man and the Thinker.* Chicago: Precedent, 1981

Phenomenological Interpretation of Kant's "Critique of Pure Reason". (GA 25). Translated by P. Emad and K. Maly. Bloomington: Indiana University Press, 1997

Piety of Thinking, The. Translated by J. Hart and J. Maraldo. Bloomington: Indiana University Press, 1976
Contains:

1. *Phenomenology and Theology.* (1927e)
2. *Theological Discussion of "The Problem of Non-Objectifying Thinking and Speaking in Today's Theology" - Some Pointers to Its Major Aspects.* (1964f)
3. *Review of Ernst Cassirer's "Mythical Thinking".* (1928g)
4. *Principles of Thinking.* (1958a)

Plato: The Sophist. (GA 19). Translated by R. Rojcewicz and A. Schuwer. Bloomington: Indiana University Press, 1997

Plato's Doctrine of Truth. Translated by J. Barlow. In: W. Barrett and H.D. Aiken (eds.), *Philosophy in the Twentieth Century.* Vol. 3. New York: Random House, 1962. (1942a)

Poetry, Language, Thought. Translated by A. Hofstadter. New York: Harper & Row, 1971
Contains:
1. *The Thinker as Poet.* (1947b)
2. *The Origin of the Work of Art.* (1935c)
3. *What Are Poets For?* (1946b)
4. *Building, Dwelling, Thinking.* (1951a)
5. *The Thing.* (1950b)
6. *Language.* (1950c)
7. *...Poetically Man Dwells...* (1951b)

Principle of Reason, The (GA 10). Translated by R. Lilly. Bloomington: Indiana University Press, 1977

Question Concerning Technology and Other Essays, The. Translated by W. Lovitt. New York: Harper & Row, 1977
Contains:
1. *The Question Concerning Technology.* (1953c)
2. *The Turning.* (1949c)
3. *The Word of Nietzsche: "God Is Dead".* (1943c)
4. *The Age of the World Picture.* (1938)
5. *Science and Reflexion.* (1953d)

Question of Being, The. Translated by J.T. Wilde and W. Kluback. Albany: New College University Press, 1958. (1955a)

Schelling's Treatise on Human Freedom. Translated by J. Stambaugh. Athens: Ohio University Press, 1985. (1971a)

Way Back into the Ground of Metaphysics, The. Translated by W. Kaufmann. In: W. Kaufmann (ed.), *Existentialism from Dostojevski to Sartre.* Cleveland: World, 1965. (1949b)

What Is a Thing? Translated by W.B. Barton, Jr. and V. Deutsch. Chicago: Henry Regnery Company, 1967. (1962a)

What Is Called Thinking? Translated by F.D. Wieck and J.G. Gray. New York: Harper & Row, 1968. (1971b)

What Is Philosophy? Translated by J.T. Wilde and W. Kluback. New Haven: College and University Press, 1968. (1956a)

Why Do I Stay in the Provinces? Translated by Th. Sheehan. In: Th. Sheehan (ed.), *Heidegger: The Man and the Thinker*. Chicago: Precedent, 1981. (1933b)

2. English Translations in Preparation

Hölderlin's Hymns "Germanien" and "The Rhine". (GA 39). Translated by W. McNeill. Bloomington: Indiana University Press

Nature of Truth, The. (GA 34). Translated by E.H. Sadler. London: Athlone Press

On the Essence of Human Freedom. (GA 31). Translated by E.H. Sadler. London: Athlone Press

Phenomenology of Intuition and Expression. (GA 59). Translated by E.H. Sadler. London: Athlone Press

Towards the Definition of Philosophy. (GA 56/57). Translated by E.H. Sadler. London: Athlone Press

III. CORRESPONDENCE

(Author's note: In Appendix I are listed some of the most important individual letters that have been published. Here are listed only collections of correspondence.)

Hannah Arendt / Martin Heidegger. *Briefe 1925 bis 1975 und andere Zeugnisse*. Edited by Ursula Ludz. Frankfurt am Main: Klostermann, 1998

Martin Heidegger / Elisabeth Blochmann. *Briefwechsel 1918-1969*. Edited by Joachim W Storck. Marbach am Neckar: Deutsche Schiller-gesellschaft, 1989

Parts of Heidegger's correspondence with Medard Boss can be found in Heidegger, Martin. *Zollikoner Seminare. Protokolle - Zwiegespräche - Briefe*. Edited by Medard Boss. Frankfurt am Main: Klostermann, [2]1994

Rudolf Bultmann / Martin Heidegger. *Briefwechsel*. Edited by Andreas Großmann and Klaus Müller. Frankfurt am Main: Klostermann (scheduled for publication in 2000)

Part of Heidegger's correspondence with Ludwig von Ficker has been published in Ficker, Ludwig von. *Briefwechsel 1940-1967*. Edited by Ignaz Zangerle, Walter Methagl, and Franz Syer. Innsbruck: Haymon Verlag, 1996

Extracts of Heidegger's correspondence with Hans-Georg Gadamer were published by Jean Grondin in his *Hans-Georg Gadamer. Eine Biographie*. Tübingen: Mohr, 1999

Heidegger's correspondence with Paul Häberlin can be found in Paul Häberlin - Ludwig Binswanger. *Briefwechsel 1908-1960*. Edited by Jeannine Luczak. Basel: Schwabe, 1997

Martin Heidegger / Edmund Husserl. *Briefwechsel 1916-1933*. In: *Husserliana Dokumente*. Band 3. Teil 4. *Die Freiburger Schüler*. Edited by Karl Schuhmann and Elisabeth Schuhmann. Dordrecht: Kluwer Academic Publishers, 1994

Martin Heidegger / Karl Jaspers. *Briefwechsel 1920-1963*. Edited by Walter Biemel and Hans Saner. Frankfurt am Main: Klostermann 1990

Martin Heidegger / Erhart Kästner. *Briefwechsel 1953-1974*. Edited by Heinrich W. Petzet. Frankfurt am Main: Insel Verlag, 1986

Parts of Heidegger's correspondence with Max Kommerell can be found in Kommerell, Max. *Briefe und Aufzeichnungen: 1919-1944*.

Aus dem Nachlaß herausgegeben von Inge Jens. Freiburg: Olten, 1967
and in:
Philosophie, No. 16. Paris: Minuit, 1987

Karl Löwith published parts of Heidegger's letters to him in Löwith, Karl. *Zu Heideggers Seinsfrage: Die Natur des Menschen und die Welt der Natur*; in his *Sämtliche Schriften*. Bd. 8: *Heidegger - Denker in dürftiger Zeit*. Stuttgart: Metzler, 1984
and
Three Heidegger letters were published in: Dietrich Papenfuss and Otto Pöggeler (Hrsg.). *Zur philosophischen Aktualität Heideggers*. Band 2. *Im Gespräch der Zeit*. Frankfurt am Main: Klostermann, 1990

Martin Heidegger / Erich Rothacker. *Die Briefe 1922-1941*. Edited by Joachim W. Storck and Theodore Kisiel. In: Dilthey-Jahrbuch 8, 1992/93

IV. BIBLIOGRAPHY AND REFERENCE

1. Bibliography

Capelle, Philippe. *Philosophie et théologie dans la pensée de Martin Heidegger*. Paris: Cerf, 1998

Franzen, Winfried. *Martin Heidegger*. Stuttgart: Metzler, 1976.

Gabel, Gernot U. *Heidegger. Ein internationales Verzeichnis der Hochschulschriften 1930-1990*. Hürth-Efferen: Gemini, 1993

Groth, Miles. *The Voice That Thinks: Heidegger: Translations and Studies with a Bibliography of English Translations, 1949-1996*. Greensburg: Eadmer Press, 1997

Guignon, Charles (ed.). *The Cambridge Companion to Heidegger*. Cambridge: Cambridge University Press, 1993

Lübbe, Hermann. *Bibliographie der Heidegger-Literatur, 1917-1955*. Meisenheim am Glan: Hain, 1957

Mehring, Reinhard. *Heideggers Überlieferungsgeschick. Eine dyonisische Inszenierung.* Würzburg: Königshausen & Neumann, 1992

Nordquist, Joan (ed.). *Martin Heidegger: A Bibliography.* Santa Cruz: Reference and Research Services, 1990

—— *Martin Heidegger (II): A Bibliography.* Santz Cruz: Reference and Research Services, 1996

Sass, Hans-Martin. *Heidegger-Bibliographie.* Meisenheim am Glan: Hain, 1968

—— *Materialien zur Heidegger Bibliographie 1917-1972.* Meisenheim am Glan: Hain, 1975

—— *Martin Heidegger: Bibliography and Glossary.* Bowling Green: Bowling Green State University, Philosophy Documentation Center, 1982

Schneeberger, Guido. *Ergänzungen zu einer Heidegger-Bibliographie.* Bern: Suhr, 1960

Sheehan, Thomas (ed.). *Heidegger: The Man and the Thinker.* Chicago: Precedent, 1981

Thomä, Dieter. *Die Zeit des Selbst und die Zeit danach. Zur Kritik der Textgeschichte Martin Heidgegers 1910-1976.* Frankfurt am Main: Suhrkamp, 1990

2. Reference

Bast, Rainer A., and Delfosse, Heinrich P. *Handbuch zum Textstudium von Martin Heideggers "Sein und Zeit".* Band 1: *Stellenindizes. Philologisch- kritischer Apparat.* Stuttgart-Bad Canstatt: Frommann-Holzboog, 1980

Feick, Hildegard. *Index zu Heidegger's "Sein und Zeit".* Tübingen: Niemeyer, [4]1991

Landolt, Eduard. *Systematischer Index zu Werken Heideggers: Was ist das - die Philosophie?, Identität und Differenz, Gelassenheit.* Heidelberg: Winter, 1992

Petkovšek, Robert. *Heidegger-Index (1919-1927).* Tübingen: Tübinger Gesellschaft für phänomenologische Philosophie, 1998

V. BACKGROUND AND BIOGRAPHY

1. Background

Adorno, Theodor W. *Jargon of Authenticity.* Translated by K. Tarnowski and Fr. Will. Evanston: Northwestern University Press, 1973

Adorno, Theodor, and Horkheimer, Max. *Dialectics of Enlightment.* Translated by J. Cumming. New York: Seabury Press, 1972

Arendt, Hannah. *Men in Dark Times.* New York: Harcourt Brace, 1971

—— *Was ist Existenz-Philosophie?* Frankfurt am Main: Betlz-Athenäum, 1990 (reprint)

Arendt, Hannah, and Jaspers, Karl. *Correspondence: 1926-1969.* Edited by L. Kohler and H. Saner. Translated by Robert Kimber and Rita Kimber. New York: Harcourt Brace Jovanovich, 1992

Babich, Babette E. (ed.). *From Phenomenology to Thought, Errancy, and Desire. Essays in Honor of William J. Richardson, S.J.* (Phaenomenologica 133). Dordrecht: Kluwer Academic Publishers, 1995

Barrett, William. *What Is Existentialism?* New York: Grove Press, 1964

Beaufret, Jean. *Introduction aux philosophies de l'existence: De Kierkegaard à Heidegger.* Paris: Denoël/Garnier, 1971

—— *De l'existentialisme à Heidegger.* Paris: Vrin, 1986

—— *Entretiens avec Frédéric de Towarnicki.* Paris: Presses universitaires de France, 1984

Becker, Oskar. *Dasein und Dawesen. Gesammelte philosophische Aufsätze.* Pfullingen: Neske, 1963

Bernet. Rudolf, Kern, Iso, and Marbach, Eduard (Hrsg.). *Edmund Husserl. Darstellung seines Denkens.* Hamburg: Meiner, 1996

Birkenstock, Eva. *Heißt philosophieren sterben lernen?: Antworten der Existenzphilosophie: Kierkegaard, Heidegger, Sartre, Rosenzweig.* Freiburg and München: Alber, 1997

Bollnow, Otto Fr. *Studien zur ·Hermeneutik.* Band I. *Zur Philosophie der Geisteswissenschaften.* Freiburg and München: Alber, 1982

Braig, Carl. *Vom Sein. Abriß der Ontologie.* Freiburg: Herder, 1896

Brelage, Manfred. *Studien zur Transzendentalphilosophie.* Berlin: Walter de Gruyter, 1965

Brentano, Franz. *On the Several Senses of Being in Aristotle.* Edited and translated by R. George. Berkeley: University of California Press, 1975

Bubner, Rudiger. *Modern German Philosophy.* Translated by E. Matthews. Cambridge: Cambridge University Press, 1981

Dallmayr, Fred R. *Life-world, Modernity and Critique: Paths Between Heidegger and the Frankfurt School.* Cambridge: Polity Press, 1991

Denker, Alfred. *Grensverkenningen. Essays over het Wezen van de Eindigheid.* Best: Damon, 1999

Diethe, Carol. *Historical Dictionary of Nietzscheanism.* Lanham: Scarecrow Press, 1999

Dilthey, Wilhelm, and Yorck von Wartenburg, Graf. *Briefwechsel 1877-1897.* Herausgegeben von Erich Rothacker. Hildesheim: Olms, ²1995. (Reprint of the 1923 edition)

316 *Bibliography*

Fleischer, Margot (Hrsg.). *Philosophen des 20. Jahrhunderts.* Darmstadt: Wissenschaftliche Buchgesellschaft, 1995

Fräntzki, Ekkehard. *Daseinsontologie. Erstes Hauptstück.* Dettelbach: Röll, 1996

—— *Daseinsontologie. Zweites Hauptstück: Vom Wesen der Wahrheit.* Dettelbach: Röll, 1998

Frings, Manfred S. *Person und Dasein. Zur Frage der Ontologie des Wertseins.* (Phaenomenologica 23). The Hague: Nijhoff, 1969

Gadamer, Hans-Georg. *Philosophical Apprenticeships.* Translated by R.R. Sullivan. Cambridge: MIT Press, 1985

Givsan, Hassan. *Eine Bestürzende Geschichte: Warum Philosophen sich durch den "Fall Heidegger" korrumpieren lassen.* Würzburg: Königshausen & Neumann, 1998

Grondin, Jean. *Sources of Hermeneutics.* Albany: State University of New York Press, 1995

—— *Hans-Georg Gadamer. Eine Biographie.* Tübingen: Mohr, 1999

Großheim, Michael. *Von Georg Simmel zu Martin Heideger. Philosophie zwischen Leben und Existenz.* Bonn: Bouvier, 1991

Gurvitch, Georges. *Les Tendances actuelles de la philosophie allemande: E. Husserl - M. Scheler - E. Lask - M. Heidegger.* Paris: Vrin, 1949

Habermas, Jürgen. *Philosophical-Political Profiles.* Translated by Fr.G. Lawrence. Cambridge: MIT Press, 1983

—— *The Philosophical Discourse of Modernity: Twelve Lectures.* Translated by Fr.G. Lawrence. Cambridge: MIT Press, 1987

Husserl, Edmund. *Logical Investigations.* Translated by J.N. Findlay. London: Routledge, 1973

—— *Ideas Pertaining to a Pure Phenomenology and to a Phenomenological Philosophy. First Book: General Introduction to a Pure Phenomenology.* Translated by F. Kersten. Dordrecht: Kluwer Academic Publishers, 1982

—— *Aufsätze und Vorträge 1922-1937.* (Husserliana 27). Dordrecht: Kluwer Academic Publishers, 1989

—— *On the Phenomenology of the Consciousness of Internal Time (1893-1917).* Dordrecht: Kluwer Academic Publishers, 1990

Jaspers, Karl. *Philosophische Autobiographie.* München and Zürich: Piper, [2]1984

—— *Psychologie der Weltanschauungen.* München and Zürich: Piper 1985 (Lizenzausgabe)

—— *How Can the Universities be Rejuvenated? Some Theses (1933).* In: Wisser, Richard, and Ehrlich, Leonard H. (eds.), *Karl Jaspers. Philosopher Among Philosophers.* Würzburg: Königshausen & Neumann, 1993

Jaspert, Bernd (Hrsg.). *Sachgemässe Exegese. Die Protokolle aus Rudolf Bultmanns Neutestamentlichen Seminaren 1921-1951.* Marburg: N.G. Elwert Verlag, 1996

Larese, Dino. *Philosophen am Bodensee. Bollnow, Schmidhauser, Heidegger, Binswanger, Jung, Häberlin, Ziegler, Mauthner.* Friedrichshafen: Gessler, 1999

Laugstien, Thomas. *Philosophieverhältnisse im deutschen Faschismus.* Hamburg: Argument, 1990

Löwith, Karl. *Das Individuum in der Rolle des Mitmenschen.* München: Drei-Masken-Verlag, 1928

—— *My Life in Germany Before and After 1933.* London: Athlone Press, 1994

Lukács, Georg. *The Destruction of Reason.* Translated by P. Palmer. Atlantic Highlands: Humanities Press, 1981

Marx, Werner. *Is There a Measure on Earth? Foundations for a Nonmetaphysical Ethics.* Translated by Th.J. Neno and R. Lilly. Chicago: University of Chicago Press, 1987

Megill, Allan. *Prophets of Extremity: Nietzsche, Heidegger, Foucault, Derrida.* Berkeley: University of California Press, 1985

Merleau-Ponty, Maurice. *Notes des cours au Collège de France: 1958-1959 et 1960-1961.* Paris: Gallimard, 1996

Misch, Georg. *Lebensphilosophie und Phänomenologie. Eine Auseinandersetzung der Diltheyschen Richtung mit Heidegger und Husserl.* Darmstadt: Wissenschaftliche Buchgesellschaft, ³1967

Müller, Andreas. *Der Scheinwerfer. Anekdoten und Geschichten um Fritz Heidegger.* Meßkirch: Arnim Gmeiner, 1989

Müller, Max. *Existenzphilosophie. Von der Metaphysik zur Metahistorik.* Freiburg and München: Alber, 1986

Nicholson, Graeme. *Illustrations of Being: Drawing upon Heidegger and upon Metaphysics.* Atlantic Highlands: Humanities Press, 1992

Ochwadt, Curd, and Tecklenborg, Erwin (Hrsg.). *Das Mass des Verborgenen. Heinrich Ochsner zum Gedächtnis.* Hannover: Charis-Verlag, 1981

Rabinach, Anson. *German Intellecutals Between Apocalypse and Enlightment.* Berkeley: University of California Press, 1997

Ricoeur, Paul. *Time and Narrative.* 3 Vols. Translated by K. McLaughlin and D. Pellauer. Chicago: Chicago University Press, 1984-1988

—— *Oneself as Another.* Translated by K. Blamey. Chicago: University of Chicago Press, 1992

Ringer, Fritz K. *The Decline of the German Mandarins. The German Academic Community 1890-1933*. Cambridge: MIT Press, 1969

Rivelaygue, Jacques. *Leçons de métaphysique allemande. Tome II: Kant, Heidegger, Habermas*. Paris: Grasset, 1992

Roberts, Julian. *German Philosophy: An Introduction*. Atlantic Highlands: Humanities Press, 1988

Rubercy, Eryck de, and Buhan, Dominique le. *Douze questions posées à Jean Beaufret sur Heidegger*. Paris: Aubier, 1983

Sallis, John, Moneta, Giuseppina, and Taminiaux, Jacques (eds.). *The Collegium Phaenomenologicum: The First Ten Years*. (Phenomenologica 105). Dordrecht: Kluwer, 1988

Sallis, John, Seebohm, Thomas, and Silverman, Hugh J. (eds.). *Continental Philosophy in America*. Pittsburgh: Duquesne University Press, 1983

Sartre, Jean-Paul. *Being and Nothingness. A Phenomenological Essay on Ontology*. Translated and with an Introduction by H.E. Barnes. New York: Philosophical Library, 1956

—— *L'Existentialisme est un humanisme*. Paris: Nagel, ²1970

Schnädelbach, Herbert. *Philosophy in Germany, 1831-1933*. Cambridge: Cambridge University Press, 1984

Schuhmann, Karl. *Husserl-Chronik. Denk- und Lebensweg Edmund Husserls*. (Husserliana. Dokumente: Band 1). The Hague: Nijhoff, 1977

Smith, Barry, and Woodruff Smith, David (eds.). *The Cambridge Companion to Husserl*. Cambridge: Cambridge University Press, 1995

Solomon, Robert C. *From Rationalism to Existentialism: The Existentialists and Their Nineteenth-Century Background*. New York: Harper & Row, 1972

—— *Introducing the Existentialists.* Indianapolis: Hackett Publishing, 1981

Speck, Josef (Hrsg.). *Grundproblemen der großen Philosophen. Philosophie der Gegenwart 5: Jaspers - Heidegger - Sartre - Camus - Wust - Marcel.* Göttingen: UTB, ²1992

Strohm, Harald. *Die Gnosis und der Nationalsozialismus.* Frankfurt am Main: Suhrkamp, 1997

Tengelyi, László. *Der Zwitterbegriff Lebensgeschichte.* München: Fink, 1998

Wachterhauser, Brice R. (ed.). *Hermeneutics and Modern Philosophy.* Albany: State University of New York Press, 1986

Wiplinger, Fridolin. *Metaphysik. Grundfragen ihres Ursprungs und ihrer Vollendung.* Freiburg and München: Alber, 1976

Young-Bruehl, Elizabeth. *Hannah Arendt: For Love of the World.* New Haven: Yale University Press, 1982

2. Biography

Biemel, Walter. *Martin Heidegger: An Illustrated Study.* Translated by J.L. Metha. New York: Original Harvest, 1976

Ettinger, Elzbieta. *Hannah Arendt - Martin Heidegger.* New Haven: Yale University Press, 1995

Fédier, François. *Soixante-deux photographies de Martin Heidegger.* Paris: Gallimard, 1999

Larese, Dino. *Mit Heidegger im Hauptwil.* Amriswil: Amriswiler Bücherei, 1960

Meller Marcovicz, Digne. *Martin Heidegger Photos 23. September 1966 / 17. - 18. Juni 1968.* Frankfurt am Main: Klostermann, 1985

Neske, Günther (Hrsg.). *Erinnerung an Martin Heidegger.* Pfullingen: Neske, 1977

Nolte, Ernst. *Heidegger, Politik und Geschichte im Leben und Denken.* Berlin and Frankfurt am Main: Propyläen, 1992

Ochwadt, Curd. *Verirrungen eines Heidegger-Biographen. Bedauerliche Auslassungen des Professors Hugo Ott in den Jahren 1996/97.* Hannover: Charis, 1997

Ott, Hugo. *Martin Heidegger: A Political Life.* Translated by A. Blunden. New York: Basic Books, 1993

Petzet, Heinrich. *Encounters & Dialogues with Martin Heidegger 1929-1976.* Translated by P. Emad and K. Maly. Chicago: Chicago University Press, 1993

Pöggeler, Otto. *Heidegger in seiner Zeit.* München: Fink, 1999

Safranski, Rüdiger. *Martin Heidegger: Between Good and Evil.* Translated by E. Osers. Boston: Harvard University Press, 1998

Stadt Meßkirch (Hrsg.). *Zum Gedenken an Martin Heidegger 1889-1976.* Meßkirch: Schönebeck, 1976

Towarnicki, Frédéric de. *À la rencontre de Heidegger. Souvenirs d'un messager de la Forêt Noire.* Paris: Gallimard, 1993

—— *Martin Heidegger: Souvenirs et chroniques.* Paris: Rivages, 1999

Wiplinger, Fridolin. *Von der Un-Verborgenheit: Fridolin Wiplingers Bericht von einem Gespräch mit Martin Heidegger.* Aufgezeichnet von E. Fräntzki. Pfaffenheim: Centaurus, 1987

Wisser, Richard (Hrsg.). *Martin Heidegger im Gespräch.* Freiburg and München: Alber, 1970

VI. GENERAL

1. General

Ansén, Rainer. *"Bewegtheit": Zur Genesis einer kinetischen Ontologie bei Heidegger.* Cuxhaven: Junghans, 1990

Bachmann, Ingeborg. *Die kritische Aufnahme der Existential-philosophie Martin Heideggers*. München and Zürich: Piper, ²1985

Ballard, Bruce W. *The Role of Mood in Heidegger's Ontology*. Washington, D.C.: University Press of America, 1990

Ballard, Edward G., and Scott, Charles E. (eds.). *Heidegger: In Europe and America*. The Hague: Nijhoff, 1973

Barash, Jeffrey A. *Martin Heidegger and the Problem of Historical Meaning*. (Phaenomenologica 102). Dordrecht: Nijhoff, 1985

—— *Heidegger et son siècle*. Paris: Presses universitaires de France, 1995

Beaufret, Jean. *Dialogue avec Heidegger*. 4 Vols. Paris: Minuit, 1973-1985

Bernasconi, Robert. *Heidegger in Question: The Art of Existing*. Atlantic Highlands: Humanities Press, 1993

Biemel, Walter. *Le Concept de monde chez Heidegger*. Paris: Vrin, 1950

Birault, Henri. *Heidegger et l'expérience de la pensée*. Paris: Gallimard, 1978

Blust, Franz-Karl. *Selbstheit und Zeitlichkeit. Heideggers neuer Denkansatz zur Seinsbestimmung des Ich*. Würzburg: Königshausen & Neumann, 1987

Boeder, Heribert. *Heidegger and the Limit of Modernity*. Translated by M. Brainard. Albany: State University of New York, 1997

Bohrer, Karl H. *Der Ernstfall Heidegger*. Basel: Schwabe, 1997

Börig-Hover, Lina (Hrsg.). *Unterwegs zur Heimat. Martin Heidegger zum 100. Geburtstag*. Fridingen: Börsig, 1989

Boutot, Alain. *Heidegger*. Paris: Presses universitaires de France, 1991

Brandner, Rudolf. *Heidegger. Sein und Wissen. Eine Einführung in sein Denken.* Wien: Passagen, 1993

—— *Heideggers Begriff der Geschichte und das neuzeitliche Geschichtsdenken.* Wien: Passagen, 1994

Bretschneider, Willy. *Sein und Wahrheit. Über die Zusammengehörigkeit von Sein und Wahrheit im Denken Martin Heideggers.* Meisenheim am Glan: Hain, 1965

Brihat, Denise. *De l'être ou de rien: Heidegger et la philosophie de l'être.* Saint Ceneré: Pierre Téqui, 1988

Buchheim, Thomas (Hrsg.) *Destruktion und Überlieferung. Zu den Aufgaben von Philosophiegeschichte nach Martin Heidegger.* Weinheim: VCH, 1989

Busche, Jürgen, et al. *Martin Heidegger Fragen an sein Werk. Ein Symposium.* Stuttgart: Reclam, 1977

Caputo, John D. *Demythologizing Heidegger.* Bloomington: Indiana University Press, 1993

Cardorff, Peter. *Martin Heidegger.* Frankfurt am Main and New York: Campus, 1991

Carr, David. *Time, Narrative, and History.* Bloomington: Indiana University Press, 1986

Chassard, Pierre. *Heidegger: Au-delà des choses. Jenseits der Dinge.* Wesseling: Thomas, 1993

Colloque "Heidegger". Paris, les 12, 13 et 14 mars 1997. Organisé par le Collège International de Philosophie. Paris: Osiris, 1988

Cooper, David E. *Heidegger.* London: Claridge, 1996

Cordonnier, Vincent. *Heidegger.* Paris: Quitette, 1995

Corvez, Maurice. *La Philosophie de Heidegger.* Paris: Presses universitaires de France, 1961

Cotten, Jean-Paul. *Heidegger*. Paris: Seuil, 1974

Couturier, Fernand. *Monde et être chez Heidegger*. Montréal: Presses universitaires de Montréal, 1971

Dallmayr, Fred R. *The Other Heidegger*. Ithaca: Cornell University Press, 1993

Dantlo, René. *À la rencontre de Martin Heidegger*. Toulouse: Privat, 1969

Dastur, Françoise. *Heidegger and the Question of Time*. Translated by F. Raffoul and D. Pettigrew. Atlantic Highlands: Humanities Press, 1998

Dem Andenken Martin Heideggers. Zum 26. Mai 1976. Frankfurt am Main: Klostermann, 1977

Demske, James M. *Der Tod im Denken Martin Heideggers*. Freiburg and München: Alber, 1962

Derrida, Jacques. *Psyché. Inventions de l'autre*. Paris: Galilée, 1987

Dreyfus, Hubert L., and Hall, Harrison (eds.). *Heidegger: A Critical Reader*. Oxford: Blackwell, 1992

Ebeling, Hans. *Heidegger. Geschichte einer Täuschung*. Würzburg: Königshausen & Neumann, ²1991

Elred, Michael (Hrsg.). *Twisting Heidegger: Drehversuche parodistischen Denkens*. Cuxhaven: Junghans, 1993

Fay, T. *The Critique of Logic*. Dordrecht: Kluwer Academic Publishers, 1977

Fehér, István M. (Hrsg.). *Wege und Irrwege des neueren Umganges mit Heideggers Werk. Ein deutsch-hungarisches Symposium*. Berlin: Duncker & Humblot, 1991

Ferrie, Christian. *Heidegger et la problématique de l'interprétation* T1. Paris: Kime, 1999

Figal, Günter. *Martin Heidegger. Phänomenologie der Freiheit.* Bodenheim: Hain, [2]1991

—— *Heidegger. Zur Einführung.* Hamburg: Junius, [2]1996

Fischer, Kurt. *Abschied: Die Denkbewegungen Martin Heideggers.* Würzburg: Königshausen & Neumann, 1990

Forum für Philosophie (Hrsg.). *Heidegger: Innen- und Außenansichten.* Frankfurt am Main: Suhrkamp, 1989

Frage Martin Heideggers, Die. Beiträge zu einem Kolloquium mit Heidegger aus Anlass seines 80. Geburtstages. Von Beaufret, Jean, Gadamer, Hans-Georg, Löwith, Karl, and Volckmann-Schluck, Karl-Heinz. (Sitzungsberichten der Heidelberger Akademie der Wissenschaften). Heidelberg: Winter, 1969

Franck, Didier. *Heidegger et le problème de l'espace.* Paris: Minuit, 1986

Franzen, Winfried. *Von der Existenzialontologie zur Seinsgeschichte. Eine Untersuchung über die Entwicklung der Philosophie Martin Heideggers.* Meisenheim am Glan: Hain, 1975

—— *Martin Heidegger.* Stuttgart: Metzler, 1976.

Frings, Manfred A. (ed.). *Heidegger and the Quest for Truth.* Chicago: Quadrangle Books, 1968

Frynsk, Christopher. *Heidegger: Thought and Historicity.* Ithaca: Cornell University Press, 1986

Fürst, Maria (Hrsg.). *Symposion über Tendenzen und Ergebnisse der Heidegger-Forschung in Ost- und Mitteleuropa.* Wien: Braumüller, 1991

Fürstenau, Peter. *Heidegger. Das Gefüge seines Denkens.* Frankfurt am Main: Klostermann, 1958

Gadamer, Hans-Georg. *Heidegger's Ways.* Translated by J.W. Stanley. Albany: State University of New York Press, 1994

Gadamer, Hans-Georg, et al. *Denken und Dichten bei Heidegger. Fünf Vorträge gehalten am 26. und 27. September 1987 auf der zweiten Tagung der Martin-Heidegger-Gesellschaft in Meßkirch.* Jahresgabe 1988 der Martin-Heidegger-Gesellschaft.

Gander, Hans-Helmuth (Hrsg.). *Europa und die Philosophie.* (Schriftenreihe der Martin-Heidegger-Gesellschaft Bd. 2). Frankfurt am Main: Klostermann, 1993

—— *Von Heidegger her. Wirkungen in Philosophie - Kunst - Medizin.* (Schriftenreihe der Martin-Heidegger-Gesellschaft Bd. 1). Frankfurt am Main: Klostermann, 1991

Gethmann, Carl Fr. *Verstehen und Auslegung. Das Methodenproblem in der Philosophie Martin Heideggers.* Bonn: Bouvier, 1974

Givsan, Hassan. *Heidegger - Das Denken der Inhumanität. Eine ontologische Auseinandersetzung mit Heideggers Denken.* Würzburg: Königshausen & Neumann, 1998

Grede, Marjorie. *Martin Heidegger.* London: Bowes & Bowes, 1957

Greisch, Jean. *La Parole heureuse: Martin Heidegger entre les choses et les mots.* Paris: Beauchesne, 1987

Groth, Miles. *Preparatory Thinking in Heidegger's Teaching.* New York: Philosophical Library, 1987

Gruppe Nagel. *Heidegger für Barbesucher.* Bonn: Parerga, 1997

Guignon, Charles B. *Heidegger and the Problem of Knowledge.* Indianapolis: Hackett, 1983

Guignon, Charles B. (ed.). *The Cambridge Companion to Heidegger.* Cambridge: Cambridge University Press, 1993

Gunderson, Dörte. *Denken wie der Wald - von Stifter zu Heidegger: Untersuchungen zu Heideggers Denkens.* Bern and New York: Lang, 1995

Guzzoni, Ute (Hrsg.). *Nachdenken über Heidegger. Eine Bestandaufnahme*. Hildesheim: Garstenberg, 1980

Haar, Michel. *Heidegger and the Essence of Man*. Translated by W. McNeill. Albany: State University of New York Press, 1993

—— *The Song of the Earth: Heidegger and the Grounds of the History of Being*. Translated by R. Lilly. Bloomington: Indiana University Press, 1993

—— *La Fracture de l'histoire. Douze essais sur Heidegger*. Grenoble: Millon, 1994

Haar, Michel (ed.). *Cahier de l'Herne: Martin Heidegger*. Paris: Editions de l'Herne, 1983

Habermas, Jürgen. *Martin Heidegger. L'Oeuvre et l'engagement*. Traduction de R. Rochlitz. Paris: Cerf, 1988

Halliburton, David. *Poetic Thinking: An Approach to Heidegger*. Chicago: University of Chicago Press, 1981

Han, Byung-Chul. *Heideggers Herz. Zum Begriff der Stimmung bei Martin Heidegger*. München: Fink, 1996

Happel, Markus (Hrsg.). *Heidegger - neu gelesen*. Würzburg: Königshausen & Neumann, 1997

Henri, Charles. *La Notion de finitude dans la philosophie de Martin Heidegger*. Lausanne: Éditions de l'Age d'Homme, 1971

Herrmann, Friedrich-Wilhelm von. *Die Selbstinterpretation Martin Heideggers*. Meisenheim am Glan: Hain, 1964

Ignatow, Assen. *Heidegger und die philosophische Anthropologie: Eine Untersuchung über die anthropologische Dimension des Heideggerschen Denkens*. Königstein: Hain, 1979

Inwood, Michael. *Heidegger*. Oxford: Oxford University Press, 1997

Irigaray, Luce. *Forgetting Air.* Translated by M.B. Mader. London: Athlone Press, 1999

Janicaud, Dominique, and Mattéi, Jean-François. *Heidegger from Metaphysics to Thought.* Translated by M. Gendre. Albany: State University of New York Press, 1995

Jaspers, Karl. *Notizen zu Heidegger.* Herausgegeben von Hans Saner. München and Zürich: Piper, ³1989

Kettering, Emil. *NÄHE. Das Denken Martin Heideggers.* Pfullingen: Neske, 1987

King, Magda. *Heidegger's Philosophy: A Guide to His Basic Thought.* Oxford: Blackwell, 1964

Klostermann, Vittorio (Hrsg.). *Durchblicke. Martin Heidegger zum 80. Geburtstag.* Frankfurt am Main: Klostermann, 1970

Langan, Thomas. *The Meaning of Heidegger.* New York: Columbia University Press, 1961

LeMay, Eric, and Pitts, Jennifer A. *Heidegger for Beginners.* Illustrated by P. Gordon. New York: Writers and Readers Publishing, 1994

Leveque, Jean. *Heidegger, l'ontologie: Fragment 1.* Paris: Osiris, 1989

—— *Heidegger, la proximité. Fragment 2.* Paris: Osiris, 1995

Löwith, Karl. *Heidegger: Denker in dürftiger Zeit: Zur Stellung der Philosophie im 20. Jahrhundert.* Stuttgart: Metzler, 1984

—— *Martin Heidegger and European Nihilism.* Edited by R. Wollin and translated by G. Steiner. New York: Columbia University Press, 1995

Macann, Christopher (ed.). *Martin Heideger: Critical Assessments.* 4 Vols. London: Routledge, 1992

—— *Critical Heidegger*. London: Routledge, 1996

Macomber, William B. *The Anatomy of Disillusion: Martin Heidegger's Notion of Truth*. Evanston: Northwestern University Press, 1967

Marten, Rainer. *Heidegger lesen*. München: Fink, 1991

Martin Heidegger zum 80. Geburtstag von seiner Heimatstadt Meßkirch. Frankfurt am Main: Klostermann, 1969

Marx, Werner. *Heidegger Memorial Lectures*. Translated by S.W. Davis. Pittsburgh: Duquesne University Press, 1982

Marx, Werner (Hrsg.). *Heidegger. Freiburger Universitätsvorträge zu seinem Gedenken*. Freiburg and München: Alber, [2]1979

Mehta, Jarava L. *The Philosophy of Martin Heidegger*. New York: Harper Torchbooks, 1971

—— *Martin Heidegger, the Way and the Vision*. Honolulu: University of Hawaii Press, 1976

Meschonnic, Henri. *Le Langage de Heidegger*. Paris: Presses universitaires de France, 1990

Molinuevo, José L. *Die Zweideutigkeit des Ursprünglichen bei Martin Heidegger*. Übersetzt von D. Wiggert. Bern and New York: Lang, 1996

Munier, Roger. *Stèle pour Heidegger*. Paris: Arfuyen, 1992

Murguía, Adolfo. *Zweideutige Radikalität: Analyse der Heideggerschen Philosophieauffassung*. Essen: Die Blaue Eule, 1994

Neske, Günther (Hrsg.). *Martin Heidegger zum Siebzigsten Geburtstag*. Pfullingen: Neske, 1959

Neuhäusler, Anton. *Zeit und Sein*. Meisenheim am Glan: Hain, 1957

Okrent, Mark. *Heidegger's Pragmatism: Understanding, Being, and the Critique of Metaphysics*. Ithaca: Cornell University Press, 1988

Olafson, Frederick A. *What Is a Human Being? A Heideggerian View*. Cambridge: Cambridge University Press, 1995

Øverenget, Einar. *Seeing the Self: Heidegger on Subjectivity*. (Phaenomenologica 149). Dordrecht: Kluwer Academic Publishers, 1998

Panis, Daniel. *Il y a le il y a: L'Énigme de Heidegger*. Paris: Vrin, 1995

Patent, Grigorij I. *Zur Kritik der Existenzphilosophie Martin Heideggers*. Berlin: Akademie Verlag, 1979

Pathak, Chintamani. *The Problem of Being in Heidegger*. Varanasi: Bharata Manisha, 1974

Peng, Fuchung. *Das Nichten des Nichts. Zur Kernfrage des Denkwegs Martin Heideggers*. Bern and New York: Lang, 1998

Philipse, Herman. *Heidegger's Philosophy of Being: A Critical Interpretation*. Princeton: Princeton University Press, 1999

Pöggeler, Otto. *Martin Heidegger's Path of Thinking*. Translated by D. Magurshak and S. Barber. Atlantic Highlands: Humanities Press, 1987

——— *Neue Wege mit Heidegger*. Freiburg and München: Alber, 1992

——— *The Paths of Heidegger's Life and Thought*. Translated by J. Bailiff. Loughton: Prometheus Books, 1997

Pöggeler, Otto (Hrsg.). *Heidegger: Perspektiven zur Deutung seines Werkes*. Königsstein: Athenäum, ²1984

Polt, Richard. *Heidegger. An Introduction*. Ithaca: Cornell University Press, 1998

Pouget, Pierre-Marie. *Heidegger ou le retour à la voix silencieuse*. Lausanne: L'Age d'Homme, 1975

Poulain, Jacques (ed.). *Penser après Heidegger: Actes du colloque du centenaire* (Paris, 25-27 septembre 1989). Paris: L'Harmattan, 1992

Pylkko, Pauli. *The Aconceptual Mind: Heidegerrian Themes in Holistic Naturalism.* Amsterdam and Philadelphia: John Benjamins Publishing, 1998

Raffelt, Albert (Hrsg.). *Katholische Akademie der Erzdiözese Freiburg: Martin Heidegger weiter denken.* Zürich: Schnell und Steiner, 1990

Raffoul, François. *Heidegger and the Subject.* Translated by D. Pettigrew and G. Recco. Atlantic Highlands: Humanities Press, 1998

Ree, John. *Heidegger.* New York: Weidenfeld, 1998

Regvald. Richard. *Heidegger et le problème du néant.* (Phaenomenologica 101). The Hague: Nijhoff, 1987

Rentsch, Thomas. *Martin Heidegger: Das Sein und der Tod. Eine kritische Einführung.* München and Zürich: Piper, 1989

Richardson, William J. *S.J. Heidegger - Through Phenomenology to Thought.* (Phaenomenologica 13) The Hague: Nijhoff, 1963

Richter, Ewald (Hrsg.). *Die Frage nach der Wahrheit.* (Schriftenreihe der Martin-Heidegger-Gesellschaft Bd. 4). Frankfurt am Main: Klostermann, 1997

Rorty, Richard. *Essays on Heidegger and Others.* (*Philosophical Papers*, Vol. 2). Cambridge: Cambridge University Press, 1991

Rosen, Stanley. *The Question of Being. A Reversal of Heidegger.* New Haven: Yale University Press, 1993

Rothacker, Erich. *Gedanken über Martin Heidegger.* Bonn: Bouvier, 1973

Ruin, Hans. *Enigmatic Origins: Tracing the Theme of Historicity Through Heidegger's Works.* Stockholm: Almquist & Wiksell, 1994

Salanskis, Jean-Michel. *Heidegger*. Paris: Les Belles Lettres, 1997

Sallis, John. *Echoes: After Heidegger*. Bloomington: Indiana University Press, 1990

Sallis, John (ed.). *Heidegger and the Path of Thinking*. Pittsburgh: Duquesne University Press, 1970.

—— *Reading Heidegger: Commemorations*. Bloomington: Indiana University Press, 1993

Schäfer, Hermann (Hrsg.). *Annäherungen an Martin Heidegger. Festschrift für Hugo Ott zum 65. Geburtstag*. Frankfurt am Main and New York: Campus, 1996

Schirmacher, Wolfgang (Hrsg.). *Zeitkritik nach Heidegger*. Essen: Die Blaue Eule, 1989

Shahan, Robert W., and Mohanty, Norman (eds.). *Thinking About Being. Aspects of Heidegger's Thought*. Norman: University of Oklahoma Press, 1984

Sheehan, Thomas (ed.). *Heidegger: The Man and the Thinker*. Chicago: Precedent, 1981

Slaatte, Howard A. *The Philosophy of Martin Heidegger*. Lanham: University Press of America, 1984

Spaude, Edelgard (Hrsg.), und bearbeitet von Reiter, Nikolaus. *Große Themen Martin Heideggers. Eine Einführung in sein Denken*. Freiburg: Rombach, ²1994

Stambaugh, Joan. *Thoughts on Heidegger*. Washington, D.C.: University Press of America, 1991

—— *The Finitude of Being*. Albany: State University of New York Press, 1992

Steiner, George. *Martin Heidegger*. Harmondsworth: Penguin Books, 1980

Strolz, Walter. *Heidegger als meditativer Denker.* St. Gallen: Erker, 1974

Thomä, Dieter. *Die Zeit des Selbst und die Zeit danach. Zur Kritik der Textgeschichte Martin Heideggers 1910-1976.* Frankfurt am Main: Suhrkamp, 1990

Vattimo. Gianni. *Introduction à Heidegger.* Paris: Cerf, ³1985

Veauthier, Frank W. (Hrsg.). *Martin Heidegger: Denker der Post-Metaphysik.* (Symposium aus Anlaß seines 100. Geburtstag). Heidelberg: Winter, 1992

Wahl, Jean. *Introduction à la pensée de Heidegger. Cours donnés en Sorbonne de janvier à juin 1946.* Paris: Livre de Poche, 1998

Werkmeister, William H. *Martin Heidegger on the Way.* Edited by Richard T. Hull. Amsterdam and Atlanta: Rodopi, 1996

White, David A. *Logic and Ontology in Heidegger.* Columbus: Ohio State University Press, 1985

Youm, Jae-Chul. *Heideggers Verwandlung des Denkens.* Würzburg: Königshausen & Neumann, 1995

Zimmerman, Michael E. *The Thought of Martin Heidegger.* New Orleans: Tulane University Press, 1984

—— *Eclipse of the Self: The Development of Heidegger's Concept of Authenticity.* Athens: Ohio University Press, 1986

2. Early Heidegger

Beelman, Axel. *Heimat als Daseinsmetapher. Weltanschauliche Elemente im Denken des Theologiestudenten Martin Heidegger.* Wien: Passagen, 1994

Brasser, Martin. *Wahrheit und Verborgenheit. Interpretationen zu Heideggers Wahrheitsverständnis von "Sein und Zeit" bis "Vom Wesen der Wahrheit".* Würzburg: Königshausen & Neumann, 1997

Brisart, Robert. *La Phénoménologie de Marbourg: Ou la résurgence métaphysique chez Heidegger à l'époque de "Sein und Zeit".* Bruxelles: Facultés Universitaires Saint-Louis, 1991

Buren, John van. *The Young Heidegger. Rumor of the Hidden King.* Bloomington: Indiana University Press, 1994

Courtine, Jean-François (ed.). *Heidegger 1919-1929. De l'hermeneutique de la facticité à la métaphysique du "Dasein".* Paris: Vrin, 1996

Dahlstrom, Daniel O. *Das logische Vorurteil. Untersuchungen zur Wahrheitstheorie des frühen Heidegger.* Wien: Passagen, 1994

Denker, Alfred. *Omdat Filosoferen Leven Is. Een archeologie van Martin Heideggers "Sein und Zeit".* Best: Damon, 1997

Elliston, Frederick. *Heidegger's Existential Analytic.* The Hague: Mouton, 1978

Gudopp, Wolf-Dieter. *Der junge Heidegger.* Frankfurt am Main: Verlag Marxistische Blätter, 1983

Heinz, Marion. *Zeitlichkeit und Temporlität. Die Konstitution der Existenz und die Grundlegung einer temporalen Ontologie im Frühwerk Heideggers.* Würzburg: Rodopi, 1982

Imdahl, Georg. *Das Leben verstehen. Heideggers formal anzeigende Hermeneutik in den frühen Freiburger Vorlesungen (1919-1923).* Würzburg: Königshausen & Neumann, 1997

Jaeger, Petra. *Ansatz zur Verwindung der Metaphysik in der Epoche von "Sein und Zeit".* Bern and New York: Lang, 1976

Kim, In-Suk. *Phänomenologie des faktischen Lebens. Heideggers formal anzeigende Hermeneutik (1919-1923).* Bern and New York: Lang, 1998

Kisiel, Theodore. *The Genesis of Heidegger's "Being and Time".* Berkeley: University of California Press, 1993

Kisiel, Theodore, and Buren, John van (eds.). *Reading Heidegger from the Start. Essays in His Earliest Thought.* Albany: State University of New York Press, 1994

Opilik, Klaus. *Transzendenz und Vereinzelung. Zur Fragwürdigkeit des transzendentalen Ansatzes im Umkreis von Heideggers "Sein und Zeit".* Freiburg and München: Alber, 1993

Rosales, Alberto. *Transzendenz und Differenz. Ein Beitrag zum Problem der ontologischen Differenz beim frühen Heidegger.* (Phaenomenologica 33). The Hague: Nijhoff, 1970

Taminiaux, Jacques. *Heidegger and the Project of Fundamental Ontology.* Translated by M. Gendre. Albany: State University of New York Press, 1991

Thurnher, Rainer. *Wandlungen der Seinsfrage. Zur Krisis im Denken Heideggers nach "Sein und Zeit".* Tübingen: Attempo, 1997

Ucatescu Barrón, Jorge. *Die Grundartikulation des Seins: Eine Untersuchung auf dem Boden der Fundamentalontologie Martin Heideggers.* Würzburg: Königshausen & Neumann, 1992

Waelhens, Alphone de. *La Philosophie de Martin Heidegger.* Louvain: Éditions de l'Institut Supérieur de Philosophie, ³1948

3. Later Heidegger

Caysa, Volker. *Das Seyn entwerfen: Die negative Metaphysik Martin Heideggers.* Bern and New York: Lang, 1994

Fräntzki, Ekkehard. *Die Kehre, Heideggers Schrift: "Vom Wesen der Wahrheit".* Pfaffenheim: Centaurus, ²1987

Fresco, Marcel F., Dijk, Rob J.A. van, and Vijgeboom, Peter H.W. (Hrsg.). *Heideggers These vom Ende der Philosophie.* Bonn: Bouvier, 1989

Grondin, Jean. *Le Tournant dans la pensée de Martin Heidegger.* Paris: Presses universitaires de France, 1987

Guibal, Francis. *Et combien de dieux nouveaux. Heidegger*. Paris: Aubier, 1980

Guilead, Reuben. *Être et liberté. Une étude sur le dernier Heidegger*. Louvain: Nauwelaerts, 1965

Jamme, Christoph, and Harries, Karsten (Hrsg.). *Martin Heidegger: Kunst - Politik - Technik*. München: Fink, 1992

Kockelmans, Joseph J. *On the Truth of Being. Reflections on Heidegger's Later Philosophy*. Bloomington: Indiana University Press, 1984

Krell, David F. *Intimations of Mortality: Time, Truth, and Finitude in Heidegger's Thinking of Being*. University Park: Pennsylvania State University Press, 1986

—— *Daimon Life, Heidegger and Life-Philosophy*. Bloomington: Indiana University Press, 1992

Landolt, Eduard. *Der einzige Heidegger. Eine Deutung nach dem systematischen Index*. Heidelberg: Winter, 1992

Lang, Berel. *Heidegger's Silence*. Ithaca: Cornell University Press, 1996

Papenfuss, Dietrich, and Pöggeler, Otto (Hrsg.). *Zur philosophischen Aktualität Heideggers*. Band 1. *Philosophie und Politik*. Frankfurt am Main: Klostermann, 1991

—— *Zur philosophischen Aktualität Heideggers*. Band 2. *Im Gespräch der Zeit*. Frankfurt am Main: Klostermann, 1990

—— *Zur philosophischen Aktualität Heideggers*. Band 3. *Im Spiegel der Welt: Sprache, Übersetzung, Auseinandersetzung*. Frankfurt am Main: Klostermann, 1992.

Perrefort, Maria. *Opfer und Gehorsam: Kritische Untersuchungen zur Struktur von Heideggers Gelassenheitsidee*. Würzburg: Königshausen & Neumann, 1990

Pocai, Romano. *Heideggers These der Befindlichkeit. Sein Denken zwischen 1927 und 1933.* Freiburg and München: Alber, 1996

Pugliese, Orlando. *Vermittlung und Kehre. Grundzüge des Geschichtsdenkens bei Martin Heidegger.* Freiburg and München: Alber, ²1986

Shin, Syng-Hwan. *Wahrheitsfrage und Kehre bei Martin Heidegger.* Würzburg: Königshausen & Neumann, 1993

—— *Metaphysik - Kunst - Postmoderne. Martin Heideggers Rationalitätskiritk und das Problem der Wahrheit.* Regensburg: Roderer, 1996

Stadt Meßkirch (Hrsg.). *Martin Heidegger 26. September 1969.* Meßkirch: Stadt Meßkirch, 1969

Vail, Loy M. *Heidegger and Ontological Difference.* University Park: Pennsylvania State University Press, 1972

Vorläufer, Johannes. *Das Sein-Lassen als Grundvollzug des Daseins. Eine Annäherung an Heideggers Begriff der Gelassenheit.* Wien: Passagen, 1994

VII. COMMENTARIES

1. *Being and Time*

Chapelle, Albert. *L'Ontologie phénoménologique de Heidegger: Un commentaire de "Sein und Zeit".* Paris: Éditions Universitaires, 1962

Commetti, Jean-Pierre. *"Être et Temps" de Martin Heidegger: Questions de méthode et voies de recherche.* Paris: Sud, 1989

Dreyfus, Hubert L. *Being-in-the-World: A Commentary on Heidegger's "Being and Time", Division I.* Cambridge: MIT Press, 1991

Fleischer, Margot. *Die Zeitanalysen in Heideggers "Sein und Zeit". Aporien, Probleme und ein Ausblick.* Würzburg: Königshausen & Neumann, 1991

Gelven, Michael. *A Commentary on Heidegger's "Being and Time".* New York: Harper Torchbooks, 1970

Gould, Carol C. *Authenticity and Being-with-others: A Critique of Heidegger's "Sein und Zeit".* New Haven: Yale University Press, 1971

Graeser, Andreas. *Philosophie in "Sein und Zeit". Kritische Erwägungen zu Heidegger.* Sankt Augustin: Academia Richarz, 1994

Greenier, David L. *Being, Meaning and Time in Heidegger's "Being and Time".* London: Minerva Press, 1997

Greisch, Jean. *Ontologie et temporalité. Esquisse d'une interprétation intégrale de "Sein und Zeit".* Paris: Presses universitaires de France, 1994

Herrmann, Friedrich-Wilhelm von. *Subjekt und Dasein. Interpretationen zu "Sein und Zeit".* Frankfurt am Main: Klostermann, ²1985

—— *Hermeneutische Phänomenologie des Daseins. Eine Erläuterung von "Sein und Zeit".* Band 1. *Einleitung: Die Exposition der Frage nach dem Sinn von Sein.* Frankfurt am Main: Klostermann, 1987

—— *Heideggers "Grundprobleme der Phänomenologie". Zur "Zweiten Hälfte" von "Sein und Zeit".* Frankfurt am Main: Klostermann, 1991

Kaelin, E.F. *Heidegger's Being and Time: Reading for Readers.* Gainesville: University Press of Florida, 1988

Kockelmans, Joseph J. (ed.). *A Companion to Martin Heidegger's "Being and Time".* Washington, D.C.: University Press of America, 1986

—— *Heidegger's "Being and Time": The Analytic of Dasein as Fundamental Ontology.* Washington, D.C.: University Press of America, 1989

Köhler, Dietmar. *Martin Heidegger: Die Schematisierung des Seinssinnes als Thematik des dritten Abschnittes von "Sein und Zeit".* Bonn: Bouvier, 1993

Luckner, Andreas. *Martin Heidegger: "Sein und Zeit". Eine einführende Kommentar.* Parderborn: Schöningh/UTB, 1997

McDonald, Peter J. *Daseinsanalytik und Grundfrage. Zur Einheit und Ganzheit von Heideggers "Sein und Zeit".* Würzburg: Königshausen & Neumann, 1997

Mulhall, Stephen. *Routledge Philosophy Guidebook to Heidegger and "Being and Time".* London: Routledge, 1996

Pasqua, Hervé. *Introduction à la lecture de "Être et Temps" de Martin Heidegger.* Lausanne: L'Age d'Homme, 1993

Prauss, Gerold. *Knowing and Doing in Heidegger's "Being and Time".* Translated by G. Steiner. Loughton: Prometheus Books, 1998

Schubert, Rainer. *Das Problem der Zuhandenheit in Heideggers "Sein und Zeit".* Bern and New York: Lang, 1995

Vetter, Helmuth (Hrsg.). *Siebzig Jahre "Sein und Zeit".* Bern and New York: Lang, 1999

2. Other Works

Beelmann, Axel. *Heideggers hermeneutischer Lebensbegriff. Eine Analyse seiner Vorlesung "Die Grundbegriffe der Metaphysik. Welt - Endlichkeit – Einsamkeit".* Würzburg: Königshausen & Neumann, 1994

Coriando, Paola-Ludocia. *Der letzte Gott als Anfang. Zur abgründigen Zeit-Räumlichkeit des Übergangs in Heideggers "Beiträge zur Philosophie".* München: Fink, 1998

Herrmann, Frierich-Wilhelm von. *Wege ins Ereignis. Zu Heideggers "Beiträgen zur Philosophie".* Frankfurt am Main: Klostermann, 1994

Neu, Daniela. *Die Notwendigkeit der Gründung im Zeitalter der Dekonstruktion. Zur Gründung in Heideggers "Beiträgen zur Philosophie" unter Hinzuziehung der Derridaschen Dekonstruktion.* Berlin: Duncker & Humblot, 1997

Nikfar, Mohammed-Reza. *Die Erörterung des Satzes vom Grund bei Martin Heidegger.* Bern and New York: Lang, 1997

Ullrich, Wolfgang. *Der Garten der Wildnis. Eine Studie zu Martin Heideggers Ereignis-Denken.* München: Fink, 1996

Witt, Christoph. *Auf dem Feldweg Martin Heideggers: Anregungen zur Deutung mit dem Originaltext Martin Heideggers "Der Feldweg".* Meßkirch: Gmeiner, 1988

VIII. HISTORY OF PHILOSOPHY

1. General

Blattner, William D. *Heidegger's Temporal Idealism.* Cambridge: Cambridge University Press, 1999

Bucher, Alexius. *Metaphysikkritik als Begriffsproblematik.* Bonn: Bouvier, 1972

Gadamer, Hans-Georg. *Gesammelte Werke Bd. 3: Neuere Philosophie I: Hegel - Husserl - Heidegger.* Tübingen: Mohr, 1987

Haeffner, Gerd. *Heideggers Begriff der Metaphysik.* München, Berchmans, [2]1981

Huch, Kurt J. *Philosophiegeschichtliche Voraussetzungen der Heideggerschen Ontologie.* Frankfurt am Main: Europäische Verlagsanstalt, 1967

Lleras, Fernando. *Zu Heideggers Gedanken vom Ende der Metaphysik.* Bern and New York: Lang, 1986

Marx, Werner. *Heidegger and the Tradition.* Translated by T. Kisiel and M. Kisiel. Atlantic Highlands: Humanities Press, 1998

Mattéi, Jean-François. *L'Ordre du monde: Platon, Nietzsche, Heidegger*. Paris: Presses universitaires de France, 1989

Melčić, Dunja. *Heideggers Kritik der Metaphysik und das Problem der Ontologie*. Würzburg: Königshausen & Neumann, 1986

Mikulić. Borislav. *Sein, Physis, Alètheia. Zur Vermittlung und Unmittelbarkeit im "ursprünglichen" Seinsdenken Martin Heideggers*. Würzburg: Königshausen & Neumann, 1987

Mongis, Henri. *Heidegger et la critique de la notion de valeur: La Destruction de la fondation métaphysique*. (Phaenomenologica 74). The Hague: Nijhoff, 1976

Murray, Michael (ed.). *Heidegger and Modern Philosophy: Critical Essays*. New Haven: Yale University Press, 1978

Patt, Walter. *Formen des Anti-Platonismus bei Kant, Nietzsche und Heidegger*. Frankfurt am Main: Klostermann, 1997

Paumen, Jean. *Fortunes de la question de l'homme: Kant, Weber, Jaspers, Heidegger*. Paris: Vrin, 1995

Peperzak, Adriaan Th. *Platonic Transformations: with and after Hegel, Heidegger, and Lévinas*. Oxford: Rowman & Littlefield, 1997

Protevi, John L. *Time and Exteriority: Aristotle, Heidegger, Derrida*. Lewisburg: Bucknell University Press, 1994

Schüssler, Ingeborg. *La Question de la vérité: Thomas d'Aquin, Nietzsche, Kant, Aristote, Heidegger*. Lausanne: Payot, 1998

Siewerth, Gustav. *Das Schicksal der Metaphysik von Thomas zu Heidegger*. Einsiedeln: Johannes, 1959

Winter, Stefan. *Heideggers Bestimmung der Metaphysik*. Freiburg and München: Alber, 1993

Yun, Byeong-Yeol. *Der Wandel des Wahrheitsverständnisses im Denken Heideggers. Untersuchung seiner Wahrheitsauffassung im*

Lichte des husserlschen und griechischen Denkens. Aachen: Shaker, 1997

2. Ancient Philosophy

Beierwaltes, Werner. *Heideggers Rückgang zu den Griechen.* Heidelberg: Winter, 1995

Boutot, Alain. *Heidegger et Platon.* The Hague: Nijhoff, 1970

Brach, Markus J. *Heidegger - Platon. Vom Neukantianismus zur existentiellen Interpretation des "Sophistes".* Würzburg: Königshausen & Neumann, 1996

Maly, Kenneth, and Emad, Parvis (eds.). *Heidegger on Heraclitus: A New Reading.* Lewiston: Edwin Mellen Press, 1986

Sadler, Ted. *Heidegger and Aristotle: The Question of Being.* London: Athlone Press, 1996

Sallis, John, and Maly, Kenneth (eds.). *Heraclitean Fragments. A Companion Volume to the Heidegger/Fink Seminar on Heraclitus.* Huntsville: University of Alabama Press, 1980

Schlüter, Jochen. *Heidegger und Parmenides: Ein Beitrag zu Heideggers Parmenidesauslegung und zur Vorsokratiker Forschung.* Bonn: Bouvier, 1979

Seidel, George J. *Martin Heidegger and the Pre-Socratics.* Lincoln: University of Nebraska Press, 1964

Severson, Richard J. *Time, Death, and Eternity: Reflecting on Augustine's "Confessions" in Light of Heidegger's "Being and Time".* Lanham: Scarecrow Press, 1995

Starr, David E. *Entity and Existence: An Ontological Investigation of Aristotle and Heidegger.* New York: B. Franklin, 1975

Wolz, Henry G. *Plato and Heidegger: In Search of Selfhood.* Lewisburg: Bucknell University Press, 1981

3. Medieval Philosophy

Caputo, John D. *Heidegger and Aquinas: An Essay on Overcoming Metaphysics.* New York: Fordham University Press, 1982

Grassi, Ernesto. *Heidegger and the Question of Renaissance Humanism: Four Studies.* Binghamton: Center for Medieval and Early Renaissance Studies, 1983

—— *Vico and Humanism: Essays on Vico, Heidegger, and Rhetoric.* Bern and New York: Lang, 1990

Helting, Holger. *Heidegger und Meister Eckhart. Vorbereitende Überlegungen zu ihrem Gottesdenken.* Berlin: Duncker & Humblot, 1997

Lindblad, Ulrika M. *L'Intelligibilité de l'être selon saint Thomas d'Aquin et selon Martin Heidegger.* Bern and New York: Lang, 1987

Lotz, Johannes B. *Martin Heidegger und Thomas von Aquin. Mensch - Zeit - Sein.* Pfullingen: Neske, 1975

Vetter, Helmuth (Hrsg.). *Heidegger und das Mittelalter.* Bern and New York: Lang, 1999

Wagner, Jürgen. *Meditationen über Gelassenheit. Der Zugang des Menschen zu seinem Wesen im Anschluß an Martin Heidegger und Meister Eckhart.* Hamburg: Kovac, 1995

4. Modern Philosophy

Acikgenc, Alparslan. *Being and Existence in Sadrā and Heidegger: A Comparative Ontology.* Kuala Lumpur: International Institute of Islamic Thought and Civilization, 1993

Bambach, Charles R. *Heidegger, Dilthey, and the Crisis of Historicism.* Ithaca: Cornell University Press, 1995

Behler, Ernst. *Confrontations: Derrida - Heidegger - Nietzsche.* Translated by St. Taubeneck. Stanford: Stanford University Press, 1992

Benjamin, Andrew. *The Plural Event: Descartes, Hegel, Heidegger.* London: Routledge, 1993

Cobben, Paul. *Das endliche Selbst. Über Identität (und Differenz) Hegels "Phänomenologie des Geistes" und Heideggers "Sein und Zeit".* Würzburg: Königshausen & Neumann, 1998

Cristin, Renato. *Heidegger and Leibniz: Reason and the Path.* Dordrecht: Kluwer Academic Publishers, 1998

Declève, Henri. *Heidegger et Kant.* (Phaenomenologica 40). The Hague: Nijhoff, 1970

Dupond, Pascal. *Raison et temporalité: Le Dialogue de Heidegger avec Kant.* Bruxelles: Éditions Ousia, 1996

Gander, Hans-Helmuth (Hrsg.). *Verwechselt mich vor allem nicht. Heidegger und Nietzsche.* (Schriftenreihe der Martin-Heidegger-Gesellschaft Bd. 3). Frankfurt am Main: Klostermann, 1994

Gillespie, Michael A. *Hegel, Heidegger, and the Ground of History.* Chicago: University of Chicago Press, 1984

Graybeal, Jean. *Language and "The Feminine" in Nietzsche and Heidegger.* Bloomington: Indiana University Press, 1980

Grossmann, Andreas. *Kunst und Geschichte im Widerstreit zwischen Hegel und Heidegger.* Bonn: Bouvier, 1996

Iber, Christian. *Das Andere der Vernunft als ihr Prinzip. Grundzüge der philosophischen Entwicklung Schellings mit einem Ausblick auf die nachidealistischen Philosophiekonzeptionen Heideggers und Adornos.* Berlin: Walter de Gruyter, 1994

Kang, Hak-Soon. *Die Bedeutung von Heideggers Nietzsche-Deutung im Zuge der Verwindung der Metaphysik.* Bern and New York: Lang, 1990

Kaufmann, Walter A. *Nietzsche, Heidegger, and Buber.* New York: McGraw Hill, 1980

Kolb, David. *The Critique of Pure Modernity: Hegel, Heidegger, and After*. Chicago: Chicago University Press, 1986

Laruelle, François. *Nietzsche contre Heidegger: Thèses pour une politique nietzscheènne*. Paris: Payot, 1977

Meulen, Jan A. van der. *Heidegger und Hegel oder Widerstreit und Widerspruch*. Meisenheim an Glan: Hain, 1953

Ohashi, Ryosuke. *Ekstase und Gelassenheit. Zu Schelling und Heidegger*. München: Fink, 1975

Otsuru, Tadashi. *Gerechtigkeit und Dikè: Der Denkweg als Selbst-Kritik in Heideggers Nietzsche-Auslegung*. Würzburg: Königshausen & Neumann, 1992

Richardson, John. *Existential Epistemology: A Heideggerian Critique of the Cartesian Project*. Oxford: Clarendon Press, 1986

Rockmore, Tom, and Kisiel, Theodore (eds.). *Heidegger, German Idealism, and Neo-Kantianism*. Amherst: Humanities Books, 2000

Saffer, Stephan. *Untersuchungen zum Weltansichtstheorem bei Wilhelm von Humboldt und Martin Heidegger*. Mainz: Verlag Mainz, 1996

Sargentis, Dionysios. *Das differente Selbst der Philosophie. Heideggers Auseinandersetzung mit Hegel*. Berlin: Köster, 1998

Schalow, Frank. *The Renewal of the Heidegger-Kant Dialogue: Action, Thought and Responsibility*. Albany: State University of New York Press, 1992

Schmidt, Dennis J. *The Ubiquity of the Finite: Hegel, Heidegger and the Entitlements of Philosophy*. Cambridge: MIT Press, 1988

Schmitt, Gerhard. *The Concept of Being in Hegel and Heidegger*. Bonn: Bouvier, 1977

Sell, Annette. *Martin Heideggers Gang durch Hegels "Phänomenologie des Geistes"*. Bouvier: Bonn, 1998

Sherover, Charles M. *Heidegger, Kant & Time*. Bloomington: Indiana University Press, 1971

Sinn, Dieter. *Die Kritik am Identitätsprinzip. Von Heidegger zu Hegel*. Bonn: Bouvier, 1988

Skowron, Michael. *Nietzsche und Heidegger: Das Problem der Metaphysik*. Bern and New York: Lang, 1987

Smith, Gregory B. *Nietzsche, Heidegger, and the Transition to Postmodernity*. Chicago: University of Chicago Press, 1995

Wyschogrod, Michael. *Kierkegaard and Heidegger: The Ontology of Existence*. London: Routledge and Kegan Paul, 1954

5. Contemporary Philosophy

Amorim Almeida, Roberto de. *Natur und Geschichte: Zur Frage nach der ursprünglichen Dimension abendländischen Denkens vor der Hintergrund der Auseinandersetzung zwischen Martin Heidegger und Karl Löwith*. Meisenheim am Glan: Hain, 1976

Argyros, Alexander. *The Question of Truth in Sartre, Heidegger, and Derrida*. Ithaca: Cornell University Press, 1977

Baruzzi, Arno: *Philosophieren mit Jaspers und Heidegger*. Würzburg: Ergon, 1999

Bernet, Rudolf (Hrsg.). *Zeit und Zeitlichkeit bei Husserl und Heidegger*. Freiburg und München: Alber, 1983

Borchers, Dagmar. *Der große Graben. Heidegger und die analytische Philosophie*. Bern and New York: Lang, 1997

Brunnhuber, Stefan. *Der dialogische Aufbau der Wirklichkeit: Gemeinsame Elemente im Philosophiebegriff von Martin Buber, Martin Heidegger und Sigmund Freud*. Regensburg: Roderer, 1993

Buckley, Philip R. *Husserl, Heidegger, and the Crisis of Philosophical Responsibility*. (Phaenomenologica 125). Dordrecht: Kluwer Academic Publishers, 1992

Cooper, Ron L. *Heidegger and Whitehead: A Phenomenological Examination into the Intelligibility of Experience.* Athens: Ohio University Press, 1993

Davis, Walter A. *Inwardness and Existence: Subjectivity in/and Hegel, Heidegger, Marx, and Freud.* Madison: University of Wisconsin Press, 1989

DeNeef, Leigh A. *Traherne in Dialogue: Heidegger, Lacan, and Derrida.* Durham: Duke University Press, 1988

Doherty, Joseph E. *Sein, Mensch und Symbol: Heidegger und die Auseinandersetzung mit dem neukantianischen Symbolbegriff.* Bonn: Bouvier, 1972

Donkel, Douglas L. *The Understanding of Difference in Heidegger and Derrida.* Bern and New York: Lang, 1993

Edwards, James C. *The Authority of Language: Heidegger, Wittgenstein, and the Threat of Philosophical Nihilism.* Tampa: University of South Florida Press, 1990

Fell, Joseph P. *Heidegger and Sartre: An Essay on Being and Place.* New York: Columbia University Press, 1979

Furuta, Hirokiyo. *Wittgenstein und Heidegger. "Sinn" und "Logik" in der Tradition der analytischen Philosophie.* Würzburg: Königshausen & Neumann, 1996

Ganty, Etienne. *Penser la modernité: Essai sur Heidegger, Habermas et Eric Weil.* Namur: Presses universitaires de Namur, 1997

García Düttmann, Alexander. *Das Gedächtnis des Denkens: Versuch über Heidegger und Adorno.* Frankfurt am Main: Suhrkamp, 1991

Giroux, Laurent. *Durée et temporalité: Bergson et Heidegger.* Paris: Desclée de Brouwer, 1971

Glendinning, Simon. *On Being with Others: Heidegger, Derrida, Wittgenstein.* London: Routledge, 1998

Göbel, Eckart. *Konstellation und Existenz: Kritik der Geschichte um 1930: Studien zu Heidegger, Benjamin, Jahn und Musil.* Tübingen: Stauffenburg, 1996

Goldmann, Lucien. *Lukács et Heidegger.* Paris: Denoël, 1973

Huizing, Klaas. *Das Sein und der Andere. Lévinas Auseinandersetzung mit Heidegger.* Bodenheim: Hain, 1988

Huntington, Patricia J. *Ecstatic Subjects, Utopia, and Recognition: Kristeva, Heidegger, Irigaray.* Albany: State University of New York Press, 1998

Jolivet, Régis. *Le Problème de la mort chez M. Heidegger et J.-P. Sartre.* Abbaye Saint Wandrelle: Édtions de Fontenelle, 1950

Kelly, A.F. *Language and Transcendence. A Study in the Philosophy of Martin Heidegger and Karl-Otto Apel.* Bern and New York: Lang, 1994

Kuchler, Tilman. *Postmodern Gaming: Heidegger, Duchamp, Derrida.* Bern and New York: Lang, 1994

Lehmann, Karl. *Der Tod bei Heidegger und Jaspers: Ein Beitrag zur Frage: Existenzialphilosophie, Existenzphilosophie und protestantische Theologie.* Heidelberg: Comtesse, 1938

Lévinas, Emmanuel. *En découvrant l'existence avec Husserl et Heidegger.* Paris: Vrin, ³1994

Marrati-Guénoun, Paola. *La Genèse et la trace. Derrida lecteur de Husserl et Heidegger.* (Phaenomenologica 146). Dordrecht: Kluwer Academic Publishers, 1998

Mayer, Michael. *Transzendenz und Geschichte: Ein Versuch im Anschluß an Lévinas und seine Erörterung Heideggers.* Essen: Die Blaue Eule, 1995

Michalski, Mark. *Fremdwahrnehmung und Mitsein. Zur Grundlegung der Sozialphilosophie im Denken Max Schelers und Martin Heideggers.* Bonn: Bouvier, 1997

Mörchen, Hermann. *Adorno und Heidegger. Untersuchung einer philosophischen Kommunikationsverweigerung.* Stuttgart: Klett-Cotta, 1980

Mortensen, Ellen. *The Feminine and Nihilism: Luce Irigaray with Nietzsche and Heidegger.* Oslo: Scandinavian University Press of North America, 1994

Mulhall, Stephen. *On Being in the World: Wittgenstein and Heidegger on Seeing Aspects.* London: Routledge, 1990

Olson, Alan M. (ed.). *Heidegger & Jaspers.* Philadelphia: Temple University Press, 1994

Piller, Gereon. *Bewußtsein und Da-Sein. Ontologische Implikationen einer Kontroverse. Zur Relation von Sein und Denken im Ausgang von Husserl und Heidegger.* Würzburg: Königshausen & Neumann, 1996

Rapaport, Herman. *Heidegger and Derrida: Reflections on Time and Language.* Lincoln: University of Nebraska Press, 1989

Reijen, Willem van. *Der Schwarzwald und Paris. Heidegger und Benjamin.* München: Fink, 1998

Rentsch, Thomas. *Heidegger und Wittgenstein. Existenzial- und Sprachanalysen zu den Grundlagen philosophischer Anthropologie.* Stuttgart: Klett-Cotta, 1985

Rockmore, Tom. *Heidegger and French Philosophy: Humanism, Anti-Humanism, and Being.* London and New York: Routledge, 1995

Schröter, Hartmut (Hrsg.). *Technik und Kunst: Heidegger und Adorno.* Münster: Edition Liberación, 1988

Sefler, George F. *Language and the World: A Methodological Synthesis Within the Writings of Martin Heidegger and Ludwig Wittgenstein.* New York: Humanities Press, 1974

Silverman, Hugh J. (ed.). *The Horizons of Continental Philosophy. Essays on Husserl, Heidegger, and Merleau-Ponty*. Dordrecht: Kluwer Academic Publishers, 1988

Stallmach, Josef. *Ansichsein und Seinsverstehen. Neue Wege der Ontologie bei Nicolai Hartmann und Martin Heidegger*. Bonn: Bouvier, 1987

Stolzenberg, Jürgen. *Ursprung und System. Probleme der Begründung systematischer Philosophie im Werk Hermann Cohens, Paul Natorps und beim frühen Martin Heidegger*. Göttingen: Vandenhoeck & Ruprecht, 1995

Taminiaux, Jacques. *The Thracian Maid and the Professional Thinker: Arendt and Heidegger*. Translated by M. Gendre. Albany: State University of New York Press, 1998

Theunissen, Michael. *The Other: Studies in the Social Ontology of Husserl, Heidegger, Sartre, and Buber*. Translated by Chr. Macann. Cambridge: MIT Press, 1984

Tugendhat, Ernst. *Der Wahrheitsbegriff bei Husserl and Heidegger*. Berlin: Walter de Gruyter, 1970

Tuttle, Howard N. *The Dawn of Historical Reason: The Historicality of Human Existence in the Thought of Dilthey, Heidegger, and Ortega y Gasset*. Bern and New York: Lang, 1994

Vajda, Mihály. *Die Krise der Kulturkritik. Fallstudien zu Heidegger, Lukács und anderen*. Wien: Passagen, 1996

Villa, Dana R. *Arendt and Heidegger. The Fate of the Political*. Princeton: Princeton University Press, 1996

Vuillemin, Jules. *L'Héritage Kantien et la Révolution Copernicienne: Fichte - Cohen - Heidegger*. Paris: Presses universitaires de France, 1954

Wilke, Sabine. *Zur Dialektik von Exposition und Darstellung: Ansätze zu einer Kritik der Arbeiten Martin Heideggers, Theodor W. Adornos und Jacques Derrida*. Bern and New York: Lang, 1988

Wood, David (ed.). *Of Derrida, Heidegger, and Spirit.* Evanston: Northwestern University Press, 1993

Wurzer, Wilhelm S. *Filming and Judgment: Between Heidegger and Adorno.* Atlantic Highlands: Humanities Press, 1990

Yoon, Seokbin. *Zur Struktur der Mitmenschlichkeit mit Blick auf Husserl, Heidegger und Buber.* Regensburg: CH-Druck und Verlag, 1996

IX. PHENOMENOLOGY

Bernsen, Niels. *Heidegger's Theory of Intentionality.* Odense: Odense University Press, 1986

Courtine, Jean-François. *Heidegger et la phénoménologie.* Paris: Vrin 1990

—— *Phénoménologie et logique.* Paris: Presses de l'École Normale Supérieure, 1996

Dennes, Maryse. *Husserl - Heidegger: Influence de leur oeuvre en Russie.* Paris: Éditions l'Harmattan, 1998

Dümpelmann, Leo. *Sein und Struktur: Eine Auseinandersetzung der Phänomenologie Heideggers und Rombachs.* Pfaffenweiler: Centaurus, 1991

Emad, Parvis. *Heidegger and the Phenomenology of Values.* Glenn Ellyn: Torey Press, 1981

Embree, Lester (ed.). *Encyclopedia of Phenomenology.* Dordrecht: Kluwer Academic Publishers, 1997

Gier, Nicholas F. *Wittgenstein and Phenomenology: A comparative study of the later Wittgenstein, Husserl, Heidegger, and Merleau-Ponty.* Albany: State University of New York Press, 1981

Herrmann, Friedrich-Wilhelm von. *Der Begriff der Phänomenologie bei Heidegger und Husserl.* Frankfurt am Main: Klostermann, ²1988

—— *Weg und Methode. Zur hermeneutischen Phänomenologie des seinsgeschichtlichen Denkens.* Frankfurt am Main: Klostermann, 1990

Hines, Thomas J. *The Later Poetry of Wallace Stevens: Phenomenological Parallels with Husserl and Heidegger.* Lewisburg: Bucknell University Press, 1976

Hopkins, Burt C. *Intentionality in Husserl and Heidegger. The Problem of the Original Method and Phenomenon of Phenomenology.* (Contributions to Phenomenology 11). Dordrecht: Kluwer Academic Publishers, 1993

Husserl, Edmund. *Notes sur Heidegger.* Paris: Éditions de Minuit, 1993

—— *Psychological and Transcendental Phenomenology and the Confrontation with Heidegger (1927-1931): The Encyclopaedia Britannica Article, the Amsterdam Lectures.* Dordrecht: Kluwer Academic Publishers, 1997

Kockelmans, Joseph J. (ed.). *Hermeneutic Phenomenology: Lectures and Essays.* Washington, D.C.: University Press of America, 1988

Kontos, Pavlos. *D'une phénoménologie de la perception chez Heidegger.* (Phaenomenologica 137). Dordrecht: Kluwer Academic Publishers, 1996

Kwan, Tze-wan. *Die hermeneutische Phänomenologie und das tautologische Denken.* Bonn: Bouvier, 1982

Macann, Christopher. *Presence and Coincidence. The Transformation of Transcendental into Ontological Phenomenology.* (Phaenomenologica 119). Dordrecht: Kluwer Academic Publishers, 1991

Marion, Jean-Luc. *Reduction and Givenness: Investigations of Husserl, Heidegger, and Phenomenology.* Translated by Th. A. Carlson. Evanston: Northwestern University Press, 1998

Merker, Barbara. *Selbsttäuschung und Selbsterkenntnis. Zu Heideggers Transformation der Phänomenologie Husserls.* Frankfurt am Main: Suhrkamp, 1988

Orth, Ernst W. (Hrsg.). *Husserl, Scheler, Heidegger in der Sicht neuer Quellen.* Freiburg und München: Alber, 1978

Pöggeler, Otto. *Heidegger und die hermeneutische Phänomenologie.* Freiburg and München: Alber, 1983

Schmitz, Hermann. *Husserl und Heidegger.* Bonn: Bouvier, 1995

Schönleben, Erich. *Wahrheit und Existenz: zu Heideggers phäno-menologischer Grundlegung des überlieferten Wahrheitsbegriffes als Übereinstimmung.* Würzburg: Königshausen & Neumann, 1987

Seebohm, Thomas M.(Hrsg.) *Logik, Anschaulichkeit und Transparenz: Studien zu Husserl, Heidegger und der französischen Phänomenolo-giekritik.* Freiburg and München: Alber, 1990

Spiegelberg, Herbert. *The Phenomenological Movement: A Historical Introduction.* 2 Vols. (Phaenomenologica 1 & 2). The Hague: Nijhoff, 1969

Stapleton, Timothy J. *Husserl and Heidegger: The Question of a Phenomenological Beginning.* Albany: State University of New York Press, 1983

Strube, Claudius. *Zur Vorgeschichte der hermeneutischen Phänomeno-logie.* Würzburg: Königshausen & Neumann, 1993

Sundara Rajan, R. *The Humanization of Transcendental Philosophy: Studies on Husserl, Heidegger, and Merleau-Ponty.* New Delhi: Tulika, 1997

Taminiaux, Jacques (ed.). *Heidegger et l'idée de la phénoménologie.* (Phaenomenologica 108). Dordrecht: Kluwer Academic Publishers, 1988

Trawny, Peter. *Martin Heideggers Phänomenologie der Welt.* Freiburg and München: Alber, 1997

Vukicevic, Vladimir. *Logik und Zeit in der phänomenologischen Philosophie Martin Heideggers.* Hildesheim: Olms, 1988

Wang, Wen-Sheng. *Das Dasein und das Ur-Ich: Heideggers Position hinsichtlich des Problems des Ur-Ich bei Husserl.* Bern and New York: Lang, 1994

Waterhouse, Roger. *A Heidegger Critique: A Critical Examination of the Existential Phenomenology of Martin Heidegger.* Brighton: Harvester Press, 1981

Wolz-Gottwald, Eckard. *Transformation der Phänomenologie. Zur Mystik bei Husserl und Heidegger.* Wien: Passagen, 1998

Yuasa, Shin-Ichi. *Phänomenologie des Alltäglichen: vom Aspekt der Leiblichkeit des Menschen her.* Bern and New York: Lang, 1998

X. ETHICS, NATIONAL SOCIALISM, AND POLITICS

1. Ethics

Blitz, Mark. *Heidegger's "Being and Time" and the Possibility of Political Philosophy.* Ithaca: Cornell University Press, 1981

Brandner, Rudolf. *Warum Heidegger keine Ethik geschrieben hat.* Wien: Passagen, 1992

Dallery, Arleen, Scott, Charles E., and Roberts, Holly P. (eds.). *Ethics and Danger: Essays on Heidegger and Continental Thought.* Albany: State University of New York Press, 1992

Gethmann-Siefert, Annemarie, and Pöggeler, Otto (Hrsg.). *Heidegger und die praktische Philosophie.* Frankfurt am Main: Suhrkamp, 1988

Hans, James S. *The Question of Value: Thinking Through Nietzsche, Heidegger, and Freud.* Carbondale: Southern Illinois University Press, 1989

Hodge, Joanna. *Heidegger and Ethics.* London: Routledge, 1994

Kreiml, Josef. *Zwei Auffassungen des Ethischen bei Heidegger: Ein Vergleich von "Sein und Zeit" mit dem "Brief über den Humanismus"*. Regensburg: Roderer, 1987

Krockow, Christian von. *Die Entscheidung. Eine Untersuchung über Ernst Jünger, Carl Schmitt, Martin Heidegger*. Frankfurt am Main and New York: Campus, 1990

Llewelyn, John. *The Middle Voice of Ecological Consciousness: A Chiasmic Reading of Responsibility in the Neighbourhood of Lévinas, Heidegger, and others*. Basingstoke: Macmillan, 1991

Margreiter, Reinahrd, and Leidlmair, Karl (Hrsg.). *Heidegger: Technik - Ethik - Politik*. Würzburg: Königshausen & Neumann, 1991

McWhorter, Ladelle. *Heidegger and the Earth: Issues in Environmental Philosophy*. Kirksland: Thomas Jefferson University Press, 1990

Nießeler, Andreas. *Vom Ethos der Gelassenheit: Zu Heideggers Bedeutung für die Pädagogik*. Würzburg: Königshausen & Neumann, 1995

Olafson, Frederick A. *Heidegger and the Ground of Ethics. A Study of "Mitsein"*. Cambridge: Cambridge University Press, 1998

Rother, Ralf. *Wie die Entscheidung lesen? Zu Platon, Heidegger und Schmitt*. Wien: Turia und Kant, 1993

Schalow, Frank. *Imagination and Existence: Heidegger's Retrieval of Kantian Ethics*. Lanham: University Press of America, 1986

Schönherr-Mann, Hans-Martin. *Politik der Technik: Heidegger und die Frage der Gerechtigkeit*. Wien: Passagen, 1992

Scott, Charles E. *The Question of Ethics: Nietzsche, Foucault, Heidegger*. Bloomington: Indiana University Press, 1990

Thomé, Martin. *Existenz und Verantwortung. Untersuchungen zur existenzialontologischen Fundierung von Verantwortung auf der*

Grundlage der Philosophie Martin Heideggers. Würzburg: Königs-hausen & Neumann, 198

Vogel, Lawrence. *The Fragile "We": Ethical Implications of Heidegger's "Being and Time".* Evanston: Northwestern University Press, 1994

2. National Socialism and Politics

Altwegg, Jürgen (Hrsg.). *Die Heidegger Kontroverse.* Frankfurt am Main: Athenäum, 1988

Aoun, Mouchir. *La Polis heidegerrienne: Lieu de réconciliation de l'être et du politique.* Altenberge: Oros, 1996

Beistegui, Miguel de. *Heidegger & the Political: Dystopias.* London: Routledge, 1998

Bourdieu, Pierre. *The Political Ontology of Martin Heidegger.* Translated by P. Collier. Stanford: Stanford University Press, 1991

Brainard, Marcus, Jabobs, David, and Lee, Rick (eds.): *Heidegger and the Political.* New School for Social Research New York: *Graduate Faculty of Philosophy Journal* 14-15, 1991

Derrida, Jacques. *Of Spirit: Heidegger and the Question.* Translated by G. Bennington and R. Bowly. Chicago: University of Chicago Press, 1989

Ebeling, Hans. *Martin Heidegger. Philosophie und Ideologie.* Reinbek bei Hamburg: Rowohlt, 1991

Farias, Victor. *Heidegger and Nazism.* Edited, with a Foreword, by Joseph Margolis and Tom Rockmore. Translated by P. Burrell and G.R. Ricci. Philadelphia: Temple University Press, 1987

Faye, Jean Pierre. *Le Piège: La philosophie heideggerienne et la nationalsocialisme.* Paris: Éditions Balland, 1994

Fédier, François. *Heidegger. Anatomie d'un Scandale.* Paris: Robert Laffont, 1988

Ferry, Luc, and Renaut, Alain. *Heidegger and Modernity*. Translated by Fr. Philip. Chicago: University of Chicago Press, 1990

Gebert, Sigbert. *Negative Politik. Zur Grundlegung der Politischen Philosophie aus der Daseinsanalytik und ihrer Bewährung in den Politischen Schriften Martin Heideggers von 1933/34*. Berlin: Duncker & Humblot, 1992

Großheim, Michael. *Ökologie oder Technokratie. Der Konservatismus in der Moderne*. Berlin: Duncker & Humblot, 1995

Haug, Wolgang Fr. *Deutsche Philosophen 1933*. Hamburg: Argument, 1989

Hempel, Hans-Peter. *Heideggers Weg aus der Gefahr*. Meßkirch: Arnim Gmeiner, 1993

Hollerbach, Alexander. *Martin Heidegger: Ein Philosoph und die Politik*. Freiburg: Rombach, 1986

Hühnerfeld, Paul. *In Sachen Heidegger. Versuch über ein deutsches Genie*. München: List, ²1961

Janicaud, Dominique. *The Shadow of That Thought: Heidegger and the Question of Politics*. Translated by M. Gendre. Evanston: Northwestern University Press, 1996

Kemper, Peter (Hrsg.). *Martin Heidegger - Faszination und Erchrekken. Die politische Dimension einer Philosophie*. Frankfurt am Main and New York: Campus, 1990

Köchler, Hans. *Skepsis und Gesellschaftskritik im Denken Martin Heideggers*. Bodenheim: Hain, 1978

—— *Politik und Theologie bei Heidegger. Politischer Aktionismus und theologische Mystik nach "Sein und Zeit"*. Innsbruck: Veröffentlichungen der Arbeitsgemeinschaft für Wissenschaft und Politik an der Universität Innsbruck, 1991

358 *Bibliography*

Kohl, Stephan J. *Spuren. Ernst Jünger und Martin Heidegger. Das Walten des Nihilismus und die Rückkunft der Zukünftigen.* Weimar: Turm, 1994

Lacoue-Labarthe, Philippe. *Heidegger, Art and Politics.* Translated by Chr. Turner. London: Blackwell, 1990

Leaman, George. *Heidegger im Kontext. Gesamtüberblick zum NS-Engagement der Universitätsphilosophen.* Hamburg: Argument, 1933

Losurdo, Dominico. *Die Gemeinschaft, der Tod, das Abendland. Heidegger und die Kriesideologie.* Stuttgart: Metzler, 1995

Lyotard, Jean-François. *Heidegger and "The Jews".* Translated by A. Michel and M.S. Roberts. Minneapolis: University of Minnesota Press, 1990

—— *Heidegger und die Juden. Vortrag im Wien und Freiburg.* Wien: Passagen, 1990

Martin, Bernd (Hrsg.). *Martin Heidegger und das 'Dritte Reich'. Ein Kompendium.* Darmstadt: Wissenschaftliche Buchgesellschaft, 1989

Milchman, Alan, and Rosenberg, Alan (eds.). *Heidegger and the Holocaust.* Atlantic Highlands: Humanities Press, 1996

Moehling, Karl A. *Heidegger and the Nazi Party. An Examination.* Ann Arbor: UMI, 1972

Neske, Günther, and Kettering, Emil (eds.). *Martin Heidegger and National Socialism: Questions and Answers.* Translated by L. Harries. New York: Paragon House, 1990

Palmier, Jean-Paul. *Les Écrits politiques de Martin Heidegger.* Paris: L'Herne, 1968

Pöggeler, Otto. *Philosophie und Poltik bei Heidegger.* Freiburg and München: Alber, [2]1974

—— *Philosophie und Nationalsozialismus - am Beispiel Heideggers.* Opladen: Westdeutscher Verlag, 1990

Redner, Harry. *Malign Masters: Gentile, Heidegger, Lukács, Wittgenstein: Philosophy and Politics in the Twentieth Century.* New York: St. Martin's Press, 1997

Rockmore, Tom. *On Heidegger's Nazism and Philosophy.* Berkeley: University of California Press, 1992

Rockmore, Tom, and Margolis, Joseph (eds.). *The Heidegger Case: On Philosophy and Politics.* Philadelphia: Temple University Press, 1992

Roth, Michael. *The Poetics of Resistance: Heidegger's Line.* Evanston: Northwestern University Press, 1996

Schalow, Frank. *Language and Deed. Rediscovering Politics Through Heidegger's Encounter with German Idealism.* Amsterdam and Atlanta: Rodopi, 1998

Schneeberger, Guido (Hrsg.). *Nachlese zu Heidegger* [private print]. Bern, 1962

Schürmann, Reiner. *Heidegger on Being and Acting from Principles to Anarchy.* Translated by Chr.-M. Gros. Bloomington: Indiana University Press, 1990

Schwan, Alexander. *Politische Philosophie im Denken Heideggers.* Opladen: Westdeutscher Verlag, ²1989

Sluga, Hans. *Heidegger's Crisis, Philosophy and Politics in Nazi Germany.* Cambridge: Harvard University Press, 1993

Thielle, Leslie P. *Timely Meditations: Martin Heidegger and Postmodern Politics.* Princeton: Princeton University Press, 1995

Vietta, Silvio. *Heideggers Kritik am Nationalsozialismus und an der Technik.* Tübingen: Niemeyer, 1989

Ward, James F. *Law, Philosophy and National Socialism: Heidegger, Schmitt, and Radbruch in Context*. Bern and New York: Lang, 1992

—— *Heidegger's Political Thinking*. Amherst: University of Massachusetts Press, 1995

Wolin, Richard. *The Politics of Being. The Political Thought of Martin Heidegger*. New York: Columbia University Press, 1990

Wolin, Richard (ed.). *The Heidegger Controversy. A Critical Reader*. Cambridge: MIT Press, 1993

Wyschogrod, Edith. *Spirit in Ashes: Hegel, Heidegger, and Man-Made Mass Death*. New Haven: Yale University Press, 1987

Young, Julian. *Heidegger, Philosophy, Nazism*. Cambridge: Cambridge University Press, 1997

Zimmermann, Hans D. *Der Wahnsinn des Jahrhunderts: Die Verantwortung der Schriftsteller in der Politik: Überlegungen zu Johannes R. Becher, Gottfried Benn, Ernst Bloch, Bert Brecht, Georg Büchner, Hans Magnus Enzensberger, Martin Heidegger, Heinrich Heine, Stephan Hermlin, Peter Huchel, Ernst Jünger*. Stuttgart: Kohlhammer, 1992

XI. ART, HERMENEUTICS, AND LANGUAGE

Alleman, Beda. *Hölderlin und Heidegger*. Zürich and Freiburg: Atlantis, 1954

Benedikt, Michael. *Heideggers Halbwelt: Vom Expressionismus der Lebenswelt zum Postmodernismus des Ereignisses*. Wien: Turia & Kant, 1991

Bernasconi, Robert. *The Question of Language in Heidegger's History of Being*. Atlantic Highlands: Humanities Press, 1985

Betet, Serge. *Langue, langage et stratégies linguistiques chez Heidegger*. Bern and New York: Lang, 1997

Biemel, Walter, and Herrmann, Friedrich-Wilhelm von (Hrsg.). *Kunst und Technik. Gedächtnisschrift zum 100. Geburtstag von Martin Heidegger*. Frankfurt am Main: Klostermann, 1989

Birus, Hendrik (Hrsg.). *Hermeneutische Positionen: Schleiermacher - Dilthey - Heidegger - Gadamer*. Göttingen: Vandenhoek Ruprecht, 1982

Bock, Irmgard. *Heideggers Sprachdenken*. Meisenheim am Glan: Hain, 1966

Bohlen, Stephanie. *Die Übermacht des Seins. Heideggers Auslegung des Bezuges von Mensch und Natur und Hölderlins Dichtung des Heiligen*. Berlin: Duncker & Humblot, 1993

Bonzon, Alfred. *Racine et Heidegger*. Paris: Nizet, 1995

Bourgeois, Patrick, and Schalow, Frank. *Traces of Understanding: A Profile of Heidegger's and Ricoeur's Hermeneutics*. Amsterdam and Atlanta: Rodopi, 1990

Bove, Paul A. *Destructive Poetics: Heidegger and Modern American Poetry*. New York: Columbia University Press, 1980

Bruns, Gerald L. *Heidegger's Estrangements: Language, Truth, and Poetry in the Later Writings*. New Haven: Yale University Press, 1989

Caputo, John D. *Radical Hermeneutics. Repetition, Deconstruction, and the Hermeneutic Project*. Bloomington: Indiana University Press, 1987

Christopher-Smith, Peter. *The Hermeneutics of Original Argument: Demonstration, Dialectic, Rhetoric*. Evanston: Northwestern University Press, 1998

Clark, Timothy. *Derrida, Heidegger, Blanchot: Sources of Derrida's Notion and Practice of Literature*. Cambridge: Cambridge University Press, 1992

Coltman, Rodney R. *The Language of Hermeneutics: Gadamer and Heidegger in Dialogue*. Albany: State University of New York Press, 1998

DiCenso, James. *Hermeneutics and the Disclosure of Truth: A Study in the Work of Heidegger, Gadamer, and Ricoeur*. Charlottesville: University of Virginia Press, 1990

Faden, Gerhard. *Der Schein der Kunst: Zu Heideggers Kritik der Ästhetik*. Würzburg: Königshausen & Neumann, 1986

Fassbind, Bernard. *Voraussetzungen dialogischer Poesie bei Paul Celan und Konzepte von Intersubjektivität bei Martin Buber, Martin Heidegger und Emmanuel Lévinas*. München: Fink, 1995

Fóti, Véronique M. *Heidegger and the Poets. Poièsis/Sophia/Technè*. Atlantic Highlands: Humanities Press, 1992

Froment Meurice, Mark. *Les Intermittences de la raison: Penser Cage, entendre Heidegger*. Paris: Klincksieck, 1982

—— *Solitudes: From Rimbaud to Heidegger*. Albany: State University of New York Press, 1995

—— *That Is to Say: Heidegger's Poetics*. Stanford: Stanford University Press, 1998

Gedinat, Jürgen. *Werk oder Produkt: Zur Frage nach dem Seienden der Kunst*. Berlin: Duncker & Humblot, 1997

Gruber, Winfried. *Vom Wesen des Kunstwerkes nach Martin Heidegger: Eine Untersuchung über die Möglichkeit und Notwendigkeit der Kunst*. Graz: Akademische Druck- und Verlagsanstalt, 1956

Herrmann, Friedrich-Wilhelm von. *Heideggers Philosophie der Kunst. Eine systematische Interpretation der Holzwege-Abhandlung "Der Ursprung des Kunstwerkes"*. Frankfurt am Main: Klostermann, ²1994

Hollinger, Robert (ed.). *Hermeneutics and Praxis*. Notre Dame: University of Notre Dame Press, 1985

Iber, Christian. *Selbstbesinnung der philosophischen Moderne: Beiträge zur kritischen Hermeneutik ihrer Grundbegriffe*. Cuxhaven: Jungshans, 1998

Jaeger, Hans. *Heidegger und die Sprache*. Bern: Francke, 1971

Kelkel. Arion L. *La Légende de l'être: Langage et poésie chez Heidegger*. Paris: Vrin, 1980

Kiernan, Doris. *Existenziale Themen bei Max Frisch: Die Existenzphilosophie Martin Heideggers in den Romanen "Stiller", "Homo faber" und "Mein Name sei Gantenbein"*. Berlin: Walter de Gruyter, 1978

Kockelmans, Joseph J. *On Heidegger and Language*. Evanston: Northwestern University Press, 1972

—— *Heidegger on Art and Art Works*. (Phaenomenologica 99). The Hague: Nijhoff, 1985

Kusch, Martin. *Language as Calculus Versus Language as Universal Medium: A Study in Husserl, Heidegger, and Gadamer*. Dordrecht: Kluwer Academic Publishers, 1989

Lafont, Cristina. *Sprache und Welterschließung. Zur linguistischen Wende der Hermeneutik Heideggers*. Frankfurt am Main: Suhrkamp, 1994

Lambrou, Athanassios. *Von der Umkehr in die Herkunft der Kunst: Zu einer neuen Wesensbestimmung der Kunst im Horizont der Frage nach der Technik*. Bern and New York: Lang, 1994

MacCormick, Peter J. *Heidegger and the Language of the World: An Argumentative Reading of the Later Heidegger's Meditations on Language*. Ottawa: University of Ottawa Press, 1976

Maraldo, John C. *Der hermeneutische Zirkel. Untersuchungen zu Schleiermacher, Dilthey und Heidegger*. Freiburg and München: Alber, [2]1984

Marx, Eduardo. *Heidegger und der Ort der Musik*. Würzburg: Königshausen & Neumann, 1998

Müller, Tilman. *Wahrheitsgeschehen und Kunst. Zur seinsgeschichtlichen Bestimmung des Kunstwerkes bei Martin Heidegger*. München: Scaneg, 1994

Muñoz, Breno O. *Überschritt ins Unumgängliche. Heideggers dichterische Wende jenseits der Metaphysik*. Bern and New York: Lang, 1997

Payot, Daniel. *La Statue de Heidegger: Art, vérité, souveraineté*. Belfort: Circé, 1998

Pöggeler, Otto. *Die Frage nach der Kunst. Von Hegel zu Heidegger*. Freiburg and München: Alber, 1984

—— *Über die moderne Kunst. Heidegger und Klee's Jenaer Rede von 1924*. Erlangen: Palm & Enke, 1995

Pornschlegel, Clemens. *Der literarische Souverän: Zur politischen Funktion der deutschen Dichtung bei Goethe, Heidegger, Kafka und im George-Kreis*. Freiburg: Rombach, 1994

Ralston, Kenneth M. *The Captured Horizon: Heidegger and the "Nachtwachen von Bonaventura"*. Tübingen: Niemeyer, 1994

Rechsteiner, Alois. *Wesen und Sinn von Sein und Sprache bei Martin Heidegger*. Bern and New York: Lang, 1977

Rubio, Heriberto. *Tod und Tragik bei Heidegger und Aristoteles*. Münster: Uni Press Hochschulschriften, 1989

Sadzik, Joseph. *Esthétique de Martin Heidegger*. Paris: Éditions universitaires, 1963

Schrift, Alan D. *Nietzsche and the Question of Interpretation: Between Hermeneutics and Deconstruction*. London: Routledge, 1990

Schweppenhäuser, Hermann. *Studien über die Heideggersche Sprachtheorie*. München: Edition Text und Kritik, 1988

Scott, Charles E. *The Language of Difference*. Atlantic Highlands: Humanities Press, 1987

Scott, Nathan E. *The Poetics of Belief: Studies in Coleridge, Arnold, Pater, Santayana, Stevens, and Heidegger*. Chapel Hill: University of North Carolina Press, 1985

Seubold, Günter. *Kunst als Enteignis. Heideggers Weg zu einer nicht metaphysischen Kunst*. Bonn: Bouvier, 1997

Sieppe, Ellengard. *Nietzsches Deutung der Kunst im Denken Heideggers: Heideggers Kunstdenken im europäisch-philosophischen Kontext von Nietzsche, Hegel, Platon*. München: Kopierladen, 1991

Sowa, Hubert. *Krisis der Poièsis: Schaffen und Bewahren als doppelter Grund im Denken Martin Heideggers*. Würzburg: Königshausen & Neumann, 1992

Spanos, William V. (ed.). *Martin Heidegger and the Question of Literature: Toward a Postmodern Theory*. Bloomington: Indiana University Press, 1979

Spanos, William V., and Pease, Donald E. *Heidegger and Criticism: Retrieving the Cultural Politics of Destruction*. Minneapolis: University of Minnesota, 1993

Standish, Paul. *Beyond the Self: Wittgenstein, Heidegger, and the Limits of Language*. Aldershot: Avebury, 1992

Stassen, Manfred. *Heideggers Philosophie der Sprache in "Sein und Zeit" und ihre philosophisch-theologischen Wurzeln*. Bonn: Grundmann, 1973

Torno, Timothy C. *Finding Time: Reading for Temporality in Hölderlin and Heidegger*. Bern and New York: Lang, 1995

Tymieniecka, Anna-Teresa (ed.). *The Philosophical Reflection of Man in Literature*. Dordrecht: Reidel, 1982

Vandevelde, Pol. *Être et Discours. La Question de langage dans l'itinéraire de Heidegger (1927-1938)*. Bruxelles: Académie Royale de Belgique, 1994

Wachterhauser, Brice R., and Wachterhauser, Brice C. (eds.) *Hermeneutics and Truth*. Evanston: Northwestern University Press, 1994

Wahl, Jean. *La Pensée de Heidegger et la poésie de Hölderlin*. Paris: Centre de Documentation Universitaire, 1955

Warminski, Andrzej. *Readings in Interpretation: Hölderlin, Hegel, Heidegger*. Minneapolis: University of Minnesota Press, 1987

White, David A. *Heidegger and the Language of Poetry*. Lincoln: University of Nebraska Press, 1979.

Wielens, Hans (Hrsg.). *Bauen, Wohnen, Denken. Martin Heidegger inspiriert Künstler*. Münster: Coppenrath, 1994

Ziarek, Krzystof. *Inflected Language: Toward a Hermeneutics of Nearness: Heidegger, Lévinas, Stevens, Celan*. Albany: State University of New York Press, 1994

Ziegler, Suzanne. *Heidegger, Hölderlin und die Alètheia. Martin Heideggers Geschichtsdenken in seinen Vorlesungen 1934/35 bis 1944*. Berlin: Duncker & Humblot, 1991

XII. SCIENCE, PHILOSOPHY OF NATURE, AND TECHNOLOGY

Angus, Ian H. *George Grant's Platonic Rejoinder to Heidegger: Contemporary Political Philosophy and the Question of Technology*. Lewiston: Edwin Mellen Press, 1987

Astrada, Carlos, et al. *Martin Heideggers Einfluss auf die Wissenschaften. Zum 60. Geburtstag*. Bern: Francke, 1949

Barrett, William. *The Illusion of Technique: a Search for Meaning in a Technological Civilization*. Garden City: Anchor Press, 1978

Bast, Rainer A. *Der Wissenschaftsbegriff Martin Heideggers in Zusammenhang seiner Philosophie.* Stuttgart-Bad Canstatt: Frommann-Holzboog, 1986

Biella, Burkhard. *Eine Spur ins Wohnen legen. Entwurf einer Philosophie des Wohnens nach Heidegger und über Heidegger hinaus.* Düsseldorf: Parerga, 1998

Borgmann, Albert. *Technology and the Character of Everyday Life: A Philosophical Inquiry.* Chicago: University of Chicago Press, 1984

Durbin, Paul T. (ed.). *Research in Philosophy and Technology.* Vol. 2. Greenwich: JAI Press, 1979

Durbin, Paul T., and Rapp, Friedrich (eds.). *Philosophy and Technology.* Dordrecht: Reidel, 1983

Foltz, Bruce. *Inhabiting the Earth: Heidegger, Environmental Ethics, and the Metaphysics of Nature.* Loughton: Prometheus Books, 1995

Guery, François. *Heidegger rediscuté: Nature, technique et philosophie.* Paris: Descartes & Cie, 1995

Hempel, Hans P. *Natur und Geschichte. Der Jahrhundertdialog zwischen Heidegger und Heisenberg.* Bodenheim: Hain, 1990

Hildebrandt, Helmut. *Weltzustand Technik. Ein Vergleich der Technikphilosophien von Günther Anders und Martin Heidegger.* Marburg: Metropolis, 1990

Jacob, Eric. *Martin Heidegger und Hans Jonas. Die Metaphysik der Subjektivität und die Krise der technologischen Zivilisation.* Tübingen: Francke, 1996

Kockelmans, Jospeh J. *Heidegger and Science.* Washington, D.C.: University Press of America, 1985

Langenegger, Detlev. *Gesamtdeutungen moderner Technik. Moscovici, Ropohl, Ellul, Heidegger. Eine interdiskursive Problemsicht.* Würzburg: Königshausen & Neumann, 1990

Loscerbo, John. *Being and Technology: A Study in the Philosophy of Martin Heidegger.* (Phaenomenologica 82). The Hague: Nijhoff, 1981

Lovitt, William, and Brundage Lovitt, Harriet. *Modern Technology in the Heideggerian Perspective.* Lewiston: Edwin Mellen Press, 1995

Richter, Ewald. *Heideggers Frage nach dem Gewährenden und die exakten Wissenschaften.* Berlin: Duncker & Humblot, 1992

Rosales, Rodriguez. *Die Technikdeutung Martin Heideggers in ihrer systematischen Entwicklung und philosophischen Aufnahme.* Dortmund: Projekt-Verlag, 1994

Schirmacher, Wolfgang. *Technik und Gelassenheit. Zeitkritik nach Heidegger.* Freiburg and München: Alber, 1983

Schönherr, Hans M. *Die Technik und die Schwäche. Ökologie nach Nietzsche, Heidegger und dem "schwachen Denken".* Wien: Passagen, 1989

Seubold, Günter. *Heideggers Analyse der neuzeitlichen Technik.* Freiburg and München: Alber, 1986

Vogt, Christian. *Philosophische Dimension des Wohnens bei Heidegger und Flusser.* Marburg: Tectum-Verlag, 1997

Zimmermann, Michael E. *Heidegger's Confrontation with Modernity. Technology, Politics, Art.* Bloomington: Indiana University Press, 1990

XIII. THEOLOGY AND RELIGIOUS STUDIES

Ballard, Bruce W. *The Role of Mood in Heidegger's Ontology.* Lanham: University Press of America, 1991

Baum, Wolfgang. *Gnostische elemente im Denken Martin Heideggers? Ein Studie auf der Grundlage der Religionsphilosophie von Hans Jonas.* Neuried: Ars Una, 1997

Bonsor, Jack A. *Rahner, Heidegger, and Truth: Karl Rahner's Notion of Christian Truth and the Influence of Heidegger.* Lanham: University Press of America, 1987

Braun, Hans-Jürg. *Martin Heidegger und der christliche Glaube.* Zürich: Theologische Verlag, 1990

Brechtken, Josef. *Geschichtliche Transzendenz bei Heidegger: Die Hoffnungsstruktur des Daseins und die gottlose Gottesfrage.* Meisenheim am Glan: Hain, 1972

Brejdak, Jaromir. *Philosophia Crucis. Heideggers Beschäftigung mit dem Apostel Paulus.* Bern and New York: Lang, 1996

Brkic, Pero. *Martin Heidegger und die Theologie. Ein Thema in dreifacher Fragestellung.* Mainz: Matthias-Grünewald, 1994

Capelle, Philippe *Philosophie et théologie dans la pensée de Martin Heidegger.* Paris: Cerf, 1998

Caputo, John D. *The Mystical Element in Heidegger's Thought.* New York: Fordham University Press, 1986

Carlson, Thomas A. *Indiscretion: Finitude and the Naming of God.* Chicago: University of Chicago Press, 1999

Coriando, Paola-Ludovica (Hrsg.). *"Herkunft Aber Bleibt Stets Zukunft". Martin Heidegger und die Gottesfrage.* (Schriftenreihe der Martin-Heidegger-Gesellschaft Bd. 5). Frankfurt am Main: Klostermann, 1998

Cupitt, Don. *The Religion of Being.* London: SCM, 1998

Danner, Helmut. *Das Göttliche und der Gott bei Heidegger.* Meisenheim am Glan: Hain, 1971

Gall, Robert S. *Beyond Theism and Atheism: Heidegger's Significance for Religious Thinking.* The Hague: Nijhoff, 1987

Gethmann-Siefert, Annemarie. *Das Verhältnis von Philosophie und Theologie im Denken Martin Heideggers*. Freiburg and München: Alber, 1974

Hemming, Laurence P. *"No Being Without God". An Enquiry into Martin Heidegger's Thought About God and Being in the Light of Jean-Luc Marion's Work "Dieu sans l'être"*. Washington: Hänsel-Hohenhausen, 1997

Jäger, Alfred. *Gott. Nochmals Martin Heidegger*. Tübingen: Mohr, 1970

Jung, Matthias. *Das Denken des Seins und der Glaube and Gott. Zum Verhältnis von Philosophie und Theologie bei Martin Heidegger*. Würzburg: Königshausen & Neumann, 1990

Kearny, R. and O'Leary, J. (eds.). *Heidegger et la question de Dieu*. Paris: Grasset, 1980

Kovacs, George. *The Question of God in Heidegger's Phenomenology*. Evanston: Northwestern University Press, 1990

Laffoucrière, Odette. *Le Destin de la pensée et "la mort de Dieu" selon Heidegger*. (Phaenomenologica 24). The Hague: Nijhoff, 1968

Lill, Marcel. *Zeitlichkeit und Offenbarung: Ein Vergleich von Martin Heideggers "Sein und Zeit" mit Rudolf Bultmanns "Das Evangelium des Johannes"*. Bern and New York: Lang, 1987

Macquarrie, John. *An Existentialist Theology: A Comparison of Heidegger and Bultmann*. New York: Macmillan, 1955

—— *Heidegger and Christianity: The Hensley Henson Lectures*. New York and London: Continuum Publishers Group, 1994

Manzke, Karl H. *Ewigkeit und Zeitlichkeit: Aspekte für eine theologische Deutung der Zeit*. Göttingen: Vandenhoeck & Ruprecht, 1992

Noller, Gerhard. *Sein und Existenz. Die Überwindung des Subjekt-Objektschemas in der Philosophie Heideggers und in der Theologie der Entmythologisierung*. München: Kaiser, 1962

Noller, Gerhard (Hrsg.). *Heidegger und die Theologie. Beginn und Fortgang der Diskussion.* München: Kaiser, 1967

Ozankom, Claude. *Gott und Gegenstand: Martin Heideggers Objektivierungsverdikt und seine theologische Rezeption bei Rudolf Bultmann und Heinrich Ott.* Paderborn: Schöningh, 1994

Pausch, Eberhard M. *Wahrheit zwischen Erschlossenheit und Verantwortung. Die Rezeption und Transformation der Wahrheitskonzeption Martin Heideggers in der Theologie Rudolf Bultmanns.* Berlin: Walter de Gruyter, 1995

Perotti, James L. *Heidegger on the Divine: The Thinker, the Poet, and God.* Athens: Ohio University Press, 1974

Pöltner, Günther. *Auf der Spur des Heiligen. Heideggers Beitrag zur Gottesfrage.* Köln: Böhlau, 1991

Prudhomme, Jeff O. *God and Being: Heidegger's Relation to Theology.* Loughton: Prometheus Books, 1997

Robinson, James McConkey, and Cobb, John B., Jr. (eds.). *The Later Heidegger and Theology.* Westport: Greenwood Press, 1979

Ruff, Gerhard. *Am Ursprung der Zeit. Studien zu Martin Heideggers phänomenologischen Zugang zur christlichen Religion in den ersten "Freiburger Vorlesungen".* Berlin: Duncker & Humblot, 1997

Schaeffler, Richard. *Frömmigkeit des Denkens? Martin Heidegger und die katholische Theologie.* Darmstadt: Wissenschaftliche Buchgesellschaft, 1978

Shim, Kwang-Seop. *Der nachmetaphysische Gott: Überlegungen zur Problematik des Verhältnisses von Gott und Metaphysik in den Entwürfen von Martin Heidegger, Wilhelm Weischedel und Berhard Welte.* Bielefeld: Kirchliche Hochschule Bethel, 1991

Sikka, Sonya. *Forms of Transcendence: Heidegger and Medieval Mystical Theology.* Albany: State University of New York Press, 1997

Souche-Dagues, Denise. *Le Logos chez Heidegger. Philosophie et Théologie.* Grenoble: Millon, 1999

Staten, John C. *Conscience and the Reality of God: An Essay on the Experiential Foundations of Religious Knowledge.* Berlin: Walter de Gruyter, 1988

Strube, Claudius. *Das Mysterium der Moderne. Heideggers Stellung zur gewandelten Seins- und Gottesfrage.* München: Fink, 1994

Thiselton, Anthony C. *The Two Horizons: New Testament Hermeneutics and Philosophical Description with Special Reference to Heidegger, Bultmann, Gadamer, and Wittgenstein.* Grand Rapids: Erdmans, 1980

Tropea, Gregory. *Religion, Ideology, and Heidegger's Concept of Falling.* Atlanta: Scholars Press, 1987

Weber, Ludwig. *Heidegger und die Theologie.* Bodenheim: Hain, 1980

—— *Theologie als Meditation - unter "Verwendung" des Heideggerschen Denkens. Mit einem Exkurs über das Sein bei Thomas und Heidegger.* Pfaffenheim: Centaurus, 1985

—— *Heidegger und die Theologie.* Pfaffenheim: Centaurus, 1997

Weclawski, Tomasz. *Zwischen Sprache und Zweigen: eine Erörterung der theologischen Apophase im Gespräch mit Vladimir N. Lossky und Martin Heidegger.* München: Minerva, 1985

Williams, John R. *Heidegger's Philosophy of Religion.* Waterloo: Wilfrid Laurier University Press, 1977

Yannaras, Ch. *De l'absence et de l'inconnaissance de Dieu d'après les écrits aréopagitiques et Martin Heidegger.* Paris: Cerf, 1971

Zarader, Marlène. *La Dette impensée, Heidegger et l'héritage hébraique.* Paris: Sueil, 1990

XIV. PSYCHOLOGY AND PSYCHOTHERAPY

Bartels, Martin. *Selbstbewußtsein und Unbewußtes. Studien zu Freud und Heidegger.* Berlin: Walter de Gruyter, 1976

Becker, Gregor. *Philosophische Probleme der Daseinsanalyse von Medard Boss und ihre praktische Anwendung.* Marburg: Tectum, 1997

Binswanger, Ludwig. *Grundformen und Erkenntnis menschlichen Daseins.* Zürich: Niehans, 1942

Boss, Medard. *"I Dreamt Last Night..."*: *a New Approach to the Revelations of Dreaming and Its Uses in Psychotherapy.* Translated by St. Conway. New York: Gardner Press, 1977

—— *Psychoanalysis and Daseinsanalysis.* Translated by L.B. Léfèbre. NewYork: Da Capo Press, 1982

—— *Existential Foundations of Medicine and Psychology.* Translated by St. Conway and A. Cleaves. New York: J. Aronson, 1983

Condrau, Gion. *Sigmund Freud und Martin Heidegger. Daseinsanalytische Neurosenlehre und Psychotherapie.* Bern: Huber, 1992

—— *Martin Heidegger's Impact on Psychotherapy.* Oakville and London: Mosaic, 1998

Düe, Michael. *Ontologie und Psychoanalyse. Metapsychologische Untersuchungen über den Begriff der Angst in den Schriften Sigmund Freuds und Martin Heideggers.* Bodenheim: Hain, 1986

Faulconer, James E. (ed.). *Reconsidering Psychology: Perspectives from Continental Philosophy.* Pittsburgh: Duquesne University Press, 1990

Hagestedt, Jens. *Freud und Heidegger. Zum Begriff der Geschichte im Ausgang des subjektzentrischen Denkens.* München: Fink, 1993

Hoeller, Keith (ed.). *Heidegger & Psychology*. Seattle: *Review of Existential Psychology & Psychiatry*, 1988

Holzhey-Kunz, Alice. *Leiden am Dasein: Die Daseinsanalyse und die Aufgabe einer Hermeneutik psychopathologischer Phänomene.* Wien: Passagen, 1994

Kawai, Toshio. *Bild und Sprache und ihre Beziehungen zur Welt. Überlegungen zur Bedeutung von Jung und Heidegger für die Psychologie.* Würzburg: Königshausen & Neumann, 1988

Kurthen, Martin. *Synchronizität und Ereignis. Über das Selbe im Denken C.G. Jungs und M. Heideggers.* Essen: Die Blaue Eule, 1986

Leidlmair, Karl. *Künstliche Intelligenz und Heidegger: Über den Zwiespalt von Natur und Geist.* München: Fink, 1990

McCall, Raymond J. *Phenomenological Psychology: An Introduction, with a Glossary of Some Key Heideggerian Terms.* Madison: University of Wisconsin Press, 1983

Messer, Stanley B., Sass, Louis A., and Woolfolk, Robert L. *Hermeneutics and Psychological Theory: Interpretive Perspectives on Personality, Psychotherapy, and Psychopathology.* New Brunswick: Rutgers University Press, 1988

Olafson, Frederick A. *Heidegger and the Philosophy of Mind.* New Haven: Yale University Press, 1987

Riem, Ludger. *Das daseinsanalytische Verständnis in der Medizin: Von seinem Beginn bei Ludwig Binswanger bis zur Grundung des "Daseinsanalytischen Institutes für Psychotherapie und Psychosomatik (Medard Boss Stiftung)" in Zürich.* Herzogenrath: Murken-Altrogge, 1987

Rosatzin, Horst. *Archetyp und Sprache. Exkurs zu ausgewählten Themen aus dem Spätwerk Martin Heideggers, "Beiträge zur Philosophie. Vom Ereignis" im Blickfeld von C.G. Jung.* Riehen: Lung, 1996

XV. EASTERN PHILOSOPHY AND RELIGION

Blosser, Philip, Shimomissé, Eiichi, Embree, Lester, and Kojima, Hiroshi (eds.). *Japanese and Western Phenomenology*. (Contributions to Phenomenology 12). Dordrecht: Kluwer Academic Publishers, 1993

Böhler, Arno. *Das Gedächtnis der Zukunft. Ansätze zu einer Fundamentalontologie bei Martin Heidegger und Aurobindo Ghose*. Wien: Passagen, 1996

Buchner, Hartmut (Hrsg.). *Japan und Heidegger. Gedenkschrift der Stadt Meßkirch zum hundertsten Geburtstag Martin Heideggers*. Sigmaringen: Jan Thorbecke Verlag, 1989

George, Vensus A. *Authentic Human Destiny: The Paths of Sankara and Heidegger*. Washington, D.C.: Council for Research in Values & Philosophy, 1998

Grimes, John A. *Quest for Certainty: A Comparative Study of Heidegger and Sankara*. Bern and New York: Lang, 1989

Hartig, Willfred. *Die Lehre des Buddha und Heidegger: Beiträge zum Ost-West-Dialog des Denkens im 20. Jahrhundert. Mit einer Würdigung Heideggers aus buddhistischer Sicht von Hellmuth Hecker*. Konstanz: Universität Konstanz, 1997

Heine, Steven. *Existential and Ontological Dimensions of Time in Heidegger and Dogen*. Albany: State University of New York Press, 1985

Hempel, Hans P. *Heidegger und Zen*. Frankfurt am Main: Athenäum, 1992

Jackson, William J. (ed.). *J.L. Metha on Heidegger, Hermeneutics and Indian Tradition*. Leiden: Brill, 1992

May, Reinhard. *Ex Oriente Lux. Heideggers Werk unter ostasiatischen Einfluss*. Wiesbaden: Steiner, 1989

—— *Heidegger's Hidden Sources. East Asian Influences on his Work.* Translated by G. Parker. London: Routledge, 1996

Oshima, Yoshiko. *Zen anders denken? Zugleich ein Versuch über Zen und Heidegger.* Heidelberg: Lambert Schneider, 1985

—— *Nähe und Ferne. Mit Heidegger Unterwegs zum Zen.* Würzburg: Königshausen & Neumann, 1998

Parkes, Graham (ed.). *Heidegger and Asian Thought.* Honolulu: University of Hawaii Press, 1987

Seeland, Klaus. *Interkultureller Vergleich. Eine Theorie der Weltaneignung nach Heidegger.* Würzburg: Königshausen & Neumann, 1998

Sinn, Dieter. *Ereignis und Nirwana. Heidegger - Buddhismus - Mythos - Mystik.* Bonn: Bouvier, 1991

Taber, John A. *Transformative Philosophy: A Study of Sankara, Fichte, and Heidegger.* Honolulu: University of Hawaii Press, 1983

Vetsch, Florian. *Martin Heideggers Angang der interkulturellen Auseinandersetzung.* Würzburg: Königshausen & Neumann, 1992

Weinmayr, Elmar. *Entstellung. Die Metaphysik im Denken Martin Heideggers mit einem Blick nach Japan.* München: Fink, 1991

Yeow, Coo L. *An Asian Look at Martin Heidegger.* Singapore: Trinity Theological College, 1977

XVI. PERIODICALS

1. Jahresgaben der Martin-Heidegger-Gesellschaft

1988   *Denken und Dichten bei Martin Heidegger.* Fünf Vorträge Gehalten am 26. und 27. September 1987 auf der zweiten Tagung der Martin-Heidegger-Gesellschaft in Meßkirch.

1989 Heidegger, Martin. *Neuzeitliche Naturwissenschaft und moderne Technik. Grusswort an die Teilnehmer des zehnten Colloquiums vom 14. - 16. Mai in Chicago.*

1990 *Verstehen und Geschehen.* Symposium aus Anlass des 90. Geburtstages von Hans-Georg Gadamer.

1991 Heidegger, Martin. *Cézanne.* Aus der Reihe "Gedachtes" für René Char. L'Herne,1971. Spätere Fassung, 1974.

1992 Heidegger, Martin. *Die Armut.*

1993 Heidegger, Martin. *Das Wesen des Menschen. (Das Gedächtnis im Ereignis).*

1994 Heidegger, Martin. *Besinnung auf unser Wesen.*

1995 Heidegger, Martin. *Existenzialismus.*

1996 Kock, Hans. *Erinnerung an Martin Heidegger.* Meßkirch, 25. Mai 1996. Vortrag gehalten auf der 8. Tagung der Martin-Heidegger-Gesellschaft.

1997 Heidegger, Martin. *Die Herkunft der Gottheit.*

1998 Heidegger, Martin. *Ein Brief an Ernst Jünger.* (18. Dezember 1950).

2. Schriftenreihe der Martin-Heidegger-Gesellschaft
(published by Vittorio Klostermann, Frankfurt am Main)

Band 1. *Von Heidegger her. Wirkungen in Philosophie - Kunst - Medizin,* 1991

Band 2. *Europa und die Philosophie,* 1993

Band 3. *"Verwechselt mich vor allem nicht". Heidegger und Nietzsche,* 1994

Band 4. *Die Frage nach der Wahrheit,* 1997

Band 5. *"Herkunft aber bleibt stets Zukunft". Martin Heidegger und die Gottesfrage*, 1998

3. Heidegger Studies / Heidegger Studien / Etudes Heideggeriennes

ABOUT THE AUTHOR

ALFRED DENKER (B.A., Rijskuniversiteit Groningen; M.A., Universiteit van Amsterdam; Ph.D., Universiteit van Amsterdam) studied philosophy at the Universities of Groningen and Amsterdam in the Netherlands. After teaching courses on Heidegger at the University of Amsterdam, he moved to Pont de Cirou in France, where he established the philosophical center Les Trois Hiboux, which offers seminars and conferences on philosophy, including that of Heidegger. His prior books include *Een Filosofie voor Onderweg* (A Philosophy for Your Journey Through Life), *Omdat Filosoferen Leven Is. Een archeologie van Martin Heideggers "Sein und Zeit"* (While Philosophizing Means to Live. An Archeology of Martin Heidegger's *Being and Time*) and *Grensverkenningen. Essays over het Wezen van de Eindigheid* (Explorations of Limits. Essays on the Essence of Finitude). He has published numerous articles on German philosophy, and Heidegger in particular, in Dutch, German and English journals and collections of essays. In 1995 with Tom Rockmore and Theodore Kisiel he organized a conference on Heidegger and neo-Kantianism. Humanities Books will publish the proceedings of this meeting in late 1999. He is a member of numerous philosophical societies, including the British Society for Phenomenology, the Martin Heidegger Gesellschaft, the Internationale Johann Gottlieb Fichte Gesellschaft and the Internationale Schelling Gesellschaft. He is at present working on the authorized biography of Martin Heidegger and a book on his involvement with National Socialism.